CONCEPTS
OF
FOODSERVICE
OPERATIONS
AND
MANAGEMENT

CONCEPTS OF FOODSERVICE OPERATIONS AND MANAGEMENT

Second Edition

MAHMOOD A. KHAN

Department of Hotel, Restaurant, & Institutional Management
Virginia Polytechnic Institute & State University

JOHN WILEY & SONS, INC.

New York   Chichester   Weinheim   Brisbane   Singapore   Toronto

Library of Congress Cataloging-in-Publication Data:

Khan, Mahmood A.
    Concepts of foodservice operations and management / Mahmood A. Khan.
    —2nd ed.
      p.   cm.
    Revision of: Foodservice operations. c1987.
    Includes bibliographical references.
    ISBN 0-471-28402-5
    1. Food service.   2. Food service management.   I. Khan, Mahmood A. Foodservice
    operations.   II. Title.
TX943.K48   1990
647.95'068—dc20   90-11914

Printed in the United States of America

10   9   8   7   6   5   4   3

Dedicated to my father
Habib Ulla Khan
for being a continuous source of inspiration

CONTENTS

PREFACE

Concepts of Foodservice Operations and Management is the second edition of *Foodservice Operations*. It has been revised to highlight and update essential concepts in the operations and management of foodservice facilities. Its format has been changed so that it may serve appropriately as a textbook for *introductory* courses in foodservice management, restaurant management, hotel management, institutional management, dietetics, and other hospitality-related curricula. It can serve also as a basic reference book for foodservice managers, since it outlines all steps in foodservice operations in a simple and understandable fashion. The unique feature of the book continues to be the emphasis on systems, which applies to both commercial and institutional operations. This textbook can also serve as a useful resource for the foodservice management component of the registration examination for dietitians.

Each chapter introduces the concepts and essential components of a system in foodservice operations. The first chapter presents an overview, with each chapter following discussing a separate system. The integration of these systems is evidenced by the arrangement of the chapters and by the materials included in each chapter. The sequence starts from "back of the house" and goes all the way to the "front of the house," explaining all concepts involved in operations and management. An outline and key concepts at the beginning of each chapter provide a guide to comprehending the chapter contents. All definitions and terms applicable to a particular system are clearly outlined and explained. Photographs and figures are used to supplement the information. Examples of forms and materials used in the management of foodservice operations are given. In revising this textbook, current references and publications were consulted and information was updated. At the end of each chapter, review questions are provided to help students review the essential concepts and topics discussed. Also included are chapter assignments, carefully designed to give students an opportunity to understand the concepts as well as to study their practical applications. These added features make this publication a unique textbook in the field.

The author wishes to acknowledge the support and advice of colleagues and friends in this revision. He would like to thank all foodservice operations and related agencies which have been most generous in providing information and assistance. He would also like to acknowledge significant contributions by his wife, Maryam, and children, Samala, Feras, and Nufayl, who helped in the completion of this book by providing constant encouragement and affection.

PREFACE TO THE FIRST EDITION

Foodservice Operations is designed and written as a textbook for students who are majoring in foodservice-related areas. It can be used as an introductory text for junior-level courses in two- and four-year degree programs in restaurant management, dietetics, institution management, foodservice management, or hospitality management. This text is also a reference book for foodservice managers since it discusses, in depth, all aspects of a foodservice operation. A unique feature of the book is the description of systems which are applicable to both commercial and institutional foodservice operations. In addition, this volume is structured to serve as a reference for the foodservice component of the examination for Registered Dietitians (R.D.).

This book follows a systems approach; therefore, chapters are arranged in a logical sequence. The first chapter presents an overview of all systems, and each chapter that follows discusses a separate system. The integration of these systems is made evident both by the manner in which the chapters are arranged and by the materials included in each chapter. All definitions and terms applicable to a particular system are clearly outlined and explained. Photographs and figures are used to supplement the information provided in the text. Examples of forms and materials used in the management of a foodservice operation are given. Thus, the chapters explain the theoretical aspects of a foodservice operation and also their practical applications. In developing this text, current references and publications from different fields of study were consulted. As a result, the material included is comprehensive and complete.

1987

CHAPTER 1

FOODSERVICE SYSTEMS

KEY CONCEPTS AND TERMS

foodservice system
input
output
feedback
management functions
commercial foodservices
institutional foodservices

WHAT IS A SYSTEM?

A system can generally be defined as a "set or arrangement of things so related as to form a whole" or as an "established, orderly way of doing something." It can be understood by comparing "system" to the human body, where a number of organs are working independently for the welfare of the entire body—thus there are subsystems working to comprise a complete system. A system, therefore, may be defined as an entity composed of interrelated parts or subsystems that work together to achieve a common goal (Kotchevar 1981).

We can observe many systems in our daily life. Simple examples are a car, a watch, or a television set, in which several units or components work together to achieve a common goal. As noted above, the human body itself is a good example of a system, since there are several subsystems—respiratory, renal, and digestive, for example—working together to make the body function.

Foodservice may be viewed from the systems point of view described in the above definitions. Simply put, in any type of foodservice, raw products and ingredients are converted, utilizing various available resources, into foods that are acceptable to consumers and eventually fulfill set organizational objectives.

A **foodservice system** can therefore be defined as an entity composed of subsystems designed and functioning together to accomplish specific objectives. There are several units or components in any type of foodservice that are responsible for the overall functioning and the fulfilling of the objectives. Although some of these units may be small and some may be large, they are all interrelated. For example, sanitation, food storage, and service are different types of functions or activities that simultaneously work together to fulfill set objectives. A foodservice system has also been defined as an integrated program in which procurement, storage, preparation, and service of food and beverages, and the equipment and methods required to accomplish these objectives are fully coordinated for minimum labor, optimum customer satisfaction, quality, and cost control (Livingston 1966).

In the past, conventional approaches have seldom considered foodservices as an entity composed of interrelated systems. Technological advancement and sophistication have made it imperative to consider foodservice from a systems point of view, and this trend is gaining increased attention. It should be noted that the term "foodservice system" is frequently and erroneously used to describe a subsystem and is often confused with the foodservice delivery system. In a systems approach, the entire foodservice is considered as a system which, in turn, has several complex and interrelated subsystems. Rapid development of the overall foodservice industry, particularly the multi-unit chains, also demands a systems approach. This approach mandates a careful identification of all relevant aspects that must successfully interface if a system is to function smoothly, achieve customer acceptance, and be economically viable (Livingston and Chang 1979).

There are several advantages to considering foodservice as an independent system, some of which are:

1. The entire foodservice is considered as one body, including the several subsystems that work together to allow the system to function.
2. The management of any foodservice operation is facilitated by considering it as a system.
3. Employees as well as management work better as a team if they are made aware of their significance in the system.
4. Any problem within the system can be located easily by screening each subsystem and improving any that are deficient.
5. Multidisciplinary teams can be put in charge of each subsystem based on their expertise.
6. Cost control and budgeting can be facilitated by analyzing costs incurred by each subsystem.
7. For multiple chain-type operations, it is easier to plan and evaluate subsystems at various locations.
8. Training programs can be developed to ensure that all members within a foodservice system are performing the tasks that are expected of them in the most competent manner.
9. It is easier to control and monitor activities within the system and subsystems.
10. A systems approach helps in the stepwise planning of a new operation.

The typical functioning of a system and its respective components is depicted in Figure 1.1. For any system to function, there are two essential components: (1) input and (2) output. The **input** of a system is the "drive" that starts the entire system and results in an **output.** For a system to function, there should be inputs, consequently resulting in outputs, and the pace of the entire system can be adjusted by **feedback,** which is based on the nature of the outcome. Feedback helps in assessing the functioning of a system. A foodservice system is relatively complex, since it entails several variable factors, such as consumer acceptance, training and

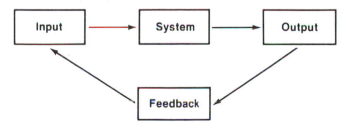

Figure 1-1.   Flow diagram showing typical components of a system.

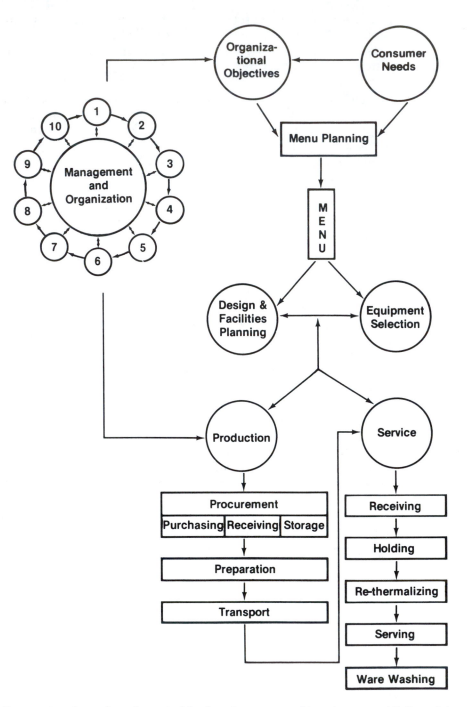

Figure 1-2. An outline of a typical foodservice system and its subsystems: (1) Organizing, (2) Staffing, (3) Directing, (4) Controlling, (5) Budgeting, (6) Developing, (7) Marketing, (8) Planning, (9) Communicating, (10) Decision making.

motivation, and quality control. As with any system, a good foodservice system is one that controls costs and produces high returns. In other words, the entire system should run smoothly and give the desired results within the set financial limits. Although there are several types of foodservice operations, a systems approach is applicable to all of them regardless of the size and nature of the operation. A typical foodservice system and its subsystems are illustrated in Figure 1.2.

Organizational objectives and consumer needs are the initial driving forces for a foodservice system. Each foodservice operation has its own objective whether it is a commercial or a noncommercial operation. In a restaurant, the objective may be to provide nutritious foods. On the other hand, organizational objectives are based on *consumer needs*, which in turn lead to the fulfillment of the needs of the consumers. Both organizational objectives and consumer needs require the preparation of a *menu*, which is the most critical focal point of all activities in a foodservice system. Practically, a foodservice operation "starts with a menu and ends with a menu." It is the sole indicator of what foods need to be produced, what needs to be served, and what methods are required for managing the entire process. The *design and facilities* and *equipment selection* are all based on the menu. Once the technical aspects are completed for a particular system, the entire system needs to be *organized and managed*. This is an entirely separate phase and one that is responsible for the maintenance and working of the system, as each subunit has varied responsibilities. The **management functions** of *planning, organizing, staffing, directing, controlling, communicating, decision making, budgeting, developing, and marketing* are all interdependent and essential in running the system.

Additional subsystems control the entire management process. In any foodservice operation, large or small, there are two primary functions: (1) production and (2) service. In a restaurant, the kitchen is the production unit and the dining area is the service or distribution unit—often referred to as "back-of-the-house" and "front-of-the-house" operations. These are two very vital subsystems within the foodservice system. *Procurement, preparation, and transport* are units which can technically be included within the production subsystem. *Receiving, holding, rethermalizing, serving, and warewashing* are the primary units within the service subsystem. Each of these subsystems is described in detail in separate chapters of this textbook. In order to understand each subsystem within the system, it is imperative to understand the growth, as well as the potential for growth, of the foodservice industry.

GROWTH OF THE FOODSERVICE INDUSTRY

The foodservice industry is an integral part of the economy of the United States. According to the National Restaurant Association (NRA), the foodservice industry is entering its tenth consecutive year of real growth. Foodservice industry sales equal nearly 5% of the U.S. gross national product. Foodservice industry sales are projected to reach $241.3 billion in 1990—an increase of 6.2% over 1989. Foodservice receives over 42% of all consumer expenditures for food. The food-and-beverage purchases by the foodservice industry are forecasted to reach $91.5 billion in 1990. The foodservice industry employs more than eight million persons, making it the number one retail employer in the nation.

Report showed that 45% of adults are foodservice patrons on a typical day, with per person check average of $3.64. It was also reported that as income increases, consumers eat away from home more frequently; singles eat out more often than families, and men eat away from home more frequently than women.

The forecast by the NRA (Table 1.1) projects another good year in 1990, with real sales continuing to show substantial growth. The total foodservice industry sales are projected to reach $240 billion in 1990. Thus the industry is predicted to record real sales growth for the tenth consecutive year.

Food-and-drink sales in the commercial foodservice group are forecast to advance to $214.0 billion in 1990—up 6.3% from the previous year. The institutional foodservice group is expected to report a real sales growth of 5.0% in 1990. Total sales for this sector are expected to reach $26.2 billion versus $25.0 billion in 1989. Food-and-drink sales in the military foodservice group are forecasted to post real sales growth of 5.8% in 1990.

Within the commercial foodservice group, sales at eating places will reach $156.4 billion in 1990, accounting for almost two-thirds of the total foodservice industry sales. Real growth at eating places is attributed to increases in the nation's population, coupled with a slowly increasing consumer propensity to purchase meals away from home. Fast-food restaurants will continue to post impressive real sales gains in 1990 and should once again lead the eating-place group, with sales projected to advance 7.4% in 1990 to $70.4 billion. Sales at restaurants and lunchrooms are estimated to reach $77.2 billion in 1990—a 5.4 percent advance from 1989. Sales at commercial cafeterias are forecasted to total $4.4 billion in 1990, a 5.0% increase over 1989. In summary the 1990 forecast is for continued but moderate growth with ample opportunities for foodservice operators and their suppliers. Consumers are predicted to be spending a larger share of their food dollar away from home.

Factors Affecting the Growth of the Foodservice Industry

Consumer Trends

Convenience.   Convenience has become a top priority for the many Americans who do not want to spend time shopping for food and preparing it at home. The increasing number of single households and working women (many with preschool-age children) has given a strong impetus to the many conveniences that foodservice operations are now providing: drive-in facilities, home-delivery service, and a variety of take-out options. Creative and gourmet type take-out foods are being included in the expanding convenience market.

Convenience is also a major concern of singles, a group that is expanding rapidly and will continue to grow throughout the decade. These consumers want meals that can be picked up in a hurry.

Discriminating Customers.   Customers are demanding more sophisticated entrees and are becoming more quality conscious. These discriminating tastes are attributable to better educated consumers and the aging of the baby boom generation. An example of this is the fact that baby boomers have grown up eating out frequently, have money to spend, and expect a high-quality, interesting dining-out experience. In order to meet the demands of these types of consumers, foodservice operations are including "gourmet burgers," ethnic menus, unusual desserts, "build-your-own" options, and exhibition cooking.

Customers are also demanding quality service, since it is a prime component of the dining-out occasion. If they do not receive the quality of service they expect, it is very unlikely that they will return to the restaurant. In a National Restaurant Association 1988 Gallup survey, three-fourths of the respondents noted that they are interested in separate sections for smokers and nonsmokers. Sixty percent find the idea of children's menus and nutritious items very attractive and slightly more than one-half of respondents expressed great interest in self-service salad or food bars. Other features that appealed to the consumers included on-premises baking; daily and seasonal menu changes; display cooking; dessert displays, and live entertainment.

Diversity.   Today's consumer also wants diversity and variety when dining away from home. This diversity may also be attributed to the growing number of immigrants. It is predicted that there will be continued population increases among Hispanics and Asians. These populations have diverse cultural backgrounds which will have an impact on the growth of the foodservice industry in the United States. Traditional ethnic flavors are "Americanized" to suit the demands of the consumers. Ethnic menus, such as Chinese, Italian, Mexican, and Greek, are gaining in popularity. New concepts and cooking methods are being developed to cater to the needs of consumers.

According to NRA research (1990), the top three ethnic foods in the United States are Chinese, Italian, and Mexican. Approximately nine out of every ten consumers have eaten each of these foods at least once in a restaurant. All this points to the diversity of consumer food preferences and the willingness of consumers to try new things.

Grazing.   Grazing refers to the food patron's desire to "try a little of this and a little of that." Simpler menus and smaller restaurants are proliferating to meet the grazing tendencies of consumers. Menu items that attract the grazing customer include hot pretzels, hot potatoes, cookies, and ice cream. In this approach to dining, consumers satisfy their appetites by choosing a lighter, more casual meal, often consisting of appetizers and desserts, rather than a regular full-course meal. According to the NRA study (1985), an adjunct to the grazing phenomena is the popularity of single-serving portions of food. Mini-pizzas, sushi, skewered grilled chicken, gourmet cookies, brownies, and salads from salad bars are some examples of foods the grazing customer might select.

Maturing Population.   According to the U.S. Department of Commerce, Bureau of the Census, the median age of the population in 1989 was 32.6 years, whereas it

Table 1.1

Foodservice Industry Food and Drink Sales Projected to 1990

	1987 Estimated F&D sales ($000)	1989 Projected F&D sales ($000)	1990 Projected F&D sales ($000)	1989–1990 Percent change	1989–1990 Percent real growth change	1987–1990 Compound annual growth rate
Group I—Commercial Foodservice[1]						
Eating places						
Restaurants, lunchrooms	$ 65,389,229	$ 73,235,148	$ 77,189,846	5.4%	1.0%	5.7%
Limited-menu restaurants, refreshment places	56,359,221	65,529,362	70,379,987	7.4	3.0	7.7
Commercial cafeterias	3,738,014	4,152,436	4,360,058	5.0	0.6	5.3
Social caterers	1,766,458	2,089,014	2,251,957	7.8	3.4	8.4
Ice cream, frozen-custard stands	1,735,592	2,033,680	2,180,105	7.2	2.8	7.9
Total eating places	$128,988,514	$147,039,640	$156,361,953	6.3%	1.9%	6.6%
Bars, taverns	8,771,229	8,982,686	9,009,634	0.3	−4.3	0.9
Total eating & drinking places	$137,759,743[2]	$156,022,326	$165,371,587	6.0%	1.6%	6.3%
Food contractors						
Manufacturing & industrial plants	$ 3,041,957	$ 3,655,370	$ 3,943,779	7.9%	3.5%	9.0%
Commercial & office buildings	1,063,465	1,239,264	1,335,926	7.8	3.4	7.9
Hospitals & nursing homes	1,348,436	1,572,749	1,711,151	8.8	4.4	8.3
Colleges & universities	2,057,454	2,426,232	2,700,784	11.3	6.0	9.5
Primary & secondary schools	988,436	1,158,803	1,225,052	5.7	1.5	7.4
In-transit foodservice (airlines)	1,067,654	1,285,502	1,406,339	9.4	5.7	9.6
Recreation & sports centers	1,508,072	1,724,969	1,838,817	6.6	2.2	6.8
Total food contractors	$ 11,075,474	$ 13,062,889	$ 14,161,848	8.4%	3.9%	8.5%
Lodging places						
Hotel restaurants	$ 10,263,299	$ 11,853,052	$ 12,684,284	7.0%	2.6%	7.3%
Motor hotel restaurants	789,780	883,214	936,207	6.0	1.6	5.8
Motel restaurants	1,274,954	1,404,296	1,467,489	4.5	0.1	4.8
Total lodging places	$ 12,328,033	$ 14,140,562	$ 15,087,980	6.7%	2.3%	7.0%
Retail host restaurants[3]	$ 7,826,994	$ 9,457,060	$ 10,326,297	9.2%	4.8%	9.7%
Recreation & sports[4]	2,212,921	2,550,506	2,735,834	7.3	2.9	7.3
Mobile caterers	664,722	757,460	799,120	5.5	1.1	6.3
Vending & nonstore retailers[5]	4,551,070	5,186,108	5,445,413	5.0	0.6	6.2
TOTAL GROUP I	$176,418,957	$201,176,911	$213,928,079	6.3%	1.9%	6.6%

Group II—Institutional Foodservice—*Business, educational, governmental or institutional organizations that operate their own foodservice*

Employee foodservice[6]	$ 1,976,272	$ 1,912,619	−5.8%	$ 1,912,108	−1.5%	−1.1%
Public & parochial elementary, secondary schools	3,189,407	3,544,167	0.6	3,703,654	4.5	5.1
Colleges & universities	3,352,208	3,699,289	−0.8	3,836,163	3.7	4.6
Transportation	885,417	1,077,893	6.8	1,190,951	10.5	10.4
Hospitals[7]	7,436,091	8,326,892	1.5	8,784,871	5.5	5.7
Nursing homes; homes for aged, blind, orphans, and the mentally & physically disabled[8]	3,224,663	3,627,546	1.8	3,819,806	5.3	5.8
Clubs, sporting & recreational camps	1,877,757	2,160,245	3.2	2,322,421	7.5	7.3
Community centers	487,558	590,083	5.2	641,420	8.7	9.6
TOTAL GROUP II	**$ 22,429,373**	**$ 24,967,734**	**0.9%**	**$ 26,211,394**	**5.0%**	**5.3%**
TOTAL GROUPS I & II	**$198,848,330**	**$226,144,645**	**1.8%**	**$ 240,139,473**	**6.2%**	**6.5%**

Group III—Military Foodservice[9]

Officers & NCO clubs ("Open Mess")	$ 633,471	$ 705,736	1.2%	$ 745,257	5.6%	5.6%
Foodservice—military exchanges	331,653	372,644	1.7	395,375	6.1	6.0
TOTAL GROUP III	**$ 965,124**	**$ 1,078,380**	**1.4%**	**$ 1,140,632**	**5.8%**	**5.7%**
GRAND TOTAL	**$199,813,454**	**$227,223,025**	**1.8%**	**$241,280,105**	**6.2%**	**6.5%**

1. Data are given only for establishments with payroll.
2. Food and drink sales for nonpayroll establishments totaled 53,794,160,000 in 1987.
3. Includes drug and proprietary store restaurants, general-merchandise-store restaurants, variety-store restaurants, food-store restaurants, grocery-store restaurants, gasoline-service-station restaurants and miscellaneous retailers.
4. Includes drive-in movies, bowling lanes and recreation and sports centers.
5. Includes sales of hot food, sandwiches, pastries, coffee and other hot beverages.
6. Includes industrial and commercial organizations, seagoing and inland-waterway vessels.
7. Includes voluntary and proprietary hospitals; long-term general, TB, mental hospitals; and sales or commercial equivalent to employees in state and local short-term hospitals and federal hospitals.
8. Sales (commercial equivalent) calculated for nursing homes and homes for the aged only. All others in this grouping make no charge for food served either in cash or in kind.
9. Continental United States only.

Reprinted from the 1990 *National Restaurant Association Foodservice Industry Forecast.*

is projected to be 34.3 by 1994. Meanwhile, the percent of the population over 65 years of age jumped from 9.8 in 1970 to 12.3 in 1987. This age group is the fastest growing group in the United States. Although average income of this age group is lower than at earlier ages, their expenditures are considerably less. Thus they spent more on food compared to other population groups. In 1986, it was reported that seniors spent almost 17% of their annual budget on food. Foodservice operations are preparing to meet the needs of this population group by providing menu items that are low in salt and sugar; easily readable menus; takeout and delivery service; and other conveniences.

Nutrition. Nutrition consciousness is growing among all consumers. There is a considerable demand for nutritious foods from students, working men and women, senior citizens, and families with small children. The first "Surgeon General's Report on Nutrition and Health" was released in 1988 by the U.S. Department of Health and Human Services. The primary conclusion of the report was that overeating is a problem for many Americans. The report recommended set guidelines, which included selection of foods on the basis of their benefit to health. These guidelines are discussed in later chapters. The foodservice industry is revising menus to meet the dietary guidelines. Special light dishes; items prepared with no or limited salt; more broiled, baked, or grilled items; and menus with calorie counts and nutritional information are being introduced by foodservice operations to meet the demands of nutrition-aware consumers. Fast-food and hotel foodservices are changing their menus to include light items. Vegetable oils or vegetable shortenings are being used by many foodservice operations. Low-fat meats are used in entrée preparation.

Participants in a 1988 Delphi study on foodservice in the year 2000, conducted by the National Restaurant Association, predicted that nutritional concerns will continue to be critical to menu development. They also believe that lower-calorie menu items will be commonplace, and that chefs will be able to achieve rich flavors without the addition of fats and salt. The Delphi panelists also see foodservice outlets offering more fish and poultry as well as fresh, natural, and wholesome foods.

Breakfast. Today's busy lifestyles have made picking up breakfast on the way to work desirable. More and more foodservice operations are including breakfast items on their menus. Muffins, biscuits, croissants, and breakfast sandwiches are gaining in popularity. In addition, weekend brunches continue to rise in popularity.

Home Activities. Many Americans are finding home a refuge from the increasing pressures at work and would like to unwind at home after a long day. This relaxation involves using food delivery and carryout service, and sitting in front of the television or videocassette recorder (VCR). Consumers are rapidly acquiring new types of home entertainment equipment. It is estimated that nearly one-fourth of America's households own a VCR, and four out of ten households have cable television. In addition, computer and electronic games are rapidly becoming commonplace. Microwave ovens are also adding to the convenience of eating at home. As a result, take-out and home delivery are becoming popular meal alternatives. According to 1988 National Restaurant Association research on consumers' dinner decisions, dinner delivery service from restaurants is popular with singles and families with children. Similarly, restaurant carryout was found to be popular with these groups as well as with individuals less than 30 years old. Both takeout and delivery services allow consumers the convenience of savoring restaurant foods in the privacy of their own homes.

Although the above trends are on the rise, there is considerable consumer inconsistency. Even though consumers are interested in exotic, international foods, there is a movement toward simple home-style cooking. Thus, there is continued demand for hamburgers with thick patties, french fries, premium ice creams, and high-calorie desserts. The foodservice industry will therefore continue to provide a diverse public with ever-changing kaleidoscopic menu choices.

Marketplace Trends

Expansion. Expansion is one of the top concerns for many foodservice operators. Expansion is needed both to meet the consumer's demands as well as to survive in a competitive and increasingly saturated market, which has led to mergers and/or acquisitions. Expansion enables operations to branch out in different directions and to convert existing facilities—often a cost-effective way to expand. Some operators are leaning toward a "mini-store" concept. Small units are relatively less expensive to build and have low overhead costs. Crowded downtowns, shopping centers, food courts, and small towns that cannot support full-size units are ideal for the development of mini-stores. Expansions are also taking place in such nontraditional places as schools, hospitals, toll roads, military bases, government buildings, and retail stores. Also, as the U.S. market becomes saturated, companies are stepping up expansion in international markets.

Management. Modern management techniques and philosophies are affecting the foodservice industries as much as other industries. Advances in computer technology are reshaping various activities and the management of foodservice operations. Financial and strategic planning are becoming increasingly centralized. Computers are used from receiving to points-of-sale and to calculate food and labor costs, employee scheduling, customer counts, check averages, menu pricing—in other words, in all aspects of control and management. Changing demographics and the shrinking number of teenage employees are affecting employee benefit policies. Management is placing more emphasis on attracting and retaining workers by providing incentives and by tapping such nonconventional pools of workers as senior citizens and handicapped individuals.

With the advancement of technologies of all types, training methods are becoming more sophisticated. Several professional foodservice training programs are now available, and many companies are developing their own training programs. This is resulting in well-trained employees, talented managers, and skilled chefs.

Productivity. New ideas and concepts are being introduced in order to maximize productivity and to increase cost efficiency. The focus of the industries is on flexible concepts that can easily be changed or remodeled to keep pace with changing trends. Also, nontraditional sales are being combined with traditional food items. Such special discounts as "early bird specials," "happy hours," and other off-peak timing sales are being introduced to keep pace with the productivity of an operation.

Alcohol Awareness. The publicity associated with "drunk driving" is having a strong impact on the foodservice industry. Foodservice operators are facing increased regulations restricting the sales of alcoholic beverages. There are minimum age limits for persons to whom these beverages can be served.

Advertising. Advertising in an extremely competitive market is an important factor affecting foodservices. Various types of consumers are being targeted for promotional and advertising campaigns. The impact of these campaigns is obvious. Promotions that include price discounts, two-for-one offers, and special events are very popular.

Economic Factors

Economic factors have a major impact on the foodservice industry. The effect of the economy's upturn during the 1980s and the modest pace of growth projected for coming years will influence the direction and development of the foodservice industry through the 1990s. In 1984, when the U.S. economy posted its best performance in 30 years, the foodservice industry was a primary beneficiary. The fact that real disposable personal income rose sharply has had an impact on consumers' expenditures on food. Thus, consumers with more money to spend and more confidence in their economic well-being opted to eat out more frequently and to spend more on dining away from home.

The rate of increase in disposable personal income is also predicted as an indicator of foodservice performance. In general it was noted that changes in disposable income are closely linked to changes in restaurant sales. Other indicators include the CPI (Consumer Price Index), labor costs, interest rates, and housing starts.

Legislative and Regulatory Factors

The foodservice industry operates in a complex legal and regulatory environment. Many laws and regulations at the federal, state, and local levels directly or indirectly affect the foodservice industry. Some of the issues the foodservice industry was facing in the 1980s were:

At the federal level:

- Labor issues, such as minimum wage and tip credit; mandated health benefits; and mandated parental leave
- Tax issues such as the deductibility of business meals and taxes on tip income
- Use of such additives and preservatives as sulfiting agents and aspartame
- Immigration reforms and policies, such as employment and resident status of the alien

At the state and local levels:

- Labor issues, such as minimum wage and tip credit
- Tax issues, such as meal tax, hotel tax, local sales and income taxes
- Liquor issues, such as minimum drinking age, hours of operation, and liability
- Smoking/nonsmoking regulations and laws
- Truth-in-menus issues
- Use of additives and preservatives
- Sanitation issues

COMMERCIAL AND INSTITUTIONAL FOODSERVICES

Since the foodservice industry is very complex, there are several ways to define and group its various components. No matter how the grouping is done, there is a considerable overlap within the groups and subgroups. These groupings are to some extent arbitrary, and it is very difficult to draw sharp boundaries between them. The NRA defines the foodservice industry as encompassing all meals and snacks prepared outside the home. This definition therefore includes all take-out meals and beverages. The major foodservice groupings by NRA, which are also commonly used, are commercial feeding, institutional feeding, and military feeding.

Commercial Foodservices

Commercial foodservices consist of establishments that are open to the public, are operated for profit, and that may operate facilities and/or supply meal service on a regular basis. This type of feeding accounts for nearly 85% of foodservice sales and includes eating and drinking places, foodservice contractors, hotel and motel restaurants, and restaurants in department stores, drug stores, and so on. These operations are run for profit on a commercial basis. Commercial foodservices therefore primarily consist of eating and drinking places run solely for profit, such as restaurants, lunchrooms, commercial cafeterias, limited-menu restaurants, fast-food chains and franchises, hotel and motel foodservice operations, ice cream and frozen custard stands, and social caterers.

Institutional Foodservices

Foodservices provided by business, educational, government, and institutional organizations are referred to as **institutional foodservices.** The foodservice is a part of an organization and is provided as an auxiliary service to complement other activities. Although some establishments may operate at a profit, this is not the primary goal of the foodservices provided at these facilities. Food is served primarily as a convenience or as a necessity for employees, students, patients, or residents. Thus the main difference between commercial and institutional foodservices is in the goals and objectives. Most of these institutional foodservices are run on a nonprofit or not-for-profit basis. The differences between the commercial and institutional types of foodservices are compared in Table 1.2. Foodservices classi-

Table 1.2

Comparison of Commercial and Institutional Foodservices

Aspect	Commercial Foodservice	Institutional Foodservice
Foodservice	Largely independent, with the main purpose of providing food only	Foodservice is only a small part of a large operation, the primary purposes of which are health care, education, etc.
Market	Facilities and menus are important to build market and repeat business	Mostly they have a "captive market" with specific consumer needs
Consumer satisfaction	Challenge is to please the guest and secure consumer satisfaction	In addition to consumer satisfaction, the requirements of the clients (institutional) are to be satisfied
Guest/client relationship	Success is directly related to pleasing the guests	Meeting requirements (clients or regulatory) as well as pleasing the guests is responsible for success
Guest needs and wants	These are general and are based on temporary goals	These are very specific and may be based on permanent goals (adequate nutrition for nursing home patients)
Profit	Profit is one of the major motivations which is sought in these operations by various means	Profit is not the major motivation, and most operations have a limited budget
Operation	Number of meals to prepare is hard, if not impossible, to predict	Number of meals and portion sizes easier to predict due to an expected number of patrons
Atmosphere	Since customer volume is unpredictable, there may be times when the facilities are very crowded	Less crowded/hurried atmosphere due to predicted number of patrons
Management	Management is under stress with long hours of work at times	Working hours are predictable, and less stress is involved
Menu	Menu planning and production is relatively easier, since patrons do not visit regularly	Menu planning, and consequently production, is more complex, since patrons eat on a regular basis, several times a day

fied as institutional include those provided by hospitals, nursing homes, schools and colleges, correctional facilities, business and industrial locations, and air and surface transportation facilities.

Military Foodservices

Military foodservices are provided to military personnel in several forms at various places such as military bases, officers' clubs, and similar installations. This is a distinct grouping so far as foodservices are concerned. Conventionally, military foodservices are grouped under institutional feeding. Military foodservices can be run either for profit or nonprofit. For example, the regular foodservice operation may be nonprofit, whereas foods and beverages provided at the clubs may be sold for profit.

The foodservice system and its subsystems are described in detail in the following chapters, using a systems approach, which is different from that followed by the majority of previously published textbooks in this field. Each chapter has in-depth discussions on each system, and there is an interrelation of one chapter with another. The intent is to highlight how small subsystems function in the operation of the entire foodservice system.

SUMMARY

Foodservice management is best understood from a systems point of view. This chapter outlines the significance of foodservice systems. Trends responsible for the growth of the foodservice industry are highlighted with particular emphasis on their impact on the U.S. economy. Certain distinct differences between commercial and institutional foodservice operations are shown in a comparative manner. However, in all types of foodservice operations, similar systems and subsystems are in existence. The management principles applicable are the same in all types of foodservice operation.

REVIEW
QUESTIONS

What are the advantages of considering foodservice management from a systems point of view?

List important factors contributing to the growth of the foodservice industry.

From the management point of view, what are the major differences between commercial and institutional foodservice operations?

What are some of the management functions that are essential for the success of a foodservice operation?

ASSIGNMENTS

Visit a foodservice facility in a restaurant, health-care facility, hotel, college, or nursing home and write a report on:

- an assessment of the foodservice operation
- an analysis of the operation into systems and a discussion of each system
- the type of operation and the basis for your classification

Collect current news items and report on recent trends in the foodservice industry.

REFERENCES

Kotchevar, L. H. 1981. Speaking of systems —What is a system? *J. Foodservice Systems* I, VII.

Livingston, G. E. 1966. Food-service system: Food technology in action. *Food Technology* 20, 644.

Livingston, G. E., and Chang, C. M. 1979. *Food Service Systems—Analysis, Design and Implementation.* Academic Press, New York.

SUGGESTED READINGS

Livingston, G. E. 1968. Design of a food service system. *Food Technology* 22, 35.

National Restaurant Association. 1982. The foodservice industry: 1980 in review. *Foodservice Trends*—a publication brochure.

National Restaurant Association. 1989–90. *Foodservice Industry Pocket Factbook.* Brochure.

National Restaurant Association. 1983. A glowing year ahead—1984 NRA forecast. *NRA News* 3, 9.

National Restaurant Association. 1983. The foodservice industry: 1981 in review. *NRA News* 3, 25.

National Restaurant Association. 1984. The 1985 NRA forecast. *NRA News* 4, 13.

National Restaurant Association. 1985. The 1986 NRS foodservice industry forecast. *NRA News* 5, 11.

National Restaurant Association. 1989. The 1989 NRA foodservice industry forecast. *Restaurants USA* 8, 11.

National Restaurant Association. 1989. Foodservice Industry 2000. *Current Issues Report.*

National Restaurant Association. 1989. The Restaurant Industry 1990. *Current Issues Report.*

CHAPTER 2

CONSUMER NEEDS AND TYPES OF FOODSERVICES

CHAPTER OUTLINE

Types of Consumers
Types of Foodservices
Summary
Review Questions
Assignments
Suggested Readings

KEY CONCEPTS AND TERMS

fast-food operations
midpriced restaurants
upscale restaurants
family restaurants
theme restaurants
take-out foodservices
captured patrons

The success of any foodservice operation is based on the extent to which consumer demands and needs are fulfilled. As mentioned in Chapter 1, a foodservice system is activated by and revolves around consumer needs. A successful manager always keeps consumer needs in mind and performs all duties with these needs in mind. Although preliminary market and site analysis provides important demographic information, it is imperative to understand the types of consumers and what they actually want. The easiest way to assess consumer needs is to question why a particular consumer, or a group of consumers, is or should be availing themselves of the foodservices provided by an operation. The answer will reveal the reasons why consumers are or will be attracted to a foodservice facility.

Consumers might be interested in the menu, convenience, atmosphere, entertainment, discounts, service, or other factors. The base line remains the fulfillment of consumer needs and their satisfaction. Once consumers and their needs are identified, it becomes important to know what they like and dislike, when it is related to food and/or foodservice. There are relatively few publications emphasizing the needs and wants of consumers availing themselves of various types of foodservices.

Since consumers represent various segments of the population, their needs can be considered from two aspects: (1) types of consumers utilizing foodservices and (2) types of foodservices serving specific consumers.

TYPES OF CONSUMERS

Since consumers represent various demographic segments, their needs and wants are subject to individual variations, which may be physiological or sociological in origin. Some consumers may avail themselves of a foodservice in order to meet their nutritional needs or requirements; others may use them as status symbols or for demonstrating affection. Therefore, it is important to understand what particular consumers want; this should be the first step in setting up any type of a foodservice system.

From the consumer-needs point of view, consumers may be categorized as follows: (1) children, (2) adolescents, (3) adults, (4) senior citizens, (5) students, (6) shoppers, (7) workers, (8) travelers, and (9) patients. Although there is a certain amount of overlap in these groups, there is still a definite distinction in the types of foodservices and foods that individuals in each of these groups prefer. For example, a family may prefer elegant service and gourmet food during a visit to a restaurant but may feel satisfied with hamburgers, hot dogs, popcorn, or ice cream while traveling or shopping. Each of the above-mentioned types of consumers and their preferences will be discussed individually in the following sections.

Children

Children are a very important and special group of consumers because they are a major influence when families eat out. Although this fact was not given much importance by the foodservice industry in the past, recently more emphasis has been placed on attracting this category of consumers, particularly by the fast foodservices. Children are very easily influenced by advertisements and are fascinated by special gift offers. Their needs and wants should be given high priority by any foodservice planning to attract families and groups. Foodservice chains have attracted children by providing special offers backed by large-scale national publicity. In addition, many foodservice chains provide playgrounds, birthday parties, and special gift packages. Some facilities provide entertainment such as games, animated cartoon characters, videogames, and other means to keep the children busy while food is being readied and served. These attractions are for adults as well and are a means of supplementing income for the owners of foodservice operations.

Fast-food or quick-service restaurants are preferred by families with children because of their convenience, informal atmosphere, and low prices. Also, since the service is relatively fast, the problem of children becoming impatient is solved. Foodservice managers must always remember that families—particularly larger ones—are looking for economy and bargains when they eat out with their children. The children, in turn, attach particular significance to eating out because they consider it a special occasion and a treat. Therefore, they prefer food items that are not frequently served at home. Also, it is important to remember that the children themselves—not their parents—usually make decisions on what they order, which should be considered when planning menus. Although children seldom accompany their parents to fine restaurants, they may frequently go to medium-priced restaurants. Special menu planning and advertisements are therefore essential to attract this target group of consumers. The menus should feature foods that are attractive, interesting, filling, and preferably accompanied by special beverages like milk shakes, ice sherbets, ice creams, and carbonated drinks.

Adolescents

Adolescents comprise a very special group of consumers, one that is passing through a stage of the life cycle in which physiological changes are taking place and social awareness is developing. Adolescents often become "calorie-conscious" at this stage, so that salads, vegetables, and low-calorie menu items are particularly preferred by them. For many foodservice managers, dealing with the diverse needs of this group of consumers is a challenge and at times an unrewarding experience. Often it is hard to please this category of consumers, particularly those who eat at an institutional foodservice. The very fact that the recipes are standardized in foodservices—compared to "home" food, which has day-to-day variability in taste—may be a reason for their displeasure. Since adolescents are becoming more and more influenced by the food provided by the fast-food chains, there is a growing trend in many institutional foodservice operations to include foods that are similar to those served by local quick-service chains. Among adolescents there is a small subgroup that prefers special foods because of different food beliefs. Special dietary foods like skim milk, yogurt, vegetarian dishes, and other low-calorie items are gaining popularity. In addition, teenagers frequently buy machine-vended food and drinks. Both alcoholic and nonalcoholic beverages, particularly carbonated ones, are important to them. On occasion, adolescents may visit fine restaurants, particularly when dating or for demonstrating self-esteem. Special entertainment is also an important attraction. Since they are the adult consumers of the future and are at a stage of life when food habits become set, it is important to consider their needs when planning menus.

Adults

Adults comprise a very broad category of consumers, the food preferences of which are often based on marital status. Thus, the needs of single, widowed, divorced, and married consumers may be very different. Singles who are largely independent often eat away from home, as most of them do not care to cook or clean up their meals. Also, they may prefer to eat at fast-food restaurants, where they will not feel lonely, as they often do at relatively fine restaurants. Singles often look for a variety of food choices in addition to fast service. Ethnic foods that are hard to prepare at home, like Chinese or Mexican foods, are preferred by consumers within this group. Singles also buy a great deal of take-out food.

Since marital status greatly affects the economic status of individuals, the frequency with which married couples eat out depends on the total income of the family, the time available for outings, and family size. Most families prefer visiting midpriced foodservice operations, primarily for economic reasons. Drinks such as beer, wine, and cocktails are popular among individuals within this category. Because the income level of families varies widely, this group can be expected to patronize a variety of foodservice operations.

Senior Citizens

Senior citizens represent a very special group of food consumers and an ever-growing market for the foodservice industry. Among the factors that affect their food habits and preferences are (1) loneliness, (2) diminished taste and olfactory sensitivity, (3) physiological changes, (4) anxiety, (5) depression, (6) dental problems, (7) rigid food habits, (8) lack of mobility, (9) lack of nutritional knowledge, (10) socioeconomic status, and (11) resistance to change. These factors seldom operate singly and so are interrelated and complex. Consideration should be given to these factors while planning menus and foodservice facilities intended for the elderly. Unfortunately, there is a considerable lack of information about the food likes and dislikes of this group. They directly or indirectly are frequent consumers, availing themselves of many different types of foodservices. Many senior citizens reside at home, while others are in nursing homes or convalescent centers, thereby using institutional foodservices.

For senior citizens, eating out may be more often a social rather than a physiological need. Eating out can eliminate boredom, pass time, and provide a change of atmosphere, since these consumers are often isolated or may be required to spend numerous hours with a spouse, roommate, or colleague. Food thus becomes an important reason for them to dress up and spend some time outside the residence. Many are tired of eating home-cooked food, leftovers, or institutionally prepared foods. Also, they may prefer convenience and do not feel like cooking or cleaning up. A main concern, however, is economy, since they often have a limited income. There is a preference for easily chewable and tasty food, probably due to a diminishing sense of taste and dental problems. Senior citizens avail themselves of special offers, coupons, early-bird specials, "buy-one-get-one-free" offers, and other bargains. Often, these food bargains prove to be less expensive than fixing meals at home. They prefer a variety of foods and often order complete meals when eating out. Cost is frequently a primary consideration and since these older food patrons often prefer staying on for long periods of time, the foodservices often patronized include coffee shops, cafeterias, and food counters within malls or shopping centers. These places provide an appealing atmosphere for them since they get an opportunity to socialize over a cup of tea or coffee and some of the soft-textured foods (cakes and toast, for example) that go well with that beverage.

Several aspects need to be considered when serving patrons in this group. One of them is the size of the food portion. Medium-to-small servings are normally preferred by elderly consumers, and therefore the emphasis should be on small serving sizes with more variety. Also, food should be attractive and of desirable texture. Since there is often a diminished sense of appetite, an appealing menu is highly desirable. Heavy meals are generally avoided by these consumers, particularly for dinner or supper; their big daily meal is usually at lunch. Therefore, nutritious and filling meals should be planned for lunch. Fried foods and dairy products are frequently avoided by older individuals. They like foods cooked simply with fewer spices and prefer such semi-liquid foods as soups, stews, or casseroles. It is advisable to add fresh fruits and vegetables to their meals whenever possible.

Comfort might be cited as the single most important factor in the selection of a foodservice operation by these consumers. Comfort may be derived from such factors as accessibility, a pleasant atmosphere in a dining area with bright lighting, less congestion and traffic, no waiting lines, an easy-to-read menu, provision of ambulatory facilities, vicinity of malls and shopping centers, good heating and/or air conditioning, cordial service, light entertainment, television, and newspapers. In other words, elderly patrons are looking for a place where they are welcome and feel at ease.

Senior citizens usually have food habits that are very much set and difficult to change at this stage of life. Frequent criticisms of the contemporary meal patterns may be expected. Foodservice managers should realize that senior citizens are their most loyal customers and as such should be expected to return frequently. On the other hand, they may be hard to please since they often get frustrated very easily. However, it should be understood that their feelings may stem from physical or socioeconomic reasons rather than displeasure with the food. Residents in such institutions as nursing homes often take out their anger (from other sources) on food and/or foodservices.

The elderly should be considered as important potential clients for a foodservice operation, since they represent an increasing segment of the population in the United States. Some of them have special dietary needs, which should be taken into account when planning meals. Most of them prefer cafeteria-style foodservices, giving them the option to regulate portion sizes and to make their selections from a variety of displayed foods. As mentioned earlier, they like a relaxed and leisurely eating atmosphere. In order to accomplish this, they may also prefer visiting at slack periods of business to avoid crowds and to have time for socialization. These customers often develop an acquaintance with foodservice personnel, particularly waiters and waitresses, which establishes repeat business. Since eating out is influenced by weather conditions, the season may play an important role in the frequency of their decision to eat away from home. There are various types of foodservices serving these consumers on a regular basis, and there are several plans for serving one or more meals at home, such as the "Meals on Wheels" program, and the "Peace Meal" plan. Several nonprofit organizations and churches also cater to senior citizens on a temporary or permanent basis.

Students

School and college students represent a hard-to-please category of consumers, as they often complain about the food provided by school or college foodservices. Common complaints include that the food is starchy, non-nutritious, loaded with calories, or monotonous. Menu planning thus becomes a challenge for school and college foodservice managers. Students often prefer convenience when selecting food-serving places, mainly because they may lack the time, the motivation, or the facilities to prepare meals. A limited student budget can be expected to influence their selection of places to eat out. They often visit local foodservice establishments; particularly on weekends, college students find it necessary to eat out. Lack of transportation causes this group to patronize eating establishments that are close to campus. Likewise, school students prefer eating lunch out at places close to their school.

Several studies have shown that breakfast is the meal most commonly skipped by this group of food consumers. There is a growing tendency for them to select low-calorie or vegetarian food, since they are becoming more calorie conscious. Salad bars are becoming popular. Carbonated beverages and certain alcoholic beverages are also very popular and are commonly preferred items by the majority of college students. School students mainly choose soft drinks, since they are below the age limit for alcoholic beverages.

Students generally prefer eating on campus—in sororities, fraternities, or dining halls—mainly because of the conveniences of living and eating they provide. Lack of time or incentive are the common reasons for selecting this type of foodservice for regular meals. On-campus foodservices should consider satisfying these consumers by providing menu items that are generally preferred by students. Inclusion of a large variety of foods should be the main consideration. Students are also value conscious and seriously consider the quality and quantity of foods provided for the price. These reasons make it advisable to include students in the menu-planning process so as to take into account their opinions and food preferences. Frequent use of standardized recipes becomes monotonous for them, and variations in the preparation methods may be desirable. Consideration should be given to the fact that students like to eat out after supper or late at night, particularly during examination periods. Also, they may have to eat at times other than the scheduled meal hours because of class schedules. For these reasons, residence halls often provide continuous foodservice for the major part of the day.

Shoppers

Shoppers represent a relatively new category of consumers, one that is growing in proportion with the increasing number of malls and shopping centers. Many franchise-type foodservices and cafeterias are expanding their operations to provide food for this category of consumers. Since shopping is their primary motive, food becomes secondary to these consumers, although at times shopping and dining may be combined. Since these consumers are interested in shopping, convenient locations of the foodservice operations are highly desirable. Many retail stores have their own foodservices, such as cafeterias or lunchrooms, and provide a limited to an extended menu. It is recognized that a "dining experience" is not the primary motive of these consumers, since they are primarily interested in refreshment and a diversion from shopping. Fast service becomes an important consideration, particularly during peak shopping hours and holiday seasons. Therefore, the menu should include items that can be prepared and served as quickly as possible. Families with children often use these types of foodservices, since the children may get restless while shopping with their parents.

Foodservices in shopping centers are unique in the sense that they provide opportunities for informal chats with acquaintances, a place to rest and become refreshed, a place for meeting, and, more important for some, a place to sit and watch the crowds. Location, therefore, plays a very important role in the selection of foodservices by these patrons. In addition to shoppers, people who work in or near these shopping centers also avail themselves of these foodservices, particularly at lunch time. The foods commonly provided by these places include sandwiches, soups, cakes, salads, desserts, doughnuts, pretzels, ice cream, and popcorn. Senior citizens also like to visit these places if conveniently located, since they provide an opportunity for them to meet each other, to watch people, and to observe the "moving scene" of the market. Shoppers are also attracted by discounts, sales, or advertised specials. Some eating places have weekly specials, and some will even offer discounts for shopping at a particular store. Much attention must be given both to menu and service if a foodservice operation wishes to attract this category of consumers.

Workers

Both blue- and white-collar workers represent a loyal and growing class of consumers for all types of foodservice. Many businesses and industries are realizing that establishing their own foodservices for their employees may result in direct or indirect benefits. An example of the benefit is the comfort and satisfaction provided by on-site meals and the resulting increase in the motivation and productivity of the workers. On-premise foodservice operations may be considered one of the fringe benefits provided by the employer. As with other groups, convenience from the consumers' viewpoint is an essential component for the success of such foodservice operations. Company cafeterias should be relaxing and have quick, efficient service, since there is a need to unwind quickly from the tensions of work. Employers prefer that the service be fast so that employees will not lose work time. Most employers provide, for a very low price, good food that can range from a snack to a whole meal. Low prices are therefore a primary incentive for workers to select foodservices on the company premises.

For many workers, the food served at the company foodservice may be the main meal of the day, since they may not have the incentive to cook at home after long and/or irregular hours on work shifts. Also, many prefer to eat hot meals rather than a cold "brown-bag" lunch. The company lunch also provides for socialization with friends and coworkers. An added attraction of company cafeterias is that they are very convenient in severe weather, because they are usually under the same roof or in the same complex as the workplace. Machine-vended foods also are purchased by this group of consumers. Workers may be in need of nutritionally sound diets, and company foodservices may be the means of providing good nutrition to them, particularly if the meals provided represent the main meal of the day.

Many businesses and industries that provide on-site foodservices also emphasize a pleasant dining atmosphere, primarily for two reasons: (1) a good, quiet atmosphere is needed as a change from noisy workplaces, and (2) management executives use the facilities for meetings and get-togethers. Many companies now have executive dining rooms that present a positive image of the business to visitors, clients, prospective employees, and the press. The food and decor in these dining areas are planned to be attractive and of superior quality. Since many of these companies are not food related, outside contractors may be hired to run the dining areas.

Foodservice establishments in businesses and industries benefit from serving a large number of employees. The foodservice is largely dependent on a large employee work pool and works best when there is on-going employment and overtime work. On the other hand, the foodservices are affected by the retrenchment of employees, slack periods, or by shutdowns. Most of these places provide varied menu items and charge low prices to consumers, since meals are partially or wholly subsidized by the employers. The company cafeteria may also have a large salad bar, sold by the ounce, or a variety of sandwiches. Some foodservices may even have "all-you-can-eat" offers, particularly in jobs where heavy physical work is required or where situations demand temporary isolation from families, as in the case of oil rigs, coal mines, and offshore drilling plants.

Quality as well as quantity of food is very important to workers of all types. The food habits of these consumers are influenced by frequent consumption of fast foods, and therefore the menus should preferably include items that are normally served by quick-service restaurants. Many of the fast-food chains are trying to attract this category of consumers for breakfast and lunch by offering special items that are often discounted. Increasing numbers of breakfast items are being offered by fast-food operations for this group of consumers, since it is very convenient for workers to have a quick, prepackaged breakfast available on their way to work. It avoids the hassle of preparing breakfast in the time available to get ready and go to work.

Travelers

People are always on the move in the United States, whether for business, leisure, or for family visits. Travel is at a peak during vacations, conventions, national holidays, or other important events. Certain travelers, like truck drivers, are constantly on the move and are therefore a continuous source of income for the food-service operations on or near highways. So far as travelers are concerned, the main incentive usually is to take a break, and a fine dining experience is not the motive. Atmosphere is usually not a primary consideration so long as the service is fast and efficient. Nevertheless, cleanliness and uncrowded conditions are still required. Facilities such as adequate washrooms and dining areas are considered by consumers when selecting food stops while traveling. Many travelers prefer franchised fast-food restaurants, because they are familiar with the type of food they offer and know they will be served quickly. Hot foods and cold beverages, mostly carbonated, are preferred by most of these consumers. Most of the items selected are medium priced, particularly foods purchased by those traveling in large groups or with families.

Truck drivers are a very important segment of this market, since they are normally repeat customers. Many foodservices try to attract these "year-round" customers by providing efficient and pleasant waitress service or discounts. Discounts may also be extended to bus drivers when they bring in busloads of passengers.

Foodservices at bus stops, train stations, or airports cater to the needs of the passengers, their guests, and transportation personnel. Passengers in transit find these foodservices to be convenient because they often have time between transportation connections; passing time is often the primary motive of these consumers. They want to sit in a convenient and comfortable spot and refresh themselves while waiting for their next ride or flight. Some might prefer a drink or two to buying food. The crew and staff of the transportation services are among the regular customers of these foodservice operations. When flights are delayed or cancelled, airlines depend on these foodservices to provide food and beverages to the detained passengers. Fast foods generally are preferred by the passengers. It is noteworthy that at some locations, particularly airports, foodservice facilities are designed either without seating or with a less than comfortable type of seating, since fast turnover is desired by the operators.

Foods selected for use in in-flight meals or on trains must be able to be stored, re-thermalized, and served without loss of quality or safety. Since this leads to limited menu choices, it becomes hard to please all consumers. Menus consist mainly of frozen entrees and other items that can be re-thermalized just before service.

Patients

Patients represent hard-to-please foodservice patrons, primarily because they usually have physiological and/or psychological problems. The fact that they are ill and hospitalized is a strain, which may have a considerable impact on their appetite or food preferences. They are more anxious to leave the hospital or to regain their health than to remember hospital food as a pleasant experience. The anxiety associated with the condition of their health or the physiological tests they might be undergoing often creates a great deal of frustration. Food often becomes the target for venting this frustration.

There are several types of meals served by health-care facilities, and they vary according to an individual's condition. Probably few other foodservices have menus as well planned as hospitals. Food items are carefully selected and arranged in menu cycles under the constant scrutiny of dietitians and other health authorities. Meals may have several dietary modifications that range from differences in food texture to caloric and specific nutrient contents. Since a large number of individuals may be on special diets—such as low-sodium, low-calorie, or other modifications, either permanently or for a prolonged period of time—there is a need for almost any foodservice operation to include special items in the menus. Foodservice managers must carefully plan the menus based on the health status of the patients. The hospital atmosphere itself interferes with the aroma and acceptability of foods. Most hospitals have cycle menus, which normally range from two to three weeks. Although many of the meals may be modified, foods are also prepared for normal patients, medical and nursing staff, and other hospital personnel. Some hospitals provide alcoholic beverages and special dinners for certain occasions and for parents of newborn babies. Special meals may also be provided for medical staff members, administrators, and visitors. There is a growing trend in hospitals to have foodservices managed by commercial foodservice contractors.

TYPES OF FOODSERVICES

Foodservices may be classified in terms of consumer need, or type of facility, which will help us assess food operations from a different viewpoint. It is assumed that there will be a considerable overlap with foodservices as classified below by foodservice type and as described by type of consumer in the first part of this chapter. The intent is to present the consumers' needs from different angles and to show that there is more than one method of classification. In order to avoid duplication, only salient features of each type of foodservice will be discussed.

Fast-Food/Quick Foodservices

In **fast-food operations,** the term "fast" refers to the service rather than to the food; it is a term commonly misunderstood by many. It is, therefore, currently being referred to as "quickservice," to attach true meaning to it. Fast service does not mean that the quality of food is inferior or loaded with calories. This fact needs emphasis, since there is misunderstanding among general consumers. Fast food is the fastest growing segment of the industry, as evidenced by sales figures and the number of projected units shown in Table 1.1. For fast service these foodservices rely heavily on automation. The need for faster service imposes a limitation on the food items and menu choices. Until very recently, the emphasis was on a single item, such as hamburgers or fried chicken. However, sophisticated market testing, advances in equipment and facilities, and consumer tastes and preferences have led to a trend whereby these foodservices are now offering a variety of food. Thus a hamburger chain may also offer chicken, ham, fish, salads, pizza, sausages, and several other combinations. There is keen competition among fast foodservice operations, which has led to the development of a varied menu as well as superior service. To help eliminate misconceptions about caloric or nutritional content, many fast foodservices are providing nutritional information or are labeling the foods they offer.

Fast food includes restaurants not considered suitable for special occasions or a fine dining experience. The very concept is based on fast service, which runs contrary to the leisurely pace of a fine restaurant. The fast service concept also carries over to the type and quality of seating arrangements, which are planned to facilitate a fast turnover rate. Seating is normally congested with less than comfortable to moderately comfortable seats. Cleanliness is more important than decor or atmosphere. Patrons usually expect fast-food places to have a crowded atmosphere.

Each fast-food chain features a fairly distinct type of menu and has a target population, thereby attempting to control a specific segment of the market. The economy has a direct impact on popularity and sales in the fast-food chains. Two-income families have resulted in an increased number of consumers using these operations. Most of the fast-food chains are popular for providing quality foods for limited money, in addition to providing quick and efficient service. This segment of the foodservice industry is the only one in which coupons, discounts, games, prizes, and other promotions are extensively used with increasing frequency. Since there are many fast-food chains and considerable competition, consumers have several options. Because these restaurants feature fixed menu items, it becomes important to provide special discounts and offers to attract repeat consumers. Some of the chains capitalize on the children's market and direct promotions to them. Some facilities provide special shows and electronic animated cartoons and characters to attract children as well as to keep them busy between the placement of the order and the serving of food. These places are gaining considerable popularity. Children normally regard fast food as a treat. Birthday parties, gifts, playgrounds, special packages, and calendars are also offered to attract children, who bring in adult consumers with them. Fast foods are not just for teenagers and children. Young families, office workers, business executives, working spouses; in short, people of all ages and sexes visit these facilities. Normally, lunch is the busiest time, particularly in an area surrounded by offices and shopping centers. Many facilities attract workers by providing breakfasts.

Drive-in facilities are considered an added convenience. To save time, many patrons prefer taking food out or eating in the car while traveling. Immediate service is the top priority. Employees are trained to serve consumers as rapidly as possible. Management of some fast-food places specify to their employees that a few minutes or even seconds is the optimum serving time per customer. A variety of foods are being offered, and there is stiff competition among various franchised operations. In order to please diet-conscious consumers, many places offer special salads and low-calorie items. On the other hand, foods like fried chicken and pizza are the choices of another group of patrons, since it is difficult to prepare these items at home in small quantities in a limited time. One can expect changes and new developments in this segment of the foodservice industry. Many franchised fast-food items are very popular in the United States. Their logos are symbolic of the

Figure 2-1. An example of a franchised fast-food restaurant. (Courtesy of McDonald's Corporation, Illinois)

type and quality of foods served by these establishments. An example of a fast-food restaurant is shown in Figure 2.1.

Midpriced Restaurants

Midpriced restaurants offer food at moderate prices, but their service is not necessarily as fast as that of the fast-food chains. Many **family restaurants** fall into this category. Almost all age groups patronize these restaurants. Those who visit midpriced restaurants want more than is offered by fast-food operations. Most of these family-type restaurants are frequented by children, and therefore a varied menu is necessary. The foods desired by these consumers are of a different nature than those normally cooked at home. Low-cost, economical food items are popular, since it is often difficult to take the entire family out to an expensive meal. There is a growing demand for calorically lighter food, particularly salads. A varied menu, a modest decor, and a pleasing atmosphere are important. All of the above factors are important to assure repeat business. Sometimes entertainment is offered, thus combining dining with music or entertainment, particularly for special occasions. Dinner is the busiest time for midpriced restaurants, for it is usually then that both spouses are able to eat away from home. Also, since these restaurants are open until late at night, their hours suit a variety of consumers. The hours are convenient for those returning from a movie, concert, work, library, or bar to stop for light meals, snacks, or beverages in a quiet atmosphere. Midpriced restaurants usually include family restaurants, coffee shops, diners, pancake houses, and theme restaurants.

The overall nature of these restaurants allows for a congenial and comfortable setting for dining with friends and relatives, or for celebrating special occasions. Overcrowding is common in some of the favorite places, and reservations are often required. Menus offered include food items suitable for all ages, usually with specials offered on each day of the week. Special parties and weddings are also catered by many midpriced restaurants. Some people are interested in different foods and appreciate having a variety to choose from. Others are attracted by the specialties and/or ethnic foods offered. Customers typically are looking for foods other than the usual "hamburger." An example of a midpriced restaurant is shown in Figure 2.2.

A cordial and quiet atmosphere with privacy is preferred by patrons visiting midpriced restaurants. Formal table settings and service are also important. Customers expect to be seated cordially and waited on as a prelude to the dining experience. Special seats or high chairs may be needed by patrons with young children. Music, games, and puzzles are often provided, to keep family members entertained while the food is being prepared and/or served.

Midpriced restaurants attract consumers who are interested in a conventional type of dining facility where family and friends can get together on an informal basis or for special occasions. A midpriced menu, reasonable service, and a pleasant atmosphere seem to be the greatest attractions.

Figure 2-2. A cafeteria-style, midpriced restaurant with desserts displayed at the counter. (Courtesy of Furr's/Bishop's cafeterias, L.P. Lubbock, Texas)

Upscale Restaurants

Fine restaurants as well as "theme" restaurants can be included in the **upscale restaurant** category. Consumers visiting these facilities are looking for a dining experience that is unique and memorable. They expect quality in both food and service and are willing to pay the price for it. They are particularly interested in menus that include foreign foods and dishes that are either difficult to prepare at home or that require special skills for their preparation. Most of the consumers visiting these places are sophisticated and have had a variety of dining experiences; they are looking for quality.

Since these restaurants are often selected for dining on special occasions, there is a demand for an elegant atmosphere and decor, such as candlelight, antiques, and unusual decorations (see Figure 2.3). Entertainment such as an orchestra, singers, or dancers is frequently offered. Shows, special guest appearances, plays, and theme nights are some of the attractions of these restaurants. Elegant preparation methods and presentations of foods from a varied menu are expected. Thus, dining at fine restaurants can be a form of relaxation, a social event, a privilege, entertainment, and fun. These places provide opportunities to go with a "special" person for a memorable occasion. Married couples may find that dining at such a restaurant

Figure 2-3.   Interior of an upscale restaurant. (Courtesy of The Levy Corporation, Illinois)

offers an opportunity to be alone together and to get away from the children, since patrons rarely bring young children to such restaurants.

Theme restaurants within this category provide special attractions. If the theme is related to a foreign country, ideally, the patrons should feel as if they are physically present in that country. This requires skillful meal preparation as well as presentation. Many restaurants coordinate decor, music, and entertainment with the particular theme. Tableside food preparation and service are also common attractions of these restaurants.

Patrons of fine restaurants do not like them to be too crowded or too brightly lit; they also do not like loud music. Colorful arrangements of plates or platters are highly desirable and expected, as is elegant service. There is a need for a sophisticated blend of all desirable attributes to make these operations successful. Patrons are willing to pay more or to travel extra miles in order to get what they want. Some businessmen find these upscale restaurants to be good places to meet with their clients. Red meats, seafood, and a variety of vegetable dishes are normally included in the menus. Upscale restaurants provide fine dining and entertainment at considerably higher prices than the average consumer either can afford or may wish to pay.

Take-Out Foodservice Facilities

Take-out foodservices purvey such items as pizza, deli sandwiches, pastas, gourmet salads, special ethnic foods (Chinese or Mexican foods, for example), hamburgers, chicken, and ice cream. These foodservices either do not provide any dining facilities or have very limited dining areas. Some consumers may prefer buying food from a drive-in and eating it at home. These take-out foodservices (Figure 2.4) are handy for getting food at times when there is neither the incentive to cook at home nor to eat out. The increasing popularity of home entertainment, such as videos, electronic games, and cable television, calls for "home eating" of restaurant foods, particularly on weekends and holidays. Also, some consumers particularly working singles, may not have the incentive to cook and may feel awkward eating alone in a restaurant; this group is a big user of take-out services. Students also find take-out services handy at late night hours, particularly during examination periods. Take-out foodservices may also provide home delivery.

Since food has to be carried a certain distance before consumption, foods most suited for take-outs include items that maintain their quality and temperature for prolonged periods of time. Pizza is the most commonly preferred take-out or home-delivered item. Breakfast items, such as doughnuts, cakes, and cookies and beverages such as cokes and coffee also are very popular take-out items. All ages use

Figure 2-4. A typical restaurant with take-out facility. (Courtesy of Kentucky Fried Chicken, Kentucky)

take-out foodservices, regardless of income bracket or marital status. Often take-out foods may prove less expensive than food eaten at a restaurant. In addition to quick service, the quality of food offered is particularly important to consumers. From the management point of view, menu selection and quick delivery are the most important factors in this type of operation. Special packaging or holding equipment may be an added expense for the foodservice operation. However, these expenses may very well be compensated for by the fact that the consumers are not being waited on and are not occupying seats in a restaurant.

Hotel/Motel Foodservices

Many hotel foodservices rely not only on in-house customers but also on outside consumers. Of course, the main target consumers are those staying in the hotel. Guests may order foods through room service, which is an important component of service in a hotel. Breakfast is the meal most often eaten in the room. Room service of foods requires attention to ensure desired temperature and quality. Rapid service is highly desirable whether it is room service or in the adjoining motel restaurants, since travelers are often on a tight schedule. Toast, scrambled eggs, sausage, and hot breads are popular breakfast items; the continental breakfast is also popular. Guests staying in hotels and motels usually do not eat lunch there, since most plan to be away during that time. However, special dinner events are well attended. Foodservices in hotels are very busy during conventions, meetings, or holiday seasons. Cost is not often a major factor for consumers, since dining is either charged to a business account or is considered to be a single-occasion expense. Courteous service is an essential amenity. Convenience is the primary reason for preferring services in the hotel. Competition may be intense if hotels are located in busy industrial or business areas. Special meals, breakfasts, and brunches are offered by hotels to attract in-house guests as well as local customers. Parties are also arranged at times by these facilities. These foodservice operations profit considerably during conventions and large banquets, which are often booked several years in advance. Hotels located in larger cities, resorts, vacation, and recreational areas offer variety in meals and services. Larger hotels often have several theme restaurants on their premises to attract guests and give them ample choices. Carts may be used to dispense foods and beverages for the convenience of patrons in lobbies of larger hotels. Foodservices provided by hotels are often very elaborate, and foods are usually prepared under the direction of skilled and well-trained chefs.

Foodservices at Leisure Facilities

Foods and beverages are very much in demand at amusement parks, zoos, sports arenas, resort areas, vacationlands, and other tourist attractions. From the foodservices point of view, tourists represent **captured patrons,** since they usually do not want to waste time looking for places to eat. Many leisure facilities do not allow food to be brought in from the outside, which increases the business of foodservices on their premises. Long lines are normally observed at food stands at amusement parks and stadiums. Fast foodservice is essential, since food is not the major source of attraction and there may be limited time to eat between activities. Cleanliness and speed are very important for repeat business. Consumers are willing to pay more than usual, and cost or variety in foods usually is not important to them. Caloric content of the foods is not very important to many, since consumption is considered to be limited to a single occasion. Customers are willing to try new and exotic food items. Carbonated beverages are popular, particularly on a hot and humid day and in open-air facilities. Consumers may be of all ages and sexes. Children are very much attracted by the types of foods and beverages served at these operations. Many consumers prefer snacks rather than a complete meal. Although more variety in foods may be desirable, increased choices will increase serving time since it becomes increasingly difficult for consumers to make up their minds. Consumers have limited expectations from foodservice at leisure facilities, except in fine restaurants in resorts and vacationlands. Many resort areas provide elegant dining facilities. The economy has a great impact on these types of foodservice facilities, since visits to them are largely dependent on available disposable income. When efficiently planned and managed, these services may be very profitable.

Foodservices in Health-Care Facilities

Health-care facilities primarily include hospitals, nursing homes, and convalescent centers. Foodservices at health-care facilities are carefully planned. There is always a need for specialized diets as well as the necessity to comply with rules and regulations of various regulatory agencies. Hospitals have a variety of food items arranged in cycle menus ranging from one to three weeks' duration. Food often becomes an easy target of criticism for patients in hospitals and nursing homes. There is a wide difference in food preferences by those in hospitals compared to those in nursing homes because of differences in length of stay and incentive to eat. The psychological impact of being in a hospital affects appetite, since there may be anxiety for many reasons. On the other hand, residents may stay for long periods of time in nursing homes, so that food plays an important role in their daily lives and becomes a frequent topic of discussion. There may be complaints because of monotony in food items served or because food is different from what patients are used to eating at home. Residents usually have few demands on their time and spend endless hours in socializing with co-residents. It becomes very important to carefully plan menus for this group. Dietitians are hired to help in menu planning as well as for consultation on diets. Because of continuing demand, health-care foodservices are regarded more or less as a "recession-proof" business. In addition to serving patients, these facilities also serve health professionals and visitors. The goals and objectives of these health-care foodservices are very different from other types of foodservices discussed earlier in this chapter.

Foodservices in Business and Industry

The numbers of cafeterias and restaurants in business and industrial locations are increasing steadily. Worker motivation is the primary reason for providing foodservice to employees. Many company cafeterias operate on a 24-hour schedule. The economy has both a direct and indirect impact on these types of foodservices. Charges at many of these facilities are nominal, since increased worker productivity compensates for the subsidized cost of the meals. Quality, quantity, and costs are carefully assessed by the employees before they use these foodservices. There is a demand for food of high quality in large portions. Snacks are also consumed frequently at these locations. In addition to increasing motivation and decreasing fatigue among workers, company-subsidized meals are often the main meals of the day for many employees. There may be special dining areas for executives and guests.

Since time for breaks and meals is limited, quick service is highly desired by employees and more so by employers. Industry interprets every minute in terms of dollars. Even a few minutes of delay may prove to be too expensive for the employers. Foodservice managers at such facilities are therefore under constant pressure. Many businesses and industries let contract foodservices manage their foodservice operations. These types of foodservices are primarily limited to employees and their guests and are not open to the general public. Variety in the menus offered is desirable to please the consumers. Special meals may also be served on special occasions and parties may be arranged. Industrial foodservices are gaining in popularity and have a potential for future development. Decoration, service, and seating arrangements are designed to facilitate serving many consumers at a time (see Figure 2.5) with fast-moving lines (see Figure 2.6).

Figure 2-5.   Seating arrangement in a business operation. (Courtesy of ARA Services)

Figure 2-6.   Cafeteria counters designed to facilitate fast movement of consumer line. (Courtesy of ARA Services)

Foodservices in Educational Institutions

School, college, and university foodservices represent another important segment of the industry. School lunch programs on a national basis are important for the health of the growing population, but consumer satisfaction becomes a problem in these types of foodservices. Menus need careful assessment to meet the requirements of regulatory agencies as well as to meet dietary goals. Variety in menus is essential. These consumers have food preferences which are much different from those of other age groups. Their preferences are affected by the food items normally offered by fast foodservices, such as hamburgers, pizza, and tacos. More and more school foodservices are including these items in their menus.

Students eating in residence halls are generally required to participate in "board plans." Food plans facilitate production and management in foodservices because they provide for a predictable sales volume over an extended period of time, such as one semester or one academic year. Advance planning helps to reduce costs and makes it possible to offer an attractive package price to students. Students often miss breakfasts or other meals for a variety of reasons. To compensate for this, some foodservices operate on a continuous basis for a certain period of time, which eliminates the possibility of rush and overcrowding. In addition to resident hall facilities, foodservices may also be provided by on-campus sororities and fraternities, as well as student unions and other private operations.

Traditionally, students have a negative image of these foodservices, partly because they compare the food with food at home or consider it monotonous. Most foodservices have student advisory groups to help in menu planning. Foodservices in educational institutions are vulnerable to student enrollment and the economy. Fluctuations in federal support to students, as well as to school lunch programs, will affect the future development of this type of foodservice.

Community Foodservices

Several government-sponsored programs provide foods or foodservices for special segments of the population or for special occasions. Examples of these types of foodservices include WIC (Women, Infant, and Children) programs and "Meals on Wheels." The needs and wants of the consumer groups may differ widely. Most of these consumers are categorized by socioeconomic status. Other foodservices are offered by religious and charitable organizations. During disasters and emergencies, foodservices are offered by various governmental and nongovernmental agencies. Convenience foods, snacks, and readily prepared foods usually are served by these foodservices. The nutritional content of these meals is given priority over texture and taste. Normally these foodservices operate on a relatively small scale, either temporarily or on an irregular basis.

SUMMARY

Success of any foodservice operation is dependent on how well consumer demands and needs are met. In this chapter all categories of consumers and their needs are separately described. From another perspective, different foodservice operations are designed to serve the needs of specific categories of consumers. These are also described in detail. It becomes clear that, in order to be successful, a manager in any foodservice operation should first define the needs of the targeted consumers and then plan carefully to fulfill those needs.

REVIEW
QUESTIONS

Outline the different needs of children, adolescents, adults, and senior citizens from the foodservice point of view.

Why are fast foodservice operations referred to as "fast"? List one recent development that you have observed in a fast foodservice operation that has helped to attract a particular category of consumer.

Compare the similarities and differences between consumer demands in a foodservice operation serving students in an educational facility and patients in a health-care facility.

What types of trends/changes will you predict in consumer demands and needs over the next ten years?

ASSIGNMENTS

Visit a foodservice operation and record the predominant types of consumers visiting that facility. Describe any two facilities provided for that particular group of consumers.

Collect photographs of different types of foodservice operations and write a paragraph on special features of each.

SUGGESTED READINGS

National Restaurant Association. 1982. How consumers make the decision to eat out. *Consumer Attitude and Behavior Study.*

National Restaurant Association. 1982. Consumer reactions to and use of restaurant promotions. *Consumer Attitude and Behavior Study.*

National Restaurant Association. 1989. The restaurant industry in 1990. *Current Issues Report.*

National Restaurant Association. 1989. Foodservice Industry 2000. *Current Issues Report.*

CHAPTER 3

MENUS AND MENU PLANNING

KEY CONCEPTS AND TERMS

menu
menu planning
Recommended Daily Dietary
  Allowances (RDA)
nutritional labeling
consumer food preferences
school lunch program
menu patterns
nonselective menus
selective menus
menu cycles
cycle menus
mechanics of menu planning
menu format
menu design and display

WHAT IS A MENU?

After assessing the consumer needs and organizational objectives of a foodservice operation, the next important step is to plan a menu. Menu planning is one of the most important tasks in a foodservice operation and an essential component of the foodservice system. Simply stated, a **menu** is a list of food items served by any foodservice operation. In more complex terms, menus are statements of the food and beverage items provided by a foodservice establishment, primarily based on consumer needs and/or demands and designed to achieve organizational objectives. Menus represent the focal point around which all components of a foodservice system are centered. The success or failure of a foodservice operation depends on the menu and how foods on it are selected and served. It can also determine the degree of profit for an operation. Thus all efforts need to be directed toward menu planning, taking into consideration all aspects of the operation. **Menu planning** is the process by which menus are planned, taking into consideration all aspects of a foodservice system. It involves selection of food and beverage items that are acceptable from the point of view of both management and consumers.

BASIC CONSIDERATIONS IN MENU PLANNING

Careful menu planning will result in consumer satisfaction, employee motivation, and success of the management. The numerous factors that should be considered prior to and while planning menus may be considered from two aspects: (1) the management's viewpoint and (2) the consumers' viewpoint, as shown in Figure 3.1.

From Management's Viewpoint

Organizational Goals and Objectives

The primary consideration in menu planning is whether the menu conforms to the goals and objectives of the operation. As evident from the discussions in the earlier chapters, the goals vary depending on whether the foodservice is institutional or commercial, and this difference need careful consideration in menu planning. For example, the menus planned for a hospital will be entirely different from the menus planned for a restaurant. The menu should reflect the purpose of the organization and the very need for existence of foodservices at that operation.

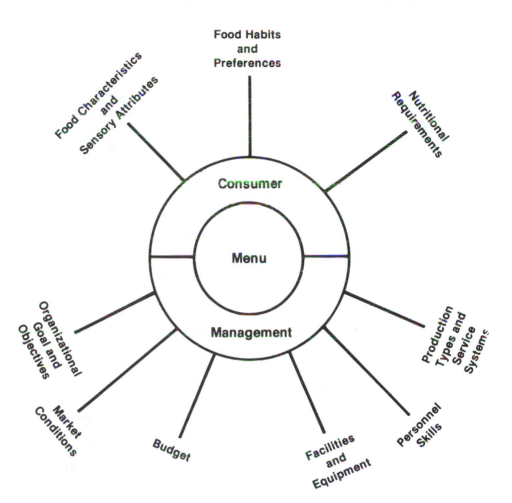

Figure 3-1.   Factors to be considered in menu planning for a foodservice operation.

Budget

Obviously, budget is an extremely important factor in menu planning. The amount of money that can be spent depends on the income from food sales and the relative food cost percentage. In turn, the income from food sales depends on consumers' available disposable income (ADI), the location of the facility, the type of service, and several other dependent factors. Menu planning requires careful consideration of the relative costs of food, labor, and equipment. There are several economic constraints, such as inflation, which have a considerable impact on the available amount at specific times. Commercial foodservices experience more fluctuations in sales/income than do most of the institutional foodservices, where budgets are primarily based on consumer counts for a relatively longer period of time. On the other hand, institutional foodservices are usually on a tight budget, and therefore menu planning becomes critical for this type of operation. This is not to imply that variety and appeal in menus cannot be planned under tight budgets. Careful planning with a blend of imagination, efficiency, and creativity is an important attribute for success in menu planning. Efficient utilization of all the available resources is essential for success.

Depending on the type of foodservice, budgets are normally projected (1) on the basis of estimated costs for serving an actual number of residents, (2) by per capita allowances for the expected number of consumers, or (3) by forecasting the number of consumers during a specific period of time. The food cost percentage is also a valuable tool in determining budgets. Pre-costed standardized recipes, when updated from time to time, help in the calculation of costs to be used in the formulation of budgets. Menu planning becomes very complex and difficult when a number of high and low cost items are included on a menu and when one or more of the items are offered as choices. Careful screening and selection of items are required in order to arrive at the desired combination that will result in a consistent average consumer check.

Food Market Conditions

Raw food products, the primary resource of any foodservice operation, are subjected to seasonal fluctuations that have an enormous impact on the demand and supply. Favorable weather conditions may result in overabundance of a product and result in lower prices. On the other hand, adverse seasonal conditions may cause severe shortages of food products and consequently higher prices. This factor is of primary importance when menus are planned, particularly for long time periods. Fruits and vegetables are the items most commonly affected by seasonal fluctuations. Menus are to be planned in such a way as to take maximum advantage of the seasonal availability or non-availability of the food products. The location of the foodservice operation and its accessibility to the market also affect menu planning. Foodservices located in large cities have fewer problems in obtaining a variety of food products or their substitutes.

Physical Facilities and Equipment

The physical facilities and plant of the foodservice and the equipment it contains dictate the type of menus that may be planned and vice versa. Not only the availability of certain pieces of equipment but their number play an important role in the selection of menu items. Based on the facilities and available research, it may not be possible to include a menu item or a variety of menu items within a desired period of time. Sometimes a major piece of equipment may be needed to prepare several items at a time. The proper type of equipment as well as its sequential arrangement in a facility results in smooth operation, with less fatigue for the employees. Such labor-saving devices and equipment as food processors and mechanical slicers, peelers, and corers facilitate menu planning by providing various choices for selection. Efficient menu planning requires a well-balanced approach toward the utilization of materials, equipment, and employees. Efficient use also results in prolonged life of the equipment. The simultaneous use of a variety of equipment facilitates smooth food production and service operations. For example, deep-fat fryers, grills, and ovens may be used simultaneously to provide a variety of food items. Trunnions may be used for preparing soups or steamed vegetables, while an adjustable and tilting skillet may be used for a variety of food preparations. Thus, planning helps in an even distribution of load to all available pieces of equipment.

The size and capacity of the equipment available are important considerations. Using the optimum capacity of equipment reduces expensive duplication of the preparation process. In addition, the type and number of table tops, counters, and work spaces determine what foods can be prepared under the desired conditions. The arrangement of the equipment in a sequence also adds to the efficient production of menu items. Much time is saved if equipment is arranged in a sequential order based on its usage. Too much crowding of the equipment results in inefficiency and exposes personnel to risky conditions. Available freezer and refrigerator space also determines the types of food items that can be stored prior to or after preparation.

A variety of items may be included in a menu by careful utilization of equipment and space. The lack of or an insufficient number of certain pieces of equipment may lead to the complete or partial omission of certain profitable and popular foods. For example, the lack of fat fryers, chafing dishes, or mobile units may restrict the serving of high-demand profitable foods. Thus, menu planning requires a careful assessment of the equipment available, as well as its capability and performance.

Personnel Skills

Efficient equipment and its layout will prove to be of little value without skilled employees to handle it. Elegant menu items requiring specific skills cannot be included if trained food personnel are not available. Any temporary or permanent lack of skilled personnel therefore restricts the number and type of menu items. In most restaurants, chefs play an important role in the success and popularity of the operation. Employees' capability and availability should be considered when planning menus. Some employees may be more skilled than others so that the average level of skills of the employees should be taken into account. Skilled and hardworking employees should be utilized efficiently without overloading them. Frustration and dissatisfaction among employees often result from an unequal distribution of work. Menu planning, therefore, seeks to eliminate these problems. On the positive side, well-planned menus are a source of motivation and challenge for the employees.

When planning menus, it is desirable to consider the time and labor required for various stages of the food-product preparation. Employee availability during a particular time period also affects the type and variety of items that can be offered. An even distribution of work helps in scheduling and forecasting the labor costs of each item on the menu. Under-utilization of employee skills may result in high labor costs, lack of employee motivation, low productivity, and/or high turnover rates. Attracting, training, and retaining good employees is very difficult and may mean the difference between making or losing money. Selection of menu items that efficiently utilize employee time and skills is therefore necessary. In other words, the menu items selected should be those that can be produced easily, utilizing the average level of skills of the available workers within a reasonable length of time. Items that require lengthy and elaborate preparation methods and a high level of skill should be considered for elimination or replacement. This does not mean that variety or elegance need be sacrificed in the food items offered.

Another important consideration is the number of employees available for work or the total number of person-hours available. Providing assistance to skilled employees, like a chef, will free their time for use in the preparation of other menu items that perhaps only they can make. Many menu items cannot be prepared and stored before service, and many items require last-minute preparation, such as hollandaise sauce. Last-minute preparation normally imposes a burden on employees at peak service times, and therefore every minor detail should be taken into consideration while planning menus. At times, permanent or temporary replacement of employees makes it necessary to modify or adjust the menus offered. It is advisable to get as much preparation as possible completed during any slack periods of time, with only essential last-minute preparation to be taken care of at a later stage. Since labor costs represent a major item of expenditure in food preparation, careful control of the above-mentioned aspects is necessary.

Types of Production and Service Subsystems

Types of production have a great deal of impact on the items that can be included in a menu. Time lag between production and service is critical. In a conventional food production and delivery system, where foods are prepared, held at serving temperature, and served on the same day, there are relatively many choices that may be included on the menu. On the other hand, in systems where food is cooked and chilled or frozen, there are severe limitations on the type of foods that can be prepared and served. The amount of time required for service is also very important. For example, in large multistoried hospitals, the time lapse between tray assembly and service may be so long that certain foods such as ice creams or omelets cannot be used. In some foodservice operations, where fast service is desired, the choices for menu items are restricted. A restaurant with table service will have a different kind of menu than that of a cafeteria. Thus menu choices are also based on the type of foodservice operation. A menu item that is suitable for one foodservice operation may not be appropriate for another.

From the Consumer's Viewpoint

The following factors are directly related to consumer needs and tastes and therefore need consideration when planning menus.

Nutritional Requirements

Almost every type of foodservice is starting to put a high priority on meeting the nutritional needs of its consumers. Until recently, institutional foodservices were the only type that was much concerned with nutritionally balanced menus, primarily because these operations are required by regulatory agencies as well as by their organizational objectives to provide well-balanced meals. Meeting nutritional needs in such institutions as hospitals, nursing homes, and schools is extremely important and must be given top priority when planning menus. Commercial foodservices are now beginning to give nutrition serious thought in the meals that they offer.

An essential guide for planning nutritional menus is the table of **Recommended Daily Dietary Allowances (RDA)** for different ages and sex groups (Table 3.1). These standards have been established by the Food and Nutrition Board, National Academy of Sciences—National Research Council for the maintenance of good nutrition of practically all healthy people in the United States. These allowances, commonly referred to as RDA, take into consideration individual variations among most normal persons living in the United States under the usual environmental stresses. Diets should be based on a variety of common foods in order to provide all nutrients, including those that are not included in the recommended dietary allowances and for which human requirements have been less well defined. Percentages of the daily RDA values should be taken into consideration when planning nutritionally well-balanced menus. Federal and state agencies require that the menus planned for certain institutions meet RDA values, as in the case of the school-lunch program, where the provision of one-third of the RDA per day is required. RDA values are updated periodically and reflect the most current requirements. RDA values are used by many foodservice managers, particularly those in hospital foodservices, for the calculation and labeling of nutrients in diets. On the basis of RDA, United States Recommended Dietary Allowances (USRDAs) are defined; they are primarily based on the average requirements, without taking into consideration the age or sex of the individuals. USRDAs are used primarily for **nutritional labeling.** Nutritional labels are printed on food packages and give information pertaining to calories per average serving; the amount of carbohydrates, proteins, and fats; and the percentage of nutrients provided in significant quantities by the specified normal serving of that food. USRDAs are often confused with RDA values, but there is a considerable difference between the two. In foodservice management, the RDA is used for menu planning, while USRDAs are helpful in purchasing and receiving of food, and in labeling menu items.

The growing nutritional concerns among many consumers have resulted in careful assessment of menu items and portion sizes served by many institutional and commercial foodservice operations. This warrants careful review of portion sizes and the percentages of the RDAs derived from them when selecting menu items. The salt, sugar, fiber, and overall carbohydrate contents provided by menu items also need careful assessment when planning menus. For certain specific nutrients, such as sodium, there are guidelines for recommended lower and higher limits of safe intake. A variety of foods, when properly used, will provide most of

Table 3.1

Food and Nutrition Board, National Academy of Sciences—National Research Council
Recommended Dietary Allowances,[a] Revised 1989
Designed for the maintenance of good nutrition of practically all healthy people in the United States

Category	Age (years) or Condition	Weight[b] (kg)	Weight[b] (lb)	Height[b] (cm)	Height[b] (in)	Protein (g)	Fat-Soluble Vitamins Vita-min A (μg RE)[c]	Vita-min D (μg)[d]	Vita-min E (mg α-TE)[e]	Vita-min K (μg)
Infants	0.0–0.5	6	13	60	24	13	375	7.5	3	5
	0.5–1.0	9	20	71	28	14	375	10	4	10
Children	1–3	13	29	90	35	16	400	10	6	15
	4–6	20	44	112	44	24	500	10	7	20
	7–10	28	62	132	52	28	700	10	7	30
Males	11–14	45	99	157	62	45	1,000	10	10	45
	15–18	66	145	176	69	59	1,000	10	10	65
	19–24	72	160	177	70	58	1,000	10	10	70
	25–50	79	174	176	70	63	1,000	5	10	80
	51+	77	170	173	68	63	1,000	5	10	80
Females	11–14	46	101	157	62	46	800	10	8	45
	15–18	55	120	163	64	44	800	10	8	55
	19–24	58	128	164	65	46	800	10	8	60
	25–50	63	138	163	64	50	800	5	8	65
	51+	65	143	160	63	50	800	5	8	65
Pregnant						60	800	10	10	65
Lactating	1st 6 months					65	1,300	10	12	65
	2nd 6 months					62	1,200	10	11	65

[a]The allowances, expressed as average daily intakes over time, are intended to provide for individual variations among most normal persons as they live in the United States under usual environmental stresses. Diets should be based on a variety of common foods in order to provide other nutrients for which human requirements have been less well defined. See text for detailed discussion of allowances and of nutrients not tabulated.

[b]Weights and heights of Reference Adults are actual medians for the U.S. population of the designated age, as reported by NHANES II. The median weights and heights of those under 19 years of age were taken from Hamill et al. (1979) (see pages 16–17). The use of these figures does not imply that the height-to-weight ratios are ideal.

the necessary nutrients. Related to the nutritional content of foods in menu planning are **consumer food preferences.** Certain foods, such as liver and organ meats, may be rich in nutrients but may not be liked very much by the average consumer. Thus, nutritional content alone does not guarantee a popular menu.

When planning menus based on nutritional requirements, consumer needs and wants discussed earlier should be taken into consideration. These needs will vary based on several factors, age being an important one. Menus for children require special consideration. The nutrient content of meals provided by the school-foodservice menus is restricted by the requirements of the National School Lunch Act, which gives guidelines for the nutritional adequacy of school lunches provided for primary and secondary school children, as well as some children in permanent-care facilities. The **school lunch program** is administered by the United States Department of Agriculture (USDA), which provides a cash reimbursement per

Water-Soluble Vitamins							Minerals						
Vitamin C (mg)	Thiamin (mg)	Riboflavin (mg)	Niacin (mg NE)[f]	Vitamin B$_6$ (mg)	Folate (µg)	Vitamin B$_{12}$ (µg)	Calcium (mg)	Phosphorus (mg)	Magnesium (mg)	Iron (mg)	Zinc (mg)	Iodine (µg)	Selenium (µg)
30	0.3	0.4	5	0.3	25	0.3	400	300	40	6	5	40	10
35	0.4	0.5	6	0.6	35	0.5	600	500	60	10	5	50	15
40	0.7	0.8	9	1.0	50	0.7	800	800	80	10	10	70	20
45	0.9	1.1	12	1.1	75	1.0	800	800	120	10	10	90	20
45	1.0	1.2	13	1.4	100	1.4	800	800	170	10	10	120	30
50	1.3	1.5	17	1.7	150	2.0	1,200	1,200	270	12	15	150	40
60	1.5	1.8	20	2.0	200	2.0	1,200	1,200	400	12	15	150	50
60	1.5	1.7	19	2.0	200	2.0	1,200	1,200	350	10	15	150	70
60	1.5	1.7	19	2.0	200	2.0	800	800	350	10	15	150	70
60	1.2	1.4	15	2.0	200	2.0	800	800	350	10	15	150	70
50	1.1	1.3	15	1.4	150	2.0	1,200	1,200	280	15	12	150	45
60	1.1	1.3	15	1.5	180	2.0	1,200	1,200	300	15	12	150	50
60	1.1	1.3	15	1.6	180	2.0	1,200	1,200	280	15	12	150	55
60	1.1	1.3	15	1.6	180	2.0	800	800	280	15	12	150	55
60	1.0	1.2	13	1.6	180	2.0	800	800	280	10	12	150	55
70	1.5	1.6	17	2.2	400	2.2	1,200	1,200	320	30	15	175	65
95	1.6	1.8	20	2.1	280	2.6	1,200	1,200	355	15	19	200	75
90	1.6	1.7	20	2.1	260	2.6	1,200	1,200	340	15	16	200	75

[c] Retinol equivalents. 1 retinol equivalent = 1 µg retinol or 6 µg β-carotene. See text for calculation of vitamin A activity of diets as retinol equivalents.

[d] As cholecalciferol. 10 µg cholecalciferol = 400 IU of vitamin D.

[e] α-Tocopherol equivalents. 1 mg d-α tocopherol = 1 α-TE. See text for variation in allowances and calculation of vitamin E activity of the diet as α-tocopherol equivalents.

[f] 1 NE (niacin equivalent) is equal to 1 mg of niacin or 60 mg of dietary tryptophan.

lunch when requirements are met by the foodservices. In addition to cash reimbursements, USDA commodities are donated through state departments of education, since student participation in such lunch programs varies from school to school. Local commercial foodservice operations, as well as snack bar and vending machines, have an impact on the students' decision to participate in the school lunch programs. Menus for school lunches have to be carefully planned with a view to the heterogeneous nature of the school population. Generally, these menus have to be planned well in advance, since they have to be publicized through various sources. The Type A lunch (Table 3.2) consists of the following meal components: (1) main dish, (2) vegetable, (3) salad, (4) bread item, (5) dessert, and (6) milk. A quick, nutritious meal can also be provided by the following permissible variation which consists of (1) protein-rich sandwich, (2) salad or raw vegetable, (3) fruit or cookie, and (4) milk. The nutrient standards are based on age groups as shown in Table 3.3.

Table 3.2

School Lunch Patterns for Various Age/Grade Groups

Components		Minimum Quantities			Recommended Quantities[2]	Specific Requirements
		Preschool		Grades K-3	Grades 4-12[1]	Grades 7-12	
		ages 1-2 (Group I)	ages 3-4 (Group II)	ages 5-8 (Group III)	ages 9 & over (Group IV)	age 12 & over (Group V)	
MEAT OR MEAT ALTERNATE	A serving of one of the following or a combination to give an equivalent quantity:						Must be served in the main dish or the main dish and one other menu item
	Lean meat, poultry, or fish (edible portion as served)	1 oz	1½ oz	1½ oz	2 oz	3 oz	Textured vegetable protein products, cheese alternate products, and enriched macaroni with fortified protein may be used to meet part of the meat/meat alternate require-
	Cheese	1 oz	1½ oz	1½ oz	2 oz	3 oz	ment. Fact sheets on each of these alternate foods give detailed instructions for use
	Large egg(s)	½	¾	¾	1	1½	NOTE: The amount you must serve of a single meat alternate may seem too large
	Cooked dry beans or peas	¼ cup	⅜ cup	⅜ cup	½ cup	¾ cup	for the particular age group you are serving. To make the quantity of that meat alternate more reasonable, use a smaller
	Peanut butter	2 Tbsp	3 Tbsp	3 Tbsp	4 Tbsp	6 Tbsp	amount to meet part of the requirement and supplement with another meat or meat alternate to meet the full requirement
VEGETABLE AND/OR FRUIT	Two or more servings of vegetable or fruit or both to total	½ cup	½ cup	½ cup	¾ cup	¾ cup	No more than one-half of the total require-ment may be met with full-strength fruit or vegetable juice. Cooked dry beans or peas may be used as a meal alternate or as a vegetable but not as both in the same meal

| BREAD OR BREAD ALTERNATE | Servings of bread or bread alternate
A serving is
• 1 slice of whole-grain or enriched bread
  • A whole-grain or enriched biscuit, roll, muffin, etc.
  • ½ cup of cooked whole-grain or enriched rice, macaroni, noodles, whole-grain or enriched pasta products, or other cereal grains such as bulgur or corn grits
  • A combination of any of the above | 5 per week | 8 per week | 8 per week | 8 per week | 10 per week | At least ½ serving of bread or an equivalent quantity of bread alternate for Group I, and 1 serving for Groups II-V must be served daily

Enriched macaroni with fortified protein may be used as a meat alternate or as a bread alternate but not as both in the same meal

NOTE: *Food Buying Guide for School Food Service*, PA-1257 (1980) provides the information for the minimum weight of a serving |
| MILK | A serving of fluid milk | ¾ cup
(6 fl oz) | ¾ cup
(6 fl oz) | ½ pint
(8 fl oz) | ½ pint
(8 fl oz) | ½ pint
(8 fl oz) | At least one of the following forms of milk must be offered.
• Unflavored lowfat milk
• Unflavored skim milk
• Unflavored buttermilk

NOTE: This requirement does not prohibit offering other milks, such as whole milk or flavored milk, along with one or more of the above |

[1]Group IV is the one meal pattern which will satisfy all requirements if no portion size adjustments are made.

[2]Group V specifies recommended, not required, quantities for students 12 years and older. These students may request smaller portions, but not smaller than those specified in Group IV.

The Child Nutrition Programs are available to all eligible children without regard to race, color, national origin, sex, age, or handicap. If you feel you have been discriminated against, write immediately to U.S. Department of Agriculture, National School Lunch Program.

USDA recommends, but does not require, that you adjust portions by age/grade group to better meet the food and nutritional needs of children according to their ages. If you adjust portions, Groups I-IV are minimum requirements for the age/grade groups specified. If you do not adjust portions, the Group IV portions are to serve all children.

49

Table 3.3

Sample Lunch Menus for 2 Weeks for Three Age Groups (Group III-V)

Monday		Group III	Group IV	Group V
Meat and Meat Alternate	Oven Fried Chicken	1 thigh 1½ oz*	1 drumstick & 1 wing 2 oz	1 drumstick & 1 thigh or ½ breast 3 oz
Vegetable and Fruit	Green Peas or Broccoli Spears	¼ cup	⅜ cup	⅜ cup
		¼ cup	⅜ cup	⅜ cup
	Fresh Fruit Cup	¼ cup	⅜ cup	⅜ cup
Bread and Bread Alternate	Hot Roll	1 small roll (1.1 oz)	1 small roll (1.1 oz)	1 small roll (1.1 oz)
	Rice Pilaf	1 serving ¼ cup ½ serving	1 serving ¼ cup ½ serving	1 serving ½ cup ½ serving
Milk	Lowfat or Whole	½ pt	½ pt	½ pt
Other Foods	Peanut Butter Cookie Butter	1 cookie	1 cookie	1 cookie

Tuesday		Group III	Group IV	Group V
Meat and Meat Alternate	Spaghetti with Meat Sauce	¼ cup 1½ oz	⅓ cup 2 oz	½ cup 3 oz
Vegetable and Fruit	Green Salad	¼ cup	⅜ cup	⅜ cup
	Cherry Cobbler or	2" × 3¾" ¼ cup	3" × 4" ⅜ cup	3" × 4" ⅜ cup
	Peach Cobbler or	2" × 3¾" ¼ cup	3" × 4" ⅜ cup	3" × 4" ⅜ cup
	Fresh Fruit	¼ cup	⅜ cup	⅜ cup
Bread and Bread Alternate	Italian Bread	1 slice (1 oz) 1 serving	1 slice (1 oz) 1 serving	1 slice (1 oz) 1 serving
	(Spaghetti)	½ cup 1 serving	½ cup 1 serving	¾ cup 1½ serving
Milk	Lowfat or Whole	½ pt	½ pt	½ pt
Other Foods	Choice of Salad Dressing Parmesan Cheese Cobbler Crust Butter			

Wednesday		Group III	Group IV	Group V
Meat and Meat Alternate	Sliced Turkey on Roll Turkey or Ham and Cheese on Roll Ham Cheese	1½ oz ¾ oz ¾ oz	2 oz 1 oz 1 oz	3 oz 1½ oz 1½ oz
Vegetable and Fruit	Lettuce on Sandwich	⅛ cup	⅛ cup	⅛ cup
	Vegetable Sticks	⅛ cup	⅛ cup	⅛ cup
	French Fries	¼ cup	½ cup	½ cup
Bread and Bread Alternate	Roll (Hard Roll)	1 large roll (2 oz) 2 servings	1 large roll (2 oz) 2 servings	1 large roll (2 oz) 2 servings
Milk	Lowfat or Whole	½ pt	½ pt	½ pt
Other Foods	Catsup/Mayonnaise/Mustard Molasses Cookie	1 cookie	1 cookie	1 cookie

Thursday		Group III	Group IV	Group V	Friday	Group III	Group IV	Group V
Meat and Meat Alternate	Burrito, Meat; Beans & Cheese or Tuna Salad	1 burrito / 1½ oz / ⅜ cup / 1½ oz	1 burrito / 2 oz / ½ cup / 2 oz	2 burritos / 3 oz / ¾ cup / 3 oz	Hamburger or Fishburger / Cheese	1½ oz / 3 oz portion / 1.6 oz / —	2 oz / 4 oz portion / 2.2 oz / —	3 oz / 4 oz portion / 2.2 oz / 1 oz
Vegetable and Fruit	Lettuce, Tomato & Onion with Green Pepper Bits or Mixed Vegetables; Strawberry Shortcake Strawberries or Fresh Fruit	— / ¼ cup / ¼ cup / ¼ cup / ¼ cup	⅛ cup / ⅜ cup / ⅜ cup / ¼ cup / ¼ cup	⅛ cup / ⅜ cup / ⅜ cup / ¼ cup / ¼ cup	Sliced Tomato & Lettuce or Carrot and Cabbage Slaw; Green Beans or Lima Beans; Fresh Orange Half	— / ¼ cup / ¼ cup / ¼ cup	¼ cup / ¼ cup / ¼ cup / ¼ cup	¼ cup / ¼ cup / ¼ cup / ¼ cup
Bread and Bread Alternate	(Tortilla) or Whole-Grain Roll	1 tortilla (1.1 oz) 1 serving; 1 small roll (1.1 oz) 1 serving	1 tortilla (1.1 oz) 1 serving; 1 small roll (1.1 oz) 1 serving	2 tortillas (1.1 oz ea) 2 servings; 2 small rolls (1.1 oz ea) 2 servings	(Hamburger Roll)	small roll (1.4 oz) 1½ servings	med roll (1.8 oz) 2 servings	med roll (1.8 oz) 2 servings
Milk	Lowfat or Whole	½ pt	½ pt	½ pt	Lowfat or Whole	½ pt	½ pt	½ pt
Other Foods	(Shortcake) Whipped Topping				Catsup/Mayonnaise/Tartar Sauce Peanut Raisin Mix			

*Italics indicate contribution to meal requirements

(continued)

Table 3.3 (*continued*)

Sample Lunch Menus for 2 Weeks for Three Age Groups (Group III-V)

	Monday	Group III	Group IV	Group V	Tuesday	Group III	Group IV	Group V	Wednesday	Group III	Group IV	Group V
Meat and Meat Alternate	Grilled Cheese Sand				Lasagna or	2½" × 3"	2" × 3¾"	3" × 4"	Barbecued Pork on Bun			
	Cheese & Ham or	1½ oz	1½ oz	1½ oz		1½ oz	2 oz	3 oz	Barbecued Pork	3 Tbsp	3 Tbsp	3 Tbsp
	Chicken Salad on Roll			1 oz	Chuck Wagon Steak with Gravy	1 steak	1 steak	1 steak		1 oz	1 oz	1 oz
	Chicken Salad	⅜ cup	⅜ cup	⅔ cup		1½ oz	2 oz	3 oz	Tuna Salad on Bun			
		1½ oz	1½ oz	2½ oz					Tuna Salad	¼ cup	¼ cup	¼ cup
	(Beef in Soup)	—	½ oz	½ oz						1 oz	1 oz	1 oz
									Black-Eyed Peas or Baked Beans	⅜ cup / ⅜ cup	¼ cup / ¼ cup	¼ cup / ¼ cup
Vegetable and Fruit	School made Vegetable Soup	½ cup	—	—	Mashed Potatoes or	¼ cup	⅜ cup	⅜ cup	Coleslaw or Collard Greens or	¼ cup	⅜ cup	⅜ cup
		¼ cup			Green Beans	¼ cup	⅜ cup	⅜ cup	Chilled Grape Juice	¼ cup	⅜ cup	⅜ cup
	School made Vegetable Beef Soup	—	1 cup	1 cup	Mixed Fruit or	¼ cup	⅜ cup	⅜ cup	Melon or Berries in Season	⅜ cup	⅜ cup	⅜ cup
			⅜ cup	⅜ cup	Fresh Plums	¼ cup	⅜ cup	⅜ cup				
	Fresh Fruit	¼ cup	⅜ cup	⅜ cup						¼ cup	⅜ cup	⅜ cup
Bread and Bread Alternate	(Bread) or	2 slices	2 slices	2 slices	(Lasagna Noodles)	⅜ cup	½ cup	¾ cup	(Bun)	med bun	med bun	med bun
	(Roll)	1 large roll	1 large roll	1 large roll		¾ serving	1 serving	1½ servings		(1.8 oz)	(1.8 oz)	(1.8 oz)
		(2 oz)	(2 oz)	(2 oz)	French Bread or	1 slice	1 slice	1 slice		2 servings	2 servings	2 servings
		2 servings	2 servings	2 servings	Whole Wheat Roll	1 large roll	1 large roll	1 large roll				
						(2 oz)	(2 oz)	(2 oz)				
						2 servings	2 servings	2 servings				
Milk	Lowfat or Chocolate	½ pt	½ pt	½ pt	Lowfat or Whole	½ pt	½ pt	½ pt	Skim or Chocolate	½ pt	½ pt	½ pt
Other Foods					(Gravy) Butter				Catsup/ Mustard			

Thursday		Group III	Group IV	Group V
Meat and Meat Alternate	Meat Ball Sub Sand Meat Ball or	*1½ oz*	*1½ oz*	*2 oz*
	Baked Fish	3 oz portion *1½ oz*	3 oz portion *1½ oz*	4 oz portion *2 oz*
	Peanut Butter (on celery)	—	*1 Tbsp*	*2 Tbsp*
Vegetable and Fruit	Celery	—	2 sticks *⅛ cup*	2 sticks *⅛ cup*
	Potato Rounds or	*¼ cup*	*⅜ cup*	*⅜ cup*
	Peas and Carrots	*¼ cup*	*⅜ cup*	*⅜ cup*
	Chilled Fruit or	*¼ cup*	*¼ cup*	*¼ cup*
	Lettuce, Tomato & Onion	*¼ cup*	*¼ cup*	*¼ cup*
Bread and Bread Alternate	(Sub Roll) or	½ roll *1¼ servings*	½ roll *1¼ servings*	1 roll *2½ servings*
	Roll	1 small roll (1.1 oz) *1 serving*	1 small roll (1.1 oz) *1 serving*	1 large roll (2 oz) *2 servings*
Milk	Lowfat or Whole	*½ pt*	*½ pt*	*½ pt*
Other Foods	Tartar Sauce/ Catsup			
	Butter			

Friday	Group III	Group IV	Group V
Cheese Pizza or Cheese & Sausage Pizza	3¼″ × 5″ *1½ oz*	3¼″ × 5″ *2 oz*	4¼″ × 6″ *3 oz*
Tossed Vegetable Salad	*¼ cup*	*⅜ cup*	*⅜ cup*
Cranberry-Apple Crisp or	2″ × 3¾″ *¼ cup*	3″ × 4″ *⅜ cup*	3″ × 4″ *⅜ cup*
Apricot Crisp or	2″ × 3¾″ *¼ cup*	3″ × 4″ *⅜ cup*	3″ × 4″ *⅜ cup*
Applesauce	*¼ cup*	*⅜ cup*	*⅜ cup*
(Pizza Crust)	*1 serving*	*1 serving*	*1½ servings*
Skim or Whole or Buttermilk	*½ pt*	*½ pt*	*½ pt*
Choice of Dressing			
Crust on Cobbler			

**Italics indicate contribution to meal requirements*

Many restaurants and fast-food chains are providing nutritive meals as well as suggesting ways through which adequate nutrition can be obtained by selecting certain menu items. Since children and the elderly are among the growing categories of their consumers, the nutritional quality of their meals is of paramount importance.

Providing nutritive foods by careful menu planning is absolutely necessary for hospital patients and nursing-home residents. Careful planning is most critical for nursing-home residents, since long-term planning has to be done, and pleasing these consumers becomes a real challenge. Menu planning for this group is not only based on nutrition, but also on food preferences.

In planning menus it is essential to consider the nutritional requirements of all categories of consumers. Closely associated with the selection of items based on nutrient contents are the different food groups, the most important of them being (1) meats, (2) fruits and vegetables, (3) milk and milk products, and (4) cereals and breads. The food items or choices selected should be such that all the food groups are included in one meal, if possible. This will indirectly ensure the nutritive content of the meals, although this may not be a very accurate way of estimating it. Many foodservices provide the caloric and nutrient contents of menu items and also express those values in terms of the percentages of the RDA. There are several ways of computing the nutritional values of the food items selected. One of the most common and economical way of estimating the nutrient composition of foods is by using the values from food composition tables. The U.S. Department of Agriculture (USDA) has published various handbooks and tables which can be used in the calculation of the nutrient values of foods. The USDA *Handbook No. 8* and *Handbook No. 456* are indispensable references for anyone involved in menu planning, since they contain tables that provide the nutrient compositions of hundreds of foods in various forms (cooked and raw, for example) expressed on the basis of commonly used portion sizes. These publications are updated from time to time so that new foods and current nutrient values can be added.

Menus should meet the nutritional needs of the patrons as well as those requirements set by the federal and state agencies, wherever applicable. Nursing homes and health-care facilities are required to meet certain requirements in order to qualify for state or federal aid. Residence halls, day-care centers, and other foodservices where quality food items are provided should serve nutritionally well-balanced and wholesome meals. Although institutional foodservices are particular about meeting nutritional requirements, many commercial foodservices as well as franchises have begun to put nutrition labels on their foods so that consumers may be made aware of the nutritive value of the foods they select. This type of information is definitely needed and will prove helpful in at least two ways: (1) by indicating the amount of the recommended daily dietary allowances provided by each meal and thereby helping in food selection, and (2) by reducing the misconception that foods provided by that foodservice operation are devoid of nutrients or are loaded with calories. Some foodservices advertise or list special types of foods they offer, such as those containing low fat or low salt. This information attracts the undecided consumer and leads to greater consumer satisfaction. Restaurants and other commercial foodservice operations offering balanced nutritious foods may prove to be valuable outlets for providing balanced diets to selected segments of the population. Inclusion of salads, fruits, and vegetables provides for nutritious meals as well as for making menus more appealing. At industrial foodservices, where workers may consume the main meal of the day, it is extremely important that the foods selected be rich in nutrition. The menu should therefore be planned taking into consideration nutritional needs.

Food Habits and Preferences

No matter how sophisticated preparation methods are or how attractively foods are served, a menu is of little practical value if the foods in it are not liked by the consumer. In menu planning, food preferences and habits play an important role. Currently, this factor is underscored by many foodservice operators primarily because of the following reasons: (1) food preferences are intricately related to several factors and are very complex, (2) data are lacking on food preferences, (3) simple methods for evaluating food preferences require expertise in several disciplines such as psychology and the behavioral sciences, and (5) the potential uses of food preferences in the management of the hospitality industry are not well defined.

To comprehend fully the intricacies involved in food and foodservice preferences it is necessary to analyze all interrelated aspects. When a menu is presented to a consumer, a variety of factors act simultaneously prior to the final selection of the menu item. "A person prefers to eat what he/she likes and likes to prefer what he/she eats" summarizes the complex nature of food preferences. Managers in the hospitality industry should recognize that all consumers have a great deal of previous knowledge and experience of food (no matter how limited that may be), which makes them highly critical of food as compared to other services or products.

Food preferences may be defined *as the selection of food items from choices available among acceptable foods*. Patterns of food selection may emerge as a consequence of temporary or permanent food preferences. Food habits may be defined as the way in which individuals, in response to social and cultural pressures, select, consume, and utilize portions of the available food supply. Food preferences are based on sensory, social, psychological, religious, emotional, cultural, health, economic, preparation, and other related factors. Food habits and food acceptances are learned, acquired, and finally become a part of oneself. They become a very strong form of individual self-expression.

Several influences start acting on one's food preferences at birth and continue to operate throughout life. The most important factors that influence consumer food preferences and that should be taken into consideration while planning menus are categorized and discussed in the following paragraphs. A summary of these factors is given in Figure 3.2.

Intrinsic Factors.   Intrinsic factors include certain influences directly associated with food, such as appearance, color, odor, texture, temperature, flavor, and quality.

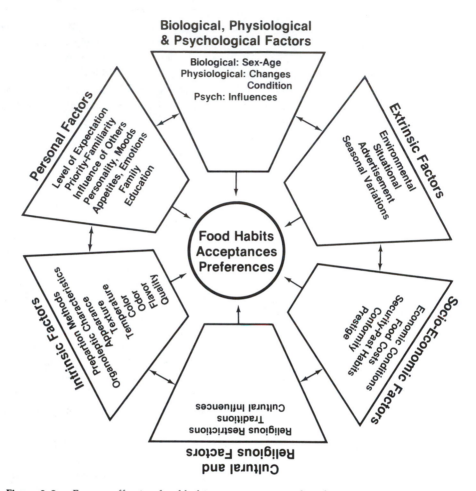

Figure 3-2. Factors affecting food habits, acceptance, and preferences.

The manner in which food is presented (including both desirable and undesirable attributes), the way food is arranged on the plate, and the temperature at which it is served all have an impact on food preferences. Standardized large-quantity food production may result in a different food preference ranking than when the same foods are prepared at home. Variability in these intrinsic factors affects food preferences.

Extrinsic Factors. Extrinsic factors include direct external factors that can affect food preferences as follows:

Environment. Food preferences are affected by the environment in which it is served, such as homes, restaurants, and clubs. A good example is the hospital environment, which has a marked effect on the selection of food. On the other hand, the effect that a candlelight environment in a restaurant has on food preference compared to that in a fast-food restaurant is obvious.

Situational expectation. The quality of food one expects is a function of the situation in which it is to be consumed. Food is expected to be good when it is associated with social, ritual, or religious occasions. Thus, the food served at a banquet or wedding party carries with it the expectation of something outstanding, in keeping with the occasion itself.

Advertising. It is evident and has been proven by many studies that advertising can influence one's attitude toward food. Many foodservice operations use this technique to attract customers. Consumers are tempted to try new food when it is appealingly advertised. Many restaurants advertise the specialties on their menus.

Time and seasonal variations. Food selections appear to be somewhat immune to the influence of certain natural phenomena such as seasonal variations, outdoor temperatures, and the day of the week. However, the availability of certain foods, particularly fruits and vegetables, affects their selection. For example, watermelons are generally preferred during the hot summer months. On the other hand, hot chocolate is not a summer favorite. Other factors, such as the hours of meal service and the length of the meal times, may also have an effect on food preferences.

Biological, Physiological, and Psychological Factors. These factors are each broad in scope but are grouped together here because they are closely interrelated. Physiological disorders can have a profound effect on food preferences by changing the appreciation, perception, or appetite toward food. These changes are often associated with psychological influences commonly related to physical well-being. Age and sex are major demographic factors that influence food preferences. A good example of this is the higher acceptance and preference of "fast foods" by the younger generation.

Personal Factors. The individual and personal attributes that affect food choice are as follows:

Level of expectation. Expectations have a definite effect on food preferences and selection. For example, patients in hospitals have a low expectation regarding food. When they find food better than they expected, the preference ratings are favorably affected. On the other hand, the level of expectation is much higher when dining at a restaurant. If the food is of lower quality than expected, the ratings can be adversely affected. This phenomenon coincides with the sociopsychological theory that the lower the level of expectation, the more easily satisfied the person is; and that people perceive things as they expect them to be, rather than as they are.

Priority. Priorities are indirectly related to the level of expectations. Airline foodservices or hospital foodservices are good examples of the consumers' priorities being to reach their destination or to recover and be well, rather than to have gourmet meals. Thus, aspects other than food are more likely to be critically evaluated.

Familiarity. The conditions (both environmental and social) under which a person initially eats a food has an impact on acceptance behavior. Earlier studies have shown that familiar terms on menus produced controversial results. Some research has shown that menu acceptance is enhanced by the use of familiar terms, whereas others have indicated that interesting or descriptive menus may increase food appeal.

Influence of other persons. Friends, relatives, and family members can influence food preferences. Even those being served on a cafeteria line can influence the food selection of a person behind them in the line. Individuals have been found to accept food advice best from those they consider friends or professionals. As would be expected, parents are quite influential in the introduction and acceptance of foods by children.

Appetites, moods, and emotions. The emotions affect a complex intermingling of preference factors. A careless server may be spared for bringing cold food to the table when one is in a good mood; the same may not be true if one is in a bad mood. Preferences for foods vary based on moods. Moods are unpredictable and constantly changing, which causes problems in menu planning. Moods and appetites are also influenced by physiological disorders, as well as such factors as satisfaction or dissatisfaction with work and other aspects of one's life. Food preferences may be a demonstration of one's personality, mood, and emotions.

Family unit. A mother's educational achievements and her employment status are associated with familial influence on food preferences. A young family usually is more concerned with economizing than a middle-aged couple, who may be primarily concerned with reducing calories, cholesterol, and salt in their diet.

Educational status. Extent and type of education affect food preferences and selection. Nutrition education also influences food preferences, but nutritional knowledge or education alone does not ensure an adequate diet or the correct selection of foods.

Socioeconomic Factors. Socioeconomic factors operate when one is following set food patterns or is altering them temporarily or permanently to meet economic limitations. Abundant evidence exists in both developed and developing countries to demonstrate that food choices are related to a great extent to income. During such short-term crises as illness or unemployment, people tend to cut back on the money they spend on food and drinks. One's sense of security can also be enhanced by retaining past food habits and resisting any change in them. Food preferences can be a means of demonstrating group acceptance, conformity, and prestige.

Cultural and Religious Factors. Cultural and religious motivations for food preferences may be transmitted from one generation to another. Various religious restrictions have resulted in stable and rigid food preferences. For examples, Muslims and Jews restrict the use of pork and pork products. In foodservice menu planning, recognizing various population groups and their food preferences can be observed among cultures in all parts of the world.

The above-mentioned factors seldom have an impact singly. They are interrelated and complex. All of these factors must be taken into consideration in menu planning, regardless of the type of foodservice. Food preferences have to be considered very carefully to avoid individual bias. Using informal and formal methods to analyze and study how consumers react to various menu items that are served can help avoid bias. Informal observations in the dining room and the cafeteria line, comments made by consumers, what is left over, and the extent of food waste provide valuable information on food likes and dislikes. Formal types of surveys may also be conducted. A typical food-preference survey form is shown in Figure 3.3. Many modifications are possible, based on the desired aspects under study. Questionnaires may be designed to suit specific foodservices by including pertinent questions. The results of such studies are very useful in planning menus. Food preferences of consumers should be assessed periodically, in order to consider changes in technology, food availability, economy, and food habits. Consideration of food preferences becomes more critical for a long-term menu planning. Menu items have to be rotated so as not to repeat food items, particularly those that are not well liked. A possible solution to food dislikes may be to include choices among menu items. A way of ranking food preferences may also be developed, and when choices are provided, foods can be selected in such a way that similarly ranked items are included on the menu as choices. This will facilitate balanced selection of items from choices provided in the menu. Choices should be carefully weighed before inclusion, since forecasting production becomes more complex with increases in the number of choices.

Food Characteristics.   Probably the most important factor to be considered in menu planning is the food itself. Characteristics of foods, which include their organoleptic (sensory) properties, play an important role in their acceptance. The most important food characteristics are discussed below.

Color. Interesting and coordinating color combinations help in the acceptance of food and, to an extent, indirectly help stimulate appetite. Planning and arranging foods so that there is a good color combination on a plate, tray, counter, or salad bar is an important aspect of menu planning. Even a small garnish, like a parsley twig or a cherry, can make an enormous difference in food appearance. Colorful foods have eye appeal, which can lead to their selection. Color also emphasizes the variety available for selection. When planning menus, different colored items should be included, and too many items with a similar color should be avoided. In some printed menus, the visual aspects of the foods are enhanced by colored pictures. Bright and desirable food combinations add to a menu's attractiveness, while dull colors convey a sense of blandness in the food. A consumer will often select food first by its eye appeal, thus color is a very important aspect to consider when planning menus.

Colors also have a psychological impact on consumers. Red, orange, peach, pink, brown, yellow, and light green are considered desirable colors for foods. Purple, violet, dark green, gray, and olive are less desirable. Artificial coloring may be added to enhance foods so long as it is safe and does not impart bitterness or any undesirable taste. Generally, natural food colors are preferred. Fruits and vegetables, in all their variety of forms and shapes, add to the colors of the menu items. Garnishings, plate decorations, and attractive counter displays add color and should be considered when planning menus.

Name: _____

Using the following scale, circle the number that most appropriately describes your like or dislike for the entrées listed below. Please try to answer as accurately as possible. Thank you.

0	1	2	3	4	5	6	7	8	9
Never Tried	Dislike Extremely	Dislike Very Much	Dislike Moderately	Dislike Slightly	Neither Like Nor Dislike	Like Slightly	Like Moderately	Like Very Much	Like Extremely

ENTRÉE	HOW MUCH YOU LIKE OR DISLIKE	COMMENTS
1. Carrot, Cheese, and Rice Casserole	0 1 2 3 4 5 6 7 8 9	
2. Cheese, Bacon, Tomato on English Muffin	0 1 2 3 4 5 6 7 8 9	
3. Cheese Fondue	0 1 2 3 4 5 6 7 8 9	
4. Cheese Rarebit on French Bread	0 1 2 3 4 5 6 7 8 9	
5. Baked Cheese Sandwich	0 1 2 3 4 5 6 7 8 9	
6. Waffle Cheese Sandwich	0 1 2 3 4 5 6 7 8 9	
7. Cheese Souffle	0 1 2 3 4 5 6 7 8 9	
8. Egg Croquette	0 1 2 3 4 5 6 7 8 9	
9. Barbecued Hamburger Squares	0 1 2 3 4 5 6 7 8 9	
10. Quiche Lorraine	0 1 2 3 4 5 6 7 8 9	
11. Sausage Patties w/Gravy	0 1 2 3 4 5 6 7 8 9	
12. Broccoli, Tomato, and Jack Cheese	0 1 2 3 4 5 6 7 8 9	
13. Chicken Livers w/Rice	0 1 2 3 4 5 6 7 8 9	
14. Roast Beef	0 1 2 3 4 5 6 7 8 9	

Figure 3-3. An example of a food-preference survey questionnaire.

Texture and shape. The textures and shapes of foods also affect consumers' preferences. Certain foods are preferred because of their hard texture and some because of their soft texture. A desirable combination of soft- and hard-textured items on the menu is essential. Impressions of the texture and shape of a particular food are formed even before tasting it. Texture can best be detected by mouth feel. "Soft," "hard," "crispy," "crunchy," "chewy," "smooth," "brittle," and "grainy" are some of the adjectives used to describe food texture. Certain combinations of food items go well together. Soups are preferred with crispy crackers, soft-textured potatoes go well with chewy steaks, and casseroles are desirable with crisp vegetables. Foods in different shapes add to the attraction of the menu as well as to eye appeal when the foods are served. Vegetable and fruit carvings provide interesting shapes and add to food appeal. Special equipment can be used to dice, cut, or carve products into various shapes and sizes. Carrots, for example, may be cut in squares, strips, circles, balls, screws, and other interesting shapes. Mixed vegetables combine interesting shapes, providing color and texture and enhancing the attractiveness of the food when placed on a plate. Even when similar products are included in the menu, different shapes can break the monotony.

Consistency. Consistency refers to the degree of viscosity or density of a product. Like texture, consistency provides for variety among menu items. "Runny," "gelatinous," "pasty," "thin," "thick," "sticky," and "gummy" are the most common adjectives used to describe consistency. These terms are most often used for sauces and gravies. Food items on a particular menu should have varying consistencies. Too many runny items on the menu may not only adversely affect their acceptance but will make it difficult to keep these items together on the plate without intermingling them. As a rule, items that have a hard texture should be complemented by items having a thin consistency. Relatively hard-textured meats go well with thin gravies, while nuts in thin items create a desirable combination of textures.

Flavor. It is obvious that the flavor of foods is an important consideration when planning menus. Foods can have sweet, sour, bitter, or salty flavors, which can be present alone or in combination. In addition, there are various off-flavors or undesirable flavors specific to certain foods. A desirable blend of flavors is essential for creating variety in the menu. The predominance of any one flavor is usually undesirable. A contrast in the types of flavors and their intensity adds to the acceptability of menu items. Bland foods may be made more appetizing by adding pungent sauces, or a blend of sweet and sour flavors may be added to a menu. Pickles and mustard add to the flavor of the foods when used in proper quantities. Too many pungent items or sweet items are not desirable. The right combinations of spices and condiments are essential in order to develop the right kinds of flavors. Frequent taste testing and standardization are needed to achieve the desired flavor combinations. Examples of foods with desirable combinations of flavor are sweet-and-sour meatballs, curried chicken with rice, lamb with mint sauce, sauerkraut and Polish sausage, chicken with orange sauce or honey, and broccoli with hollandaise sauce. Flavors can be masked or enhanced by adding contrasting items to the menu, as, for example, liver and onions, curried eggplant, and vanilla pudding.

Some recipes call for the addition of certain natural or artificial flavor enhancers, which, as the name indicates, enhance the flavors present in foods rather than provide their own flavors.

A combination of strong- and mild-flavored vegetables is desirable in menus. Broccoli, cabbage, and onions provide strong flavors and therefore should be complemented by mild-flavored vegetables. Strong-flavored sauces and gravies go well with bland items like rice or mashed potatoes.

Method of food preparation. Consideration should be given to the method of preparation in menu planning. Food can be prepared in many ways, and a variety in the methods of preparation is desirable. Some restaurants are limited or known for a certain type of food preparation, but most foodservices have the option of preparing foods in different ways. Methods include frying, baking, broiling, boiling, steaming, grilling, braising, or a combination of these methods. In each of these types of preparation, there may be variations based on the sauces or gravies or the equipment used, to produce dishes such as flame-broiled chicken with barbecue sauce or roast duck with gravy, for example. It is advisable to group by method of preparation all the recipes offered by a foodservice operation. This makes it easier to select items for preparation and to avoid items that are similar in preparation. From the management point of view, it is essential that there be a uniform distribution of the methods selected for food preparation to facilitate optimal use of employee skills and equipment. A fried item on the menu may tie up the deep-fat fryer or the skilled cook, thereby limiting the possibility of including other food items similarly prepared. Predominant use of a single preparation method is not desirable for many other reasons. For example, too many fried items on the menu — even with variability in the types of foods — is undesirable and unappetizing. Also, from the nutritional point of view, many consumers dislike fatty foods and/or may prefer steamed items. A balance in the methods of food preparation is therefore desirable so that a variety is provided.

Serving temperature. Temperature is probably the most easily controlled and least complex component in planning menus based on food characteristics. Food temperatures preferred by individuals vary with age and other personal factors. Both hot and cold foods are desirable on the menu. A chilled gazpacho appetizer is desirable with hot entrées, a cold salad may go well with hot bread, or a cold sandwich may be more desirable with hot soup. Similarly, cold desserts are preferred after hot entrées. There is no strong evidence that season or weather has an impact on the selection of particular temperatures of food, but it may be desirable to include a lemonade or sherbet on a hot day. Similarly, hot chocolate may be preferred on a relatively cold day. Seasonal availability of foods will also affect their inclusion on menus. Strawberry milk shakes, watermelon, and peach desserts are preferred in warm or hot seasons.

Presentation. The final appearance of food — whether on a plate, cafeteria counter, serving tray, buffet table, or in a display case or take-out package — is an important factor in the final selection of the item. Consumers buy with their eyes. A three-dimensional appearance adds to the attractiveness of food whether on paper or in actuality. All-flat food items on the plate, regardless of their taste, are unappealing and, to a great extent, undesirable. Similarly, all-tall food items on the plate are unappetizing and do not contribute to contrast and sequence in arrangement. A meat chop with a baked potato, a dressed whole tomato, a rectangular cornbread piece, and cut celery stalks is unappealing, regardless of colors or flavors. Thus the heights of the foods and the overall appearance of the menu items should be taken into consideration. A combination of tall, flat, and variously shaped items, arranged in a symmetrical pattern, is eye-appealing and should be considered when planning menus.

MENU PATTERNS AND TYPES OF MENUS

A **menu pattern** is the outline of food items and choices to be included in each meal. Menu patterns are based on the types of foods to be included on the menu, taking into consideration all the different factors influencing menu planning. Menus based on patterns may be divided into three principal types.

Set or Nonselective Menus

Nonselective menus are set and therefore do not provide choices among food items offered. Institutional foodservices normally have a set menu pattern, and some commercial operations may also opt to have set menus, particularly if their specialty is based on one or a limited number of food items. Sometimes set menus are referred to as simple menus, since they do not provide for choices and are simple in nature. Set menus are most suited to situations where the consumer is not qualified to make a decision, as in the case of young children, the incompetent elderly, or medical patients; or where there is limited time available for service, as in the case of banquets or foodservices at parks, tourist attractions, and sports arenas. In some other operations, production costs, the type of delivery service, available equipment, and personnel skills may make it necessary to have set menus.

Set menus facilitate easy production forecasting—saving management time and reducing waste to a certain extent. Planning set menus is relatively difficult, since such factors as variety, nutritional quality, and consumer satisfaction have to be considered while selecting from the choices available, which in certain situations may be limited. Consumer dissatisfaction may result if set menus are not carefully planned. Plate waste is indicative of the popularity and consumption of these menus. Set menus allow little potential for accommodating different categories of consumers, their food habits, and food preferences. Limited flexibility in the cost of food items is also a characteristic of set menus.

Selective (or Free-Choice) Menus

Selective menus provide two or more choices for each meal, and choices may also be provided for each course of the meal. These menus have enough flexibility and provide sufficient choice to fulfill the food preferences of most consumers. Selective menus are most commonly available in restaurants, fast-food franchises, and cafeterias. Ordinarily these menus result in greater consumer satisfaction than set menus. Because numerous choices may be involved, planning a well-balanced selective menu is demanding. Forecasting demand and, consequently, production, are difficult mainly because of the uncertainty in grouping choices. Preference ratings for food items may help in ranking foods and providing combinations. The process of selection by the consumer leads to increased contact and interaction with personnel, which may be desirable. Thus, a person in a cafeteria line, restaurant, or hospital will get an opportunity to interact with those providing service. This interaction allows the food server to promote the sale of food items by helping in the selection. From management's point of view, a selective menu is complex to plan and serve. This type of menu may include several choices among appetizers, soups, salads, vegetables, entrées, and desserts. Increased production imposes a load on the equipment and personnel which requires careful planning. Free-choice menus normally require more production and service equipment than set menus. Efficient portion-control methods are needed to control costs when this type of menu is used.

Partially Selective (or Partial Choice) Menus

Partially selective menus provide choices among entrées, vegetables, or desserts but not other menu items. Partial-choice menus provide answers to some of the problems inherent in the two types of menus discussed earlier. Several types of foodservice operations use this type of menu. Most often the choices are provided among entrées. Menu planning is facilitated by planning all other items and then selecting the partial-choice food items. It not only makes forecasting easier but also helps in planning production. Where there are limitations on the kind of equipment and the availability of skilled personnel, the partial-choice menu may be most suitable.

MENU CYCLES AND CYCLE MENUS

Menu cycle refers to the time period for which menus are planned, which may range from a few days to several weeks. It is advisable to have menu cycles based on odd-numbered days so that the serving of similar food items on certain days of the week is not repeated. The term "menu cycle" is often confused with another term, **cycle menus,** which refers to a set or different sets of carefully planned menus that are rotated at fixed intervals of time. Menus are planned for various periods, ranging from two weeks to several months, and are rotated at fixed intervals. Typical menu cycles in foodservices are based on a three- or four-month cycle, mostly in accordance with the seasons. An advantage of using cycle menus is that they provide for changes based on seasonal variations. A set of menus may be planned for each season and repeated at a set period of time, providing for the inclusion of seasonal foods. Within each set cycle, the menus can also be rotated.

The length of the cycle should be selected carefully, since the entire rotation is based on the cycle. The cycle has a beginning, middle, and an end period. The food items selected should be adequately balanced throughout this cycle. The cycle may be short or long. Short cycles may be of three weeks' duration or less and may be repeated at least four times per season. Separate cycles may be planned for each season. Thus, three-week cycles may be planned for fall (September, October, and November); winter (December, January, and February); spring (March, April, and May); and summer (June, July, and August). Long cycles may range over an extended period of time, such as six-week cycles within a year or more.

Cycle menus are commonly used in institutional foodservices, particularly hospitals and nursing homes. Where consumers are likely to utilize foodservices for a short period of time such as in hospitals, short menu cycles are appropriate. On the other hand, cycle menus may cause problems and create monotony due to repetition. The advantages of cycle menus may be summed up as follows:

1. If menus are carefully planned, cycle menus reduce the need for frequent menu planning, which avoids a tedious procedure and frees time for other management functions.
2. The repeated use of menu items in the cycle helps to standardize production and service.
3. The workloads of employees and the equipment used may be distributed evenly on a long-term basis and can be balanced uniformly.
4. Food purchasing and inventory control are facilitated, since purchase orders are easy to prepare and the inventory can be controlled accordingly. Well-planned and formal methods of food purchasing may be utilized since long-term needs are known.
5. Production forecasting and control becomes relatively easier.
6. Comparative evaluations of the cost of production can be made between menu cycles as well as between set periods within the cycles.
7. It is easy to make changes and troubleshoot problems.

On the other hand, there are several disadvantages associated with the use of cycle menus. The greatest problem stems from the fact that food may become monotonous due to the lack of variability over a period of time. Further, if the cycles are not carefully planned, errors or problems keep repeating. Short cycles may result in too frequent repetitions and monotony. If the cycle is too long, planning and management may become difficult and complicated. Therefore, the length of the menu cycle is extremely important and should be carefully assessed before and after its implementation. The first cycle of the newly planned menu should always be regarded as a test period, and adjustments should be made after careful assessment based on the problems encountered and/or observed deficiencies. Frequent adjustments may be necessary in subsequent cycles. New food items, when possible, should be included in the menu cycle to break the monotony. Adjustments should also be made for food costs based on inflation and other economic conditions. If this is not done, an expensive item may keep rotating in the cycle and impose an additional burden on the available budget. Cycles should be adjusted or arranged, keeping in view forthcoming special occasions and holidays. Once cycle menus have been carefully planned and evaluated, they become established and provide all the advantages listed earlier. Their proper use saves money, increases profitability, and facilitates efficient management.

MECHANICS OF MENU PLANNING

Menu planning is one of the most important responsibilities of management. Those planning menus should be aware of all aspects of production and service and must be experienced in the **mechanics of menu planning.** Since each foodservice operation is different in some respects, it will be necessary for a new manager to understand the unique situations and problems at the new foodservice facility regardless of his or her previous experience. Much can be learned from the successes and failures of past menus. In health-related foodservices, menus are checked and/or planned by dietitians. In any setting, it is advisable to have a group meeting for menu planning of all those concerned so that different ideas can be explored. Consideration should be given to having those in charge of purchasing and production at these meetings, which should be planned at a convenient time and location, well ahead of time, with no distractions or interruptions. Sufficient lead time should be allowed for food ordering, production planning, and employee scheduling.

Some reference materials that should be readily available for menu planning include:

1. Standardized recipe files, showing in detail method of preparation, portion sizes, portion costs, and nutrient content
2. Copies of previous menus
3. Cookbooks
4. Pictures of prepared foods, if available
5. Food preference data, if available
6. Market statements
7. Consumer comments, if available
8. Food delivery schedules
9. A comprehensive list of menu items, preferably with prices
10. Food sales record
11. Production records
12. Professional and trade journals
13. Organizational manual
14. Other pertinent publications

Since most of these items are readily available in the foodservice manager's office, it may be advisable to have the menu planning meeting there. Copies of the materials may also be placed in the library or conference room. Although not all of the above-mentioned references may be needed at one time, all those listed provide important information for menu planning. Consumer preferences and comments should be analyzed and reviewed first and, if possible, before the meeting. It is also advisable to arrange the menu items in categories based on one or more of the following attributes: cost, nutritional value, possible choices, color, seasonal availability, texture, and flavor. There are computerized programs that can categorize menu items based on the above-mentioned attributes and also provide a ranking among the items.

To start the process of menu planning, it is important to have several blank menu forms for use, since planning may involve several trials and errors. These forms should be based on the menu patterns and the number of choices planned for each meal. Careful planning of forms will avoid much inconvenience. They may be printed on regular size paper or incorporated on a large blackboard. Erasable ink, chalk, and pencils will be needed. An example of a menu planning form used on a weekly basis is presented in Figure 3.4, where meal types are listed on the right-hand side with the number of choices available under each (entrées, vegetables, salads, hot breads, and desserts) for each meal. This is the simplest type of menu form. Similar forms with modifications may be prepared for all three meals, as shown in Figure 3.5. These forms, which may be modified to suit individual needs, are very useful, since the food items selected are based on the type of items included on the preceding day and the succeeding day. These interrelations should be considered on a day-to-day and week-to-week basis. A typical menu pattern (Figure 3.6) should be outlined on the basis of which menu forms can be designed. A menu form should therefore include meal pattern(s), number of meals, days of the week, and types of food items.

When planning menus, care should be taken to avoid food leftovers. In cycle menus, it will be difficult to utilize leftovers until the cycle is repeated. It is advisable to keep a record of leftover items and consider it when planning menus. Leftovers are also indicative of the popularity or the lack of it of certain menu items.

An early decision in menu planning is which meal or type of food should be considered first. Certain meals and food items have priority and should be considered first. It is advisable to follow the same sequence every time a menu is planned. Steps that have proven successful in menu planning are summarized on the following pages.

STEP 1. Entrées, or main courses, of dinners for entire menu cycle

Dinner entrées should preferably be selected first because (1) other food items for each meal are chosen to complement the entrée, (2) they are often the most expensive items on the menu, (3) good balance among the menu items is maintained by planning food items that complement the entrée, and (4) the entrée cost will be indicative of the average meal price that can be set.

Entrée selection should be based on cost, maintaining a good balance between high- and low-priced menu items. This balance should bring about an average price for these items on a day-to-day basis. What an average price should be depends on the type of foodservice and what is considered to be a desirable average meal check.

Breakfast/Lunch/Dinner (circle one)	Dates: From _____ through _____	Week: _____			
Food Items	MONDAY	TUESDAY	WEDNESDAY	THURSDAY	FRIDAY
SOUP					
ENTRÉES 1. 2.					
VEGETABLES 1. 2. 3.					
SALADS 1. 2.					
HOT BREADS					
DESSERTS 1. 2.					

Figure 3-4. A typical blank form for planning menus.

Large fluctuations in menu prices could affect the reputation of the foodservice operation.

If the menu pattern does not provide for choices, a weekly menu should be planned using different entrée items from meats or meat substitutes. Care should be taken to see that the same type of meat is not offered on the preceding or the succeeding day of the week, even if the preparation methods are different. For example, a casserole with ground beef should not be followed by hamburgers. If there are several choices provided for the same meal, combinations may be selected on the basis of preference ratings. An example of the preference rating collection is shown in Figure 3.3. Food items with a similar or close rating to each other should be included in choices in order to avoid overselection of one popular item placed against relatively less popular items. Variety should be considered when providing more than one entrée choice on the same day. Barbecued beef, turkey divan, and cheese omelet; or fried chicken, roast beef, and fish are good examples of variety among choices. Even when choices are provided, care should be taken to see that there are no repetitions on preceding or succeeding days. For example, fried fish and fried chicken or curried veal with rice and a carrot-and-rice casserole should preferably be avoided as choice combinations even though they are somewhat different. Similar variations in preparation methods should be provided for each day of the week. Items with similar garnishes and/or gravies also should be avoided. Garnishes or gravies should be limited since they add to labor cost.

Texture is an important consideration when selecting entrées. For example, it is not advisable to select casseroles as the only choices on a particular menu. Both soft- and hard-textured entrées should be offered so that there are enough variations to suit the demands of consumers. Foods that are fried, baked, broiled, poached, and steamed should be evenly distributed. Choices should include highly seasoned and relatively less seasoned items in order to provide variety. Gravies or drippings may be added to improve the flavor of the entrées or other menu items as well as to supplement their nutrient content. Organ meats provide variety as well as good nutrition.

STEP 2. Entrées for second most important meal of the day

In most cases lunch is the second most important meal, except in foodservice operations where the employees or the elderly are served. In these cases, lunch may be the most important meal of the day. Most people prefer salads or light meals for lunch. If choices are provided, there should be a balance among these items. In the final selection of foods, all aspects discussed in selecting dinner entrées should be taken into consideration. Variety in type of meat, preparation methods, texture, and color should all be considered. A cost balance should be maintained by selecting both high-cost and the low-cost entrées. For example, if a high-cost entrée was selected for dinner, a relatively low-cost entrée may be selected for lunch, and vice versa. The item selected should complement the previously selected most important meal of the day.

DATES: From ———— through ————				NAME OF THE OPERATION:			
Meal and Food Items	MONDAY	TUESDAY	WEDNESDAY	THURSDAY	FRIDAY	SATURDAY	SUNDAY

BREAKFAST
Cereal
  1.
  2.
**Meat or
Meat alternative (s)**
  1.
  2.
Breads
  1.
  2.
Beverages/Fruit
  1.
  2.
  3.							

LUNCH
Appetizer
  1.
  2.
Entrées/Salads
  1.
  2.
  3.
Vegetables
  1.
  2.
  3.
Breads
  1.
  2.							

Desserts
1.
2.
3.
Beverages
1.
2.
3.

DINNER
Appetizer
1.
2.
Entrées
1.
2.
3.
Vegetables
1.
2.
3.
Breads
1.
Desserts
1.
2.
3.
Salads
1.
2.
Beverages
1.
2.

Figure 3-5. Suggested blank form for use in planning a menu for a week.

```
BREAKFAST
   Juice or fruit
   Hot or cold cereals
   Meat or meat alternative(s)
   Bread w. butter or margarine
   Hot and/or cold beverages

LUNCH
   Soups or appetizers
   Entrée
   Vegetable and/or salad
   Bread w. butter or margarine
   Dessert
   Hot and/or cold beverages

DINNER
   Appetizers
   Soups
   Entrée
   Salad
   Potato, rice, or pasta
   Vegetables
   Bread w. butter or margarine
   Dessert
   Hot and/or cold beverages
```

Figure 3-6.   A typical menu pattern. Note that choices may be provided within each category.

STEP 3. Starchy food

Starchy food such as potatoes, grains, pasta, and yams should be selected to complement the entrée, to provide variety in color, texture, consistency, shape, and flavor. If the entrées are relatively dry, moist and creamed dishes should be selected; on the other hand, if the meats have drippings or juice, bland foods such as mashed potatoes should be included to complement the flavor. Care should be taken to see that there are only a limited number of starchy items on the menu. It is possible that the entrée may be a casserole with a starchy food like rice or potatoes; under these circumstances, a separate starchy course should not be included. From the nutritional point of view this step should be carefully controlled since starchy foods are often loaded with calories. When the main entrées are low in calories, starchy foods provide good variety and may be used as "fill-ins." It is also possible to include one such item in the overall combinations provided in the menu. The judgment and experience of the menu planner(s) are needed to make these decisions.

STEP 4. *Vegetables*

Vegetables should complement the entrée items and should be selected on the basis of color, shape, size, texture, preparation method, and flavor. The food characteristics discussed earlier in this chapter should all be taken into consideration. In addition to contributing nutritive value, vegetables play an important role in making the total meal appealing. The variety and versatility of vegetables add to their desirability. Vegetable colors, textures, and preparation methods provide many possibilities and alternatives for the menu. They may be served whole, halved, quartered, sliced, diced, cubed, julienne, or carved into attractive shapes. They may be combined to give color variety. Carrots, broccoli, peas, cauliflower, beans, and other vegetables provide rich colors and interesting combinations. They may be prepared by steaming, boiling, or sautéeing. They may be creamed or added with other gravies. Many sauces and seasonings go well with vegetables. When more than one vegetable choice is provided, texture should be considered, and alternatives should be provided between soft- and hard-textured vegetables. Contrast in color, shape, and preparation methods is essential when choices are provided or when more than one vegetable is included in the menu. Flavors should also be considered, since some vegetables are pungent and have strong flavors as compared to others. For example, onions or vegetables belonging to the cabbage group are strong flavored and should preferably be used with vegetables that are relatively bland. Vegetables should complement the entrées of the day. Highly seasoned entrées should be complemented with mild-flavored vegetables and vice versa.

Nutritionally, vegetables are an important food group, and more than one type of vegetable should be included each day. A menu that provides for dark green and deep yellow vegetables daily ensures a high content of certain required vitamins. Vegetables should be served raw or cooked for the least possible time to preserve their nutritional content. Various types of plate garnishes may be provided by careful selection and carving of vegetables. Vegetables add visual appeal in addition to complementing the entrées in other ways.

STEP 5. *Salads*

Salads may consist of one or more combinations of vegetables, fruits, meats, fish, cheese, and gelatin molds. They may be accompanied by different kinds of dressings and garnishes. Salads add color, flavor, and texture to the meal. When selecting salad, entrées and vegetables for the meal should be considered to avoid repetition. All aspects should be taken into consideration; for example, the meat in a salad, even if in small quantities, should be different from that selected for entrées. The same rule applies to vegetables and fruits used in salads. Salad temperature also plays an important role. Chilled salads complement hot entrées, and this variation in serving temperature adds to the variety and appeal of the menu. Salads may also be selected as the main item of the meal. If choices are included, there should be at least one large salad, and possibly a variety of other salads in smaller serving sizes. A small salad may be preferred with a filling entrée or a large salad may be desirable with a sandwich. Salads such as tunafish, meats, vegetables, or cheese can become popular attractions or specialties of an operation. In general, if salads complement the entrées, smaller serving sizes are usually adequate. Salads contribute greatly to the overall nutritional value of a meal, and this fact should be considered when planning menus. Although salads do not require elaborate equipment, a good deal of hard labor is involved in preparation and arrangement. Salads require relatively large amounts storage space as well as careful handling during holding.

STEP 6. *Soups and appetizers*

As with salads, there are numerous types and kinds of appetizers and soups from which to choose. These items precede entrées or the main item of the meal. As evident from their name, appetizers are for stimulating the appetite. Soups, to a great extent, serve the same function. Since these foods are included to "whet" the appetite, it is essential to select recipes for soups that will increase the appetite for the main course of the meal. Soups and appetizers can be light or heavy based on their ingredients. A light appetizer should be planned when heavy and filling entrées are offered and vice versa. Light entrées or sandwiches may be complemented by heavier soups. Leftover vegetables, juices, and drained syrups from canned foods may be effectively utilized in soups. Soups for the succeeding meal should be planned with consideration of possible leftovers and their utilization. However, costs should be considered in utilization of the leftover items. It will be necessary to determine whether leftover vegetables would be more profitable as an accompaniment to entrées or as ingredients in soups. Various spices, condiments, and garnishes are used to complement appetizers and soups. As in the case of other menu items, it is necessary to plan appetizers and soups in such a way that there is no repetition with other items that may be on the menu. Creamed soups should not be served with creamed entrées. Fish chowders should not be included when other fish dishes are on the menu. The temperature at which soups are served is important, since the preferences for temperature requires equipment and labor which must be considered in menu planning. It is essential that soups maintain desirable temperatures until they reach the consumers.

STEP 7. *Desserts*

Since most of the menu items have already been selected, it is relatively easy to plan desserts. It is always preferable to select desserts last. Desserts are important because many patrons look forward to them. Desserts not only add a final touch to the menu, but also provide a lasting impression of the meal. Careful menu planning is essential, as a well-planned meal may be spoiled by a disappointing dessert. It is primarily the taste of the dessert that is important rather than the quantity. A tasty, small serving is sufficient to leave a lasting impression of the meal.

Desserts may consist of fruits (whole, part, or combination), cakes, pies, cheese, puddings, ice creams, cookies, nuts, or liqueurs. Many interesting combinations are possible. It is important to consider the caloric value in planning desserts. A light dessert should be planned with heavy meals and vice versa. There should be no duplication with any of the foods already included in the menu. The color, consistency/texture, and shape should be considered, as well as the intensity of sweetness. A hot, spicy, entrée may be followed by an intensely sweet dessert, or a hot meat item may be followed by ice cream. Sweet and soft desserts go well with filling entrées. Entrées and desserts are usually the main items that a food patron considers when selecting items from the menus, so they need to be carefully planned. When choices are provided among desserts, consider the type of dessert as well as its consistency, texture, color, and flavor. A pie, cake, and pudding are good choice combinations. Appearance of desserts is very important when they are displayed on a dessert cart or in display cases. Nuts, condiments, and syrups add to the appeal. Ice cream, sherbets, liqueurs, and frozen drinks are also popular dessert choices.

STEP 8. *Breads*

Breads can be of many different kinds and shapes. Their preparation methods and final texture also vary considerably. Breads complement the entrée and should be planned accordingly. The shape, size, and texture of the bread should be taken into consideration. Among the many varieties of breads are yeast, quick, sweet-dough, sourdough, flat, and several specialty breads. Several types of foreign breads are especially good with foreign entrées. The serving size of the bread should vary with the type of entrées. Since most breads are eaten with butter, greasy items should be limited when breads are provided. Bland breads may be included when spicy and/or juicy items are on the menu. Breads may be used in entrée items, such as cheese rarebit on rye bread. In these situations bread duplication should be avoided.

STEP 9. *Beverages*

Selecting beverages is probably the easiest step in menu planning, as several hot and cold beverages are usually included on the menu. Most beverages can be made relatively easily and frequently, or are readily available for serving, so little effort is needed in planning. At many operations the list of beverages is standardized. Seasonal availability and variations should be taken into consideration in planning beverages for the menu. Beverages may be selected from alcoholic or nonalcoholic beverages, carbonated beverages, fruit juices, lemonade, coffee, milk shakes, hot tea, iced tea, and various types of milk products. Herbal teas are also increasingly popular. Selection is complex for alcoholic drinks because of the wide variety of beverages available and the many possible combinations that may be requested.

STEP 10. *Breakfast menus*

Breakfast items are relatively simple to plan. Normally, there are fixed breakfast items that need to be included on the menu, although variations in the method of preparation are desirable. In institutional foodservices, breakfast is very important. Breakfast items should be such that they can be prepared easily on short notice. Several choices may be included, since preferences vary, and there are standard foods desired for breakfast by many consumers. Juices, cereals, toasts, eggs, sausage, ham, and biscuits are among popular breakfast items. Duplication and repetition of the items should be avoided as much as possible.

```
┌─────────────────────────────────────────────────────────────────────────┐
│  [  ]  Is menu consistent with the management's goals and objectives?     │
│  [  ]  Does the menu include all choices planned in the menu pattern?     │
│  [  ]  Does the menu have a balance between the low-priced and high-priced items? │
│  [  ]  Are all the equipment and facilities adequately utilized?          │
│  [  ]  Are all the personnel skills effectively utilized?                 │
│  [  ]  Are seasonal foods effectively used in the menu?                    │
│  [  ]  Will there be sufficient time for production of all the menu items planned? │
│  [  ]  Are the work loads balanced from the personnel and equipment point of view? │
│  [  ]  Does the menu meet the desired nutritional requirements?           │
│  [  ]  Is the menu well balanced from the nutritional point of view?      │
│  [  ]  Are the color combinations of the menu well planned, attractive, and pleasing? │
│  [  ]  Does the menu include items with varying consistencies and texture, thereby │
│        providing well-balanced meals?                                     │
│  [  ]  Are attractive and appealing garnishes and accompaniments included wher- │
│        ever possible?                                                      │
│  [  ]  Are all the flavors well selected to provide a well-balanced meal? │
│  [  ]  Are items selected of different shapes and sizes?                  │
│  [  ]  Is there a balanced distribution of food items based on their preparation │
│        methods?                                                            │
│  [  ]  Does the menu include hot and cold items distributed evenly?       │
│  [  ]  Are choices provided according to food preferences or popularity?  │
│  [  ]  Is the menu free of duplication, repetition, and blanks as to the food items │
│        included in the menu on the same day as well as the same week?     │
│  [  ]  Does the overall menu represent high quality, wholesome, appealing, and │
│        manageable food and beverage items?                                │
│                                                                            │
│  Comments: _____  │
│                                                                            │
│                                                                            │
│  _____  │
│                                                                            │
│  _____  │
│                                                                            │
│  Date:                                          Checked by:               │
└─────────────────────────────────────────────────────────────────────────┘
```

Figure 3-7.   Checklist for use in planning menus.

These steps outline the recommended procedure for menu planning. A final menu check is essential, taking into consideration all the factors mentioned in this chapter. The horizontal and vertical lines of the menus should be checked and rechecked. It is recommended that the menu be planned in two different sessions, one for active planning and one for finalization. A trial menu may be offered for the first few weeks, particularly if the foodservice facility is new. Modifications and

Considerations	MON	TUES	WED	THURS	FRI	SAT	SUN
1. *Management's point of view*							
a. Conforms to the menu pattern							
b. Provides balance in the cost of items							
c. Meets nutritional adequacy							
d. Is based on seasonal fluctuations							
e. Provides optimum work load							
f. Provides optimum equipment load							
g. Utilizes personnel skills							
h. Facilitates production							
i. Facilitates fast and efficient service							
j. Appears promising and profitable							
2. *Consumer's point of view* Variety in:							
a. Color							
b. Texture							
c. Shape							
d. Flavor							
e. Consistency							
f. Preparation							
g. Other _____							
3. Conforms with food habits							
4. Is targeted toward consumers							
5. Overall acceptability							
6. Other aspects _____							

7. Remarks: _____

Yes: ✓   No: ×   Needs Improvement: NI

Figure 3-8.   Final menu checklist.

changes in the menus may be necessary. Enough flexibility must be built into the menu to accommodate future changes and/or unexpected conditions. A final checklist is desirable for every type of foodservice operation. Examples of such checklists are provided in Figures 3.7 and 3.8. Either one of these checklists or one planned along these lines, should be used for ensuring that everything essential for the success of the menu has been considered.

COMPUTERS IN MENU PLANNING

With the development of computer technology and the availability of many different types of computers, more and more foodservices are utilizing these instruments for various aspects of management. The menu planning process becomes greatly simplified if a computer is used. However, all aspects of menu planning mentioned in this chapter need to be considered. Final judgment should come from management rather than the computer. Computers respond only to the information fed onto them, therefore accurate input of information is vital for the success of computer-planned menus. Using computers, menus may be planned on the basis of data on food preferences, food characteristics, production time, labor needs, nutritional quality, overall costs, selling prices, inventory control, and forecasting. Efficient programming to include all of this information as well as careful handling of data is essential. Both skill and experience are required.

The major advantages of using a computer for menu planning are:

Storage of a voluminous amount of data. Inventory records, lists of recipes and ingredients, cost of ingredients and prepared menu items, serving sizes of menu items, nutritional and food preference data may all be stored in the computer and recalled for use in planning menus.

Financial savings. If properly used, computers may save significantly the costs incurred in planning menus.

Calculations using the stored data. Using a computer, it is relatively easy to calculate the cost of the menu items, or the nutritional value of the menu; both procedures would almost be impossible to do by other methods in a limited amount of time.

Selection of menu items or choices at random. Selection can be facilitated if a sequential rating/ranking is provided.

Avoidance of human bias. Any bias related to use of menu items and employee scheduling can be avoided by using computers. Employee complaints and dissatisfaction can frequently be eliminated by using computers in planning.

Recommended dietary allowances. RDAs provided by meals can be very easily calculated by computers.

Cost calculations. Cost of the items, food cost percentages, selling price, percent profit, and other such calculations can be made easily.

Forecasting. Different forecasting can be done by using the stored data.

Consumer data. Popularity of the menu items can be calculated from consumer demand data.

Use in problem solving. Graphs, charts, bar diagrams, pie diagrams, and tables are easier to interpret than raw data. Thus computers may be utilized to get the information in any or all of the above-mentioned formats.

The use of computers as well as the type of computers to be used is a decision of management and must be based on several factors. The fact remains, however, that computers are becoming increasingly popular and, considering the complexity of the foodservice operation, they should be utilized in menu planning. Several types of software are available which can be used to conduct one or more of the above-mentioned functions. However, care should be taken to select programs that are appropriate for a particular foodservice operation. Buying software that is too complicated and has more functions than needed will prove to be time-consuming, complex, and most likely very costly. On the other hand, software should be selected taking into consideration future expansion and uses, ease of operation, and compatibility to existing or easily available hardware.

MENU FORMAT

After menus are written, revised, refined, and finally approved, they are ready to be tested and implemented. The menus have to be rewritten in two different **menu formats,** although the menu items themselves will remain unchanged. These two different formats are written (1) for foodservice personnel and (2) for consumers. Menus written for foodservice personnel are supplemented by such pertinent technical information as recipe file number, name of recipe, production schedule (if not included separately), equipment usage, and prepreparation schedule, etc. In many foodservices, this information is included on production sheets. Simple names of the menu items are included in this format, with which all foodservice personnel are familiar. From the consumers' point of view, menus are designed to "sell," and therefore foods are described to attract consumers' attention. The descriptions are planned to create an appeal for the items served. Examples of menu descriptions are presented in Figures 3.9 and 3.10.

Since the purpose of the menu is to *communicate* with the consumer, a good menu format is one which is effective in presenting its message. Careful word selection is required, and it should be remembered that words have different meanings for different people. A well-planned menu is of no value until the consumer "buys" it in all respects. Menu items should be described as accurately and honestly as possible. Overemphasis or masking of descriptions may create a negative effect. It is advisable that nothing be left for consumers to assume, since they are likely to avoid unfamiliar or unclear items on the menu. "Chef's Delite" or "Fisherman's Catch," with no adequate description, leaves a lot to consumers' imaginations and may adversely affect a good-quality product. Interesting or "eye-catching" terms should convey an accurate description of the menu item. Foreign terms used in menus should be followed by translations and/or descriptions. When foreign dishes are included, the cooking methods or concepts related to that food should arouse interest and, it is hoped, a desire to try those food items. Correct spellings with accents are essential when foreign terms are used. A list of the most commonly used foreign menu terms, with correct pronunciation and meaning, is given in Appendix A.

The art of Chinese cooking is based on three fundamental techniques: *t'i wei* ("enhancing the flavor"), *chieh wei* ("borrowing the flavor"), and *ju wei* ("absorbing the flavor"). To enhance the flavor, it is necessary to use the correct seasonings. Among the seasonings used in Chinese foods are ginger, garlic, and soy sauce. Some ingredients are used more for their interesting texture or nutritional value than for their flavor. In that case, the flavor is borrowed from other ingredients. To get optimum absorption of flavors, the seasonings must be allowed enough time to produce just the right aroma and taste. In preparing today's selections, we've used all three of these techniques to bring you an authentic Chinese meal.

APPETIZER

Egg Rolls—a filling containing cabbage, bean sprouts, bamboo shoots, and greens wrapped in an egg roll skin and deep fried

SOUP

Sizzling Rice Soup—a soup made of chicken, snowpeas, and mushrooms in chicken broth; it sizzles when deep-fried rice is added

ENTRÉES

Gingered Chicken—chicken baked in a soy sauce, ginger, and garlic marinade; served with rice

Moo Shu Pork—pork loin, bean threads, cabbage, string beans, eggs, soy sauce, sherry, and *wing yee* served on *pao ping* (a Chinese pancake) with a delicate plum sauce; a serving of rice is included

VEGETABLES

Cannelini Stir Fry—a combination of American vegetables, zucchini, tomatoes, cabbage, onions, cannelini (white kidney beans), prepared by the traditional Chinese stir-fry method and topped with Parmesan cheese

Spinach Stir Fry—spinach stir fried in the Oriental fashion

DESSERT

Almond cookies—a crisp almond-flavored cookie with a whole almond on top

Served with your choice of coffee, hot or iced tea, or milk

Figure 3-9.   An example of menu descriptions.

It may be difficult to describe salads accurately in written menus, since there can be numerous varying ingredients and it can be hard to come up with a representative term. Every effort should be made to describe the dish. Terms that are unfamiliar or nondescriptive will be a continual problem for management because consumers will always be asking questions. This can delay service, particularly in a cafeteria line. If the server is unable to provide an instant answer to menu questions, the consumer will be tempted to avoid the item, which may affect the restaurant's

APPETIZERS

Herring in White Wine

Smoked Rainbow Trout
  with dill mayonnaise

Gazpacho
  Cold and spicy vegetable soup

Seafood Crêpe
  A variety of seafood in a crêpe
  with shrimp and lobster sauce

Quiche Lorraine
  with fresh fruit garnish

New England Seafood Chowder

Turkey-Vegetable Soup

SALADS

Spinach with bacon

Tomato Salad
  with cucumbers and red onions

ENTRÉES

Yellowfin Tuna de Jonghe
  Fresh East Coast tuna baked with herbed bread crumbs, garlic, and sherry

Tuna Gratinée
  Fresh tuna baked with a zesty lobster velouté, tomato, and Parmesan cheese

Coquilles St.-Jacques
  Sea scallops sautéed with mushrooms, scallions, Parmesan cheese, and sherry

Shrimp and Lobster Sauté
  Lobster and jumbo shrimp sautéed with aromatic vegetables and finished with herb
  butter

Seafood Crêpes
  A variety of seafood stuffed in two crêpes with shrimp and lobster sauce

Breast of Chicken Milan
  Boneless breast of chicken sautéed with prosciutto, zucchini, and tomato

Breast of Chicken Gloria
  Boneless chicken breast stuffed with shrimp mousse and baked in puff pastry

Top Sirloin Milan
  7-oz. top sirloin steak broiled with prosciutto, zucchini, and tomato

Top Sirloin Steak Rossini
  7-oz. top sirloin steak broiled with pâté maison, served with a rich brown sauce and
  mushrooms

New York Strip Steak
  10-oz. steak
  13-oz. steak

Duck with Pepper Sauce
  One-half Long Island duckling in a rich hot sauce of Port, mustard, and hot pepper

DESSERTS

Strawberries Monte Carlo

Strawberries with Ice Cream

Grand Marnier Créme Caramel

Watermelon Sorbet

Figure 3-10. An arrangement of menu items and their descriptions.

reputation. These expensive delays can be avoided to an extent by careful planning of the menu format. Pictures are sometimes more effective than written descriptions.

In general, menus should be simple and easy to read, informative, attractive, self-explanatory, and complete. The menu should portray accurately the quality and richness of the items that were carefully planned and executed by the entire staff of the facility.

MENU DESIGN AND DISPLAY

Menu design and display primarily depend on the type of menu and the foodservice facility. Menus that are "á la carte" allow for the selection of food items by the consumer from a list of foods presented on the menu with prices. "Table d'hote" menus offer complete meals at a fixed price. There may be choices provided in one or more categories. There are different sets of menus in the hospitals for regular meals and for modified diets. Some menus are printed in such a way that more than one copy of the menu is produced when the consumer makes his or her selections. Patients are asked to indicate their choices in advance and copies are used on the tray assembly line, in record files, and in production. Cafeteria and fast-food restaurant menus usually consist of a listing of items on a menu board or printed sheets.

Menu design needs careful planning since the menu is almost the first thing the consumer sees, and it may easily be the source of a first impression of the foodservice facility. The outside cover tells a lot about the facility, since the design, colors, and the quality of the paper provide an overall impression of the restaurant. Menus with spilled foods and soiled paper are not only indicative of poor management but also a commentary on the type of consumers visiting it. For theme and ethnic restaurants, the design and colors of the menu should be reflective of the particular theme or culture. Many eating establishments have menus designed to match the decor, napkins, and tablecloths, the theme, and/or the trade symbol of the organization. A well-planned and designed menu is expected at an elegant restaurant. Cafeterias and stands may display menus on boards at the entrance or the back wall of a counter. Lighted, boldly printed, or electronically displayed menus are essential for drive-in facilities. The letters, whether in printed or displayed menus, should be of such a size that the menu can be easily read. Dark printing is also needed in restaurants that have candlelight or soft lighting in their dining rooms. Penciled-in changes are not desirable since they cannot be read easily. It also is advisable to provide pictures of the menu items, preferably colored.

Some restaurants prefer to have two different sets of menus, one with prices to be given to the principal host and one without prices to be given to the rest of the customers in a party. Many places prefer special clip-ons to the menus. The important items or specialty of the day can be conveniently added by using clip-ons without changing the main menu. The sequence in which items are listed on the menu is very important and affects selection. An easy way to list items is to follow the sequence in which they are to be served. In other words, menus should effectively communicate with consumers of all categories and all age groups.

Foreign languages may be used to describe menu items if the facility caters to an international audience or is located near or in an airport or seaport. It is also advisable to have special menus for those with poor eyesight. The size of the menu itself should be such that it can be easily handled. Too small a menu with items crammed on it is undesirable. On the other hand, too large a menu creates problems in handling and unfolding. Creativity in menu design pays off by providing a positive image of the restaurant. Some people even collect menus as souvenirs. Menus may also be printed on place mats, napkins, match boxes, electronic billboards, and handkerchiefs. Good-quality durable materials should be used for menu printing. Washable or easily wipeable materials are preferable.

It is also advisable to highlight specials or special nutritive value of the menu items. Menus should always be updated and kept current as to food items offered and their prices. Too many hand-written changes on the menu give a poor impression. Ingredients should be listed, if possible, particularly those ingredients—such as monosodium glutamate (MSG)—that may cause allergy or illness in specific individuals. Special items, such as the low-calorie or low-sodium foods, should be pointed out on the menu.

The menu should also include information pertaining to the facility such as phone numbers; address; location of other chains or restaurants; hours of operation; special events; map of the area; and credit card, check, or cash payment policy. In the case of elegant restaurants or those at historic sites, it may be advisable to include a short history or discuss the theme. If special items or antiques are on display, some description of them should appear on the menu. These aspects add to the prestige of the foodservice operation.

Finally, it should be considered that the success of a menu is evident only when the food on it is selected, served, and consumed, rather than when it is written. Careful assessment of consumer reaction is necessary for success of the written menu.

SUMMARY

Factors to be considered in menu planning are highlighted and discussed in detail in this chapter. Emphasis is placed on menu planning from the point of view of the consumer as well as the organizational/management goals of a foodservice operation. Steps in menu planning are explained in detail with examples of menu pattern, menu format, and design. A checklist is provided for menu evaluation based on all the requirements. Different terms used in menu planning are defined, and all essential concepts are explained in detail.

REVIEW
QUESTIONS

What is the significance of menu planning in foodservice operation? What factors should be considered in planning menus? Differentiate these factors based on the consumers' and management's point of view.

Compare the differences in menus and menu planning between institutional and commercial foodservice operations.

In view of the expected labor shortage by the year 2000 and beyond, what factors and changes do you forecast in menus and menu planning of the future?

What are the factors influencing consumer food preferences? How much significance should be placed on those factors while planning menus?

What is the difference between menu cycle and cycle menus? List all possible advantages and disadvantages of cycle menus.

Why should entrees be selected at initial stages of menu planning? List and describe the steps to be considered in menu planning.

Comment on the role of "menu" as a communicator between (a) consumers and management; and (b) management and employees.

ASSIGNMENTS

Critically analyze and evaluate a menu from a selected foodservice operation. Follow the checklist provided in this chapter in support of your critique.

Develop a menu pattern and plan a menu for a fine dining restaurant, selecting an appropriate theme. List all the assumptions you had to make while planning this menu. Use computers in this planning and submit the disk and a hard copy.

Collect at least five menus from different types of foodservice operations and comment on their layout and design. What factors would you consider in the layout and design of a menu targeted toward elderly consumers?

SUGGESTED READINGS

Crusius, V. C. 1981. Planning the menu. In *Quantity Food Management—Principles and Applications*, Chapter 7, pp. 96–114. Burgess Publishing Co., Minneapolis, MN.

Eckstein, E. F. 1983. *Menu Planning*, 3rd edition. AVI Publishing Co., Westport, CT.

Food and Nutrition Board. National Research Council. 1989. *Recommended Dietary Allowances*, 10th edition. U.S. Government Printing Office, Washington, DC.

Kotschevar, L. H. 1987. *Management by Menu*. National Institute of the Foodservice Industry, Chicago, IL.

Kreck, L. A. 1975. *Menus: Analysis and Planning*. Cahners Books, Boston, MA.

Miller, J. E. 1987. *Menu Pricing and Strategy*, 2nd edition. Van Nostrand Reinhold, New York, NY.

Peryam, D. R., and Pilgrim, F. J. 1957. Hedonic Scale method of measuring food preferences. *Food Technology* 11, 9.

Seaberg, A. G. 1973. *Menu Design, Merchandizing, and Marketing*, 3rd edition. Cahners Books, Boston, MA.

U.S. Department of Agriculture and U.S. Department of Health, Education and Welfare. 1980. *Nutrition and Your Health: Dietary Guidelines for Americans*. Office of Government and Public Affairs, Washington, DC.

U.S. Department of Agriculture. 1975. *Handbook No. 8 and No. 456, Nutritive Value of American Foods in Common Units*. Washington, DC.

West, B. B., Wood, L. V., Harger, V., and Shugart, G. 1977. Menu planning and food standards. In *Food Service in Institutions*, 5th edition. John Wiley & Sons, New York, NY.

CHAPTER 4

LAYOUT, DESIGN, AND FACILITIES PLANNING

KEY CONCEPTS AND TERMS

facilities planning
market data
site-analysis data
zoning
area characteristics
physical characteristics
actual and potential competition
food flow
flow diagram
flow pattern
shopping center design
space allocation
centralized kitchen
functional planning
templates
color combinations

Adequate layout and well-planned facilities are so essential for the efficient running of any foodservice operation that they must be considered early in the planning stages. The better these facilities are planned, the easier it will be to achieve goals and/or profits with smooth functioning of all subsystems within a foodservice system. A primary objective is to utilize these facilities for a long period of time, therefore possible future technological developments and advancements should be taken into consideration while planning. Layout, design, and facilities planning directly influence (1) worker productivity, (2) labor and energy costs, and (3) consumer satisfaction.

POINTS TO BE CONSIDERED IN FACILITIES PLANNING

The economy has a direct impact on the type of design and facilities selected for foodservices. The following aspects should be considered in **facilities planning:**

1. The layout, design, and facilities should be based on the selected menus and menus patterns. A plan good for one operation may not necessarily be workable for another operation.
2. The design should be such that future redesign and modeling is possible, facilitating new menu items and future development in equipment and machinery.
3. There should be options available for the selection of various forms of energy as well as energy-efficient appliances and equipment. The design and the resulting facilities, such as kitchen or dining room, should provide for an environment in which work may be done efficiently. A good design should lead to optimal worker productivity and consumer satisfaction.

In many operations, facilities planning and design are left solely to architects or engineers, who may not be familiar with the needs of a foodservice operation. Foodservice administrators or managers can help architects and engineers by providing practical information before a facility is designed. A team approach should be employed, with foodservice personnel constantly evaluating the plans and approving them at every step. If possible, personnel who will work in the units or with the equipment should be consulted and plans adjusted accordingly. This important consideration is often ignored, resulting in expensive and continuous inconvenience and losses. It is necessary to look into the future when planning facilities, so that additions or improvements can easily be made later.

Once the goals are established and the menu selected, a planning team consisting of architects, engineers, interior designers, and foodservice personnel should be assembled. In designing and planning foodservice facilities, it is essential to consider scientific and technological data. In addition, imagination and creativity are needed to produce an efficient and workable plan. Appearance, safety, and sanitation features must also be considered. For example, textured walls are attractive, but they may hide dirt and may be difficult to clean. Stainless steel is both attractive and utilitarian for surfaces in food-handling areas. Dirt can be easily detected on white or shiny surfaces. Thus, what is needed is a balance between utility and attractiveness.

MARKET DATA AND SITE ANALYSIS

Before any facilities planning is done, it is essential to collect **market** and **site-analysis data** (Figure 4.1). This is more important for planning new facilities than for remodeling existing facilities. Several factors must be considered to assure successful functioning and, therefore, profit. These factors are discussed below.

Zoning

Zoning is a most important consideration. Various areas have specific zoning laws, which differ in definition and interpretation. It is essential to know exactly what the available zoning permits allow. Many aspects of a site are regulated by zoning laws, such as the height of the structure, backyard and sideyard requirements, and what sort of activity can be pursued in that area. From the foodservice point of view, zoning laws also control two other important aspects—parking and use of signs. Laws specify the minimum number of parking spaces required for foodservice operations on the basis of the number of guests that can be served. Some areas have restrictions on the size, height, and/or type of signs that can be used, whether as name displays or as advertisement. Liquor permits are also sometimes based on zoning laws for the area.

Area Characteristics

The profitable functioning of a commercial foodservice as well as an institutional foodservice is dependent to an extent on **area characteristics.** The type of neighborhood provides preliminary information on the type of consumers that can be expected. One of the factors that needs to be considered is the growth potential and growth pattern of an area. Many foodservice operations have benefited enormously from adequate prediction of the growth pattern of a neighborhood. Future development of large industries, shopping centers, a main highway, development of resort areas, sites for entertainment facilities, or newly constructed subdivisions should be considered, since they promise potential future development and consequent increased profitability.

Physical Characteristics

Although **physical characteristics** of a site are particularly important to engineers, a foodservice operator may also get certain clues from prevailing physical characteristics. These characteristics include soil types, the nature of the subsoil, surface drainage, and direction of slope. Low-lying areas with poor soil drainage may pose problems during possible flash flooding. Similarly, the depth of the water table

Date: _____ Proposed Site:_____
Types of Foodservice: _____

CHARACTERISTICS	COMMENTS

ZONING
1. Current zoning _____
2. Anticipated changes in zoning _____
3. Height restrictions _____
4. Parking restrictions _____
5. Back and side yard restrictions _____
6. Sign restrictions _____
7. Other restrictions _____

LOCATION. Driving time and/or distances from:
1. Residential areas _____
2. Office complexes _____
3. Business districts _____
4. Educational facilities _____
5. Major market(s) _____
6. Sports and recreational activities _____
7. Historical sites and attractions _____
8. Interstate highways _____
9. Industrial centers _____
10. Shopping centers _____

AREA
1. Type of population _____
2. Future growth pattern _____
3. Type of businesses _____
4. Development of nearby areas _____
5. Target population(s) _____
6. Labor outlook _____
7. Planned development(s) _____

PHYSICAL CHARACTERISTICS
1. Top soil _____
2. Subsoil _____
3. Water table _____
4. Surface drainage _____
5. Slopes _____
6. Landscaping _____
7. Elevation _____
8. Distance from river, creek banks _____
9. Other characteristics _____

LAND MEASUREMENTS
1. Length _____
2. Width _____
3. Total area _____
4. Total usable area for: Building _____
                         Parking _____
                         Open space _____

Figure 4-1. Market and site analysis form.

CHARACTERISTICS	COMMENTS

VISIBILITY
  1. Obstructions
  2. Visibility from different directions
  3. Visibility of signs
  4. Visibility affected by location (e.g., within a mall or a tall structure)
  5. Improvements needed for visibility	

TRAFFIC PATTERNS AND REGULATIONS
  1. Traffic counts on site street
  2. Traffic counts on closest main street
  3. Peak traffic timings
  4. Type of traffic
  5. Distance to nearest highway
  6. Traffic regulations: one-way, stop-signs, no-turns, speed limits
  7. Parking regulations
  8. Public transportation	

SERVICES
  1. Police
  2. Fire
  3. Trash
  4. Garbage
  5. Security	

STREETS
  1. Width
  2. Pavements
  3. Curbs
  4. Sidewalks
  5. Lighting
  6. Grades
  7. Hazards
  8. Overall conditions	

UTILITIES
  1. Water
  2. Sanitary sewer
  3. Storm sewer
  4. Electricity
  5. Gas
  6. Steam	

COMPETITION
  1. Number of food facilities
  2. Type of facilities and menu
  3. Service style
  4. Number of seats
  5. Average sales
  6. Type of competition
  7. Impact of competition	

dictates whether a basement can be used for storage or other purposes. Landscaping is also extremely important. Natural landscaping, trees, and lakes not only improve the aesthetic and commercial value of a facility but save money needed in future maintenance. The most attractive side should face the dining area and the least attractive side used for storage and less used areas. Characteristics that should be considered are the length, width, and square footage or, in general, the size and shape of the lot.

Cost Considerations

Some of the above-mentioned characteristics affect the cost of the land. In addition to purchase price, the cost of land improvement and landscaping must be added. For example, it may be necessary to provide an expensive access road to the facility. Renovations can also be very expensive. Foodservice facilities have special requirements, and not all buildings are suitable for foodservice operations without extensive alterations.

Utilities

Obviously, utilities play an important role in any foodservice operation and access to energy and the type of energy available are important. Thus, the location of such major utilities as electricity, gas, telephone, water, and steam must be considered. Access to storm sewers should also be considered. Once utilities are installed, recurring costs may be involved, so it is essential to check beforehand. For example, a foodservice located in the vicinity of a large university campus or industry should consider the use of steam, which is a relatively inexpensive form of energy. Drainage and sanitation should be considered in the light of local public health regulations.

Access

Access routes to foodservice establishments are important, particularly in areas where severe weather occurs. The type and the condition of the streets, curbs, gutters, and pavements must be studied. The types of transportation available (i.e., bus, train) also are significant, since they are necessary not only for consumers and employees but also for deliveries. In addition, it is necessary to consider street lighting, since dark and lonely streets are potentially hazardous and forbidding to customers.

Position of Site

Location should be considered on the basis of driving distance as well as time to and from various centers, such as industrial, residential, recreational, sports, educational facilities, and central business districts. The proximity of the foodservice operation to these centers can give the planner some idea of the number of consumers that can be expected. A careful assessment of the site characteristics is imperative.

Traffic Information

In addition to site characteristics, traffic-flow patterns are important. Traffic counts should be recorded and used in the final analyses of the site data. A survey of traffic patterns indicates the time and direction of traffic flow. In addition to the pattern, it is also necessary to measure the frequency patterns of the traffic flow. One-way streets, speed limits, and availability of parking influence the patrons' decision to visit a foodservice operation. The types of transportation used, such as cars, trucks, and buses, should also be taken into consideration. Anticipated changes in the flow of traffic should be studied.

Availability of Services

Access to services is a factor often ignored in the analyses of data. One of the most important services for a foodservice operation is trash and garbage pick-up. Frequent waste removal is highly desirable. In addition, such services or service facilities as police, security, fire stations, fire hydrants, and sprinklers should be checked out.

Visibility

A foodservice operation can be greatly enhanced by good visibility, which is extremely important on highways and in remote areas. High-placed and lighted signs on highways are major attractions. Some states permit food facilities to advertise on road sites at appropriate intervals. Sometimes, wooded or shaded areas can be arranged to provide landscaping, in addition to providing good exposure for the foodservice operation. Any obstruction of signs or visibility should also be checked out. Signs—their location, type, distance between, and size—are all-important considerations.

Competition

It is obvious that a foodservice operation, to be successful, must consider its **actual and potential competition.** Major competitors should be considered in the light of their number, number of seats, turnover rate, type of menus offered, average check, and annual sales. A good operation may prove unsuccessful if it does not properly evaluate its competition. Competition should be studied thoroughly before final decisions on site selection and consequent planning are made by management.

THE PLANNING PROCESS

After collecting market data and making site analyses, the actual planning process should take place with an emphasis on product and consumer data. The following aspects need to be considered in the planning process.

Market

A detailed analysis of the potential users of the planned foodservice facility is essential for success. This information may be collected by actual counts, published reports, or data available from city agencies. Types of consumers and their preferences are discussed in Chapter 2. Information on consumers should include their age, sex, occupation, income, food preferences, access and transportation facilities to the proposed area, and any anticipated changes and development that might occur. Possible future development is an important consideration, and timely action may prove to be very profitable, particularly in or near malls, highways, offices, schools, and recreational or residential areas. The type of existing foodservice facilities and their availability to consumers should be considered. Because the functioning and profitability of an operation is dependent on the market, this study should be given prime importance, and all possible care should be taken in the collection of the data pertaining to it.

Type of Menu

Based on the market study, the menu must be selected, using the guidelines outlined in Chapter 3. The type of food items on the menu, methods of preparation, number of choices, portion sizes, and other related facts all have an impact on the layout, design, and the planning of the facilities. For example, if pizza is the main menu item, different layout, design, and facilities would be needed than for a restaurant primarily serving steaks. Similarly, if some of the food items on the menu require tableside or other display—flaming, for example—a different design would be essential. The seating arrangement, the equipment layout, and the overall foodservice design depend on the type of menu and on the service procedures to be followed.

Type of Operation and Service

The type of foodservice operation will dictate the type of facility needed. For example, a restaurant, cafeteria, coffee shop, drive-in, hospital room service, or fast-food counter all need different types of operational design. Planning for the kitchen and service areas must also contribute to the creation of the desired atmosphere. Careful selection of the colors of walls and furnishings, tablecloths and napkins, lighting, and decorations is required. All of these elements have an impact on the atmosphere which, in turn, is dependent on proper planning of the facilities.

When the above-mentioned preliminary aspects have been agreed upon, further planning will have to be done. The information collected from feasibility studies should be used to finalize plans, taking into consideration the type of facility and the menu. Once these aspects are decided, the space allocation for various functions of the operation should be considered. In any type of foodservice operation, the major functional areas include receiving, storage (dry, refrigerated, and frozen), production (of entrées, soups, vegetables, salads, and baked items), service, warewashing, sanitation, management facilities, and employee facilities. Careful planning is essential if all these functions are to run efficiently and to provide a smooth progression of all coordinated functions. It must be remembered that all systems are interrelated, and logical designs are necessary for their functioning.

The path that the food products follow from procurement to service is referred to as **food flow**. This path has to be considered in all plans made for the operation and service of the facility so that a smooth food flow is assured. It is advisable to have an outline of the facility on a drawing board so that the food flow can be examined

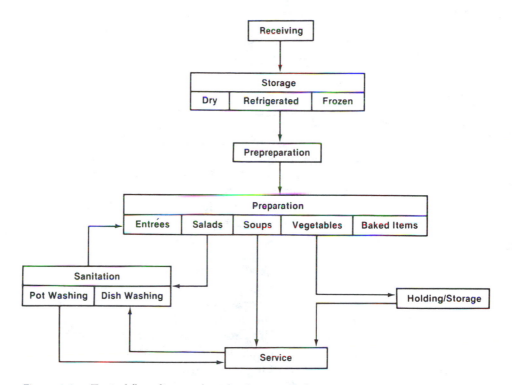

Figure 4-2.   Typical flow diagram for a foodservice facility.

visually. This will help to allocate space for all the different activities. The characteristic needs of different types of foodservice facilities are discussed below. Layout designs and plans must be based on these characteristics.

An overall **flow diagram** for a typical foodservice operation is shown in Figure 4.2. Such a diagram helps in planning work spaces and selecting equipment as well as in providing controls for the general **flow pattern.**

The design, layout, and overall plans for a foodservice operation should, therefore, be based on the type of facility and its goals. Although foodservice operations have similar flow diagrams, it may be difficult to use the flow diagram from one type of foodservice facility for another type. Equipment needs and activities to be carried out should be considered in the plans. A market and site analysis form is given in Figure 4.1.

CHARACTERISTIC NEEDS OF DIFFERENT TYPES OF FOODSERVICE FACILITIES

Although there are similar layouts and facilities in many foodservices, individual variations exist among different types of operations. These variations are dependent primarily on the type of consumer. Characteristic differences in the layout of various types of foodservices, as well as points to be considered when planning layouts, are outlined below.

College and University Foodservices

Layout plans for college and university foodservices are dependent on present and future student enrollment and the financial capability of the institution. Securing and keeping labor is a major problem, since high labor turnover is probable when students are employed on a part-time basis. The operation should be designed for high-volume feeding within fixed intervals of time. There are peaks and valleys in production times, with considerable stress during the peak-meal periods. Limitations on the times available for service exert considerable pressure on the employees as well as the equipment. Extended meal hours and continuous service solve some of the problems associated with feeding a large number of students. Single-service ware may prove to be economical and should be considered in order to cut costs due to breakage and to assure fast service.

Prompt service is highly desirable in college and university foodservices (Figure 4.3). Salad bars are very popular. At many colleges and universities, newer foodservice operations have a **shopping center design,** with several self-service and/or partially serviced islands. This design helps to distribute customers based on their choices and to facilitate fast service by reducing long lines. Food patrons are free to move from station to station. The "shopping center" system facilitates fast movement, since customers may go directly to the items they want without waiting in a single line for the whole foodservice area. It also provides time for better selection (Figures 4.4 and 4.5). However, if the shopping center system is not well controlled or designed, it may create more problems than it solves. Self-service operations have also been found to be economical. Counters may be planned in a zigzag fashion to provide more space, to facilitate easy movement of the customer line, and to add to an attractive interior design.

School Foodservices

Although the needs of school foodservices are similar to those for colleges and universities, there are distinct differences. Many school foodservices are limited to operation during the lunch hour, and many facilities have to be designed based on the school lunch program requirements. Since operations may be limited to lunch and many schools are under the jurisdiction of the school district, central kitchen and satellite types of foodservice operations are common. "Central kitchen" or **centralized kitchen** refers to a centralized food preparation area from which food is distributed to several locations or schools scattered within a set geographical region. Food prepared in the central kitchen is carried in bulk and then transported for serving at different schools. Thus the layout and design for a central kitchen should be based on the size of the operation, need for storage facilities, and equipment needed for transportation of bulk foods. Schools using the central

Figure 4-3. Layout of a cafeteria foodservice in an educational institution. (Courtesy of ARA Services)

kitchen or satellite operation need adequate holding, re-thermalizing, and service facilities. Shipping and receiving services must be planned accordingly.

Cafeteria-style service is common in many schools, and the limit of choices provides a fast traffic pattern. Seating arrangements should be such that there is a smooth flow of traffic.

Industrial Foodservice

Industrial foodservices are becoming increasingly important, since many industries realize that they are a good investment. The purpose is to provide wholesome, hot food to employees with the expectation of increased productivity. Time wasted looking for places to eat is also greatly reduced. Many industries maintain their own foodservices, while others use outside contractors. Industrial foodservices are usually subsidized, with food provided at relatively low prices. Some industries provide meals at no charge, particularly at sites such as oil rigs, offshore drilling plants, or coal mines that require employees to stay away from home for periods of time.

Most industrial facilities have cafeteria-style services with a menu providing choices. Time is an important factor, so efficient and fast services are desirable. Cafeteria service allows a variety of foods to be served at low cost in a short period of time. Either a line cafeteria or the shopping-center style is suitable. Snack bars and salad bars are also very popular. One of the advantages of a salad bar is that it allows individual choice and permits a variety of foods to be served. In some situations, it may be necessary to provide heating equipment, particularly microwave ovens. Disposable service ware may be desirable. Many establishments have attractive dining room facilities, primarily for executives and for business meetings. The food in these dining rooms is usually elegant, with table service provided. Foodservice should be planned for a 24-hour operation, or at least should make food available at times other than at regular meals.

Convenience is the main criterion to be considered in planning the layout for an industrial foodservice. Provisions for fast and efficient service with a variety of menu items should be considered in any plans. Workers frequently use dining room facilities as a convenient meeting place, a waiting room, or a common place for socializing at breaks. The atmosphere, therefore, should be such that it is conducive to unwinding, helping the hardworking employee to relax in a short period of time. Delays add to frustration in both workers and employers due to time lost. Since the work atmosphere in some industries is extremely noisy, it is desirable to provide several small rooms or areas with relatively quiet surroundings. Transportation of food from one facility to another must be taken into consideration, since many industries have several food stations spread out over a large area. Layout, design, and equipment selection should be based on efficient management and smooth flow through all aspects of foodservice. The dining areas should also be arranged for efficiency (Figure 4.6).

Figure 4-4. A Deli corner in a foodservice operation. (Courtesy of ARA Services)

Figure 4-5.   A specialized foodservice facility. (Courtesy of ARA Services)

Figure 4-6.   Seating in a dining room that provides for smooth and easy movement. (Courtesy of ARA Services)

Fast-Food Restaurants

Site selection and market studies are conducted carefully by fast-food chains. Many fast-food franchises have special teams to work on site and market studies. Fast-food operations are normally located in population centers and business districts where space is at a premium. The equipment needs of these operations are very specialized. Since fast turnover is desired, the atmosphere is brightly illuminated with minimally comfortable seating. Most of the menu items are preprepared or partially prepared and therefore require re-thermalizing. To provide fast service, it is necessary to cluster the equipment as well as to arrange the operation in a sequential manner. Thus, the most important aspect to be considered in a fast-food operation design is the "flow." Durable materials for both the equipment and walls and floors are essential. At many fast-food franchises, design and layout as well as equipment are standardized.

Specialty Restaurants

Specialty restaurants plan their menus around a theme, ethnic dishes, or other specific food items. Design and layout are variable and depend on the type of food specialties offered, as does equipment selection. Decor and atmosphere primarily depend on the theme of the restaurant. Interior design is often conducive to leisurely dining. Many operations offer tableside preparations requiring special layout and equipment.

Hospital Foodservices

Sanitation and safety are the primary considerations when planning hospital foodservice facilities. Menu items and their variations call for specialized equipment. An assembly line with conveyorized belts is desirable for setting up meal trays. Relatively large dishwashing and cleaning facilities are needed. Many hospital foodservices use centralized kitchens, and food may need to be transported in bulk. Since carts are involved in food transportation, aisles and spaces should be wide enough to facilitate smooth movement. Several hospital foodservices utilize "cook-chill" or "cook-freeze" systems for production and service, requiring large freezer and/or refrigerated storage areas.

Providing a special atmosphere for dining is not critical, since most hospitals have room service. However, special dining areas for guests and doctors are often provided. For around-the-clock operations, vending machines or limited service is desirable, particularly for the hospital staff working on evening or night shifts.

FUNCTIONAL PLANNING AND SPACE ALLOCATION

After the feasibility study is completed, the next aspect to be considered is **functional planning.** As depicted in Figure 4.2, the general functions of a foodservice operation are receiving, storage, prepreparation, preparation, postpreparation storage and holding, service, and sanitation. These functions can further be broken down into subfunctions. The fundamental criterion in planning a foodservice operation is to understand and visualize each and every function within that facility. Each function will be carried out by performing several tasks, and each one of these tasks should be considered. The next step is to arrange these tasks in a way that allows a smooth and sequential flow within that area. This is represented in the flow diagram in Figure 4.2, which outlines functions in a sequential arrangement. It is imperative to develop a flow diagram in order to plan the physical facilities and space allocation for each function. Although each foodservice is individual, there are general functions common to all. These are described below.

Receiving Area

The receiving area for foods, beverages, and supplies must be planned for maximum efficiency. The type and frequency of deliveries play an important role in planning. The number of deliveries is determined by the availability of personnel, space in the storage area(s), and other related aspects. Adequate space is needed for receiving, checking, weighing, moving, stacking, and transporting the items received. Space for such needed equipment as scales and inspection tables should be planned.

Loading docks should be planned on the basis of the type of deliveries expected. The truck-bed height should allow goods to be transferred efficiently from trucks to storage areas by using carts or other mobile equipment. The delivery platform should be of a convenient height and preferably about 8 ft deep. Movable platforms are preferable so that the heights can be adjusted. Gravity slides, conveyors, electric cars, elevators, and escalators may also be used for transport from receiving areas. The receiving area should be located away from and preferably out of sight of the main guest entrance or dining area. It should be easy to find, but away from congested traffic areas. Facilities for disposal of cartons, boxes, and other wastes are necessary. Some provision for limited temporary storage is desirable.

Storage Areas

Storage areas will vary according to the types of foods and beverages being stored and the temperature required for their storage. Sanitation and safety should be considered in planning all storage areas. Since quick and easy location of all stored products is highly desirable, they should be arranged conveniently and in a logical sequence. Standard patterns are recommended by certain professional organizations and franchised restaurants for uniform arrangement within storage areas. Stacks should be neatly arranged and easily movable. A well-organized storage area will reduce movement as well as labor and material costs.

The space required for storage area is dependent on

1. Type of menu
2. Temperature and humidity requirements
3. Frequency of deliveries
4. Maximum volume required to be stored and
5. Desired duration of storage

Ample aisle space is needed for the efficient movement of foods and personnel.

Dry Storage Areas

Dry storage areas are used for foods and various supplies to be kept at a temperature range of 50° to 70°F (10° to 21°C). The desired relative humidity for this area is approximately 50%. Many foodservice operators make the mistake of putting this area in the basement or near heat-generating equipment, such as motors or compressors, or near steam pipes. These areas are not suitable for dry storage, since the temperatures may be undesirable for the goods. Also, any leakage or sweating may lead to spoilage of stored items. Adequate ventilation is needed for such foods as root vegetables or unripe fruits. Certain supplies, such as linens, towels, paper goods, glassware, silverware, and furniture may also be stored in dry storage. However, detergents and other cleaning supplies should be stored away from food items.

Refrigerated Storage Areas

Refrigerated areas are needed for products that have to be stored at temperatures of 35° to 40°F (1.7° to 4.4°C). These temperatures are essential for storing fresh meats, fruits, vegetables, dairy products, leftover items, and beverages. Refrigeration space is also used for thawing meats. Walk-in and reach-in refrigerators are ideal for refrigerated storage. Walk-in refrigerators are desirable for foodservice operations serving 300 to 400 meals per day.

Generally, a refrigeration space of 15 to 20 ft^3 per 100 meals is recommended. Storage shelves should range from 2 to 3 ft in width. Aisle widths should be a minimum of 3 ft. Space requirements for refrigerator storage areas depend on the volume and type of products to be stored and the number of meals served per day.

Frozen Storage Areas

Frozen storage is required for foods to be stored at temperatures of 10° to 20°F (−23° to −28.9°C) and is mainly used for frozen foods. Since the use of frozen food items by many foodservice operations is increasing, a frozen storage facility should be carefully planned. Space requirements for frozen storage may be less than for refrigerated storage. Freezers may be of the walk-in or reach-in type. A walk-in freezer may be desirable for a foodservice operation serving 300 to 400 meals per day. Normally, both walk-in freezers and walk-in refrigerators are made as one unit, with an entrance door leading to the walk-in refrigerator. There is a separate door to the freezer unit inside the walk-in refrigerator. This helps conserve energy, since each time the freezer door is opened, the cold air from it goes into the refrigerated area, which is desirable. Sufficient aisle space and space for door opening should be provided. In order to conserve energy, it may be advisable to have plastic curtains or strips at the entrance.

Prepreparation Area

Many foodservice operations have a prepreparation area to accommodate activities such as peeling and coring vegetables and trimming meat. The space allotted to this area is dependent on the number of meals served and the amount of prepreparation needed at the facility. In some operations, this space is also used for ingredient weighing and other preliminary preparations such as mixing and marinating. Sinks, water lines, and other equipment will need to be included in this area.

Production, or Preparation, Area

The preparation area is the principal activity center of any foodservice operation and normally has several functions. Usually areas are assigned for the preparation of different foods such as entrées, salads, soups, vegetables, and baked goods. The amount of space required for each of these functions will be dependent on the menu and the number of meals served per day. These functions may be combined if space is limited, as it is in many restaurants. Space should be allocated based on the importance and priority of the function.

Space required for preparation is based on (1) type of menu and the items included in the menu, (2) type of preparation and the extent of the required preparation, (3) number of items and the quantity of each item to be prepared, (4) type of service, such as hospitals, restaurants, or cafeterias, and (5) equipment available for preparation.

Facilities serving a small number of meals require a relatively larger square footage per meal than those serving a large number of meals. For a foodservice operation serving 300 meals, the average production area needed, based on the type of facility, is given in Table 4.1.

It is evident that the space requirements for various types of food preparation facilities are based on a number of different factors. Once the areas for different types of preparations are designated, work spaces should be designed. Design should be based on the principles of work engineering and such human aspects as height and reachability.

A work area 4 to 6 ft long is usually convenient for an average person. The width of work tables may range from 24 to 30 in. A height of 34 to 36 in is adequate. However, whenever possible, adjustable table heights are desirable. All these facts should be taken into consideration while planning, since they directly affect the

Table 4.1

Foodservice Production Area Space Requirements[a]

Type of Facility	Require Space (ft^2/meal)	Total Space (ft^2)
Cafeterias	4.0–5.0	1200–1500
Restaurants	3.0–5.0	900–1500
Hospitals	5.0–12.0	1500–3600
Hotels	3.0–8.0	900–2400
Lunch counters	1.5–2.0	350– 600

[a]For 300 meals

productivity of employees and help reduce fatigue. Aisle spaces, which may range from 36 to 42 in in width, should be planned between work spaces, and should be wide enough to permit the movement of carts. They should allow free movement of traffic without interfering with work. Aisles should preferably be perpendicular to work areas and be limited to a minimum, since from a service point of view these are nonproductive spaces. Aisles should be used only for the traffic associated with service or production linked to food preparation. Through traffic should never be allowed through work areas. As a general rule, equipment in the preparation center should occupy a maximum of 30% of the total area. It is important to plan the placement of equipment in the preparation area as well as to plan the work spaces. **Templates,** which are small models or scale drawings, should preferably be used in the layout and design of the facilities.

Serving and Dining Areas

Serving and dining areas are dependent on the style of service of the particular foodservice operation. Since there are many styles of service, there are a variety of plans. Most service areas are designed to take into consideration the likes and dislikes of the food patrons, with particular emphasis on atmosphere.

In most restaurants, the service areas are attached to the preparation areas, and there is a pick-up center through which food is served to the customers. Particular emphasis should be given to planning so that the dining area is not affected by the smoke, heat, or sound of the food production areas. Preferably the door of the preparation area should not open directly into the dining area.

Estimating the space requirements for dining areas may be difficult, since different types of foodservices require different space allowances. In general, the space requirements for dining areas are based on

1. Type of service
2. Number of consumers to be served per meal
3. Largest number of consumers to be served at one time
4. Type of menu offered and number of choices
5. Turnover rate (Turnover rate per hour is the number of times a seat is occupied in one hour. Turnover rate per hour multiplied by the number of seats available will give the number of patrons served per hour.)
6. Type and pattern of seating arrangement
7. Table and seat sizes, shapes, and numbers
8. Aisle spaces between seats
9. Number and location of service stations
10. Special table preparation before service

Service and dining facilities should be planned using all the above-mentioned factors. The best possible plan for a dining room will take into consideration the maximum number of consumers that can be accommodated within the dining area, without any disruption of service or inconvenience to the patrons. Planning must consider the safety of everyone within that facility. Sufficient exit areas, as well as aisle spaces, for movement are essential. There should be adequate spacing between rows of chairs. Service aisles should be about 3 ft wide, and the access aisle (for the consumers) should be 1.5 to 2.0 ft wide. At least one aisle for patrons should be wide enough to allow for the passage of wheelchairs.

For cafeterias, the counter length should be based on convenience in serving by the employees as well as for food selection by the consumers. "Scatter," "shopping," "herringbone," or "sawtooth" cafeteria styles are names for counter arrangements.

In general, the comfort of consumers should be given primary importance. For comfort, adults require approximately 12 ft^2 of space. However, this may vary based on the type of foodservice operation. A deluxe restaurant may require as much space as 20 ft^2 per person, whereas a coffee shop may allow 10 ft^2 per person. At some foodservice operations, fast turnover is needed, and at such places seating that is too comfortable may not be desirable. Airports, where people may have to wait for a considerable period of time, are a good example of places where people may use eating establishments for sitting and spending time. For that reason, foodservices may have stand-up food bars or less comfortable seats to discourage their use as waiting areas. The same is true for certain fast foodservice operations, where seating is planned to encourage rapid turnover. Place settings at counters should preferably be 20 to 24 in apart. Sufficient elbow room should be provided for the comfort of consumers, as well as for smooth service by food servers.

Seating in a dining room should be planned so that a maximum number of customers can be served without inconvenience. If possible, the seating arrangement should allow a party of two, four, six, or eight guests to be easily accommodated. This type of seating will prevent unnecessary waste of space. In general, the seating capacity of a cafeteria is greater than a restaurant with table service using the same amount of space. Seating arrangements for banquets will naturally have to be specially planned to accommodate a greater than usual number of guests in the same space.

Service stations should be planned at convenient locations so that maximum consumers are served in the minimum possible time. These areas should have space for storing foods and equipment prior to and during service. Space must be provided for temporary storage of soiled dishes or trays.

Sanitation Areas

Sanitation areas include the dishwashing and pot-and-pan washing facilities. Space requirements will vary based upon (1) the volume of dishes, pots, pans, and other utensils to be cleaned at one time; (2) space available for holding clean dishes and utensils; (3) type of washing facilities and dishwasher; (4) methods used for cleaning and sanitizing; and (5) the number of personnel available for work.

The sanitation area should be organized so that there is room for stacking clean dishes and utensils. In addition to dishwashing and pot-and-pan cleaning, the area should include garbage disposal space and a place for keeping mops, brooms, and other housekeeping equipment. The space allocated for sanitation is primarily dependent on the type of foodservice. Public health department regulations must be considered when planning this area.

In addition to the above-mentioned areas, space should be allotted for employee facilities, such as lockers, lounges, showers, rest rooms, dining rooms, and office space. The space allowance for these facilities is based on several factors, including the type of foodservice operation.

PLANNING THE OVERALL ATMOSPHERE

Once layout and design are finalized, the next step is to plan the atmosphere, taking into consideration both the future food patrons and the employees. Atmosphere provides the overall impression of a foodservice operation. Planning involves the creative efforts of architects, engineers, interior designers, and foodservice managers. Management should play the key role in planning the desired atmosphere. Atmosphere is responsible for repeat consumers and results in long-term paybacks. Since a good atmosphere is something consumers will be talking about long after they have visited a foodservice operation, it is a form of publicity. The impact may be negative if atmosphere planning is neglected, regardless of the type of menu. Many customers are willing to travel extra miles to dine at an attractive restaurant.

Selecting the Atmosphere

Many factors have to be considered when planning the atmosphere of a restaurant. The type of foodservice operation is the focal point. A theme restaurant will naturally have a different atmosphere from that of a neighborhood coffee shop. If the restaurant is an ethnic one, special planning will be necessary to carry out the ethnic theme. The following aspects should be considered in planning.

Appearance

The overall visual perception of a facility includes, among many things, arrangements, interior displays, lighting, colors, light on the dining tables, screens, mirrors, chandeliers, signs, plants, and indoor and outdoor fountains.

Color is the single most important part of restaurant decor and one to which customers have an immediate first response. Color can be effectively used to create different types of feelings, and contrast in colors is more important than a single color itself. Primary colors (red, blue, and yellow) and secondary colors (green, orange, and violet) may be combined to produce intermediate colors. Red, orange, and yellow are considered "warm" colors, whereas green, blue, and violet are considered "cool." Planning should be based on effective **color combinations.** Light has an impact on color, and each should complement the other.

Selection of Colors

A number of factors must be considered when selecting colors or color combinations. Certain warm colors, such as red, orange, brown, or yellow, enhance the appearance of foods, especially meats. Food items on the menu should therefore be considered when selecting colors.

Dark colors may be used to make large or partially vacant dining areas look smaller. Conversely, light colors make rooms appear larger than they are. High ceilings may be made to appear lower and long, narrow rooms or passages may be made to look shorter by using dark colors. Undesirable objects or surfaces, such as pipes and supporting beams, may be made less conspicuous by using colors similar to those used for the background. Colors that are too dark, particularly those that are reflective, should be avoided. They are tiring to the eyes of customers as well as to employees.

At foodservice operations where fast service is desired, warm colors and bright lights should be used. On the other hand, relatively cool colors and soft lights are suitable for restaurants with table service and for elegant establishments. Cool colors are also suitable for operations serving seafood, as well as for facilities located in areas with a warm climate. Light colors and bright lights are preferable in all work areas. Dark colors and insufficient light can cause employee fatigue. Blue and green are considered refreshing and are recommended for work areas.

Ideally a combination of warm and cool colors should be used in decorating a foodservice facility, particularly when several different rooms are involved. Although a desirable, harmonious contrast in colors is preferred, care should be taken to see that there are not too many colors or designs in the same area. Linen, china, and glassware should be coordinated with the colors selected for the dining area, as should centerpieces, draperies, and other decorative items.

Colors and lighting selected for the dining area should be such that they complement the colors of the clothing worn by customers, particularly women. Colors should not detract from the attire worn for special dining occasions.

For room lighting as well as for color selection, emphasis should be given to focusing on objects that are designed to be highlighted, such as display cases, art objects, musical instruments, and decorative signs. Objects should be clearly delineated, with a background color that enhances their appearance. Lighting levels and placement of light should be such that there is no glare or strain on the eyes. If colored lights are used, they should coordinate with the colors used in the area.

Color may also be used effectively for color coding or for distinction between areas in a foodservice operation.

Odor

Odors in a dining area can be of two types—pleasant and unpleasant. The pleasant odors from food, candles, fabrics, linen, and plants should be so developed that they contribute to an elegant dining atmosphere. On the other hand, undesirable or too harsh odors must be controlled. An effective exhaust system should be used for air circulation and the elimination of undesirable odors, smoke, or fumes. Good air circulation is of particular importance in restaurants that serve highly spiced or ethnic foods. Aroma is also an important aspect in deciding what foods to order from the menu. The appetite-whetting aromas from charcoal-broiled foods and seafood are good examples. Desirable odors in foods served at hospital foodservice operations lead to greater acceptability and consumption of foods by patients. Linen and napkins should be immaculate in order to provide an odor of freshness. Frequent clearing and efficient ventilation of the dining areas are desirable to remove the odors of smoking. Table preparation and open display kitchens add to the desirable odors that stimulate the appetite and contribute to food appeal.

Sound

Sound may originate from the washing of dishes, rattling of trays, falling of silverware, or soft music played for the customers' pleasure. The origin of all sounds must be considered while planning the atmosphere of a restaurant. In order to avoid sounds from the kitchen or sanitation areas, sound barriers should be appropriately located. Doors opening into the dining area should not allow sound penetration each time they are opened. Silent and self-closing doors are preferred.

Music appropriate for the facility should be included as part of the atmosphere, as it has a direct effect on customer mood. Music may be used to reduce or inhibit an undesirable sound level originating in other areas as well as to enhance the atmosphere. The intensity and the quality of the sound are of particular importance. Music preferably should be soft and in the background to cause the least possible distraction. Speakers should be located in such a way that they do not intrude on the customers.

Comfort

A well-planned atmosphere should convey a feeling of comfort. There should be a perception of soft seats; the nice touch of draperies, linens, and napkins; a pleasant air temperature and relative humidity—all these contribute to an overall feeling of welcome and pleasure. The ideal temperature within the dining room should be between 70° and 75°F (21.1° to 23.9°C), with a relative humidity of approximately 50%. Temperatures vary depending on the outside climate and temperature and may be slightly higher or lower. The temperature of the dining area will also depend on the type of clothing worn by the customer. At formal dining places, slightly lower temperatures may be desirable as compared to informal places where light clothing may be worn. However, dining room temperatures must be adjusted according to the type of attire worn by customers. Elegant table settings, decorative napkin folding, and attractive place settings provide a feeling of welcome.

In short, it is the combination of all these factors that results in the atmosphere desired for a foodservice operation—something that can come about only by careful planning. The exterior design should be coordinated with the inside decor. Parking areas and entrances should be attractive and designed to provide all possible convenience to customers. Landscaping obviously adds to the appeal and complements the interior atmosphere of any foodservice operation.

SUMMARY

This chapter focuses on the layout, design, and facilities planning of a foodservice operation. Factors to be considered in collecting market data and site analysis are outlined and discussed in detail. Characteristic needs of different types of foodservice facilities are described with illustrations and examples. The significance of space allocation and functional planning is emphasized. Finally, the factors to be considered in planning of the overall atmosphere are discussed, highlighting points to be given specific importance.

REVIEW QUESTIONS

What factors would you consider in collecting a market data and site analysis for a foodservice operation?

How do the characteristic needs of an industrial foodservice operation differ from those of a hospital foodservice?

Outline factors that need consideration in functional planning and space allocation for different types of storage facilities.

Describe how color combinations can be effectively used in enhancing the atmosphere of a foodservice operation.

ASSIGNMENTS

Complete the market data and site analysis form for an existing foodservice operation and add your comments.

Visit one type of foodservice operation and evaluate facilities, layout, and design. Write a paper describing salient features and stressing any needed improvements.

Critically evaluate the overall atmosphere of a dining room and comment on the basic principles followed in its planning.

SUGGESTED READINGS

Kazarian, E. A. 1979. *Work Analysis and Design for Hotels, Restaurants, and Institutions*, 2nd edition. AVI Publishing Company, Westport, CT.

Kazarian, E. A. 1983. *Foodservice Facilities Planning*, 2nd edition. AVI Publishing Company, Westport, CT.

Kotschevar, L. H., and Terrell, M. E. 1977. *Food Service Planning: Layout and Equipment*, 2nd edition. John Wiley & Sons, New York, NY.

Wilkinson, J. (Ed.). 1975. *The Anatomy of Foodservice Design 1*. Cahners Publishing Company, Boston, MA.

Wilkinson, J. (Ed.). 1978. *The Anatomy of Foodservice Design 2*. Cahners Publishing Company, Boston, MA.

CHAPTER 5

EQUIPMENT SELECTION

KEY CONCEPTS AND TERMS

installation
depreciation
gauge
stainless steel
galvanized steel
finish number
hertz
horsepower
Btu
food contact surfaces
amperes
volts
watts
kilowatt-hour
resistance
ohms
infrared energy
templates
headspace

Selection of the proper equipment for a foodservice operation is extremely important. The type of equipment selected depends on the area in which it is to be used. The flow diagram in Figure 4.2 can be helpful in selecting equipment for the different units within a foodservice operation. Since equipment represents a fixed asset, which depreciates the moment it is purchased and installed, equipment selection requires careful planning and decision making. If improperly selected, equipment may tie up much needed cash and lead to the failure of the operation. A variety of restaurant equipment is available with varying degrees of modifications and a wide price range. Whether a particular piece of equipment is really needed and whether it is a good investment is one of the most difficult decisions a foodservice manager must face. In addition to experience, careful calculations are needed before such a decision is made. The volume of food production and handling, employee productivity, and profitability of a foodservice operation directly depend on the type of equipment available at the facility. Considering the systems approach, the main process within a foodservice operation is the conversion of raw food into finished product, based on the organizational objections. This process is not possible without proper equipment. Thus, the entire operation of a foodservice system is based on the availability of suitable equipment.

FACTORS IN EQUIPMENT SELECTION

Factors to be considered in the selection of equipment are discussed in the following sections.

Need

It is obvious that need should dictate the purchase of any equipment. Need and planned use of equipment should be evaluated on the basis of whether the purchase or addition of that particular equipment (1) will result in desired or improved quality of food, (2) will result in significant savings in labor and materials costs, (3) will result in increased quality of finished food products, (4) and/or will contribute to the overall profitability of a foodservice operation.

Essential equipment should be given priority and preliminary selection should be based on the basic needs of an operation. Need for a particular piece of equipment should be assessed from different points of view as, for example: (1) whether the equipment will be used for prolonged periods of time, (2) whether it has the potential for meeting the future needs of the foodservice operation, (3) whether the equipment will require maintenance, (4) and whether there exist alternate, less expensive versions of a similar piece of equipment that can meet the demands.

In other words, the need and essentiality should be calculated and well established. It is not financially advisable to buy more expensive or larger, more sophisticated equipment than that which is essential for a foodservice operation.

Cost

Several costs are incurred in the purchase, installation, and maintenance of equipment in any type of foodservice operation. The major costs incurred in the purchase of equipment are (1) purchase or initial cost; (2) **installation** cost; (3) insurance costs; (4) repair and maintenance costs; (5) **depreciation** costs; (6) initial financing costs, interest, and other charges; (7) operating costs; and (8) costs of benefits and losses derived by addition of the equipment. Installation of equipment may require extensive remodeling that can be more expensive than the cost of the equipment itself.

Market prices vary, based on the type of equipment, manufacturer, and the utility of the equipment. A comparative assessment of these costs is essential before making any decision regarding purchase. Some of these costs are calculated by the manufacturers and are available for consideration before purchasing or making a decision to purchase. Expensive equipment, like dishwashers, requires more careful assessment than relatively less expensive equipment.

There are various methods of calculating the profitability of equipment based on costs. A foodservice manager may derive an equation that can be used for calculating the profitability of equipment based on factors most pertinent to that particular operation. A common equation used for calculations is:

$$E = \frac{A}{B + C + D}$$

where E = calculated value

$\qquad A$ = savings in labor over the expected life of the equipment

$\qquad B$ = cost of the equipment (including installation) minus the resale value of the equipment at the end of the expected life

$\qquad C$ = cost of operation and maintenance of the equipment

$\qquad D$ = interest or gains possible from investments instead of purchasing the equipment

In the above calculations, if the value of E is 1.0 or more, then it is advisable to purchase the equipment, since it should more than pay for itself. If the value of E is more than 1.5, it is highly desirable — even necessary — to purchase that equipment. However, if the value of E is less than 1.0, it may not be advisable to purchase that particular equipment. Thus, the higher the value, the more potentially profitable it is to buy that equipment.

It should be noted that in the above-mentioned formula, the expected life of the equipment has to be included. Figures for the life expectancy of equipment are available from the manufacturer or the U.S. Internal Revenue Service. Normally, the life of common foodservice equipment ranges from 9 to 15 years. Various modifications of the formula may be made based on the factors directly pertaining to a particular foodservice operation. One such modification would be:

$$H = \frac{L(A + B)}{C + L(D + E + F) - G}$$

where H = calculated value
$\quad L$ = expected life of the equipment in years
$\quad A$ = savings in labor per year
$\quad B$ = savings in material per year
$\quad C$ = total cost of the equipment, including installation costs
$\quad D$ = cost of utilities per year
$\quad E$ = projected cost of maintenance and repair of the equipment per year
$\quad F$ = annual projected interest on the money in C, if invested elsewhere for the life of the equipment
$\quad G$ = turn-in value at the end of the life of the equipment

As in the case of the previous formula, if the calculated value H is higher than 1.0, it is a "Good Buy"; if it is less than 1.0, it is advisable to say "Good-Bye" to the deal. Normally, the higher the value of H the more advisable it is to purchase that equipment.

The following example will illustrate the application of the above formula. A restaurant owner is contemplating buying a steam-jacketed kettle for his operation. The data available indicates:

Expected life of the steam-jacketed kettle	12 years (L)
Projected savings in labor per year due to the purchase of the equipment	$500 (A)
Projected savings in materials per year due to the purchase of the equipment	$300 (B)
Purchase and installation cost of the equipment	$3500 (C)
Projected costs of utilities per year to operate equipment	$57 (D)
Projected costs of maintenance per year for equipment	$15 (E)
Annual projected interest on the purchase and installation cost of the equipment (assuming rate of simple interest to be 6%) will be $3500 × 6%	$210 (F)
Projected turn-in value after 12 years	$200 (G)

The value of H may be calculated by substituting the data in the formula as follows:

$$H = \frac{12(500 + 300)}{3500 + 12(57 + 15 + 210) - 200}$$

$$= \frac{9600}{3500 + 3384 - 200} = 1.44 \text{ ("Good Buy")}$$

This figure, as mentioned earlier, should preferably be higher than 1.0, but a foodservice operation management may decide to set this value to be much higher than 1.0. This will provide a standard basis for decision making when purchasing equipment. Also, it should be noted that the life expectancy of equipment may be much more than calculated, and so the final value of H may be higher. A conservative figure should preferably be used for the expected life of equipment. On the other hand, equipment may not last as long as expected or may get outdated before the expiration of the projected life period.

Functional Attributes

Since equipment is selected to fulfill certain functions of a foodservice operation, it is necessary to evaluate each piece of equipment based on its functional attributes in the light of the desired needs. Performance of the equipment should be assessed based on the cost as well as the availability of other equipment. Maximum possible functions as compared to the costs should be given preference. The possibility of modifying the equipment by attachments and other changes should be considered as an asset. Both present and future anticipated menu changes will also dictate the type of equipment to be selected. If relatively large sums are being invested in the purchasing of equipment, future changes and development should definitely be taken into consideration. Functioning of equipment is also based on the type of energy required for its operation as well as the extent to which it is planned to be used.

Sanitation and Safety

Sanitation and safety are primary considerations in purchasing equipment. Ease of cleaning and sanitation should be given high priority. No matter how sophisticated a piece of equipment is, if it cannot be cleaned properly, it is not suitable for a foodservice operation. All materials used in the manufacture of the equipment, particularly food-contact surfaces, should be made of nontoxic materials. Equipment used in food production should be such that safe temperatures can be maintained easily and at all times. Sufficient accessories such as lights and dials should be integral parts to ensure that the proper temperatures are reached and maintained. All parts should be easily accessible for cleaning. Wherever applicable and possible, the parts of the equipment should be able to be disassembled and reassembled easily and quickly to facilitate easy cleaning. Self-cleaning types of equipment are preferable. The National Sanitation Foundation (NSF) certifies foodservice equipment that meets defined sanitary standards. Whenever possible, equipment that has been approved by NSF should be given preference.

All equipment selected for a foodservice operation should have built-in safety feature(s). Electrical equipment should be used with proper voltage and should be free from any hazards. All moving and sharp parts should be properly protected. There should not be any rough or sharp edges. Safety locks and devices should be used on all equipment wherever possible, such as in steamers, steam-kettles, and carts. Equipment should be free of crevices or holes, which may either harbor insects or microorganisms or hinder proper cleaning and sanitation. All factors related to sanitation and safety should be checked before making any decision regarding purchase.

Size, Appearance, and Design

The size of the equipment should be such that it can easily be accommodated in the space available in the layout of the facility. It may be difficult to place equipment where limited space is available. Improperly located equipment will be a continuous source of inconvenience and even a hazard. The doors and openings of the equipment should be designed in such a way that they do not create any problems or hazards.

The design and appearance of the equipment should be attractive and it should perform the maximum functions with a minimum of problems. Durability should be given consideration in the design, since the equipment used in foodservice operations is subject to constant use and abuse. Although functional characteristics should be given priority over design, the latter should be such that it facilitates smooth functioning. The appearance of the equipment should be congruous with the type of facility, with matching colors whenever possible.

Overall Performance

Foodservice equipment should be selected on the basis of its overall performance, including such aspects as quietness of operation, easy mobility, remote control operations, computerized controls, variety of functions, availability of parts, and ease of maintenance. Those pieces of equipment that are known for their superior performance should be given priority. It may be advisable to purchase equipment with proven efficiency, rather than relatively new equipment with no history of use.

MATERIALS USED IN EQUIPMENT CONSTRUCTION

Foodservice equipment may be made from a variety of materials. The cost will largely be dependent on the type of materials used in construction. Some of the most common materials are described below.

Wood

Wood has both advantages and disadvantages for use in foodservice equipment. However, its disadvantages outweigh advantages because one of the major drawbacks associated with wood is problems with sanitation. Since wood absorbs moisture and is subject to cracking from the humidity of the atmosphere, it is unsafe from the sanitary point of view. On the other hand, wood has advantages. It is light in weight, it can be designed into different shapes, it can cushion noise, it can provide beauty, and it is relatively economical. Its use in foodservice is mainly restricted to cabinets, shelvings, handles, treated cutting boards, and other surfaces that do not come into contact with food.

Metal

Various types of metals are used in the construction of foodservice equipment. Metal sheets, plates, and plates with varying degree of polishing are used in various forms. Metal sheets and plates are usually specified in a standard measure referred to as **gauge,** which indicates the weight of the materials per square footage. Gauge is an indication of the durability of the material. Electroplating is the most common method used for plating metals. Such pure metals as aluminum, black and cast iron, or copper may be used, though most of the metals used in the construction of foodservice equipment are alloys, such as **stainless steel** (steels are iron and carbon in various combinations), brass (copper, zinc, and other metals), and Monel (two-thirds nickel and one-third copper). The use of pure copper has been practically discontinued in foodservices because it requires polishing, is expensive, is relatively heavy in weight, and it reacts with certain food products. Nickel is used for equipment trim, cafeteria railings, and counters. Aluminum is used for utensils, equipment interiors and exteriors, and steam-jacketed kettles. It is light in weight, has high thermal and electrical conductivity, does not corrode easily, is hard and durable, and can withstand pressure at high temperatures. It may be used in combination with other metals to form alloys having higher tensile strength. Cast iron is used in stands and supports of equipment and other surfaces that do not come into contact with food. Iron is used in pots, pans, griddles, range tops, gas burners, and similar equipment. Brass is used in faucets and shutoff valves. Steel is used for ovens, range interiors, exteriors, shelving, frames, and supports. **Galvanized steel** and iron, which is steel and iron treated with acid (by pickling) and coated with zinc, is used in dishwashing machines, sinks, tables, equipment legs, and supports. Noncorrosive metals formed by the alloys of iron, nickel, and chromium may also be used in the construction of foodservice equipment.

Stainless Steel

The extent to which stainless steel is used in foodservice operations and its importance justifies its discussion in detail. Stainless steel is preferred in foodservices because it can be easily cleaned, is bright and attractive, and can be kept sanitary because its bright surfaces show dirt easily. Like other steels, it is made by the

Table 5.1

Thickness of Stainless Steel of Various Gauges

Gauge	Inches	Millimeters
8	0.1644 (11/16)	4.1758
10	0.1345 (9/64)	3.4163
12	0.1046 (7/64)	2.6568
14	0.0747 (5/64)	1.8974
16	0.0598 (1/16)	1.5189
18	0.0478 (3/64)	1.2141
20	0.0359 (1/32)	0.9119
24	0.0239 (1/40)	0.6071

combination of iron and carbon in a proportion that results in a material resistant to oxidation or corrosion. Thus, it resists rust and stain formation. It can resist high temperatures, provide a shiny appearance, and is relatively easy to maintain. These desirable attributes have made stainless steel one of the most desirable and expensive materials used in foodservice operations. Most of the stainless steels used have a low carbon content and a relatively high chromium content. Common stainless steels have 11.5 to 27% chromium and a low carbon content. A higher chromium level provides a higher degree of hardness. Numbers are assigned to different types of stainless steels to designate their composition. The most commonly used stainless steel in foodservices is No. 302, which is composed of 18% chromium, 8% nickel, and 0.15% carbon. Since stainless steel is expensive, thickness is an important consideration in its selection. Common thicknesses of stainless steels are given in Table 5.1.

It should be noted that as the number of the gauge increases, the thickness decreases. Selection of the stainless steels should be based on their thickness. In general, Gauges 8, 10, and 12, because of their thicknesses, make good supports; and Gauges 12 and 14 make good table tops. Gauges 20 and above are primarily used for facing and exteriors. The cost of stainless steel is based on the extent of polishing desired, since polishing requires labor, material, and energy. The extent of polishing is designated by **finish number.** The common finish numbers and their descriptions are given as follows:

1	Hot rolled, annealed and pickled, dull rough
2B	Full finish, bright, smooth, cold rolled
2D	Full finish, dull, smooth, cold rolled
4	Standard finish for use in foodservices
6	High tampico, brush finish with velvety luster, used for specific tableware
7	High glossy polish with mirror or highly reflective finish

As specified, Finish No. 4 is most commonly preferred for foodservice use and is considered best for use in production areas. Higher finishes are preferred in serving areas. Higher finishes produce glare, particularly under light, which may be undesirable for use in such areas as kitchens. Polishing makes stainless steel very attractive and helps in cleaning.

Plastic

With technological advancement, more and more plastics are being used in foodservice equipment. The most common advantage of plastic is that it is available in different forms and can be molded into different combinations. Some of the commonly used plastics are acrylics (used in food covers), melamines (used for a variety of dishes and glassware), fiberglass (used in boxes, bus trays, and trays), nylons (used in equipment and mobile parts), phenolics (used in trays and containers), polyethylene (used in storage containers and bowls), polypropylene (used for dishwashing racks), and polystyrene (used for cups, covers, and packages). There are many different brand names for plastics, so it is important to select them on the basis of their use and durability. Some of the plastics are very hard and durable. Their sanitary properties should be given consideration in selection.

Coatings

Coatings are placed on certain base metals to provide desired properties which would be difficult to achieve if only metal was used. They may be enameled, painted, glass-coated, bonded, or baked on. Acrylic enamel, baked enamel, and porcelain enamel are commonly used in foodservice equipment. Silicone, which is an intermediate substance between organic and inorganic materials, is primarily used for making nonsticking surfaces, such as ice cube trays and ice buckets. One of the coatings that is becoming very popular is Teflon, which is fluorocarbon resin sprayed on oven interiors, pans, griddles, and other surfaces to facilitate good food release from these surfaces.

In general, for foodservice use, selection of materials for equipment should be based on their intended use. Guidelines for material selection based on interior surfaces may be summarized as follows:

Food contact surfaces. Materials should be smooth, nontoxic, corrosion resistant, stable, nonabsorbent, relatively heat resistant, and easily cleanable. They should not impart any color, odor, or taste to the foods with which they come into contact. They should not be affected by the pH of the foods and should not interact with any substances commonly present in foods or formed during food processing.

Splash-contact surfaces. Materials should be smooth, easily cleanable, corrosion resistant, noncracking, nonchipping, nonspalling, and resistant to relatively high temperatures. These surfaces should preferably be unpainted.

Surfaces not in contact with foods. Materials should be corrosion resistant, of a noncracking, nonchipping, and nonspalling type.

TYPES AND SOURCES OF ENERGY

Energy plays a very important role in the selection of equipment for use in foodservices. With increased emphasis on energy conservation, it is important to select equipment that is energy efficient. In order to understand energy, it is necessary to know its common sources as well as the common terminology used for the sources of energy.

Energy is available in different forms and can be transferred from one form to another. The common sources of energy primarily used in foodservices are electricity, gas, steam, and oil. The most important definitions and concepts related to the sources of energy are described below.

Electricity is the most common form of energy used in foodservices. It runs by a flow of electrons in an electric current, which is analogous to the flow of water in a pipe. As in the case of water, electricity can be quantitatively measured by the number of electrons flowing from a particular point at a given time. This flow of electrons per second is measured in **amperes** (amp or I). As the force of water from a pipe can be measured in pounds per square inch (psi), electricity can be measured in **volts** (V).

A volt can be defined as the force required to push 1 amp of electricity by a given point in one second. Thus, the voltage is indicative of the force with which electricity is flowing. There are different ranges in voltage, such as 110–120 V and 220–240 V. Voltage requirement is an important consideration in the purchase of any equipment. Before plugging in any electric equipment, voltage should be checked, since serious damage may result from using improper voltage. Foodservice equipment is frequently available in different voltages and some comes with dual voltages, in which a switch is provided to change to the desired voltage.

The force behind the flow of electrical current (V) multiplied by the amount flowing (amp or I) gives the measure of electricity in **watts** (W). In other words, $W = V \times I$. This is an important relationship and can be used for different calculations pertaining to electricity:

$$W = V \times I$$
$$I = W/V$$
$$V = W/I$$

The required amperage can be calculated using the above relationship. For example, if 2000 W of electricity is on a 110-V line, the amperage requirement would be I/V, or 2000/110, which is equal to 18.2 amp. A 25% safety factor, for possible fluctuations in electric current, should be added to this figure. Thus a 25-amp fuse will be needed for this circuit. In planning electrical outlets for equipment use, these calculations are very helpful. It should be noted that as the voltage increases, amperage decreases. For example, if the voltage in the above example is 220, the amperage would be 2000/220 = 9.09.

The watts and volt required for any electrical equipment are specified on a plate affixed to the equipment. For calculating the cost of the electricity, watts per hour are used. Thus a **watt-hour** (Wh) is one watt of electricity flowing steadily for an hour. Since there are a large number of watts involved in the use of electricity, a **kilowatt-hour** (kWh) is used, which is 1000 W of electricity flowing steadily for an hour. Costs of electricity are usually given in cents per kilowatt-hour, from which energy costs of any equipment or electrical appliance may be calculated.

Many of the electrical appliances, particularly those used in foodservices, have a grounding system. Since electrons in electricity carry a negative charge, they can be attracted toward a positive charge. Electricity may become free (due to various reasons) and flow to undesirable places. Thus, in order to provide for safety, measures are taken to ground negatively charged electrons by attracting them to a positive charge. It is advisable—even necessary—to use a grounding system. Usually the three-pronged plugs have grounding in them. In foodservice operations, all electrical equipment should be grounded for safety reasons.

When there is a resistance to the flow of water, there is an accumulation of water. Similarly, when there is a resistance to electricity, it accumulates to form heat. This principle is used when resistance elements are used for heating ovens, fryers, and similar equipment. **Resistance** (R) is set up against electricity by using certain metal wires, such as nickel, chromium, or their alloys. Resistance is measured in **ohms.** One ohm is equal to 1 amp at 1 V. Ohms can be calculated as:

$$R = V/I$$
$$I = V/R$$
$$V = I/R$$

Electricity may exist as a direct current (DC), or as an alternating current (AC). The type of electricity in the United States is in the form of AC. An AC generator of electricity sweeps masses of electrons that are sent in alternating pulses. Most alternators in the United States set up 60 alternating pulses per second which is referred to as "cycles" (c) or **hertz** (Hz). Cycles are important for equipment that has motors or revolving parts, such as blenders and recorders. Their speed and performance are affected by the number of cycles. This information is usually provided by the manufacturer and is often placed on a plate on the equipment. For motors, the power is expressed in the form of **horsepower** (hp). One hp is equal to 746 W.

The flow of steam, which is another form of energy, is measured in pounds per square inch. Heat may be measured by the temperature or by the amount expressed in British thermal units (Btu) or calories. A **Btu** is the quantity of heat required to raise the temperature of one pound of water by 1° F. A calorie is the amount of heat required to raise the temperature of one gram of water by 1° C; it is equal to 3.968 Btu. (This type of calorie should not be confused with the calorie used in nutritional sciences.)

Once the energy requirements of all appliances and equipment are known, it is relatively easy to calculate the energy costs or to conduct an audit. In order to

| Month / Date | Electricity | | | Oil | | | Natural gas | | | Coal/steam/wood | | Total |
	Quantity (kWh)	Cost $kWh	Total	Quantity (gal.)	Cost $/gal.	Total	Quantity (MCF, CCF)	Cost $/MCF	Total	Quantity unit	Cost Total	Energy costs

Figure 5-1. A typical energy and management form.

conserve energy, it is desirable to conduct energy audits at periodical intervals and to conserve energy wherever possible. A typical energy audit form is shown in Figure 5.1.

TYPES OF EQUIPMENT

In order to select equipment for a foodservice operation, it is necessary to have a complete set of data on the types of equipment available for each category of function. Long-term durability should be considered in the selection of the equipment. Figure 5.2 shows different types of ovens, which are indispensable in any type of foodservice operation. A brief description of the factors that should be considered in the selection of commonly used equipment is given below. Such equipment as

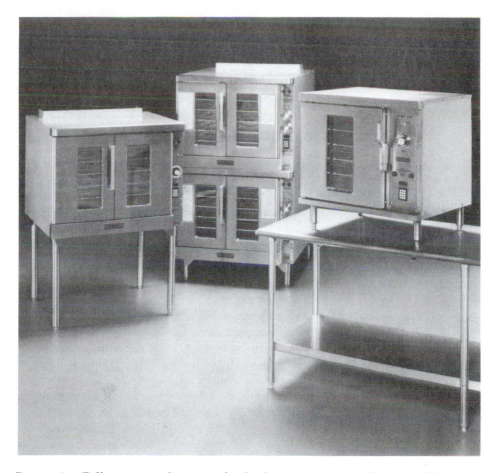

Figure 5-2. Different types of ovens used in foodservice operations. (Courtesy of Hobart Corporation)

Figure 5-3. Commercial glass-door refrigerated display case. (Courtesy of Hobart Corporation)

refrigerators and freezers are deliberately excluded since they are common household items. However, Figure 5.3 shows a glass-door refrigerator, which may be used for food displays. It is also convenient to see the food inside the refrigerator without opening the door.

Ranges

The range is the most basic piece of equipment needed by practically every type of foodservice operation; it may be gas or electric. Most ranges are mounted on the floor, and the cooking is done in pots or pans directly placed on the range top. Since ranges are among the most frequently used equipment, heavy-duty framework is preferred. Tops of gas ranges come in a variety of forms, shapes, and arrangements of elements. Ranges that can be cleaned easily and those with drip trays that can be removed for clean-up are the most practical. Reflectors are also desirable. Several attachments and modifications are available; for example griddle attachments are often used. Some ranges have ovens below and/or above. It is difficult to assess the capacity of the ranges desirable for a foodservice operation, since capacity need depends on several factors, including the type of menu and the number of meals served. However, for most types of foodservice operations, the recommended number of refrigerators and freezers may be calculated based on the number of meals served per day.

Under 300 meals	1
300–400	2
400–500	3
4500–1000	4

The exact requirement will only be known after assessing the precise needs of the foodservice operation. Refrigerators and freezers should be easily accessible to employees working in the production areas as well as in the service areas. Modifications and special attachments are desirable.

Conventional Ovens

Conventional ovens are among the most important pieces of equipment in any type of foodservice operation. Basically, an oven is a heated chamber in which foods may be cooked at various temperatures. In conventional ovens, the heat may be distributed by conduction, convection, or radiation. As in the case of ranges, durability is of prime importance in the selection of ovens. The frame, door, exterior, and interior materials should contribute to the longevity and cleanability of the equipment. Several types of attachments are also possible for conventional ovens. Heating elements should be selected on the basis of the desired use.

Since energy conservation is an important consideration, insulation materials and their thickness should be considered. It is desirable to have 4 to 5 in of insulation. Commonly used insulating materials are fiberglass, rock wool, or vitreous fiber. Temperature-regulating controls are desirable, as are panel lights and computerized controls.

To save much needed space, ovens may be installed in decks or stacks. In deciding the requirement for the number of ovens, recommendations as mentioned for the range may be followed. The capacity should be based on the type of products for which the ovens will be needed. The following formula can be used to calculate the number of ovens needed:

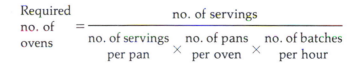

$$\text{Required no. of ovens} = \frac{\text{no. of servings}}{\frac{\text{no. of servings}}{\text{per pan}} \times \frac{\text{no. of pans}}{\text{per oven}} \times \frac{\text{no. of batches}}{\text{per hour}}}$$

For example, if a total of 400 servings is desired and there are 24 servings per pan, and the cooking of one batch requires 20 minutes, assuming there are three batches per hour and that two pans can be accommodated per oven, the number of ovens or the number of decks required for an oven may be calculated as follows:

$$\text{Required no. of ovens} = \frac{400}{24 \times 2 \times 3} = 2.8 \text{ or } 3$$

When calculating the capacity, the number of items on the menu and possible staggering of time should be considered.

Convection Ovens

The conventional ovens discussed earlier are designed to be heated by an element either at the bottom or at the top or both. The problem associated with this type of heating is that heat is not uniformly distributed within the oven cavity. In order to facilitate uniform distribution of the heat, other methods are used in convection ovens. There are several types of convectional ovens, of which the most common are:

Forced-air convection ovens, in which a fan is used to circulate heat in the oven cavity. The velocity of air circulation helps in the uniform distribution of heat.

Roll-in type convection ovens, in which carts or a large assembly of racks may be rolled into a large-size oven, Figure 5-4. Heat is so circulated as to reach all racks, thereby facilitating uniform heating.

Pulse-type convection ovens, in which alternating gusts of hot air followed by cold air are used. The hot air facilitates the baking or cooking of the foods, whereas the cold air helps in the cooling of the products and controlling overcooking of the products.

The advantages of convection ovens are:

1. Because heat is uniformly distributed, product quality is greatly improved.
2. Because the surfaces are heated, there is a desirable browning effect.
3. All parts of the oven may be fully utilized, so that the efficiency and capacity of the oven are greatly improved.
4. Relatively lower temperatures are needed for cooking food in comparison to conventional ovens.
5. Less labor and space is required in comparison to conventional ovens.
6. They are more energy-efficient.

There are certain disadvantages to convection ovens which can be corrected to some extent. Ovens now on the market have been modified to eliminate or reduce these drawbacks. Some of the disadvantages of convection ovens are:

1. Foods may be overcooked and a thick layer may form on top.
2. Surfaces of foods may be cooked more than lower portions.
3. Because there is air flowing with a certain velocity, batters or soft foods may be blown to one side, giving an undesirable appearance.

Figure 5-4.   Roll-in Rack convection oven. (Courtesy CRES-COR, Crown X Corp.)

4. Certain foods cannot be prepared in these ovens because the circulation of heat and the temperature of the air affects food surfaces. Thus, baked breads or cupcakes may have an uneven appearance or may be burnt.

In selecting convection ovens, the source of heat distribution should be considered. Other aspects of their use are similar to those of conventional ovens.

Infrared Ovens

The use of **infrared energy,** which is a form of radiant heat, is relatively new and innovative in foodservices. The top as well as the bottom of the oven may be heated depending on the location of the source of energy. A conveyor belt may be used for the introduction and removal of the food products. The advantages of these ovens are:

1. Foods are cooked in a relatively short period of time.
2. The quality of certain foods is improved due to high temperature provided in a short period of time to the surface and/or bottom, resulting in an even cooking of the product.
3. The ovens occupy relatively less space.
4. Due to the high temperatures that can be reached, most of infrared ovens have self-cleaning mechanisms.
5. Either glass or metal pans may be used.
6. The outside environment does not get heated.
7. Because of shorter cooking time, these ovens are energy-efficient.
8. Special preparations and flavors may be achieved by this specialized cooking. This is particularly true for such an infrared oven as the conveyorized broiler.

As with convection ovens, there are certain disadvantages to infrared ovens, and the manufacturers are trying to improve them. Low-chamber height is one of the drawbacks in table-top ovens. Since foods are heated to a high temperature, care must be taken to prevent overcooking. The interior of the oven may get very hot and become a safety or fire hazard. Recent improvements have made infrared a potentially useful source of energy that can be utilized effectively in the cooking of foods in foodservice operations. Special applications of these ovens should be considered in comparison to other types of ovens.

Mechanical and Pizza Ovens

Mechanical ovens are similar to other ovens except that they have a larger capacity and certain mechanical parts that help in the movement of the food products within the oven. Moving trays facilitate inspection of the products and provide for benefits of the forced-air convection oven. These ovens may be heated by gas or by electricity. Several modifications may be provided. Some of the common forms of the mechanical and pizza-type of ovens are:

Reel oven. These ovens have trays that travel vertically within the oven. There is an opening and a glass door through which food products may be inspected.

Rotary oven. These ovens have circular shelves that rotate horizontally around a central axis.

Traveling tray oven. These are fairly large-sized ovens in which the products are placed in trays that travel through the oven.

Pizza oven. These ovens are similar to other types of ovens except that they have more depth and are placed horizontally. This facilitates the placement and removal of pizza trays.

Mechanical ovens provide special functions which add to efficiency in quantity food production. The factors to be considered when purchasing these ovens are similar to those for other types of ovens.

Microwave Ovens

Microwave ovens, like the infrared ovens, are based on the use of radiation to cook foods within the oven chamber. Microwaves are very short electromagnetic waves that have a wavelength between the ultrahigh bands and the infrared bands. The wavelengths assigned to microwave ovens are (1) 915 MHz, which are 13 in or 32 cm long, and (2) 2450 MHz, which are 5 in or 12 cm long. Megahertz (MHz) are a million cycles per second (cps). The penetration of a 915-MHz wave is greater than that of a 2450-MHz wave, but the food is cooked slower in 915-MHz wave than in 2450-MHz wave.

Advantages and disadvantages of microwave ovens are listed below.

Advantages	*Disadvantages*
Foods can be cooked faster.	An inability to cook large quantities of foods is the greatest drawback from the foodservice point of view.
The surrounding atmosphere is not heated.	Certain foods are cooked unevenly.
The ovens are very useful for reheating food portions in a very short period of time.	Additional cooking, using other types of ovens, is required for browning.
Several applications make microwave ovens very useful in foodservice operations. For example, they can be used to thaw meats and reheat foods.	Special utensils are required. Repair is expensive. Extra care is required because the oven may get damaged easily if improperly cleaned.

To overcome some of the disadvantages, a combination of convection and microwave ovens is being manufactured. It has electronic digital control, and the extent of cooking by one or both of the ovens can be programmed (Figure 5-5).

In selecting microwave ovens, wavelengths, electrical current requirements, capacity, and safety features should be considered. There are several special applications to consider from a foodservice point of view. Some applications are:

1. Reheating portions of foods
2. Making sauces and gravies
3. Warming syrups
4. Drying bread crumbs and making croutons
5. Drying hard cheese
6. Softening jellies and spreads
7. Crisping potato chips
8. Reheating coffee in cups
9. Decontaminating flour and cereals
10. Heating wet towels for the customers

Figure 5-5. Jet-Wave combination convection microwave oven. (Courtesy of Microwave Products of America, Inc.)

Deep-Fat Fryers

The distinctive flavor and appearance of fried foods make deep-fat fryers one of the most valuable pieces of equipment in many foodservice operations. The points to consider in the selection of deep-fat fryers include

1. They should be made of sturdy materials and noncorrosive metals.
2. Their heating elements should be appropriate for the type of desired frying.
3. Their temperature controls should be located at a place that is protected from spattering and which can be reached safely without contact with the heated fat.
4. They should have an easy and convenient fat-drainage system.
5. They should use fat economically, without contributing to the breakdown or smoking of the fats.
6. They should have a good mechanism for the removal of crumbs and other food particles from fats.
7. They should have an easy to handle or automatically controlled frying basket.

There are a number of different kinds of deep-fat fryers available on the market; these include pressurized fryers that reduce cooking time and improve the quality of the fried products. Fat can be saved and reused if the fryer is designed with such features as siphoning and other cleaning devices. Other accessories may be selected if fried foods are particular specialties on the menu. Fryer basket lift-out devices are highly desirable, since they help to produce products of uniform quality, in addition to being convenient. Other accessories include crumb trays, fat filters, thermometers, infrared holding light, and siphons. Determination of the capacity of the fryers needed should be based on the number of deep-fat fried items on the menu as well as frequency of use.

Tilting Skillets

Tilting skillets, also called tilting fry pans, have a variety of uses in all types of foodservice operation. They are one of the most versatile and indispensable pieces of equipment. Multiple applications make them very valuable in the restaurant; they also save considerable space. Most tilting skillets are mounted on the floor or on brackets attached to the floor. Their source of heat may be gas or electricity. Since they have multipurpose functions, skillet capacity should be selected based upon possible applications. A tilting skillet may be used for several purposes.

1. Griddle cooking, since the frying pan may also be used as a griddle. Thus, such products as hamburgers, eggs, and cheese sandwiches can be easily prepared.
2. Both deep-fat and shallow-fat frying. In general, it is very convenient and safe for shallow-fat frying.
3. Stewing meats and vegetables as well as cooking or steaming vegetables.
4. Sautéeing foods.
5. Holding foods either at room or higher temperatures. This is a special advantage of the tilting skillet.
6. Poaching.
7. Proofing, since the temperature can be adjusted.
8. Preparing sauces, casseroles, mixed foods, baking (to a limited extent), heating water, boiling eggs, and cleaning fruits and vegetables.

Thus, the tilting skillet is one of the most useful pieces of equipment in a foodservice operation. The decision to purchase it should be based on its potential uses within a particular operation.

Griddles

Griddles provide heated surfaces that may be used for a variety of cooking tasks, and are particularly useful for short-order cooking. They may be heated by gas or electricity. Table space near the griddle is highly desirable for convenient placement of various food items and equipment. Griddles are useful in cooking meats, particularly patties, pancakes, eggs, steaks, and sausages. If a griddle is not required for frequent use, other, perhaps more versatile equipment that may be substituted for a griddle should be explored.

Broilers

Broilers that are used in dry heat cooking provide a special desirable flavor. Their source of heat may be gas, electricity, or infrared energy; charcoal and wood may also be used in certain types. They are available in many shapes and sizes. The charred or smoked flavor in meats is provided by broiling. The principal part of a broiler consists of a grid and a mechanism through which fat drips and is partially burnt to produce a smoked flavor. Broilers may be of an upright or back-shelf type. Their source of heat may be located at the top and/or bottom. In order to produce a charbroiled effect, charcoal, metal, or ceramic tiles may be used. Infrared energy is used in recently developed broilers. There are conveyorized and rotisserie broilers that are suitable for specialized broiling. When purchasing broilers, the source of heat, grid temperatures, safety features, fat-drainage system, and efficiency should be checked. Choice of broiler size will depend on the extent to which broiled foods are included in the menu.

Steam-Jacketed Kettles

In any type of foodservice operation, steam-jacketed kettles are indispensable. These kettles are heated by using moist heat within the jacket. The kettle may be one-third, half-, or full-jacketed. When the steam is let into the jacket, it condenses on the outside of the inner shell, thereby giving up its heat to the metal, from which it is transferred to the foods. Thus, steam does not come directly in contact with the food being heated. Steam-jacketed kettles are commonly referred to as "work-horses" in foodservices and are very useful in cooking foods that do not require high temperatures. From the nutritional point of view, their use in cooking is preferred since there is minimum nutrient loss. Specifications for the steam-jacketed kettle should be based on the size needed; type of jacketing; type of stands; pressure of the steam; and type of drawoffs, covers, and other desired accessories. Relatively small steam-jacketed kettles are commonly referred to as "trunnions." Mixers, blades, scrapers, paddles, whips, or beaters are available as attachments for steam-jacketed kettles. Multiple baskets for preparing two or three different products at one time are also available as attachments to the kettle. The source of steam should be checked before purchasing a kettle. If the foodservice operation is located at a place where there is a steam supply, steam should be used from that source. If not, a special generator for heat will need to be purchased; this adds to the cost of the kettle. Larger steam-jacketed kettles are very useful in preparing quantities of soups or sauces. Adequate devices for tilting and controlling breaks will be required. The capacity of the kettle required for a foodservice operation may be calculated as follows:

$$\frac{\text{Capacity}}{\text{kettle}} = \frac{\text{total no. of servings} \times \text{portion size} \times \% \text{ headspace}}{128 \text{ oz (1 gal) or } 1000 \text{ ml (1 liter)} \times \text{no. of batches}}$$
(in gal or liters)

The headspace allowed is normally 15%, which is needed to prevent overflow, spillage, and/or spattering.

Steam-jacketed kettles are very useful, since they heat in a very short period of time and may be used for cooking or reheating foods rapidly. Also, they can be used for making hot preparations, such as tea and coffee, or cold preparations, such as iced tea. It is advisable to have an adjustable water faucet over the steam-jacketed kettle and a drainage line close to the bottom.

Steamers

Steamers are very useful because of their efficiency, cleanability, and for the quality of food they produce. There are several advantages and a few disadvantages of steamers from the foodservice point of view.

Advantages and their applications	*Disadvantages*
Foods are cooked rapidly, so that large quantities of foods may be prepared in a relatively short period of time.	The types of foods suitable for steam cooking are limited.
Nutrients are retained to a high degree.	Steamers do not provide for the formation of crusts on foods.
Labor need is reduced, since once the products are placed in the steamer, they do not have to be watched.	Foods cannot be observed while cooking.
The quality of food is uniform when similar settings are used.	Adjustment is required to get the exact desired food quality.
Foods, particularly vegetables, can be cooked directly from the frozen stage.	
Rice and pasta products may be prepared easily.	
Special desserts such as custards can be easily made.	
Foods may be cooked in the same pan in which they are to be served.	
Fragile vegetables that require careful handling, such as asparagus, broccoli, and brussels sprouts, may be cooked successfully.	
Steamed vegetables have an attractive color, texture, and crispness.	

Points to be considered in buying steamers include the source of steam, pressure of the steam, electrical requirements, number of racks, type of door, and overall dimensions of the equipment.

Blenders and Mixers

Blenders and mixers (Figure 5.6) are needed by all types of foodservice operations. Many types of commercial equipment are available. The horsepower of the motor is one of the most important considerations. An adequate-sized blender should be

Figure 5-6.   Commercial mixer. (Courtesy Hobart Corporation)

selected, to save labor and other costs. A large blender may be more desirable than a smaller size which will require more batches to be run. A variety of attachments may be purchased, such as a flat beater, wire whip, dough arm, pastry knife, wing whip, blades, and scrapers. These attachments are used for a variety of preparations and are indispensable for a foodservice operation. Long-term usage should be considered when selecting blenders or mixers. If properly selected, they will prove to be a good investment for any foodservice operation. Vegetable cutters or choppers are also very commonly used.

Dishwashers

Dishwashers are among the most expensive and useful pieces of equipment in any type of foodservice operation. Many types of dishwashers with a variety of functions are available. The most common types are

Immersion dishwashers, in which racks of dishes are immersed for cleaning

Single-tank, stationary-type dishwashers, in which dishes are placed on racks and washed with jets of water within a single tank (see Figure 5.7)

Conveyor-rack dishwashers, in which a conveyor carries the racks of dishes through the dishwasher

Flight-type dishwashers, in which the conveyor is one continuous rack and the dishes are placed on pegs or bars (see Figure 5.8)

Carousel-type dishwashers, in which there is a closed circuit conveyor where dishes are loaded and unloaded

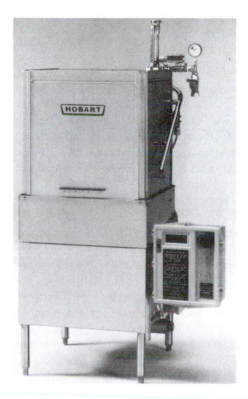

Figure 5-7.   Single-tank, stationary-type dishwasher. (Courtesy of Hobart Corporation)

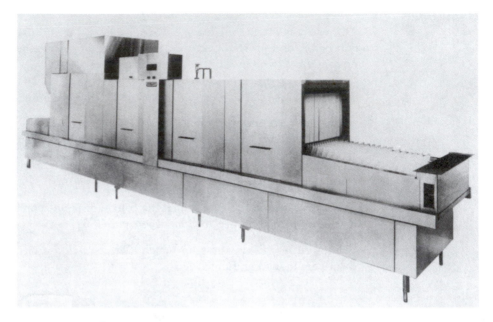

Figure 5-8.   Flight-type dishwasher. (Courtesy of Hobart Corporation)

The function of dishwashers for washing, rinsing, drying, and overall cleaning should be understood before making any purchase decision. The literature from various manufacturers should be read and comparatively evaluated. The design of the dishwasher should be such that it fits in the overall layout of the foodservice operation. The capacity needed will depend on the number of dishes to be cleaned. Specifications are provided by manufacturers for different types of dishwashers. When making a selection, the cost of installation and maintenance should be considered.

Other pieces of equipment used in foodservice operations include coffee makers, waste disposers, trash compactors, meat slicers, and various types of service equipment. In addition to large equipment, several smaller pieces of equipment and utensils are shown in Appendix B at the end of the book. The principles of selection should be based on the factors discussed for other related equipment.

An important task after the selection of equipment is to itemize exact specifications, since inadequate specifications can lead to expensive losses. Specifications should be clear, concise, and complete, and should include every possible explanation. An example of a specification for equipment purchase is given in Table 5.2. Examples of the details to be included with the specifications are categorized. Many manufacturers' catalogs have specifications listed for each model. Selections should be based on the suitability of the particular model for use within a particular foodservice operation. Some manufacturers provide **templates,** or small models, of

Table 5.2

Example of the Specifications for Equipment Purchase

1. Title	Fryer, deep-fat (electric) *(example)*
2. Scope	Its intended use
3. Classification	Types, sizes, styles, models, mountings, etc. counter model, 30 lb fat capacity for 60 lb potatoes to be fried in 1 hr (0.5-in. strips)
4. Specific requirements	51 cm wide × 76 cm deep × 38 cm high, including legs
a. General	Temperature ranges 250°–450° F thermostatically controlled
b. Materials	Metal, gauges, finishes, insulation, soldering, welding, and fasteners (16 gauge; Type 304 — stainless steel No. 4 finish; heat resistant insulation)
c. Electrical requirements (Utilities)	Voltage, phase, amperage, and resistance (230 V, 3 phase with 33 amp)
d. Controls	Regulations, and displays range 250°–400° F with increments of 5° F control on top, lighted device
e. Performance	Use for fish squares, doughnuts, and shrimp
f. Special details	Motors; accessories and heating elements
g. Certification	UL, AGA, NSF, ASME
h. Warranties	Type
i. Maintenance and repairs	Parts and labor
j. Manuals	Number required
5. Quality assurance	Inspection; performance tests
6. Delivery requirements	Delivery date and installation date
7. Administrative details	Accounting and contracts
8. Drawing and illustrations	Important if custom made
9. Contact person	

the equipment that are helpful in designing a layout. Warranties and certification by agencies such as the Underwriters Laboratories (UL), the National Sanitation Foundation (NSF), and the American Gas Association (AGA) should be checked. Plates installed on equipment contain most of this information. It is also advisable to purchase extra copies of the manuals for future use and for each of those handling equipment. Procedures for the maintenance and handling of equipment should be clearly understood and strictly enforced by management. Written procedures and instructions may be attached to each piece of equipment.

SUMMARY

This chapter provides an in-depth review of the basic considerations needed in selection and purchase of equipment for a foodservice operation. Also described are the most common materials used in the construction of equipment, providing a basic understanding of the usefulness of different types of materials. Types of energy and sources which are utilized for running the equipment are discussed. Calculations for the cost effectiveness of the equipment are shown. How to estimate the size and capacity of the equipment needed is shown with examples. Common types of equipment used in foodservice operations are described in detail, with their advantages and disadvantages.

REVIEW
QUESTIONS

What factors would you consider before deciding to purchase a piece of equipment for a restaurant?

What is the difference in utility of the following materials when used in the construction of foodservice equipment: (a) nickel, (b) aluminum, (c) wood, (d) plastic, and (e) stainless steel?

What is the difference between conduction and convection ovens?

List different types of application of microwave ovens in foodservice operations.

How will you estimate the capacity of a steam-jacketed kettle?

What are the advantages and applications of steam as a source of energy? Describe foodservice equipment in which steam is used as a major source of energy.

ASSIGNMENTS

Select a piece of equipment in a foodservice operation and record the information provided on its plate. Explain in detail what you understand by each piece of information.

Call restaurant equipment dealers in your area and ask for the details of one type of equipment. Record all information that you consider essential prior to that equipment purchase.

Calculate the cost of the equipment selected in the above assignment and determine if it is a good buy for your operation. List all costs assumed in your calculations.

Write detailed specifications for the purchase of a dishwasher for a fine dining operation serving five hundred meals per day. You may have to assume some facts and figures. Consult a manufacturer's catalog for help in writing these specifications. Attach a copy of the page(s) from the catalog used.

SUGGESTED READINGS

Avery, A. C. 1980. *A Modern Guide to Food-service Equipment.* CBI Publishing Company, Boston, MA.

Kotchevar, L. H. 1977. *Foodservice Planning: Layout and Equipment*, 2nd edition. John Wiley & Sons, New York, NY.

Scriven, C., and Stevens, J. 1982. *Food Equipment Facts: A Handbook for the Food Service Industry.* John Wiley & Sons, New York, NY.

CHAPTER 6

FOOD PURCHASING

KEY CONCEPTS AND TERMS

AP (as purchased)
EP (edible portion)
percentage yield
shrinkage
inventory on hand
buying methods
specifications
standards of quality
standards of identity
standards of fill
ethics in buying
U.S. grades
drained weight
syrup density
IMPS (Institutional Meat Purchase
    Specifications)

IMPORTANCE OF PURCHASING

Controlled food purchasing is an important function in any type of foodservice. Operations could conceivably go out of business because of improper purchasing. How purchasing affects the entire foodservice operation must be considered at every stage of systems planning.

The primary function of a foodservice operation is to convert raw food into cooked products. Thus, the success of an operation depends on how efficiently and profitably raw ingredients are converted into edible cooked products and subsequently served to the consumer. Food quality depends directly on the quality of the raw ingredients. It has been said that one can produce a low-quality food from high-quality ingredients, but it is impossible to get a high-quality food from low-quality ingredients. A manager must therefore give prime importance to food purchasing. This task is difficult because the quality of raw ingredients varies from day to day and can be unpredictable. Foodservices also deal with perishable items, whose quality deteriorates with time and inadequate handling practices. Foodservice purchasing is a precarious job when compared to purchasing raw ingredients for other industries. Thousand of dollars may be lost overnight by improper food purchasing and/or handling. Foodservice purchasing requires knowledge of terminology, specifications, processing requirements, and a thorough objective and subjective assessment of quality.

Food purchasing has been described as an *art*, since it requires talent and sophistication in judging the right combinations of color, shape, size, and consistency of food; as a *science*, since it requires skill in the overall utilization of resources. Food purchasing requires a variety of skills and experience, tasks usually handled best by persons who have had overall management or food-purchasing experience. Because food purchasing is a vast subject, this chapter will provide only a summary of the most important aspects.

PLANNING PURCHASING

A critical step, once the menu is finalized, is to decide how many servings of each item on the menu are needed for a particular meal. The quantity of each ingredient to be ordered depends on the "number of servings," for which accurate forecasting is essential—this requires skill and experience. Among the several methods of forecasting, which range in complexity and accuracy, the simplest is based on the averages or means derived from data on number of servings. Since forecasting is one of the important functions of management, it is discussed in detail in a later chapter. Forecasting is so important that it is often said that the test of a good manager is how skilled he is in forecasting. In institutional foodservice with set menus, forecasting is easier than in a commercial operation. A typical restaurant can almost never predict when there may be unexpectedly large crowds. For example, for a restaurant located on a highway, it is virtually impossible to predict when a busload of consumers may stop by. Forecasting becomes even more difficult when the menu offers many choices. A manager must realize the problems associated with over- or underproduction of food. Overproduction may result in waste and/or spoilage, while underproduction may result in dissatisfied consumers. Both results have serious economic consequences. Although it is difficult, with experience the number of servings may be forecasted with reasonable accuracy.

Once the number of servings for each item is determined, the next step is to prepare a complete list of items to be purchased. A number of sources of information are necessary to accomplish this task. Several types of records and forms make the task easier. It is also important to know the meaning of certain technical terms used in purchasing. Food **as purchased** (AP) refers to food as it is purchased without any peeling, coring, or cutting. On the other hand, **edible portion** (EP) refers to food as it will be finally available for direct use, in edible form after processing. Thus EP represents the actual usable portion of the AP foods. For purchasing food it is, therefore, necessary to know the relative percentages of AP and EP. EP of the food should be calculated prior to placing a food order.

Tested and standardized recipes would normally indicate the amount to be used in preparing a fixed number of servings. Waste and shrinkage losses may also be included in the recipe. If not, calculations are needed before determining the amount of each ingredient to purchase. The final yield may be calculated by:

$$\text{percentage of yield} = \frac{\text{weight after cooking}}{\text{weight before cooking}} \times 100$$

For example, if 65 lb of cooked ground beef can be prepared from 90 lb of raw beef, the **percentage yield** for the ground beef in this type of preparation will be 65 divided by 90 and multiplied by 100, which will be 72.2%. Thus, 27.8% more ground beef in raw form is needed to get the desired cooked ground-beef servings. This is also referred to as **shrinkage,** a fact that has to be considered in ordering food. Yield percentages are dependent on various factors, such as temperatures used for cooking, types of ovens, and time, which will vary with the type of the foodservice operation. Serious shortages in prepared food will result if this factor is not considered when planning purchasing or production. Sufficient margins should be provided in order to compensate for these losses. The fat content of meats will also affect the percentage of yield. It becomes convenient to include the range of the yield percentages on the recipe, so that the final EP can be calculated. This can be derived as follows:

$$EP = AP - \text{shrinkage (or preparation) losses} =$$

$$\text{percentage shrinkage or prepreparation losses} =$$

$$\frac{\text{losses due to shrinkage or prepreparation (wt)}}{AP \text{ (wt)}} \times 100 =$$

$$\frac{AP \text{ (wt)} - EP \text{ (wt)}}{AP \text{ (wt)}}$$

Although there are several procedures used for determining the amount of food to be purchased, a recommended standard procedure is outlined in the following paragraphs.

1. From the recipe, determine the factor to be used in calculating the desired number of servings. For example, if the recipe is for 100 servings and the desired number of servings is 300, the factor will be 300 divided by 100, which is 3. If only 50 servings are desired, the factor will be 50 divided by 100, i.e., 0.5. This factor is important in further calculations.

2. Multiply all the ingredients in the recipe by the factor derived in paragraph 1. For example, the recipe for 100 servings requires 30 lb of chicken; the amount to be purchased for 300 servings will be $3 \times 30 = 90$ lb (EP) of chicken. Calculate the AP amount of chicken by dividing the EP by the percent yield or the amount of EP provided by 1 lb, or a standard unit of the commodity. Such calculations should be done for all the ingredients in the recipe.

3. Convert the AP value to the nearest possible wholesale purchase unit (such as carton, case, box, lug, basket, crate, flat, dozen, bushel, or sack). The quantity selected should be such that the remainder of the commodity is easily utilizable and is not wasted. Sometimes, ordering in larger units may be economical and desirable. Items included in the menu for the following day or within that week should be taken into consideration. On the other hand, when items are for one-time use only, the nearest possible unit size should be used, or alternate uses for the remainder of the commodity should be planned in advance.

4. Once the amounts are determined for one menu item, the same procedure should be followed for other items on the menu, and daily totals for each item should be calculated.

5. Finally, totals for the week, month, or any fixed period of time may be calculated and used for ordering. This duration should be decided by management, based on the purchasing methods selected by an operation. Convenience should be given top priority when making this decision.

These steps may be facilitated by the use of several types of forms. Figure 6.1

shows a daily meat order form, which should be completed as a first step to determine the actual amount needed. Similar forms may be used for other types of products. Quantities in nearest weight/measure units should be included. Based on the totals obtained for each item, a quotation and order sheet should be prepared (Figure 6.2). This form is useful only if bids are not solicited, and a comparison of prices quoted by different vendors is desired. The selected price is circled and any comments are added. If bids are requested, complete information should be provided. An example of the request for bid proposal and specifications for meats is given in Appendix C and Figure 6.3. When the decisions for purchasing are finalized, either by bidding or other methods, a purchase order (Figure 6.4) is filled out. Upon receiving the products, a receiving report (Figure 6.5) giving all details should be completed. The details of purchasing methods are given elsewhere in this chapter. Similar forms could be custom designed based on the needs by a particular type of foodservice operation.

MANAGEMENT DECISIONS

Management should decide, on the basis of previous experience, how frequently foods and supplies should be purchased. Too-frequent food purchasing may add to the total cost, whereas a long delay in purchasing may result in shortages and other problems. An optimum frequency of buying should be established for each operation. Some of the factors that should be considered in deciding frequency of purchasing are discussed below.

Inventory on Hand

A complete and continuous turnover of inventory is highly desirable, based on the type of the facility. Some facilities want to maintain a week's **inventory on hand,** while others may like to have a month's supply. The volume of business also dictates the inventory required. At times, it is tempting to purchase commodities when discounts are offered by purveyors. This is an important decision and should be made after considering all factors, since tying up money in inventory may reduce the amount of much-needed cash flow.

Storage Capacity

The capacity of the dry, refrigerated, and frozen storage areas primarily dictates quantities to be purchased. It may be desirable to rotate items frequently in order to provide adequate storage for all items. With limited storage capabilities, frequent buying may be essential. Some vendors will store purchases of commodities until needed by the buyers; this fact should be considered in purchasing if storage space is a problem.

Department: _____ Week: _____

Item	SUNDAY			MONDAY			TUESDAY			WEDNESDAY			THURSDAY			FRIDAY			SATURDAY			TOTAL
	C	L.R.	Cat.	C	L.R.	Cat.	C	L.R.	Cat.	C	L.R.	Cat.	C	L.R.	Cat.	C	L.R.	Cat.	C	L.R.	Cat.	
BEEF Beef Liver, 4 oz																						
Beef Soup Bones, 4 in. length																						
Beef Tongues, 2–3 lb																						
Beef Turnovers w/Dressing, 5 oz																						
Butt Tenders, Beef $1\frac{1}{2} - 2\frac{1}{2}$ lb																						
Corned Beef, 6–8 lb																						
Corned Beef, canned																						
Cubed Steaks, special (Minute) 4 oz																						

Cubed Steaks, 5 oz							
Diced Beef, 1 in.							
Diced Sirloin Tips, 1 in. extra lean							
Filet Mignon Steaks, 8 oz							
Filet Mignon Steaks (petite steaks), 4 oz							
Flank Steaks, 5 oz							
Ground Beef							
Ground Beef Patties, 6 lb							
Ground Beef Patties, round shape, 5 oz (chopped)							

Key: C, Cafeteria; L.R., Lunchroom; Cat., Catering.

Figure 6-1. A daily meat order form.

Date Needed: _____

Delivery Deadline: _____

Item	Specifications	Amount Needed	Amount on Hand	Amount to Order	Unit	Price Quoted/Units Vendor					Comments
						1	2	3	4	5	
MEATS											
1.											
2.											
3.											
4.											
5.											
PRODUCE											
1.											
2.											
3.											
4.											
5.											
6.											
7.											

Figure 6-2. An example of a quotation and order sheet.

	Item	Quantity
Preorder Date: _____ Bid Opening Date: _____ Delivery Date: _____ *All portioned steaks and roasts must not exceed a 0.3 in. surface fat thickness.*		
	BEEF BEEF HEARTS, cap off	
	BEEF LIVER, frozen, layer pack, 10-lb package 1 solid 4-oz piece	
	BEEF SOUP BONES, femur or neck, 4 in. length	
	BEEF, TONGUES, fresh (short cut), 2–3 lb	
	BEEF TURNOVERS WITH DRESSING, 5 oz	
	BUTT TENDERS, BEEF, all fat tissue removed, USDA Choice, $1\frac{1}{2}$–$2\frac{1}{2}$ lb	
	CORNED BEEF, canned	
	CUBED STEAKS, special, produced from prime cuts, solid pieces of meat (no knitting of small pieces during cubing), all fat and connective tissue removed, 4-oz, 10-lb package	
	1195 - DICED BEEF, 1 in. extra lean. Each cube must contain 80% lean, 10-lb package	
	DICED SIRLOIN TIPS, 1 in. extra lean. Each cube must contain 80% lean, 10-lb package	
	FILET MIGNON STEAKS, U.S. Choice, 8 oz (individually cello wrapped)	
	FILET MIGNON STEAKS, (petite steaks), U.S. Choice, 4 oz (individually cello wrapped)	
	FLANK STEAKS, cubed twice, 5 oz. All fat and connective tissue removed. Solid piece of meat, 10-lb package	
	1137 - GROUND BEEF PATTIES, 75-25 blend (no additives) 6 patties per pound, frozen, 10-lb package	
	GROUND BEEF PATTIES, 75-25 blend (no additives) round shape, 5 oz, frozen, 10-lb package	

Figure 6-3. A typical form for specifications accompanying bid requisition.

Name of Operation: _____ Address: _____ _____	Ship to: _____ _____ _____ _____	No. _____ (Use this number in all correspondence)		
Delivery desired by _____ or sooner	Vendor No., FEIN/Soc. Sec. No.	Date:		
Ship Via _____ _____ Please pack all shipments to avoid damage in transit	Vendor: _____ _____ _____	Price F.O.B.: Terms: As Per _____ Date: _____		

Description	Quantity	Units	Unit Price	Amount
Total				

Comments:

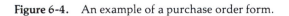

Figure 6-4. An example of a purchase order form.

Name of the Operation:								

Received from:			Ticket No.	For Dept.	Date: 19____

| Freight | Truck Line | Express | P.P. | Charges | | Trans Chgs. $ | P.O. No. |
| | | | | Pre-paid | Collect | | Received by: |

Quantity Rec'd	Unit Doz lb Each	Description of Commodity Received	Price	Amount

Entered in Inventory Record by	Food Cost Report	Total	

Figure 6-5. A typical receiving report.

Seasonal Fluctuations

Since agricultural commodities and perishable items are used in foodservices, seasonal availability is an important aspect to be considered. It may be economical to buy certain items when there is an abundant supply. Again, storage of such items should be considered before making any decisions.

Type of Market and Proximity

The type of market and its location with respect to the foodservice are important considerations. For foodservices close to a larger market, such as a seaport or livestock market, large inventories may not be necessary. For foodservices that have access only to smaller markets, such as farmers' markets, only small inventories may be possible. Seasonal items often may be purchased at bargain prices at farmers' markets.

BUYING METHODS

Once the foodservice manager has decided on the quantities of items needed, he or she must select the most appropriate method of purchasing. The best method for one operation may not be best for another. **Buying methods** should be incorporated into the policy of the facility, based on the objectives of the operation. Before establishing a buying method, it is essential to know the market. Markets are often classified as primary, secondary, and tertiary, based on their level of operation. Primary markets are those which are large, central markets of a particular commodity. All other markets are dependent on primary markets for prices as well as for the availability of specific commodities. Secondary markets are more numerous but relatively smaller and are located geographically to facilitate easy distribution of a commodity. These markets may act as distribution centers for a variety of products. Tertiary markets are local markets that deal in a variety of products at a local level.

In general, the functions of a market include (1) the exchange of commodities; (2) the physical transfer of the commodities; (3) the supply of information pertaining to all aspects of the commodities; (4) the supply of information on rules and laws pertaining to the exchange of the commodities; and (5) facilitation of transactions essential for the exchange, such as the financial procedures involved.

A buying method may be selected based on the needs of a foodservice operation — accessibility to the market, type of market, and mode of delivery. Selection of a method is primarily based on the type of operation and management policies. Some foodservice managers prefer placing orders by phone, without comparing prices from different purveyors, while others use more formal procedures for placing orders. There are advantages and disadvantages in using any purchasing method, and these should be considered before making a selection. A good buyer should evaluate the prevailing methods continuously and should be prepared to change from time to time, in order to avail himself or herself of optimum market conditions. Some of the more common buying methods are discussed below.

Informal Buying

Informal purchasing is usually based on informal agreements that often involve oral negotiations. The transactions are usually completed on the phone. This type of buying is most suitable for small operations, since it does not involve paperwork and is much faster than other methods. For the most part, orders are placed orally, and, therefore, buyers may take immediate advantage of price fluctuations and other market conditions. On the other hand, these fluctuations may result in higher costs, since there is no prior agreement about purchasing. The primary advantage of informal buying is that it saves time and is very convenient. Quick comparison of prices from a limited number of purveyors is also possible. The buyer selects the vendor and places orders for the quantity of the specific item(s) that need to be purchased. In addition to using the telephone, contacts may be made by visits to the market by the buyer or by salespersons calling on the buyer. There are several variations of informal buying.

Cash-Buying

Cash-buying is the simplest type of informal buying and is preferred for smaller operations, such as family restaurants or nursing homes. Food and other commodities may be purchased at supermarkets, farmers' markets, auctions, or other local places. Since vendors are mostly local, it is easy to find bargains, both immediate and forthcoming. Where regular farmers' markets are accessible, foods may be bought at relatively low prices, and the quality may be excellent, since most of the items are fresh. Fresh foods, such as hand-picked strawberries, vine-ripened melons, garden-fresh sweetpeas, fresh corn, and so on, make very attractive menu items. Supermarkets have the advantage that almost everything is available under one roof. Supplies may be picked up when needed or desired, particularly if the foodservice facility is close to a supermarket. Buying food at auctions may also prove to be profitable, although large quantities have to be purchased and one must be familiar with the methods used at auctions. The importance of experience and sound planning cannot be overlooked in cash-buying, even if the method is simplistic.

Advantages	*Disadvantages*
Reduces the amount of money tied up in large inventories	Some items and/or brands may not be available on a regular basis
Reduces waste, since buying can be done in the exact amounts needed	Possible fluctuation in prices
Eliminates the middleperson and his commission, and therefore is usually economical	Considerable time involved in buying, depending on the frequency of purchases

Advantages	*Disadvantages*
Makes portion control easier, since items are bought in small quantities as opposed to bulk	Special transportation and delivery methods may be needed
Facilitates the analysis of food cost and other bookkeeping, since daily receipts are available	Menu planning is difficult, since there is a lot of unpredictability
Reduces chances of going into large debt, since small cash amounts are involved and there can be periodic checks on the amount spent	Food production may be delayed due to such unforeseen problems as snowstorms, and the unavailability of personnel or transportation
Easy to check the quality before buying and decisions may be made on the spot	Not practical for large-size foodservice operations

Quotation Method

With the quotation method the buyer prepares a list of items that are needed, their quantities, and their specifications, and asks selected vendors, usually three or four, to quote prices. When all quotations are in, prices are compared and the most suitable price (not necessarily the lowest one) is selected. After all decisions are made, orders are placed with the selected vendors for the commodities. A quotation-and-order sheet, which can be used for ordering different types of products, is given in Figure 6.2. As an example, the prices quoted by the vendors are recorded next to each other for comparative assessment. The price selected is usually circled, preferably in red, so that it is easy to order the product from that particular vendor. A list of specifications set by an operation may be provided to all possible vendors and reference may be made to those specifications while placing orders. This saves time and avoids any confusion or misunderstanding when specifications are quoted over the phone.

Advantages	*Disadvantages*
Provides for comparison of prices on an informal basis	Time-consuming and requires relatively elaborate record keeping
Buyer is assured of the best possible price, regardless of fluctuations	May create problems if specifications are not clear
Informs the purveyor that purchasing is not irrespective of price and thus reduces the chances of overcharging	No written record of quoted prices, since these are primarily oral transactions
Competitive prices and better quality may be secured since selection is based on competition	

Blank-Check Method

With the blank-check method, vendors are authorized to deliver specific items at specific times and to bill the buyer without quoting prices beforehand. This method is usually used for limited commodities, particularly those that are in short supply or for which there is no strong competition. This method also may be used when price regulations exist and when there is an insignificant difference in prices on a long-term basis for the commodity among various vendors. This kind of privilege buying is restricted to reputable vendors who have established business with a foodservice operation. With this method it is advisable to give vendors price ranges, or maximum prices to be charged, in order to eliminate overcharging or any misunderstanding.

Advantages	*Disadvantages*
Convenience, as it avoids price comparison and record keeping	Since there is only one vendor involved for specific commodities, there is no control over prices charged
Easy to deal and communicate with one vendor	Method is applicable only to limited reputable vendors
For certain commodities, like bread and dairy products, it may be advisable to use this method for uninterrupted supply	No competition involved, so the quality for the price paid may not be assured
Saves a considerable amount of time	If proper records are not maintained, it becomes difficult to assess the amount spent at a particular time on that commodity

Cost-Plus Method

Cost-plus informal buying is also known as the "fixed mark-up" method. A mark-up factor is charged above the cost of the item, particularly for those items with very unstable market prices. This arrangement provides safety for both buyers and vendors. Buyers are assured that they are not overcharged because of a rise in the market prices, and vendors are assured of a fixed amount of profit. The cost-plus method is very useful for imported commodities or for those that are scarce and subject to seasonal fluctuations. When prices are inflated for these items, the buyer is assured of a mark-up factor that has been established earlier. This factor may range from 10% to 30% over cost. An operation may benefit from this method of purchasing if it is carefully utilized. The buyer may decide on purchases based on market trends for that commodity. Normally, the interest of the vendors lies in the large volume of business that is assured by such an arrangement. Over the long run, a buyer may find this method to be extremely useful, particularly for certain food items that are included in cycle menus. The cost-plus method is also useful for restaurants that have their own specialties, such as seafoods and steaks.

Advantages	*Disadvantages*
Buyer is assured of the commodity at a reasonable cost regardless of price fluctuations (a good example may be beef, where the prices may rise at a rapid pace, even doubling at times)	Mark-up factor needs careful consideration based on a study of market trends; otherwise a buyer may end up paying more for the products
Delivery of special items is assured without interruption	If there is no competition, the mark-up factor may be very high
Applicable for items that are special and that are included on a long-term basis in a menu or menu cycle	

Formal Buying

Formal buying is also referred to as "bid-buying" or "competitive buying." Most of the procedures involved in this type of buying are formal and, therefore, conducted in writing. Written sets of specifications are distributed to vendors. Formal invitations or requests for bids are circulated among all possible vendors. Since bids are requested in writing, this procedure is complicated and time-consuming, as compared to the informal method. Formal buying is usually only applicable to large operations and when large quantities of products are purchased. Often additional staff, based on the size of the foodservice operation, becomes necessary to handle the formalities and paperwork required. Records of all transactions have to be maintained, since any claims and legal actions have to be supported by documents. The main advantages of this method are that it provides for competition and that it promotes fair purchasing policies. This method is necessary when a large amount of money is involved in purchasing or when foodservices are operated for a state or federal agency. There are several methods of formal buying.

Competitive Bid

The competitive-bid method is commonly used by large foodservice operations, institutional foodservices, armed forces foodservices, and government agencies. In fact, this method is mandated by many agencies. Vendors are invited to submit bids based on written specifications of the commodities to be purchased. These requests are published in newspapers, industry-related publications, and/or mailed to a list of vendors. Regulations require that equal opportunity be provided to all interested vendors. An example of the bid request form is given in Appendix C. Clear and easily understood specifications are a must for bid requests. Many places maintain a list of approved vendors and the policy for approval is outlined in all fairness to the interested vendors. The bids may be sealed or unsealed and are to be submitted by a set deadline. The bids are opened—possibly in public—at a specified time. The bids should include details regarding general conditions, delivery methods, billing, and discounts. Bids may also be reviewed by a committee before they are finalized.

Some bids call for samples of the products that have been prepared and tested in test kitchens, which are special sites used for preparing and testing food products. Objective as well as sensory evaluations are conducted. The kitchens are equipped with all the materials required for food production and evaluation. In large operations, testing is conducted on a continuous basis, with skilled personnel and dietitians in charge. The identity of the bidder is not disclosed during testing and evaluation. Based on the results obtained, final bids are accepted, which need not be the lowest priced ones, since quality and other criteria influence the final decisions. After bids are selected, the successful bidder is announced, and the price quoted on the bid is made public. This method ensures fair handling and awards of bids. Purchase orders are then completed and sent to the successful bidder. Generally, the lowest bidder is selected, unless the product does not meet the designated specifications or proves to be of inferior quality. This method of buying is very effective and is thorough from the legal and procedural point of view.

Negotiated Buying

Negotiated buying may take place under the informal as well as the formal method, since both types of buying are involved. Informal negotiations are conducted prior to the formal written bids or purchase order. This method is used when time limits the formal requests for bids. It may also be used for the purchase of products whose prices are not subjected to fluctuations and for which there is a narrow margin in price difference. Buyers may initiate negotiations with several vendors and finally select one. This allows for competitive bidding and competition among the vendors contacted. As in the case of most formal methods, prices are set for a long period of time and this helps in the management of the foodservice operations by setting selling prices and keeping menu price fluctuations to a minimum. It also helps the management by eliminating the need for frequent quotations, price selection, food testing, fluctuating prices, and a lot of paper work. Since a long-term commitment is involved, purveyors agree to enter negotiations only with long-standing, reputable organizations and/or when large-quantity purchasing is involved.

Standing Order

In the standing order method, the purveyor continuously sends merchandise at predetermined, fixed intervals. The purchase may involve a fixed quantity or may involve stock replenishing. Milk and bakery product purchases are normally made by this method. Often the delivery person will replenish the stock, thus saving a considerable amount of time for the receiving person. Formal agreements are made in advance for this type of delivery and reviewed from time to time. One of the disadvantages of this system is that there is dependence on one vendor, and delays may be caused by unexpected problems in delivery. However, it works out well for those items that must be purchased daily or several times during a week.

Future Contract

The future contract method is similar to those discussed earlier in this type of buying. Future deliveries of the products are assured at a fixed price by entering into a future contract. Although the quantity to be purchased is not set, the prices to be charged are fixed. As and when needed, the particular commodity is ordered and bought at the set price. This, again, assures the delivery of product at a reasonable price without fluctuations in the amount charged to the foodservice operation. This method should be used only after careful consideration and evaluation of the supply and anticipated fluctuations in prices of a commodity.

Buy-and-Hold

The buy-and-hold method is used when large quantities of a product are available at bargain prices. The buyer pays the price of the stock, and the vendor is responsible for its storage, delivery, insurance, and losses due to spoilage. This method provides for the purchase of commodities at the most opportune time, as well as for their storage without obligation. However, one should consider the amount of money that may be tied up by the purchase. This method is desirable for products that are abundantly available in peak seasons and that cannot be readily stored by the foodservice operation.

SPECIFICATIONS

Specifications may be defined as the description of a particular commodity in terms of its size, quality, or condition. Specifications, which are very important in purchasing any product, especially foods, represent the technical language in which the buyer communicates with the seller as to what is actually needed. Since there are numerous products and different types and varieties within a product, it is essential to use distinct and specific terminology. An effective communication is completed when it is understood and acted on by the receiver. Thus, effective specifications are those that are complete and full in all respects.

Specifications, commonly referred to as "specs," are pieces of information that should be readily understood by most foodservice personnel. Specs have to be written and selected very carefully, since they determine the quality of food to be served. They have an impact on food costs and, consequently, the profits to be made by the operation. Specifications also serve as a means of identification of the products and their verification upon receiving. They eliminate any misunderstanding or friction all along the food flow and in the management process. Since they are specific, it is desirable to record them in writing. They should be accessible and placed at convenient locations for ready reference. It is imperative to plan and select specifications very carefully and to consider them as statements of management policy. They should be planned for the operation and, in fact, are custom-made for that facility. To blindly follow the specifications of another foodservice operation often leads to expensive problems. Some of the factors necessary in writing specifications are

1. They should be clear, concise, complete, and simple.
2. They should be based on management policy and should be viewed as requirements.
3. They should be based on tests and objective measurements that are recognized and are relatively easy to conduct.
4. They should be accurate and specific with no room for misinterpretation.
5. They must comply with the standards set by local, state, and/or federal regulatory agencies.
6. They must be used and revised to increase their usefulness.
7. They must be based on consideration of technical advancements and improvements (such as new packaging methods).

In addition, specifications should include the following information wherever applicable:

1. Common, trade, or brand name of the product
2. Amount to be purchased in the most commonly used units, such as case, crate, pound, carton, or lug
3. Recognized trade, federal, or local grade
4. Name and size of the basic container
5. Count and size of the items or units within the basic container such as 12/2's, 6/#10 cans, 12/3-lb packages, or number of dozens
6. Ranges in weight, thickness, or size, wherever applicable, such as 8 to 10 lb, ¼ to ½ in thick
7. Minimum and maximum trims, or fat content/percentages/ratios, wherever applicable
8. Degree of maturity or stage of ripening
9. Type of processing required, such as freeze-dried, cooked, or peeled
10. Type of packaging desired
11. Any additional information pertaining to nutrients or any modifications to the common specifications and additional clarifications to describe the exact item desired

Specific factors to be considered when ordering various types of food products are discussed later in this chapter. In short, the specifications should describe the item to the fullest possible extent.

Since buying is a specialized function, the person in charge of it should understand the various systems within the foodservice operation as well as their interrelationship. The food purchaser should possess the following skills and experience:

1. Awareness of the markets and market procedures
2. Ability to forecast needs and to respond to fluctuating market situations

3. Knowledge of items to be purchased and how they will be used
4. Ability to understand and set specifications, understand test data, and experience in the proper use of such specifications
5. Comprehension of the laws and regulations governing all aspects of purchasing
6. Knowledge of food processing, food labeling, nutrition, and other related information
7. Knowledge of different food grades and food qualities
8. Ability to judge quality by objective or subjective evaluations
9. Decision-making capability

REGULATORY AGENCIES

Several regulatory agencies have as their primary responsibility the assurance of food quality. They set standards and regulations designed to provide wholesome food and safe food processing. These regulations are very useful to a food buyer in setting specifications and ensuring that the products are safe and of desired quality. Federal agencies establish standards on a national basis and also provide regulatory control for these standards. They also set regulations for foods intended for interstate commerce. Regulations established by these agencies are instrumental in controlling food quality, food sanitation, and overall food marketing. Some of the agencies, as well as their regulations as they affect food purchasing, are described.

U.S. Department of Agriculture (USDA)

The Agricultural Marketing Services Act of 1953 (revised in 1957), implemented by the USDA, is probably the most important law to have a direct impact on food purchasing. It provides for grading and inspection of agricultural commodities. Since there are numerous agricultural commodities, they are categorized for inspection purposes and are handled by different departments. For most of the commodities, grading is voluntary. However, inspection is mandatory for meats, poultry, and other processed foods distributed through interstate commerce. Inspection agencies are located at several points, particularly at the shipping centers, markets, ports, or other marketing terminals. A stamp is placed on the product (as in the case of meat), container, tape, invoice, or other easily identifiable place. The presence of an approval stamp is indicative of the fact that the product meets the federal standard(s) set by the agency and/or by the buyer. Thus, the products can be verified by the agency for quality. This service is referred to as the "Acceptance" service. Individual specifications, which meet and excel the federal standards, may be set by any operation, and an agent from the agency will certify when those specifications are met. An inspection certificate may also be requested. Fees for this service may be paid by the buyer or the seller. This is a very useful service for the buyer, since quality is assured. Specific standards may be set by the organization to meet its requirements when the regulations are considered too general.

The Agricultural Marketing Service also helps in stabilizing prices, based on supply, demand, and fluctuations in prices. Stabilization is accomplished in three ways: (1) by grading commodities less stringently when in short supply, and by tightening grading during the peak supply period; (2) by paying subsidies to farmers for not planting; and (3) by purchasing surplus commodities, which are then distributed free or at a nominal cost to schools, the military, and other organizations. One or more of the above-mentioned methods may be used to stabilize prices. Many school foodservices take advantage of the commodities offered through this service, thereby reducing food costs.

The Wholesome Meat Act of 1967, which is an amended form of the Meat Inspection Act of 1906, requires inspection, at least as stringent as federal inspection, of all meat, whether it moves within or between states. It also provides technical and financial assistance for meat-inspection programs.

The Wholesome Poultry Products Act of 1968 requires inspection of all poultry and provides assistance to the state to improve inspection procedures. Tests are conducted to check for contamination of poultry products. The Egg Products Inspection Act of 1970 requires mandatory inspection of egg-processing plants and pasteurization during the freezing and drying of liquid eggs.

Food and Drug Administration (FDA)

The FDA, as part of the Department of Health and Human Services, has regulations which pertain to various practices in the food industry and which have considerable impact on the foodservice industry. One of the pioneer laws enacted by this agency is the well-known Food, Drug, and Cosmetic Act of 1906, which was later revised to the Food, Drug, and Cosmetic Act of 1938. It was designed to provide "safe and wholesome," honestly labeled, and properly packaged products. Further revisions were made to this act, the significant ones being the revision in 1958, commonly referred to as the "Delaney Clause," which states that "producers may not use any additives found to induce cancer in man or animals." This clause has been the cause of controversy from time to time and is often debated. The FDA regulations have a profound influence on the market, and a foodservice manager should be aware of them and any changes in them. Introduction of new analytical methods and technological advancements may require future changes in these laws.

Another important regulation under this act deals with the labeling of food products. The Food, Drug, and Cosmetic Act states that the labels of packaged items must include

1. Common name or names of the food item
2. Name and address of the manufacturer, packer, or distributor
3. Net contents of the package, either by count, fluid, or avoirdupois measure

4. Use of language that is easily understood with no foreign language that might circumvent label requirements
5. Specific, not collective, names for ingredients, unless the product is commonly known
6. Labels that are sufficiently prominent and easily understood
7. A list, in order of the greatest to least proportion, of all the ingredients used
8. The exact definition of the dietary properties if claims are made for any dietary value
9. The term "artificial," if artificial coloring or flavoring is used, or the term "chemical preservative," if a chemical preservative is used.

For more information, the actual regulations should be consulted.

The Food, Drug, and Cosmetic Act also defines "adulteration and misbranding" and in so doing provides important standards for processed foods. Inspectors can ascertain the quality of processed foods by (1) inspecting food samples sent to their laboratories, resulting in the certification of particular samples; (2) inspecting random samples withdrawn from lots, in which case the entire lot is certified; (3) "continuous" inspection in the food plant, thereby certifying on a continuous basis; and (4) intermittent inspection, where only a grade certificate is issued.

Three important standards are checked by food inspectors as follows: (1) standards of quality, (2) standards of identity, and (3) standards of fill. Detailed descriptions of these standards are given below.

Standards of Quality

Standards of quality refer to the quality of the food products, which may be measured by objective as well as subjective methods. Various instrumental, chemical, and other methods are used for assessing the quality of foods. Since attributes vary from one food to another, grades are based on different factors and the grading system varies from one food to another. Some of the attributes considered in grading include color, texture, tenderness, and freedom from defects. Grades for processed food items are different from those for fresh foods. For most processed foods, a scale ranging from 1 to 100 is used, with a product scoring 90 and above being designated as A, 80 to 89 as B, 70 to 79 as C, and below 70 as below standard. This grading system may vary from product to product. It should be noted that the "below standards" does not mean "unwholesome." Reasons for such grading are normally given, and it may be economical at times to use these products, especially when their appearance in the finished food product is not very important. Broken foods which may be perfectly wholesome are graded as "below standard," and these may be used in products where appearance is not significant. Grades also depend on the type of fruit or vegetable; these grades are discussed later in this chapter. Each food product is graded based on different factors, such as marbling in meats, bacterial counts for milk, and color of apples.

It should be noted that providing quality grade is entirely voluntary, but most food processors prefer grading to authenticate the quality of their products. A distinction should be made between grading for quality and inspection for wholesomeness, which are entirely different procedures. A food product must be wholesome in order to be graded for quality.

Standards of Identity

Standards of identity have been set to describe or distinguish a product. They are the means of identifying a product and differentiating it from other products. These standards prevent misrepresentation and misbranding. Exact descriptions of the products and their contents are required. The USDA sets standards of identity for meat, poultry, and egg products, while the FDA sets standards for other foods. Certain products may have several common names, but these standards identify the products by one specific name. For example, fruit cocktail may mean different things to different processors, and the contents may vary widely. These standards precisely describe the contents required before a product can be labeled and identified as fruit cocktail. Thus salad dressings, ice creams, preserves, jams, and jellies are all identified and must meet specific standards. The word "artificial" is used when additives fitting into this category are used. A product is designated as "misbranded" if the identity names are used without meeting the standards.

Standards of Fill

Standards of fill refer to the quantity required in packaged foods or how "full" a container must be to prevent deceptive filling practices. As with standards of quality, containers that do not meet the standards are labeled as "below standards of fill." Use of federal grades for quality are voluntary, but standards of fill are mandatory. Criminal action, conviction, fines, and other penalties are imposed on food manufacturers when these standards are violated. Offenders may be ordered to go out of business, pay fines, and/or go to jail. Precise weights and volumes are specified for different containers. The approved label ensures that the container is legally full to the quantity stated on the label.

In addition to fill standards, the FDA has other regulations that deal with the food processing and nutritional labeling of products. The FDA has introduced a set of regulations grouped under Good Manufacturing Practices (GMPs). These guidelines list practices for the maintenance of sanitary conditions involving food plants, grounds, equipment, utensils, facilities, controls, processes, and personnel.

U.S. Department of Commerce (USDC)

A voluntary grading system is maintained by the USDC, mainly for fish and fish products. The grades assure that there is in-plant inspection during processing. For seafood, the inspection is conducted by the National Marine Fisheries Service (NMFS). The FDA and United States Public Health Service (USPHS) are indirectly involved with the inspection of certain types of fish and shellfish. Since grading is voluntary, a product that is not graded is not necessarily unwholesome or unfit for consumption. Various grades and technical terms are used for grading and defining seafood products. These foods are handled by the USDC, since they are largely imported from other countries.

Other regulatory agencies and regulations govern many of the state and local areas. The milk, shellfish, and foods served by foodservices are frequently inspected by local public health agencies. Regulations and inspections are designed to ensure the quality and the quantity of products, encourage good marketing practices, promote good practices related to advertisements and promotions, establish fair trade practices and prices, ensure the safety and health of the consumer and the worker, and promote healthy competition. A foodservice manager or a person in charge of food purchasing should know and utilize these regulations advantageously.

ETHICS IN BUYING

In foodservice operations, large amounts of food and other items are purchased and there are often large quantities of products in storage. To avoid losses, management has a responsibility to ensure **ethics in buying** at all levels, to include all employes as well as purveyors and their agents. A continuous minor loss may erode the profits of an operation very rapidly. Loss of a pound from a 100-lb container may seem negligible, but if carried out over a period of time, will prove to be very expensive. Listed below are some of the points management should consider and implement to promote ethical standards:

1. Put an emphasis on honesty and make it a policy. It should be clear to the purchasing and receiving department that honesty is the only policy and that management is willing to go as far as necessary to see that it is implemented.
2. Set an example and be sincere in all its dealings. A manager who walks away with a loaf of bread every day leaves a very poor impression and affects overall morale.
3. Assign precise responsibilities to employees dealing with purchasing and receiving. Specific persons should be designated to deal with purveyors. No other persons should be allowed to interfere with the purchasing and the receiving functions.
4. Make a policy of not accepting personal gifts or favors from purveyors directly or indirectly. These offers should be politely declined, and the purveyors should be discouraged from making such offers. Any gifts, private offers, club memberships, charge cards for personal use, and other such offers to any employee or manager should be discouraged.
5. See that employees are satisfied to the maximum possible extent because many ethical problems arise with job dissatisfaction.

6. Ensure that specifications are clear and complete and well understood by persons in charge of purchasing and receiving. Frequent revisions and updating of specifications should be conducted.
7. Check the credentials and the authority of the dealers or their salespersons. Before entering into any contracts with the purveyors, check their reputation and, if possible, visit their facilities. A manager can learn a lot about the purveyor by talking to involved personnel and/or visiting their premises.
8. Provide the facilities and equipment needed for purchasing and receiving. Adequate physical facilities are essential. Procedures for testing should be clearly defined and placed at a convenient location for easy reference.
9. Set specific times, preferably during working hours, for visits by salespersons. Representatives of as many purveyors as possible should be encouraged to visit to demonstrate that management is fair and to promote the spirit of competitiveness. On the other hand, home visits by these representatives should be discouraged.
10. Check prices, discounts, and other deals very carefully and do not play one purveyor against the other. Equal opportunity and fair dealing should be the policy.
11. Be vigilant at all times and conduct spot checks frequently. Management should be willing to demonstrate the best possible methods.
12. Investigate promptly any complaints either from the purchasing department or the purveyors. The results of such investigation should be made known to all concerned parties as soon as possible. The very fact that an operation is willing to investigate promotes positive ethical standards.
13. Take prompt action against any offenders and take measures to avoid recurrence of the offense.
14. Reward those who are honest and sincere. This action will boost the morale of outstanding employees and encourage others to follow suit.
15. Provide security for the personnel. See that all products are stored securely so that there are no temptations for stealing.

In the following part of this chapter, examples of specifications and the points to be considered while ordering commodities are listed. The intent is to provide general information that is necessary for food purchasing. Examples are provided within each category. In actual purchasing situations, it is wise to become familiar with all details and specifications for that commodity.

PURCHASE OF SPECIFIC COMMODITIES

Fresh Fruits and Vegetables

The perishability of fresh fruits and vegetables makes these commodities unpredictable, not only from the purchasing point of view but also for the grading and setting up of specifications. Since there are numerous variations among types of fresh fruits and vegetables, it is impossible to have one set standard of specifications. The grading system, the terminology in use, and other specifications are different for individual types of fresh fruits and vegetables. In general, the following factors need to be considered.

Grade

There are different sets of United States standards that are specific for each fruit and vegetable. The quality varies within each set of these grades. These **U.S. grades** may be listed by numbers such as No. 1, No. 2, or by such terms as U.S. Fancy and U.S. Extra Fancy. Since perishable items are involved and quality is subject to deterioration in transport, it is essential to specify that the grade desired is at the time of delivery, rather than at the time of shipping. U.S. grades are handy tools and reference sources for buyers, since they avoid the use of lengthy specifications and eliminate misunderstandings. Any special requirements of a foodservice operation can always be added to the specified grade(s). The standards for both fruits and vegetables may be obtained from the USDA.

Quality

Additional factors of quality that are not specified in the food grades should be included in food orders. Grades may be supplemented by an explanation of what is desired, and many times it helps if the intended use is given. Examples of such explanations are: lettuce for salads, tomato for relishes, and parsley for garnishing. It is important to specify and insist on freshness. Wilted, stale, blemished, dry, or cut fruits and vegetables are undesirable. Although it varies for the type of fruit or vegetable, desirable characteristics include: bright, attractive colors, good shape and appearance, good proportion of weight and size, and absence of any mechanical damage or signs of decay. Lack of freshness may also be a sign of poor handling and transportation. This may result in shortened storage capability and useful life of the fruits and vegetables, even though they may be suitable for immediate use. Seasonal availability should be considered when ordering fresh produce, since storage capability is also dependent on seasonal variations. Most fresh fruits and vegetables may have undesirable attributes at the beginning and the end of the growing season. These attributes may include sourness, lack of juiciness, lack of flavor, lack of texture, unripeness, or overripeness. Quality at every stage should be compared with the price, and the decision to buy should be based on overall considerations.

Variety

Variety and type of fruits and vegetables are important, since they identify a specific item among several available kinds. For example, Golden Delicious or McIntosh specifies the exact type of apples desired without any misunderstanding.

Variety and type are also helpful in selecting the best fruits and vegetables for a particular purpose. A good example is Russet or Katahdin potatoes, which are different in appearance, specific gravity, and cooking qualities. Although the varietal names of most fruits and, particularly, vegetables are seldom used, type is very commonly used and helps in specifications.

Size

Size is one of the most important aspects of specification, particularly for fruits. The optimum size desired for the purpose should be selected, since the cost of many commodities depends on size. Normally, smaller sizes are preferable when appearance is not significant, whereas larger sizes are recommended when whole or large portions of fruits and vegetables are used. Also, larger sizes are preferred for carvings and artistic displays and presentations. Sizes also determine the count that is packaged in a container. For example, apple sizes may vary from 56 to 252 per western apple box. Similarly, many fruits are sized by count per box or by diameter. The diameter is measured not around the girth but transversely from stem end to blossom end. Some vegetables, especially greens, may be shipped in large bunches and may be specified in dozens of bunches per container. Terms used for specification should be carefully used from the prevalent terminology. Care should be taken to avoid terms that are not included in the standards for that product. "Small" or "large" should only be used if they fit in the definition of a standard grade.

Packaging

Numerous types of packaging are available for fruits and vegetables. Buyers should be specific as to the type of packaging or the container desired. An item may be available in more than one kind of package such as bushel baskets, boxes, lugs, sacks, crates, cardboard containers, and so on. Specifications should be clear as to what kind of packaging is desired, such as apples by counts per box, cantaloupes in counts per crate, or broccoli in bunches per baskets. In some cases, the type of packaging selected indirectly indicates the quantities desired. Special packaging, such as ventilated containers or containers for hydrocooled vegetables, may also be requested and specified. Packaging selected should be based on the quality and the quantity of the products desired and also on the time and distance involved in transportation. Storage space within the facility should be considered. Smaller packaging may be easier to shelve in some cases, compared to large containers, and vice versa.

Other Information

Other pertinent information, wherever applicable, should be included to enhance the specifications, such as the brand name or the growing area of the product. Produce from one area may have different qualities than that from other areas. For

Table 6.1

Guidelines for Specifications of Fresh and Packaged Fruits and Vegetables

Description	Example
Geographical area of production	California peaches; Florida oranges
Variety	Golden Delicious; Valencia
Type	Long-cut or short-cut
Style	Slices or pineapple tidbits; whole-kernel corn
Size	Large, small, medium; 20–25 lb watermelon
Count	Number per gallon; 80-count apples per box
Syrup density	Light, medium, heavy, extra-heavy syrup or water. May be given in Brix
Specific gravity	Given specifically for potatoes and tomatoes
Mix percentage	Types of fruits in fruit cocktail
Container/package	Can, case, package, or lug
Weight tolerance	Struck full or rounded full
Cut	Diced, Julienne
Condition upon receipt	Fresh, internal temperature, frozen, or in ice
Type of flavor	Sweetened, unsweetened, salt-free, or salted
Federal or other grades	U.S. No. 1, or U.S. Fancy
Other specific factors	Pitted, sun-dried

example, fruits from California may be different from the same type of fruits from Florida. As an illustration, apple varieties and their uses are shown in Table 6.2. A list of specifications to be used in purchasing fresh fruits and vegetables is given in Table 6.1.

Processed Fruits and Vegetables

Standards for processed fruits and vegetables have been well developed. Minimum quality standards, set by the federal Food, Drug, and Cosmetic Act, are the standards of identity, fill, and quality. In addition to these standards, grades used to classify processed fruits and vegetables based on their quality have been developed by the USDA.

Fruits	Vegetables
U.S. Grade A or U.S. Fancy	U.S. Grade A or U.S. Fancy
U.S. Grade B or U.S. Choice	U.S. Grade B or U.S. Extra-Standard
U.S. Grade C or U.S. Standard	U.S. Grade C or U.S. Standard

Those processed foods not meeting the minimum requirements are graded as substandard. Labeling a product as substandard does not mean it is unfit for consumption or that it is of inferior nutritional quality. In fact based on usage, it may even be economical to use such products, particularly where the identity of the fruit or vegetable is not of prime importance. Grades are based on a number of factors used in scoring, which may vary according to the fruit or vegetable. These

Table 6.2

Apple Varieties and Their Uses

Variety	Flavor-Texture	Season	Fresh/Salad	Pie	Sauce	Baking
Red Delicious	Sweet-Mellow	Sept.–June	Excellent	Poor	Fair	Poor
Golden Delicious	Sweet-Semi-firm	Sept.–May	Excellent	Excellent	Very good	Very good
McIntosh	Slightly tart-Tender	Sept.–June	Excellent	Excellent	Good	Fair
Rome Beauty	Slightly tart-Firm	Oct.–June	Good	Very good	Verg good	Excellent
Jonathan	Tart-Tender	Sept.–June	Very good	Very good	Very good	Poor
York Imperial	Tart-Firm	Oct.–Apr.	Fair	Good	Very good	Good
Stayman	Tart-Semi-firm	Oct.–Mar.	Very good	Good	Good	Good
Winesap	Slightly tart-Firm	Oct.–June	Excellent	Good	Good	Good
Newtown Pippin	Slightly tart-Firm	Sept.–June	Very good	Excellent	Excellent	Very good

factors include color, size, consistency, symmetry, finish, maturity, absence of defects, character, flavor, uniformity of size, type of liquor, cut, and wholesomeness.

Several factors are considered in grading processed fruits and vegetables. The following aspects, which may or may not be used in grading, are important to consider when purchasing processed fruits and vegetables.

Fill of Container

Unless defined by the Food and Drug regulations, USDA grades recommend generally that cans be filled as full as practicable without impairment of the quality; and the product and the packaging medium occupy not less than 90% of the water capacity of the container. For objective assessment and for all practical purposes, this percentage of fill is determined by measuring the headspace inside the can. "Headspace" is the space between the top of the container and the packaging medium. Containers that fail to meet this requirement are designated as "below standard in fill." Maximum gross headspaces for various can sizes are specified, for example, 27/32 in for No. 10 cans and 19/32 in for No. 2 cans.

Drained Weight

Except for a few products, drained weight is not considered as an attribute in the evaluation of grade, since it is not a factor related to quality. However, recommended minimum drained weights are included in the specifications. **Drained weight** refers to the weight of the canned products after the liquid is allowed to drain for 2 min on a standard sieve under specified conditions. The test is done after the product has been allowed to equalize for 30 or more days after canning. Drained weights are important, since the actual yield from a canned product can be determined, and this helps in the calculation of portion sizes.

Syrup Density

Syrup density is not considered in grading a canned product, since syrup, or any other liquid medium, is not a factor of quality. The type and density of syrup or the packaging medium, which is specified on the label, are important from two points of view: (1) The quality of the canned product is dependent on the density of the syrup. The heavier the syrup, the less the chance of the products' breaking up, particularly fruits. Therefore, for higher-quality products, heavier syrup should be recommended. (2) From the dietetic point of view, it is important to know the density of the syrup, particularly when it will be used in special diets.

The scale used to measure the density of a syrup is Brix, which relates the specific gravity of a solution to an equivalent concentration of pure sucrose. Roughly, for every degree Brix, a fruit has 1% sugar. Brix tables should be used for the accurate determination of Brix and the sugar content. The taste or tartness of fruits or fruit juices may be described in terms of Brix, or Brix-to-acid ratio. The higher the Brix, the greater the sugar concentration in the juice; and the higher the Brix-to-acid ratio, the sweeter and less tart is the juice.

Although canned fruits are not graded on the basis of syrup density, they are certified as meeting the declared syrup designation. The densities of the syrup may be measured by a refractometer or a Brix hydrometer.

Scoring Factors

Grades are assigned to each type of product based on several scoring factors (Table 6.3). These factors are dependent on the type of product and may be different for fruits or vegetables or their combination. Scores are for such factors as color, character, flavor, size, symmetry, absence of defects, maturity, texture, consistency, finish, liquor, or clearness of liquor, wholeness, and cut. It should be understood that these scores are based on the factors and are indicative of the products based on these qualities. Lower scores are not indicative of poor nutritional quality, since that is not what is described by these factors.

An example of a scoring system is given in Table 6.4, which represents a score

Table 6.3

Scoring Ranges for Grades of Canned Foods

Grades	For Foods Where There Is a Grade B	For Foods Where There Is No Grade B
A (Fancy)	90 to 100	85 to 100
B (Choice, Extra Standard)	75 to 89	—
C (Standard)	60 to 74	70 to 84
Substandard	0 to 59	0 to 69

Table 6.4

Score Chart for Canned Fruit Cocktail

Factors	Points (Max)	Grade A Fancy	Grade B Choice	Substandard
Clearness of liquid media	20	17–20	14–16	0–13[c]
Color	20	17–20	14–16[a]	0–13[c]
Uniformity of size	20	17–20	14–16[b]	0–13[c]
Absence of defects	20	17–20	14–16[c]	0–13[c]
Character of fruit	20	17–20	14–16[c]	0–13[c]
Minimum Score	—	85	70	—

[a]*Partial limiting rule:* Cocktail falling into this classification because of the staining or dullness of color cannot earn higher grade regardless of the total score.

[b]*Partial limiting rule:* Cocktail in which more than 15% by weight of the peach units, or of the pineapple units, if diced, fail to conform to the dimensions for the diced fruits cannot earn higher grade regardless of the total score.

[c]*Limiting rule:* Cocktail failing in this classification cannot earn higher grade regardless of the total score.

chart for canned fruit cocktail. As evident, the scoring factors used for canned fruit cocktail include clearness of the liquid media, color, uniformity of size, absence of defects, and the character of fruit. Based on these factors, points are given based on a maximum of 20 points. Grades assigned are Grade A (Fancy), Grade B (Choice), or Substandard. For each of the factors, scores are given, and the final grading is based on the total score. Under each factor, there are descriptions of the desirable attributes, such as those with reasonably clear and bright liquid assigned Grade A and those with slightly dull or pink color assigned Grade B, and so on. Other factors used in grading and scoring are all well defined. Although the final grading is based on the total score, there are certain limiting and partially limiting rules. As in the case of fruit cocktail, the "limiting rule" restricts those products failing in the specified classification from earning a higher grade regardless of the total score. "Partial limiting" rules similarly restrict the grading of a product to a higher grade irrespective of the total score.

For most canned fruits and vegetables the grades are based on the following scores:

USDA Grade A must be practically perfect in every respect, allowing a tolerance of from 15% to 18% within the grade which is scored between 85 and 100 points inclusive.

USDA Grade B must be reasonably perfect in every respect, allowing a tolerance of from 16.7% to 20% within the grade which is scored between 75 and 89 points inclusive.

USDA Grade C must be fairly perfect in every respect, allowing a tolerance of from 20% to 25% within the grade which is scored between 60 and 74 points inclusive.

For certain products, there are only two USDA Grades and in those instances the scoring for the grades is as follows:

USDA Grade A must be practically perfect in every respect, allowing a tolerance of from 15% to 18% within the grade which is scored between 85 and 100 points inclusive.

USDA Grade B must be fairly perfect in every respect, allowing a tolerance of from 18% to 22% within the grade which is scored between 70 and 84 points inclusive.

Frozen Fruits and Vegetables

Frozen fruits and vegetables are graded in practically the same way as canned products with minor exceptions. Frozen products are packed in a variety of packages and are available in different weights. Frozen fruits may be packaged in sugar or syrup. It is important to know the medium in which they are packaged. They may also be treated with an antioxidant to avoid browning on the surfaces. Vegetables may have added salt as a preservative.

Meats and Meat Products

In any type of foodservice operation probably no single item is as expensive as, or as important as, meats and meat products. Meat purchases may range from 30% of the total food expenditure (in institutions) to 70% (in commercial establishments). Meat purchasing may represent as much as 20% of all operating expenditures for the institutional foodservice to 40% for the commercial establishment. Thus meat plays an important role in the menu; and the ultimate profitability of many operations depends on how meat items are purchased, prepared, and served to consumers. It is essential to have well-planned and controlled methods of purchasing, receiving, preparing, and serving meat items in order to be successful in the foodservice industry. Well-defined and clear standards and regulations help in purchasing wholesome and safe meats and their byproducts. However, it should be emphasized that meat buying is complex and requires considerable experience. To be an effective buyer, an understanding of the processing of meats from the slaughterhouse to the processing plant is vital. An understanding of the terminology, grading procedures, inspection, and safety regulations pertaining to meat products is very important.

All animals intended for food are inspected and approved for normal slaughter. Antemortem and postmortem inspections are conducted to certify the wholesomeness of the meat. Soon after the death of the animal, several chemical changes occur in meats, starting with the stiffening of the muscles or "rigor mortis." Meat at this stage is referred to as "green." The main meat structures responsible for tenderness are the connective tissues and the muscle myofibrils. The connective tissues found in muscle are composed of the proteins collagen, elastin, and reticulin. Collagen is a tough fibrous protein, which upon hydrolysis yields hydroxyproline. Specific plant enzymes, such as papain (found in papaya), ficin (found in figs), and bromelin (found in pineapples), will attack tissue collagen and render it soft and tender. Meat from very young animals, such as calves, contains a large amount of collagen in proportion to other muscle fibers, so that this meat is relatively more tender. This tissue also undergoes changes due to the inherent enzymes, which make the meat tender during the process of aging. Elastin is a yellow protein which is very elastic and which is practically unaffected by normal heat during cooking. The amount of elastin present, therefore, affects the tenderness of the meat. Reticulin fibers are also similar to elastin and are very tough. Muscle tissues normally present in meats contain the muscle proteins actin, myosin, and tropomyosin. The number and size of muscle fibers as compared to connective tissues are responsible for the tenderness of meats. In other words, large fibers will have less connective tissues than small fibers. Thus, both muscle and connective tissues play an important role in the overall tenderness of meats.

Different types of retail cuts are obtained from beef, lamb, or pork carcasses. The main cuts of beef are

Hindquarter	Forequarter
Round	Rib
Rump	Chuck
Sirloin or loin end	Plate
Short loin	Brisket
Flank	Shank

Retail cuts obtained from beef and lamb are shown in Figures 6.6 and 6.7.

Meat Grades

In general, meats are graded on two important aspects: *quality*, mainly indicative of palatability; and *yield*, mainly indicative of the cutability for major retail cuts.

When writing specifications for meats, either a quality grade or a combination of quality and yield grades is required. The overall grades for meats and their descriptions are:

U.S. Prime. Highest grade; meats have fine texture and firm muscles.

U.S. Choice. High in eating quality; less fat than prime.

U.S. Good. Greater proportion of lean to fat; lacks juiciness but relatively tender.

U.S. Standard. Thin fat covering; high proportion of lean to fat; tender.

U.S. Commercial. From mature animals; lacks tenderness; relatively more wastage.

U.S. Utility. From animals advanced in age; lacks tenderness and juiciness.

U.S. Cutter and U.S. Canner. Useful for processed meat products.

It is required that the beef carcass be "ribbed" at least 10 minutes before it is graded, this allowing some of the grade-determining factors the time to become evident. "Ribbing" is splitting the carcass down the center of the backbone and cutting between the twelfth and the thirteenth rib bones to expose *longissimus dorsi* muscle. The *longissimus dorsi*, or rib-eye muscle, is the longest muscle, extending from the neck to the end of the animal body (rump). The quality grading is based on:
Classes of animals. Some of the classes and grades are given below.

Heifer or steer—Prime, Choice, Good, Standard, Commercial, Utility, Cutter, Canner

Cow—Choice, Good, Standard, Commercial, Utility, Cutter, Canner

Bullock—Prime, Choice, Good, Standard, Utility

Calf or veal — Prime, Choice, Good, Standard, Utility, Cull

Lamb — Prime, Choice, Good, Utility, Cull

Pork — U.S. No. 1, 2, 3, 4, Utility

Mutton — Choice, Good, Utility, Cull

Maturity. Maturity is indicated by bone size, shape, and ossification. Maturity grades are given from A to E, with A being the youngest and E being the oldest.

Flesh color and texture. White fat and cherry-colored lean are considered top quality. Lean flesh will have fine texture and a light grayish color.

Marbling. Streaks of fat running through lean meat is referred to as "marbling." Good marbling is indicative of well-fed animals and of meats that will be tender, juicy, and flavorful when cooked. Although marbling is desirable to an extent, overabundant marbling imparts an oily taste. The degrees of marbling for grading are abundant, moderately abundant, slightly abundant, moderate, modest, small, slight, traces, and practically devoid.

The yield grades are based on:

Amount of external fat: The thickness of fat over the rib-eye muscle measured perpendicular to the outside surface at a point three-quarters of the length of the rib eye from its chine bone end.

Amount of kidney, pelvic, and heart fat: Calculated as 3% of the carcass weight.

Area of the rib eye: Measurable by a special grid.

Hot carcass weight: Calculated by multiplying chilled carcass weight by 1.02.

The formula used for the calculation of yield grade is:

Yield grade (1 to 5) = [2.50 + 2.50 × adjusted fat thickness (in.)] + (0.20 × percentage of kidney, pelvic, and heart fat) + [0.0038 × hot carcass weight (lb)] − [0.32 × the area of the rib eye (in.^{2})]

Yield grades 1 to 5 are applicable to all quality grades. The yield grades (Table 6.5, p. 176) reflect differences in yields of boneless, closely trimmed retail cuts. Yield grade 1 represents the highest yield of cuts and yield grade 5, the lowest. However, the ones indicated by X in Table 6.5 are the yield grades most commonly available for the quality grades. It should be noted that U.S. Prime beef does not usually have a yield grade of 1 or 2.

When writing the specifications for meats the following aspects should be included:

1. Class of animal
2. USDA grade and the division of grade

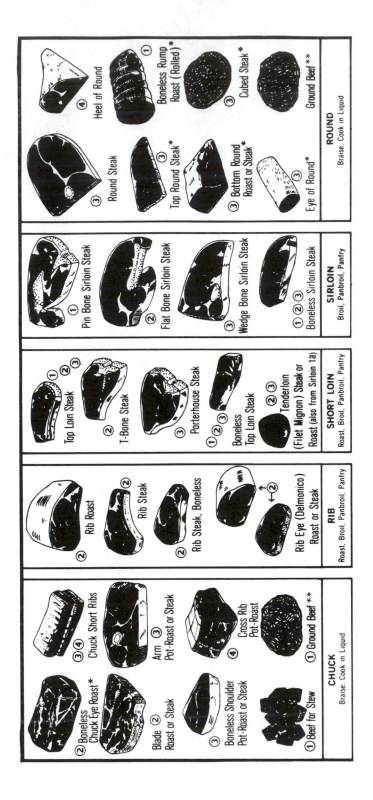

CHUCK
Braise. Cook in Liquid

② Boneless Chuck Eye Roast*

② Blade Roast or Steak

③ Boneless Shoulder Pot-Roast or Steak

① Beef for Stew

③④ Chuck Short Ribs

③ Arm Pot-Roast or Steak

④ Cross Rib Pot-Roast

① Ground Beef**

RIB
Roast, Broil, Panbroil, Panfry

② Rib Roast

② Rib Steak

② Rib Steak, Boneless

②→ Rib Eye (Delmonico) Roast or Steak

SHORT LOIN
Roast, Broil, Panbroil, Panfry

①②③ Top Loin Steak

② T-Bone Steak

③ Porterhouse Steak

①②③ Boneless Top Loin Steak

②③ Tenderloin (Filet Mignon) Steak or Roast (also from Sirloin 1a)

SIRLOIN
Broil, Panbroil, Panfry

① Pin Bone Sirloin Steak

② Flat Bone Sirloin Steak

③ Wedge Bone Sirloin Steak

①②③ Boneless Sirloin Steak

ROUND
Braise. Cook in Liquid

④ Heel of Round

① Boneless Rump Roast (Rolled)*

③ Cubed Steak*

③ Round Steak

③ Top Round Steak*

③ Bottom Round Roast or Steak*

③ Eye of Round*

Ground Beef**

172

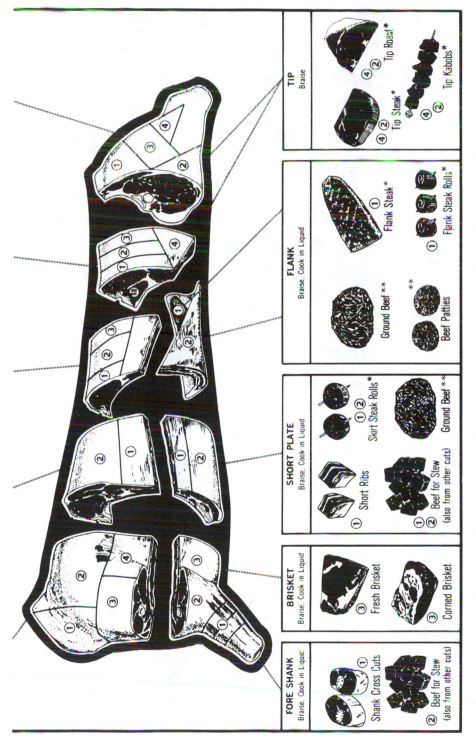

Figure 6-6. Retail cuts of beef: where they come from and how to cook them. (Courtesy National Livestock and Meat Board)

173

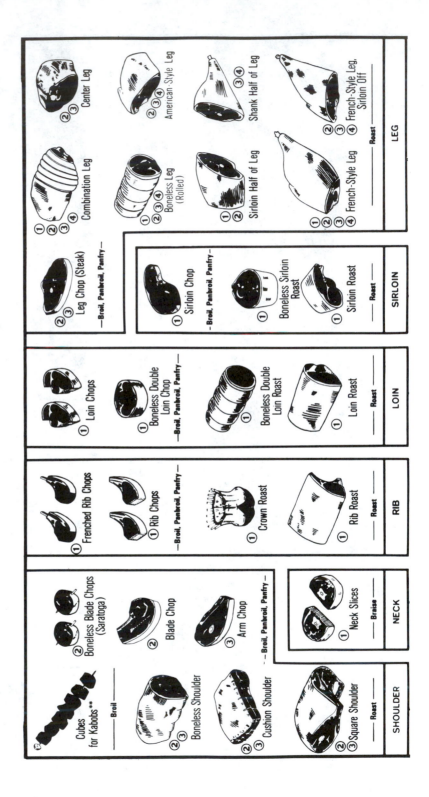

LEG

- ② ③ Center Leg
- ② ③ ④ American-Style Leg
- ③ ④ Shank Half of Leg
- ② ③ ④ French-Style Leg, Sirloin Off
- ① ② ③ ④ Combination Leg
- ② ③ ④ Boneless Leg (Rolled)
- ① ② Sirloin Half of Leg
- ① ② ③ ④ French-Style Leg

—Roast—

SIRLOIN

- ② ③ Leg Chop (Steak)
  —Broil, Panbroil, Panfry—
- ① Sirloin Chop
  — Broil, Panbroil, Panfry —
- ① ② Boneless Sirloin Roast
- ① Sirloin Roast
  —Roast—

LOIN

- ① Loin Chops
- ① Boneless Double Loin Chop
  —Broil, Panbroil, Panfry—
- ① Boneless Double Loin Roast
- ① Loin Roast
  — Roast —

RIB

- ① Frenched Rib Chops
- ① Rib Chops
  —Broil, Panbroil, Panfry—
- ① Crown Roast
- ① Rib Roast
  — Roast —

NECK

- ① Neck Slices
  — Braise

SHOULDER

- ② Boneless Blade Chops (Saratoga)
- ② Blade Chop
- ③ Arm Chop
  -- Broil, Panbroil, Panfry --
- Cubes for Kabobs***
  — Broil —
- ② ③ Boneless Shoulder
- ② Cushion Shoulder
- ② ③ Square Shoulder
  — Roast —

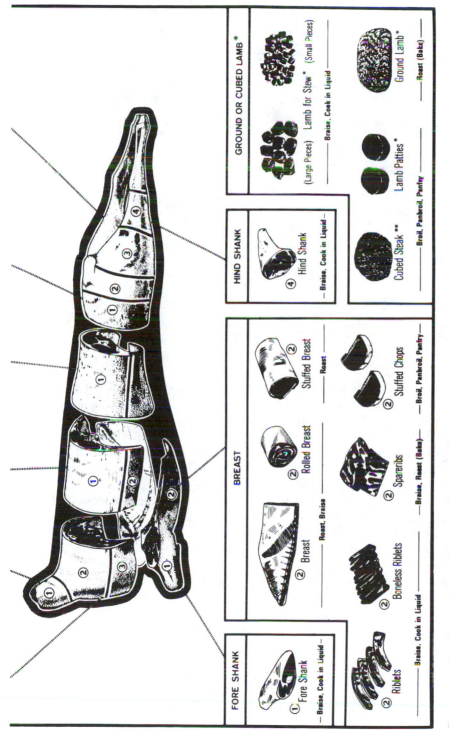

Figure 6-7. Retail cuts of lamb. (Courtesy of National Livestock and Meat Board)

175

Table 6.5

Quality and Yield Grades of Beef

U.S. Quality Grades	Yield Grades				
	1	2	3	4	5
Prime			X	X	X
Choice		X	X	X	X
Good		X	X		
Standard	X	X	X		
Commercial		X	X	X	X
Utility		X	X	X	
Cutter		X	X		
Canner		X			

3. USDA yield grade
4. Acceptance weight range
5. Fat limitations
6. Condition upon delivery
7. Temperature and packaging upon delivery
8. Weight
9. IMPS No. (explained below)

The above specifications may be enhanced by using IMPS numbers. IMPS stands for the Institutional Meat Purchase Specifications, which are the official USDA requirements for the inspection, packing, packaging, and delivering of specific meats and meat products. IMPS are also used for the certification or "acceptance" of these products by the USDA meat graders. Several publications are available that describe the IMPS specifications. One very commonly used publication is *The Meat Buyers' Guide*, published by the National Association of Meat Purveyors (NAMP), which contains meat specifications. These guides are available for standardized meat cuts and for the portion-controlled meat cuts. They are written to simplify the IMPS and to supplement overall meat grading standards. These guides also have colored pictures of the actual cuts of meats that make it easier to understand the IMPS. IMPS are based on a numbering system that facilitates easy identification of different types of meat products. As an example, the numbers and descriptions of the meat are given below:

IMPS No.	*Description*
100	Fresh beef
200	Fresh lamb and mutton
300	Fresh veal and calf
400	Fresh pork
500	Cured, smoked, cooked pork products

IMPS No.	Description
600	Cured, dried, smoked beef products
700	Edible by-products
800	Sausage products
1000	Portion-cut end products

As specific examples, the following numbers and descriptions are given to clarify the IMPS numbering system:

100	Beef carcass
101	Beef side
102	Beef forequarter
137	Special ground beef
200	Lamb carcass
234	Oven-prepared leg of lamb
300	Veal carcass
400	Pork carcass
500	Cured regular ham
600	Corned Spencer roll
613	Cured tongue
701	Beef liver
713	Lamb liver
1100	Beef cubed steaks
1103	Beef rib steak
1189	Tenderloin steak

Poultry and Eggs

Grading of poultry is based on class, quality, quantity, condition, or any combination of these factors. The U.S. Consumer grades for poultry are listed below:

U.S. Grade A. A lot of ready-to-cook poultry or parts consisting of one or more ready-to-cook carcasses, or parts of the same kind and class, each of which conforms to the requirements for A Quality, may be designated as U.S. Grade A.

U.S. Grade B. A lot of ready-to-cook poultry or parts consisting of one or more ready-to-cook carcasses, or parts of the same kind and class, each of which conforms to the requirements for B Quality or better, may be designated as U.S. Grade B.

U.S. Grade C. A lot of ready-to-cook poultry or parts consisting of one or more ready-to-cook carcasses, or parts of the same kind and class, each of which conforms to the requirements for C Quality or better, may be designated as U.S. Grade C.

There are also two procurement grades: U.S. Procurement Grade I and U.S. Procurement Grade II.

There is a voluntary USDA grading and inspection service for poultry. Poultry should be specified by part as follows: breasts, breast with ribs, wishbones, legs, wings, drumsticks, thighs, halves, quarters, and backs. The specifications for poultry should, therefore, include (1) name of the part, (2) quantity, (3) weight, (4) detailed description, (5) required inspection, (6) condition upon delivery, and (7) type of packaging.

The grading of eggs is based upon size, which is determined by weight per dozen. Since most eggs are packed in 30-dozen, corrugated-fiber cases, it is easier to determine and compare their case weights.

Large and medium eggs are the sizes most frequently used in foodservices. They are suitable for frying, poaching, hard or soft cooking, and for dishes where appearance is of primary importance. If eggs are to be used in mixed salads or for baking, size is not so important. If one uses large-sized eggs as a base, medium eggs are the better buy if they are 12% or more cheaper than large eggs. If not, there is no savings and the larger size should be selected. Similarly, small eggs are a better buy if they are 24% or more cheaper than large eggs. Size should not be confused with grading. A jumbo egg refers to its size and not to its quality. In other words, both quality and size should be considered in purchasing eggs.

The quality of eggs depends on their exterior as well as their interior condition. The shell should be sound, clean, and unbroken. Eggs lose carbon dioxide and moisture upon storage. The air cell, which is visible under light, enlarges as moisture and carbon dioxide are lost. The white becomes thin and watery and the yolk flattens out. As a result of these storage changes, an old egg covers a wide area when broken, compared to that of a fresh egg. The yolk is also weak and may break. A test known as *Haugh Unit Breakout Test* is based on the height of the white at the yolk, which is measured using a micrometer. All of these factors are considered

Table 6.6

Egg Grades

	Wt (oz) per doz	Wt (lb) per 30-doz case
Jumbo	30	56
Extra large	27	50.5
Large	24	45
Medium	21	39.5
Small	18	34
Peewee	15	28

in the grading of eggs, which are designated as consumer grades and procurement grades. The consumer grades are:

U.S. Grade AA. Clean, unbroken, and practically normal shells, the air cell almost regular in shape, no more than ⅛ in deep; clear and firm white; yolk practically free from defects with outline slightly defined. No less than 85% U.S. Grade AA at point of origin, and no less than 80% U.S. Grade AA at destination. Individual cases to be no less than 75% U.S. Grade AA, and no more than 15% U.S. Grade A and 10% U.S. Grade B at the point of origin, and no less than 70% U.S. Grade AA, but no more than 20% U.S. Grade A and 10% U.S. Grade B at destination.

U.S. Grade A. Clean, unbroken, and practically normal shells, practically regular air cell, ³⁄₁₆ in deep or less; clear and reasonably firm white; yolk outline fairly well defined and practically free from defects. No less than 85% U.S. Grade A at point of origin, and no less than 80% U.S. Grade A at destination. Individual cases to be no less than 75% U.S. Grade A and no more than 25% U.S. Grade B at the point of origin, and no less than 70% U.S. Grade A and no more than 30% U.S. Grade B at destination.

U.S. Grade B. Clean-to-slightly-stained shells, which may be slightly abnormal in shape, air cell may be free or bubbly, but not more than ⅜ in deep; the white may be clear, but may be slightly weak; yolk may be slightly enlarged, and have a well-defined outline. No less than 85% U.S. grade B at point of origin, and no less than 80% U.S. Grade B at destination. Individual cases to be no less than 75% U.S. Grade B at the point of origin, and no less than 70% U.S. Grade B at destination. No eggs that are less than Grade B can be included.

There are two procurement grades that are mainly used by large processors and rarely by foodservice operations. Thus, for writing specifications for eggs the aspects to be included are (1) size of the eggs, (2) grade of the eggs, (3) type of packaging, (4) condition upon delivery, (5) inspection requirement, and (6) detailed description.

Milk and Milk Products

There are various USDA grades for milk and milk products which should be considered in purchasing these products. In addition to grading, the processing method is also specified on milk packages. Milk is pasteurized by heating to at least 145°F and holding at, or above, this temperature continuously for at least 30 min. It can be also pasteurized by the high-temperature short-time (HTST) method by heating to a temperature of 161°F and holding at, or above, this temperature continuously for 15 sec. After heating, milk is immediately cooled to a temperature of 45°F or lower. Milk is also homogenized by passing it through small orifices under pressure in order to break the fat globules uniformly. Cream formation is thus prevented, and the milk so obtained has a slightly better flavor. It should be noted that nothing is added to homogenized milk. The grades for milk and milk products are different. Many places restrict the sale of milk lower than U.S. Grade A. Thus, grades should be checked before purchasing milk and milk products. Grading is particularly important for such products as butter, margarine, and cheese. State and local authorities have different grading systems, as well as different regulations pertaining to dairy products.

A foodservice manager should be familiar with the following types and descriptions of milk and milk products:

Whole milk. In many states this consists of milk that contains not less than 3.25% milk fat and not less than 8.25% milk solids-not-fat.

Skim milk. Milk from which fat has been removed by centrifugation. Ordinarily, skim milk contains 0.1% fat.

Two-percent milk. Contains 2% milk fat.

Certified milk. Special milk with a very low bacterial count, used specifically for patients after surgery or for nursing homes.

Low-sodium milk. Sodium is removed from milk by the process of ion exchange.

Fortified milk. Milk to which nutrients that are present in milk are added.

Vitamin D milk. Milk to which Vitamin D is specifically added.

Concentrated milk. Milks that are concentrated to different proportions. These may be fresh, frozen, evaporated, condensed, or dried.

Cream. Separated from milk. Contains not less than 16% to 18% milk fat.

Half-and-half. Equal parts of whole milk fat (3.25%) and cream fat (18%). This milk product has approximately 10.5% milk fat.

Evaporated milk. Slightly more than half of the water is removed from milk.

Condensed milk. Sugar is added to the milk before it is evaporated.

Cultured milk. Certain desirable bacterial cultures are allowed to grow in pasteurized milk under controlled conditions.

Buttermilk. Cultured milk, containing chiefly *streptococcus lactis*. The milk has a tangy, smooth flavor.

Acidophilus milk. Cultured milk with *Lactobacillus acidophilus.* Used for its therapeutic value for patients that have been treated with antibiotics.

Yogurt. Manufactured from fresh, partially skimmed milk, enriched with added milk solids-not-fat. It has a smooth texture and is available in many flavors.

Chocolate milk. A chocolate-flavored milk.

Filled milk. Milk in which milk fats are replaced by other fats, mostly fats of vegetable origin.

Dry whole milk. Milk from which the water has been removed.

Instant nonfat dry milk. Prepared by removing fat and water from the milk.

In writing specifications for milk, the type of product, grade, milk fat content desired, and the type of packaging should be included.

Fish and Shellfish

Seafoods are among the most popular items in any type of foodservice operation. Unfortunately, their quality deteriorates very rapidly, so that there is a lot of variation as far as quality is concerned among the same species of a product. Therefore, care should be taken when purchasing seafood, since there are no standard specifications such as exist for meats. Grading and inspection of fish products are entirely voluntary and are conducted by the National Marine Fisheries Service program of the U.S. Department of Commerce. This inspection and grading is done in addition to the requirements and inspections conducted by the Food and Drug Administration, which apply to all types of processing plants. The products manufactured under such inspection have a federal seal which signifies that (1) the product is clean, safe, and wholesome; (2) the product is of a specified quality, identified by the appropriate U.S. Grade designation, as determined by the federal inspector in accordance with the established requirements of the U.S. Grade standards; (3) the product was produced in an acceptable establishment, with proper equipment and in appropriate processing conditions; and (4) the product was processed and packaged using good manufacturing practices.

Grading is based on several factors, depending on the type of product. General factors used in evaluations are odor, flavor, packing, bones, color, appearance, size, broken pieces, texture, and skin. The U.S. grades for seafoods and their descriptions are:

U.S. Grade A. Means top or best quality. The products are uniform in size, practically free of blemishes and defects, in excellent condition, and possess good flavor for the species.

U.S. Grade B. Means good quality. The products are uniform in size or as free from blemishes and defects as Grade A products. Grade B may be termed a general commercial grade, quite suitable for most purposes.

U.S. Grade C. Means fairly good quality. Products are just as wholesome as higher grades. They are graded low because of minor factors, such as breakage. Where appearance is not important, these may be good buys.

Normally, U.S. Grade A products are easily available on the market. Those with a lower grade are often marketed without any grading on them. Fish may be bought in any one of the following forms:

Whole fish are sold just as they come from the water. They have to be dressed before cooking. This involves scaling, eviscerating, and removal of head, tail, and/or fins. The smaller fish are pan-dressed and heads are not removed.

Drawn fish have entrails removed, which are the cause of rapid deterioration.

Dressed fish are completely cleaned fish with head on and ready for stuffing, if desired.

Chunks are cross sections of large dressed fish, having the cross section of the backbone as the only bone.

Steaks are cross-section slices from large dressed fish, which are ⅝ to 1 in thick.

Fillets are sides of the fish cut away from the backbone. They are practically boneless.

Butterfly fillets are the two sides of the fish cut lengthwise away from the backbone and held together by the uncut flesh and skin of the belly. These steaks do not have any bone.

Fish sticks are pieces of fish flesh cut into uniform width and length, usually 3 in by 1 in.

Fish portions are larger than fish sticks but uniform in size and weight.

Breaded fish are available in a number of cooked, frozen, and other pan-ready forms.

In writing specifications for seafoods, the following aspects should be considered:

1. Name of the product
2. Species
3. Size and thickness
4. Grade
5. Style (skinless or skin-on)
6. Type (fresh, chilled, or frozen)

7. Form
8. Packaging
9. Conditions upon delivery
10. Inspection requirements

Other Products

The same procedures described above should be applied when writing specifications for other products, such as miscellaneous groceries, beverages, cereals, fats, oils, and nonfood supplies. Brochures, specification manuals, manufacturers' literature, and other publications are available for various products. Up-to-date information for these commodities should be available in the manager's office and/or in the food-purchasing office.

MECHANICS OF BUYING

The mechanics of buying are concisely described in the following paragraphs and explained with examples.

1. *Start with the Menu.* For each food preparation on the menu, prepare a list of items needed. A separated form for different types of food products is very useful. Recipes should be consulted for the most important ingredients. Based on the important categories, such as meats and vegetables, the quantities needed for the food preparation should be listed.

2. *Fill in Daily Requirements and Calculate Totals for Each Item.* Complete the daily requirement and then total the amounts needed. A daily meat order form is shown in Figure 6.1 and a total meat requisition form (quotation and order sheet) in Figure 6.2.

3. *Request Bids and/or Quotations.* Quotations and bids for the total amount of products should be prepared based on the requirements. Examples of quotation forms, bids, and their requirements are given in Figure 6.3 and Appendix B.

4. *Select the Vendor for Particular Item Selected.* Based on the outcome of the paragraph 3 and criteria outlined in this chapter, select the vendor for that particular item.

5. *Prepare and Send the Purchase Order.* Using *complete* specifications as described in the quotation or bid requests, fill in the purchase order. Examples of the purchase order are given in Figures 6.4 and 6.8.

6. *Collect Invoices and/or Receiving Reports.* An example of an invoice form is shown in Figure 6.9 and a copy of a receiving report is given in Figure 6.5.

7. *Transfer Information to Inventory Records.* Based on the forms collected in paragraph 6, prompt entry into an inventory sheet is desirable. An example of an inventory sheet is shown in Figure 6.10.

8. *Use Requisition Forms for Issuing from Storage.* Any item used from any of the storage areas should be recorded.

University of Illinois at Urbana-Champaign

REQUISITION

184

ACCOUNT NUMBER & TITLE	USER REFERENCE 1	USER REFERENCE 2	CUSAS	AMOUNT	REQUISITION NO.
					DATE
					COLL. & DEPT. NO.
					BUS. OFF. REF.

Name of Dept. Requisitioning

Dept. Address

PURCHASE ORDER NO.

Room No.	Building Name	Street Address	Building Code No.

DELIVER TO

Date Delivery Desired

For Additional Information

Call _____ Ext. _____

COMMODITY CODE

SHIP VIA

F.O.B.

TERMS	AS PER	BUYER CODE

Suggested Vendor(s) (if Available) and Special Instructions:

VENDOR NO.-FEIN/SOC. SEC. NO.		ZIP CODE	TYPE CODE

CATALOG NUMBER	ITEM (Give Complete Specifications or Performance Characteristics)	QUANTITY	ESTIMATED COST	
			UNIT	TOTAL

☐ TYPE P.O. FROM REQ.

☐ TYPE P.O. FROM BID

☐ TYPE P.O. FROM ROUGH DRAFT

☐ TYPE BID FROM REQ.

☐ TYPE BID FROM ROUGH DRAFT

Chief Accountant/Contracts Office

Comptroller

Buyer

Director of Purchases

SEALED BID

Open Date

Bid No.

C.C. No.

I hereby certify that there is an unobligated balance available for the above expenditures in the amount indicated.

Requested by _____ (In Charge)

Approved by _____ (Dean or Adm. Officer)

Approved by _____

Figure 6-8. Requisition form.

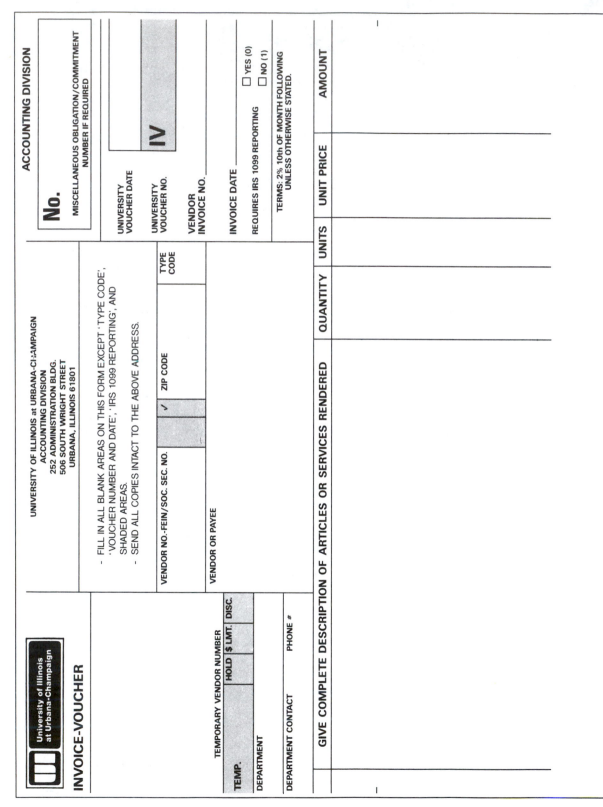

ACCOUNTING DIVISION

University of Illinois
at Urbana-Champaign

INVOICE-VOUCHER

No.

MISCELLANEOUS OBLIGATION/COMMITMENT
NUMBER IF REQUIRED

IV

UNIVERSITY
VOUCHER DATE

UNIVERSITY
VOUCHER NO.

VENDOR
INVOICE NO.

INVOICE DATE

REQUIRES IRS 1099 REPORTING
☐ YES (0)
☐ NO (1)

TERMS: 2% 10th OF MONTH FOLLOWING
UNLESS OTHERWISE STATED.

UNIVERSITY OF ILLINOIS at URBANA-CHAMPAIGN
ACCOUNTING DIVISION
252 ADMINISTRATION BLDG.
506 SOUTH WRIGHT STREET
URBANA, ILLINOIS 61801

- FILL IN ALL BLANK AREAS ON THIS FORM EXCEPT 'TYPE CODE',
  'VOUCHER NUMBER AND DATE', 'IRS 1099 REPORTING', AND
  SHADED AREAS.
- SEND ALL COPIES INTACT TO THE ABOVE ADDRESS.

VENDOR NO.-FEIN/SOC. SEC. NO.   ✓   ZIP CODE   TYPE CODE

VENDOR OR PAYEE

TEMPORARY VENDOR NUMBER

TEMP.	HOLD	$ LMT.	DISC.

DEPARTMENT

DEPARTMENT CONTACT   PHONE #

GIVE COMPLETE DESCRIPTION OF ARTICLES OR SERVICES RENDERED	QUANTITY	UNITS	UNIT PRICE	AMOUNT

186

VENDOR: PLEASE DO NOT WRITE BELOW THIS LINE

TC	DUE DATE MM DD YY	DISCOUNT	% OR $	HOLD	ENC	FUND OVERRIDE	CK CODE	CK FLAG	AP SPLIT CODE	1099	FUND	BUSINESS OFFICE REFERENCE

ITEM ACCOUNT NUMBER & TITLE

USER REFERENCE 1 USER REFERENCE 2

EXPENSE AMOUNT

CAP CUSAS

SUB-TOTAL

CASH DISCOUNT

TOTAL VOUCHER AMOUNT

COLLEGE DEPT. NO.   REQ. NO.   E/C   OBLIGATION NO.

TOTAL EXP/TOTAL PAY

P/F

ADDITIONAL APPROVAL

AUTHORIZED DEPARTMENT SIGNATURE

ACCT. PAY   EXT.   FOR CHIEF ACCOUNTANT

Figure 6-9. Invoice-voucher form.

Item:		Brand Name:			Purchase Unit:		Company:		
Date	No. In	Unit Price	Out	Balance	Date	No. In	Unit Price	Out	Balance

Figure 6-10.   An example of a perpetual inventory card.

SUMMARY

This chapter describes in detail all processes involved in purchasing for a foodservice operation. It outlines the buying methods used and factors to be considered before purchasing. Quality standards and regulatory agencies, which have an impact on the purchasing function of any operation, are described in detail. The significance of specifications as a language used in purchasing is emphasized. Giving examples of important commodities, aspects to be considered before buying are explained. Finally steps involved in buying are described in detail.

REVIEW QUESTIONS

How does the final product yield affect the purchase of any commodity in a foodservice operation?

Discuss all factors that you will consider before making any purchasing decisions.

List important aspects that you will consider in writing specifications for (a) fresh fruits and vegetables, (b) meats, (c) milk and milk products, and (d) canned products.

What steps are critical in the process of buying? Describe one method of formal buying and one method of informal buying. Discuss pros and cons of each method.

ASSIGNMENTS

Select a one-day menu of a foodservice operation and write specifications of all items needed. You may have to review earlier chapters in working with this assignment.

Select a foodservice operation and review the purchasing procedures followed. Comment on the procedures in light of the discussion in this chapter. Collect a copy of all forms (if any) used in record keeping.

Pick up a canned product from a foodservice operation or purchase one from a supermarket and comment on all information related to quality grade, quantity, ingredient labeling, and nutritional labeling. Record how labels conform to the necessary requirements.

SUGGESTED READINGS

The Almanac of Canning, Freezing and Refrigeration. 1982. Edward E. Judge & Sons, Inc., Westminster, MD.

Kotchevar, L. H., and Levinson, C. 1988. *Quantity Food Purchasing*, 3rd edition. Macmillan Publishing Co., New York, NY.

National Association of Meat Purveyors. 1988. *Meat Buyers Guide.* McLean, VA.

National Fisheries Institute. 1984. *Retail Training Manual.* National Fisheries Institute, Inc., Washington, DC.

Peddersen, R. B. 1977. *Specs: The Comprehensive Foodservice Purchasing and Specification Manual.* CBI Publishing Co., Boston, MA.

Peddersen, R. B. 1981. *Foodservice and Hotel Purchasing.* CBI Publishing Co., Boston, MA.

Warfel, M. C., and Waskey, F. H. 1979. *The Professional Food Buyer: Standards, Principles, and Procedures.* McCutchan Publishing Corp., Berkeley, CA.

CHAPTER 7

FOOD RECEIVING AND STORAGE

KEY CONCEPTS AND TERMS

invoice receiving method
blind receiving method
FIFO (first in — first out)
dry storage
refrigerated storage
frozen storage
physical inventory
perpetual inventory
inventory turnover rate
good receiving practices

FOOD RECEIVING

Efficient food purchasing methods demand good receiving procedures in order for the total system to work. The dollars saved by careful food purchasing may be lost by inefficient receiving practices. In many operations, purchasing and receiving are controlled by a single department so that both of these important functions can be coordinated. The ideal situation would be for the person(s) who place the orders to be responsible for receiving and checking, but this is not practical in large operations. Receiving must be handled by competent and knowledgeable persons. The link between purchasing and receiving is critical for the functioning of the entire system and is an excellent example of how subsystems are interdependent.

Functions of a Receiving Department

The functions of a receiving department can best be understood by studying the responsibilities of the person(s) in charge.

1. Receiving personnel should be aware of the commodities ordered and when they are expected to be delivered. In many operations a copy of the purchase order is sent to the receiving department.
2. Person(s) in charge of purchasing should have experience in checking and should know relevant testing procedures. Materials and methods used for testing should be readily accessible to the receiving personnel.
3. Receiving personnel should follow good sanitary practices in handling foods so that any chances of contamination or spoilage are avoided.
4. Receiving personnel should know the time and temperatures at which different products can be stored. They should also know the shelf life of various commodities. It is advisable to have this information in the form of wall charts, posters, illustrated brochures, and handbooks.
5. Receivers should also be aware of specifications, descriptions of terms, weights and measures, and possible use of the products. Instructions should be given to those in charge of receiving that these specifications should be adhered to rigidly.
6. Receiving personnel should be aware of the general legal procedures and prepare papers pertaining to the buying and receiving functions. In particular, insurance liabilities and responsibilities should be well understood. This is important since union regulations may have restrictions as to how and up to what point in the receiving area goods are to be delivered.

Certain receiving procedures are important to note.

1. Inspection and receiving should be completed in a reasonable amount of time. This is important for the person receiving the merchandise as well as for the delivery person.
2. If possible, deliveries should be scheduled so that there is even and smooth transfer of goods. Too many shipments at one time will interfere with adequate receiving and may result in food spoilage and other losses.
3. Adequate arrangements should be made to relocate the received shipments either to the receiving areas or to where they are needed. Refrigerated freezer space should be particularly checked. Last-minute arrangements may cause confusion and expose the food for an undesirable length of time at incorrect temperatures.
4. Scheduling of deliveries is also important to prevent the docking area from getting blocked, causing delays in the proper location of the goods, particularly under adverse weather conditions.
5. Receivers should have the copy of the invoice or the delivery ticket listing the product(s) being delivered. A stamp and/or signature are helpful in recording and verifying the goods delivered and received.
6. The purchasing department should be promptly informed of any items that were not delivered; those that do not meet required specifications; or those that were rejected, giving reasons for such action.

Receiving Methods

Receiving methods can primarily be divided into three types: invoice, blind, and partially blind.

Invoice Receiving

In the **invoice receiving method,** an invoice accompanies the shipment. An invoice is a slip or form that accompanies an order, prepared and delivered by the vendor or his agent. In this method of receiving, the invoice is checked against the delivered merchandise. The specifications, quantities, prices, and other details are listed on the invoice. The person receiving the goods should verify these particulars against the items received. If properly administered, this method ensures the quality and quantity of the goods delivered.

The disadvantages of invoice receiving include the chances of negligent practices being followed by the receiving person, either intentionally or unintentionally. Under pressure of checking deliveries, the receiving clerks may glance through the invoice and accept it. This method may also encourage the delivery person or the vendor to employ undesirable practices.

Blind Receiving

In order to overcome some of the disadvantages of invoice receiving, a **blind receiving method** may be followed. In this method a blank invoice or an invoice with only the list of items being delivered is sent. The quantity, quality, and other characteristics are omitted. This makes it essential for the receiving person to check and fill in this information in order to complete the receiving process. Thus the quality and the quantity of the delivered goods are checked and recorded. A separate invoice with all details is sent directly to the person in charge of purchasing. For the sake of convenience many vendors print the copies of the invoice in such a way that certain information is blacked out in selected copies. This is a very rigid and accurate method of ensuring the quality and quantity of the goods received. When the copy of the invoice, checked and filled in by the receiving department, is received by the purchasing department, it is checked against the complete invoice sent by the vendor. Any discrepancies are reported directly by the purchasing department to the vendor or the receiving clerk. This method demands sincerity from all concerned parties. However, the time and cost involved may be considerable and prove to be the major disadvantage of this method. It requires the time of the receiving personnel, as well as additional work for the purchasing department. This method should be followed after careful assessment of the costs and benefits involved.

Partially Blind Receiving

The partially blind method combines some of the advantages of the earlier two methods and eliminates some of the drawbacks of the blind receiving procedure. The invoice sent with the delivery contains partial information only. The list of items is included with all pertinent information except quantities. This makes it necessary to check quantities while receiving. The quantity of goods received, the most important factor in receiving, is checked and recorded in this method. This saves a considerable amount of time. In this method partially blacked-out invoices may also be used. When blind or partially blind receiving methods are followed, it is essential that management inform the vendors that completely filled-in invoices should be sent separately and should not accompany deliveries.

MECHANISM OF RECEIVING

1. When shipment is received, a proper invoice or delivery sheet should be used for verification and checking.
2. All merchandise should be carefully checked for the following aspects pertaining to the quantity and quality of the delivered goods:
   a. Each container should be checked carefully for any signs of external damage. Any signs of damage, leakage, improper packaging, or breakage are indica-

tive of poor packaging and delivery practices, and all such packages should be opened and carefully checked to ensure the quality of the merchandise.

b. Each item should be weighed and/or counted, checked, and recorded properly. Any shortages or overages should be recorded against the item. It is advisable to check and record each item separately. The quantity indicated on the label should be checked, particularly from open packages.

c. For some products it may be necessary to calculate the quantities after weighing, as in case of eggs and baked goods. Appropriate conversion tables should be readily available or prominently displayed at convenient places.

d. When items are received in bulk, all packaging materials, such as paper, ice, or foam, should be removed before weighing. If several items (such as ground beef and organ meats) are packaged in one large container, they should be sorted out and weighed separately.

3. The quality and wholesomeness of the delivered goods should be ascertained. This may be achieved by random inspection of selected representative samples of the goods and may be undertaken as follows:

a. The goods should be verified for quality against specifications. Some aspects that should be considered include USDA stamps, USDA certification, USDA shield, brand names, ingredient labels, nutritional labels, and name of the variety on labels. The grades should be checked and verified.

b. In the case of the fresh fruits and vegetables, the color, freshness, freedom from damage, and overall quality of the products should be checked. Representative samples may be cut, peeled, cored, or sliced to examine freshness, maturity, juiciness, and apparent spoilage indicators. For some products such as potatoes, specific gravity or density may be measured to assess the quality of the product. Size, thickness, and diameter may also be significant of the quality of the products and should be checked.

c. For canned products, packaging date, expiration date, batch number, and labels should be checked. Any signs of bulging, damage, or leakage need action. A can should be cut open for further inspection and experimentation. Any signs of discoloration, undesirable odor, frothiness, and mold or spore growth should be checked. All labels should be carefully verified as to the contents. Based on the ultimate use of the products, other factors should be subjectively or objectively evaluated. There are several tests as well as testing equipment that can be used in such evaluations. Tests may be conducted on representative samples for drained weights, syrup concentrations, and acidity. It is advisable that all products be dated as to the date received in order to facilitate a **FIFO (first in—first out)** procedure.

d. Since meat items are expensive and easily perishable, it is indispensable to have efficient receiving procedures. While inspecting, all barriers such as ice, plastic wraps, and papers should be removed. Whenever applicable, the inspection stamp should be checked and verified. Packages should be checked for ingredients, as in the case of processed meats such as sausages and hamburgers. Randomly, representative samples should be checked for meat trim, fat content, fat cover, weight, thickness, and lean percentage. Specifications, particularly IMPS (Institutional Meat Purchasing Specifications) numbers may be indicative of all or some of the attributes listed above and therefore should be verified at the time of receiving. Checks should be made for any signs of discoloration, odor, sliminess, mold growth, and freezer burn. For special kinds or cuts of meats, checks should be made for special characteristics, such as the color of the eyes for whole fish and skin tears in the case of chicken. It is advisable to use a procedure that automatically or conveniently facilitates the FIFO system. One of the efficient procedures followed by many foodservices to facilitate FIFO includes the tagging of meats. Meat tags are cards that can be attached to meat packages and which contain necessary information in duplicate parts as shown in Figure 7.1. Each half contains information pertaining to date, item, grade, dealer's name, weight, and price. Other information may be added to suit the requirements of a particular operation. Both sides of the tag are filled in by the receiving person after checking the meat in. This tag is filled in for each package, box, or container. The duplicate half of the tag is removed and sent to the accounting department or to the manager. The tags are used to store the items on shelves in order to issue them when needed in the sequence in which they were received based on the specified dates. Finally, the person using meat in

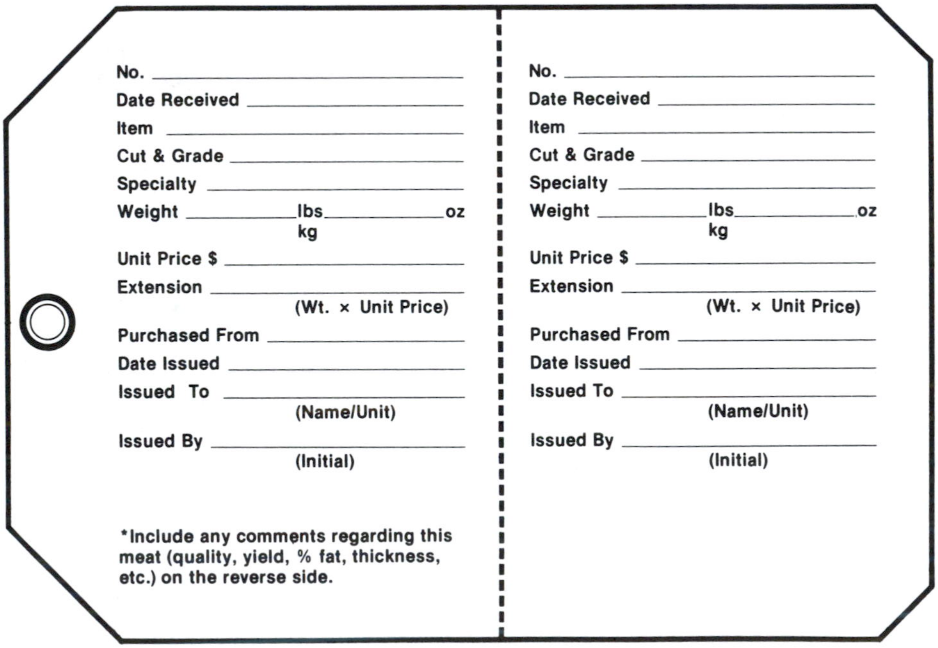
No. ______
Date Received ______
Item ______
Cut & Grade ______
Specialty ______
Weight ______ lbs ______ oz
kg
Unit Price $ ______
Extension ______
(Wt. × Unit Price)
Purchased From ______
Date Issued ______
Issued To ______
(Name/Unit)
Issued By ______
(Initial)

*Include any comments regarding this meat (quality, yield, % fat, thickness, etc.) on the reverse side.

No. ______
Date Received ______
Item ______
Cut & Grade ______
Specialty ______
Weight ______ lbs ______ oz
kg
Unit Price $ ______
Extension ______
(Wt. × Unit Price)
Purchased From ______
Date Issued ______
Issued To ______
(Name/Unit)
Issued By ______
(Initial)

Figure 7-1. An example of a meat tag.

the production unit will remove the tag and return it to the accounting department or the manager where it is verified with its original counterpart.

The advantages of using meat tags are listed below:

(i)   Facilitation and supplementation of inventory records and the checking process, since the quantity and dollar value of the meats received can be calculated daily by adding the data recorded on the tags.

(ii)   Shortages and disappearances of meat items can be easily traced or accounted for.

(iii)   Assurances of checking procedures at time of receiving, since the items are required to be weighed and recorded.

(iv)   Assists the FIFO procedure, in effective rotation, as well as in the aging of particular type of meats, because date of receipt is on the tag.

(v)   Reweighing of the meat items is eliminated since weights are included on the tags.

(vi)   Help in calculating meat costs per day or for any desirable length of time. Also, meat costs per meal can be calculated.

(vii)   Help in computing and updating of costs incurred on the recipes prepared.

(viii) Help in the comparative evaluation of the cost of meats.

(ix)   Help in tracing the origin of meat, if any problems occur.

(x)   Assists in meat purchasing by indicating the frequency of use of the items and, consequently, the amount to be ordered.

It should be noted here that the use of meat tags, as such, is becoming outdated. With the use of computers in foodservice operations, many other forms of tagging can be used. The description above is given to outline the principles involved and the advantages of using such a process. Other methods, including the use of optical scanning and computerized controls, may be devised on the same guidelines.

e. For dairy products, the fat percentages, density, and acidity may be checked based on the product(s). It is essential to check dates on milk and milk-product containers and place them accordingly. Checks should be conducted randomly for any signs of spoilage. Rancid odors in butters, margarines, or other fatty products should be checked carefully.

f. Random cartons of eggs need to be opened and checked for any signs of cracking, soiling, and oiling. Grades and sizes need to be checked in addition to the weights. Eggs should be broken at random and checked for quality and blood spots.

g. Quality checks should be made for other merchandise and non-food items based on the desirable attributes and the specifications used when placing orders. Dates should preferably be placed on all items to facilitate stock rotation.

4. Since most deliveries to foodservice operations include frozen or refrigerated items, it is imperative to check the temperatures at the time of the delivery. It is

Date _____

Weight/Count _____ o.k.☐

Quality _____ o.k.☐

Temperature _____ o.k.☐

Prices _____ o.k.☐

Received By _____

Figure 7-2. Receiving stamp.

also advisable to have these temperatures listed on the purchase order or the invoice in order to facilitate checking. Temperature charts in the receiving units are very helpful in checking the required temperatures for various products upon receipt. Spot checks should be made for temperatures, since quality is dependent on the conditions in which the items are handled at various stages of delivery. For certain products, the shape and size of ice crystals are indicative of thawing and refreezing that may have occurred during transportation. Some of the desirable temperatures for products are: meat and poultry, 33° to 38° F; fish and shellfish, 23° to 30° F.

5. Any shortages, excesses, missing items, and items that are unacceptable should be recorded. The invoice or receiving document should be signed, dated, and stamped. A copy may be sent to management and another copy may be handed over to the delivery person, based on the situation. An example of a stamp useful in receiving is shown in Figure 7.2.

6. All items received and checked should immediately be sent to their respective storage areas. Deliveries should be scheduled at convenient times, since deliveries received late in the day or during mealtimes may be held longer prior to checking and storage.

7. Finally, all invoices are checked for correctness and filed individually under their respective receiving records.

STORAGE AREAS

Foodservice operations store raw or cooked ingredients in storage areas before production or service. Since the food items stored can represent a great deal of money, it is imperative to see that all items purchased are properly stored and are issued in a definite sequence. Loss or waste of food or non-food items may occur due to improper storage, theft, insect infestation, and non-accessibility. Products piled without any logical arrangement may be subject to loss in addition to posing a safety hazard. It is advisable to set limits on the number of persons who have access to storage areas. In other words, the fewer people that go in and out of the storage areas, the more secure and efficient the foodservice operation will be.

Storage areas should have easy access from the receiving area and from the prepreparation and production areas. Storage areas should be clean and neatly arranged. They should have capability to store all goods ordered; conversely, quantities ordered should be based on the amount of storage space available. Various guidelines and sanitary requirements must be complied with and are discussed in a later chapter. The temperatures and humidity in storage areas have to be controlled and should be kept at the optimum level so that losses are prevented. In any type of foodservice operation, three different storage areas are essential: (1) dry, (2) refrigerated, and (3) frozen.

Dry Storage

Dry storage should be adequately ventilated, clean, with sufficient air circulation and the desired humidity. Shelves should be made of materials approved by local public health agencies and should be placed at proper distances from the floor, walls, and ceilings. The arrangement of the items on the shelves should be well organized to facilitate air circulation. In many foodservice operations, dry storage areas are also used to store non-food supplies such as paper goods, dishes, utensils, and silverware. However, it is advisable to place non-food items, particularly detergents, laundry supplies, and cleaning solutions, away from food supplies.

Foods normally stored in dry storage areas include canned goods, flour, sugar, shortenings, spices, cereals, certain fruits like bananas, and certain vegetables like onions and potatoes. Due to a lack of space, many operations locate dry storage areas in the basement or utility room of the operation or in areas close to heating, cooling, or ventilation equipment. In these cases, care should be taken to see that there is enough air circulation and that the food products are not affected in any way by being near heating, drainage, or other utility pipes. Regulations also require that the products be placed in such a way that they are not on the floor or in contact with walls or ceilings. One of the problems of dry storage area is their vulnerability to vermin, rodents, and insects that can survive and thrive at the prevalent temperatures. Periodic checks and steps are necessary to protect stored products.

Proper utilization of space is also necessary. Any space lost due to improper utilization may be costly and may cause recurring problems since the quality of foods will be affected. Proper labeling of the shelves helps in organizing as well as in proper storage. An alphabetical or sequential arrangement will prove helpful in finding things when needed and for replacing them.

Temperatures in dry storage areas should range from 40° to 75° F (5° to 24° C). Some perishable foods, such as potatoes and onions, should be stored at slightly lower temperatures (40° to 55°F or 4.5° to 13°C) to prevent spoilage. Circulation of air is necessary to maintain freshness of the perishable goods. Air circulation also helps in the elimination of odors and the removal of moisture. Large containers or packages that might hinder the flow of air should be replaced or removed. Sufficient space should be allowed in the storage areas for free movement of carts, pallets, and motorized lifts, particularly in the centers of all aisles.

Storage areas should be kept clean and a regular cleaning schedule followed. Spills, leakages, or breakages should be cleaned promptly. To facilitate cleaning, large storage containers should have wheels. Containers with lids that can be closed easily should be used for items such as sugar, flour, shortenings, and cereals. Lids should be tightly closed after every use. Slidable lids, self-closing lids, or half-opening lids are desirable for items not stored in their original containers. As with any item in the storage area, these containers should always be labeled properly.

Refrigerated Storage

Since proper temperatures are critical for **refrigerated storage,** it is imperative to have a regular check on temperature. It is wise to have an automatic mechanism to alert the staff to refrigerator failure. The efficiency of refrigeration is based on several factors, including the type of refrigerator, type of compressor, extent of insulation, capacity of the storage area, and amount of food and its arrangement in the storage area. Energy conservation is also important, and the number of times the doors are opened and closed should be controlled. Plastic-strip curtains are useful in conserving energy. The convenient and logical arrangement of items on shelves helps reduce time spent in the storage area. Automatic temperature-recording devices or thermometers should be conveniently and permanently located in refrigerated areas. Since temperatures may vary in different parts of the refrigerator, it is advisable to monitor temperatures at different positions. If this is not possible, the temperatures should be checked at points where the warmest temperatures are expected. Also, items placed near doors should be checked for maintenance of the desired temperature. It may be advisable to have a walk-in refrigerator, depending on the number of meals prepared and served.

To reduce moisture or ice deposits, it is necessary to keep refrigerated areas as clean as possible. Spills should be cleaned immediately to prevent chances of contamination or accidents. For optimum operation of the refrigerator, regular defrosting and the avoidance of overcrowding are vital. As in dry storage areas, no item should be placed on the floor or in contact with the ceiling or walls.

Refrigerated storage areas may be used for storing cooked or partially cooked foods in addition to thawing meats. Care should be taken that there are no leakages from or on the containers in which these items are placed. Cooked foods should be placed so that there is no chance of contact with raw food products or ingredients. Raw food items should not be stored over cooked food products. Cooked foods or leftover cooked foods should be covered and labeled immediately. It is not advisable to store hot items in refrigerated storage, because it may take a long time for them to reach safe temperatures, and the surrounding temperatures will be affected by hot food. Rapid cooling techniques and the use of shallow and wide containers are recommended for cooling hot foods. Certain products easily pick up odors; such items should be segregated. An example would be dairy products, which absorb odors from apples very easily. Fish and fish products impart strong odors and should be stored separately. As in other storage areas, it is important to date products before placing them in the refrigerator. It is convenient to use reach-in or roll-in refrigerators, particularly for short-term storage. Separate refrigerators may be desirable for dairy products or frozen desserts.

Frozen Storage

The number of foods being placed under **frozen storage** is increasing rapidly. Many items are available in the market in frozen form, making it important for a foodservice operation to have adequate frozen storage. Many facilities have walk-in freezers. Ideally, walk-in freezers should open into walk-in refrigerators. Because not all foods are suitable for frozen storage, it is important to consider the physical and chemical properties of a product before deciding to place it in the freezer. Frozen storage areas normally have temperatures ranging from 0° to 20° F. Arrangement of foods in the freezer is important, to help reduce the time and labor required to locate the needed items.

Whenever possible, frozen food items should be ordered in optimum size containers or packages, to avoid the risks of thawing large quantities of foods. Individual packages may be desirable in order to facilitate thawing and re-thermalizing. IQF (Individually Quick Frozen) items should be purchased whenever possible. IQF refers to such items as fish that are frozen individually as opposed to bulk, with the advantage that they do not stick to each other. Some foods are available in portion-controlled sizes. Thawed food items should not be refrozen, since the appearance, flavor, nutritive value, and cooking quality may be adversely affected. If any products must be frozen, they should preferably be placed in their original container or other clean and clearly labeled utensils. FIFO procedures should be strictly enforced in the frozen storage area. Based on the location of the blast fan, foods should be placed in an order that will utilize the varying degrees of cold temperatures. Any accumulation of ice should be cleared as frequently as possible; this will ensure maintenance of the desired temperatures in the storage area.

Many menu items are suitable for frozen storage soon after cooking, particularly in the "cook-freeze" system. With this method, foods are continuously prepared, often portioned, and then kept in the freezer until use. Freezer space becomes a major consideration in this system. Care should be taken to see that these prepared items are placed so that there is no chance of contamination. They should be placed away from raw food items and should be adequately protected from contamination. It should be noted that there are optimum periods of time for which different food products can be stored.

A planned system should be used for removing products from the freezer, so that there is adequate rotation of food items. Dating and labeling of containers are imperative. One of the problems commonly observed in freezer-stored foods is "freezer burn," which occurs when fat under the surface becomes rancid, causing a brown discoloration or patches.

Freezer temperatures should be recorded periodically and should be maintained at the desirable level. Automatic signaling of freezer failures is desirable, particularly for large-size operations. Since most expensive items, such as meats, are stored in the freezer, it is important to have the best possible arrangement of items for optimum utilization of space. Freezer space is also needed to store large quantities of items purchased as bargains.

ISSUING SUPPLIES

Ingredients and other supplies are issued from storage areas to the area of temporary or permanent usage on a continuing basis. In many large-sized operations, special personnel are responsible for issuing; in small operations this may not be feasible. It is advisable that the fewest possible number of persons have access to storage areas and assume the responsibility of issuing items. Some items, most particularly liquor, need strict control, and one assigned person should be in charge of issuing. The issuing person weighs out, measures, or counts items before distribution. A record of products issued helps in inventory control and cost analysis. A requisition sheet may be used for this purpose. An example of a requisition sheet is given in Figure 6.8.

INVENTORIES

Inventories are lists of items available in various areas of an operation. Food inventories are lists of food items available in storage areas. These lists should be as accurate as possible, since financial accounts and various calculations are based on them. These lists may be extremely lengthy, and various methods are used for categorizing and recording inventories. For the purpose of calculation, inventories are converted and interpreted on the basis of their dollar values. Inventories are helpful in providing information pertaining to (1) quantities available for use, (2) amounts of particular items to be ordered, (3) the dollar value of products used and on hand, (4) the food cost incurred, and (5) the food cost percentage.

Two types of inventories are commonly maintained by foodservice operations: (1) physical and (2) perpetual.

Physical Inventory

Physical inventory, as the name implies, deals with the physical count of all items on hand at the end of a specified period of time. In general, this period is one month, and the inventory is taken on the last day of the month. It is helpful to have at least two persons to efficiently complete this inventory, one recording and the other checking. Managers or their representatives may be present at the time the inventory is done. It is easier to complete the inventory if items are arranged and listed in a set pattern. A preprinted blank list arranged in the same sequence as foods are stored is helpful. Categorization also helps considerably in completing the inventory. Printed forms, books, spring-type folders, or computer sheets are needed to record the inventory. Forms with a carbon copy may also be used. Since all items must be accounted for, a physical inventory requires a considerable amount of time.

Perpetual Inventory

Perpetual inventories are continuous records of purchases and issues. If properly maintained, such inventories are efficient records and indications of the items on hand. Perpetual inventories can be maintained on cards or computer discs or other software. This type of inventory is easy to maintain with the use of computers. An example of the care used in maintaining perpetual inventory is shown in Figure 7.3. A Cardex-type file may also be used. Colored riders or markers may be used to indicate special items as well as those items that are running low or need to be ordered. This makes ordering easier and more efficient.

Perpetual inventories are used in conjunction with the physical inventories set at specific times. Perpetual and physical inventories, when combined, provide a double check. They help in calculating various costs pertaining to items used in an operation.

Since various types of items are used in foodservice operations, and cost depreciation is involved, inventories are always converted to dollar value at the time of interpretation. Every item in the foodservice operation is accounted for. Such items as silverware, napkins, tablecloths, glassware, and chinaware are checked and revalued, regardless of the method used for inventories. Depreciation costs, based on several factors, are computed and applied toward the cost of items such as equipment and other furnishings.

Perpetual inventory, particularly if manually maintained, is costly in time, labor, and materials. However, several advantages outweigh the costs. Advantages include the convenience of knowing almost instantly items and amounts needed to reorder and the control of over- or underbuying of products. A perpetual inventory also helps indicate items that are not used for a considerable period of time.

Perpetual inventories are helpful if they are properly maintained and constantly updated. Serious problems may result from negligence or improper recording. Adequate training for personnel responsible for inventories is essential. If properly designed, perpetual inventory can provide valuable information for each item, such as purveyor's name, batch number, date ordered, and date received. Some foodservice operations prefer perpetual inventories only for items that are expensive and that are needed in large quantities.

Received						Issued					Balance	
Date	Received From	Qty.	Unit	Price	Amt.	Date	Issued to Req. No.	Qty.	Amt.		Qty.	Amt.

Figure 7-3. An example of a card used in maintaining perpetual inventory.

The food costs incurred by an operation may be calculated by assessing the value of the inventory as follows:

value of opening inventory + food purchases after opening inventory =
value of total inventory on hand − value of closing inventory =
cost of food during the specific period

Inventory turnover rate can also be calculated and is useful because it indicates the number of turnovers for an inventory during a specific period of time. High or low turnover are indicators of the performance of a foodservice operation and are often used in financial analysis, as discussed in Chapter 11. The turnover rate for a specified period of time can be calculated as follows:

$$\text{food inventory turnover} = \frac{\text{total value of food sold}}{\text{value of average food inventory}}$$

If the value of food sold in a month is $80,000 and the average cost of food inventory is $5,000, the food inventory turnover rate for that month will be 80,000/5,000 = 16. This indicates that the inventory turned over 16 times that month. Food inventory turnover needs careful assessment and should be considered on a comparative basis if previous data are available. A low turnover rate coupled with high food cost may indicate poor management practices and require reassessment of forecasting and purchasing policies. It may also indicate the nonuse or the slow movement of certain food items. On the other hand, a high turnover rate may show more demand and indicate the popularity of certain foods. There are no fixed optimum rates for inventory turnover since it is based on several factors. It should be evaluated on an individual basis, mainly by comparing previous rates for the same period of time and determining the reasons for any change. A careful analysis of the turnover rate is essential.

Good receiving practices pay off in the long run. A checklist containing a list of these practices is shown below.

Schedule hours of delivery whenever possible

Check instruments, equipment, or papers needed for inspection of deliveries

Make delivery person feel welcome

Count, weigh, and mark all items received

Weigh and inspect all meats, fish, and poultry items individually

Use meat tags whenever possible

Open cartons of products at random to inspect the quality as well as to check the quantity

Check all items against purchase specification

Check invoice prices against purchase order (if available)

Stamp and sign (by receiving clerk) all receiving invoices after verification

Place unit price on each item before putting it in storage (if possible)

Place a receiving stamp, as shown in Figure 7.2, on all possible items. If not, place a date on all packages of items received

Management should periodically check and revise (if needed) receiving policies

SUMMARY

This chapter continues the discussion of the foodservice subsystem that deals with receiving and storage. It emphasizes the role receiving personnel play in efficient receiving. Different methods that can be used for receiving and storage are discussed. Types of inventories and inventory controls are highlighted.

REVIEW QUESTIONS

Outline the method of receiving that ensures the quality of products ordered.

What are some of the factors that should be considered before storing products in the dry storage area?

What is the difference between physical inventory and perpetual inventory?

List good receiving practices that you would recommend to a foodservice operation.

ASSIGNMENTS

Visit a foodservice operation, outline the receiving practices, and comment on the efficiency of methods used.

Observe different items stored in dry, refrigerated, and frozen storage areas and comment on the efficient use of storage areas. Record temperatures prevalent in all of the storage areas.

Calculate the food inventory turnover rate of a selected foodservice operation. Observe and record all paperwork and forms used in inventory maintenance.

SUGGESTED READINGS

Kotchevar, L. H., and Levinson, C. 1988. *Quantity Food Purchasing*, 3rd edition. Macmillan Publishing Co., New York, NY.

Peddersen, R. B. 1977. *Specs: The Comprehensive Foodservice Purchasing and Specification Manual*. CBI Publishing Co., Boston, MA.

Peddersen, R. B. 1981. *Foodservice and Hotel Purchasing*. CBI Publishing Co., Boston, MA.

Spears, M. C., and Vaden, A. G. 1985. *Foodservice Organizations—A Managerial and Systems Approach*. John Wiley & Sons, Inc., New York, NY.

Warfel, M. C., and Waskey, F. H. 1979. *The Professional Food Buyer: Standards, Principles, and Procedures*. McCutchan Publishing Corp., Berkeley, CA.

West, B. B., Wood, L., Harger, V. F., Shugart, G. S., and Payne-Palacio, J. 1988. *Food Service in Institutions*. MacMillan Publishing Co., New York, NY.

CHAPTER 8

FOOD SANITATION

KEY CONCEPTS AND TERMS

foodborne illness
food sanitation
pathogens
spores
infection
toxin
intoxication
danger zone
potentially hazardous food
cross-contamination

Although food sanitation is a topic for a separate foodservice textbook, it is included here to show the important link it has with the different subsystems discussed in earlier chapters. All systems of a foodservice operation are concerned in one way or other with food sanitation. Because of its significant role, all major concepts of food sanitation are outlined and discussed in this chapter.

FOODBORNE ILLNESS

Foodborne illness may be defined as illness transmitted or caused by food. Any type of food may be the source of illness, but several food items have a greater potential for causing foodborne illnesses than others. Although most foodborne illnesses are caused by microorganisms, there can be other causes.

Foodborne illness is one of the major problems confronting a foodservice manager. Illnesses caused by foods consumed away from home are increasing in the United States. Apart from the loss of reputation resulting from such outbreaks, an operation may incur heavy financial damages as a result of problems caused by such illnesses and any related consequences. Avoiding catastrophe is not difficult if foodservice managers are aware of the basic principles of **food sanitation** and follow them in day-to-day practice. Foodservice managers and their employees must understand the principles behind sanitary practices. Many states require that foodservice managers be trained in food sanitation and also encourage training sessions for employees. With the development of new technologies and processes, continuous sanitation training is vital. Sanitation is made easier by the system approach, which allows procedures to be checked at various stages and controls to be designed based on the system. Foodservice operators have serious responsibilities because their actions can affect the health of millions of people. Sanitation must become a way of life for those in foodservice. Several definitions pertaining to food sanitation are highlighted in this chapter.

Foodborne illnesses may be attributed to several causes. These may be divided into three main categories:

1. Biological sources, such as illnesses caused by microorganisms or their toxins.
2. Chemical sources related to constituents that may be directly associated with foodborne illnesses, such as pesticide, detergent, or metal contamination of foods.
3. Physical sources associated with contamination by objects such as glass or metal in food.

Although all these sources are significant, biological sources cause the major problems in foodservice operations. All of the above-mentioned sources will be discussed in detail in this chapter.

The word "sanitation" is derived from the latin word *sanitas* meaning "health." Foodservice sanitation refers to the handling of food in a healthy and hygienic manner. A distinction should be made between "clean" and "sanitary." "Clean" refers to appearance only and does not refer to sanitation. In other words what is clean may not be sanitary, which requires freedom from any illness-causing agents.

MICROORGANISMS AS CAUSES OF ILLNESS

Since the majority of foodborne illnesses are caused by microorganisms, it is important to understand their growth and survival. Microorganisms are microscopic life forms that take in nourishment, give off waste products, and multiply under favorable circumstances. They are of numerous types and are widely present in soil, air, and water, in fact, almost everywhere. The microorganisms responsible for food contamination are bacteria, viruses, fungi, and parasites. Not all microorganisms are harmful. Some microorganisms are beneficial and widely used in food preparation, such as yeast in baking, bacteria in sour cream, and mold in making selected types of cheese. Microorganisms that are harmful to human health and cause disease are called **pathogens.** Since microorganisms are living things, they need the right kind of environment in order to grow and multiply. In the following sections, the ways in which various types of microorganisms survive and multiply are discussed, with emphasis on food-related microorganisms.

Bacteria

Bacteria are single-celled, living organisms that multiply by binary fission, or the splitting of the cell to form two new cells. Bacteria occur in different shapes and sizes, the most common being (1) cocci, or spherical bacteria, which may be arranged singly (monococci), in pairs (diplococci), in chains (streptococci), or in clusters (staphylococci); (2) bacilli, or rod-shaped bacteria; and (3) spirilla, or spiral or comma-shaped bacteria.

Bacteria having a thin wall around the cell are called "vegetative" cells. Some rod-shaped bacteria have the capability to form a thick wall as a means of protection against unfavorable conditions. These cells are called **spores.** Spores are capable of resisting heat, cold, drought, chemicals, and other adverse conditions which normal vegetative cells cannot withstand. On return of favorable circumstances, spores multiply to form vegetative cells. The fact that bacteria can form spores is reason for concern in foodservice operations where food products are continuously being heated and/or cooled.

Microorganisms that enter the human body and multiply are called infectious microorganisms, and the resulting illness is called an **infection.** Salmonella is an example of an infectious microorganism. When salmonella enter the human body through food or water and multiply, their presence in the intestines causes certain specific symptoms.

On the other hand, some microorganisms do not have to be physically present in the body to cause illness. They can grow and multiply in food and produce a substance called **toxin,** which when ingested causes illness. Thus, it is the toxin rather than the microorganism that causes the illness. This is referred to as food **intoxication.** *Clostridium botulinum* is an example of a microorganism that can produce a deadly toxin in foods. Food containing infectious bacteria can be heated to a temperature that destroys the bacteria by disrupting the cells. Although food can be made safe from bacterial infection by killing the bacteria, it may not be possible to eliminate toxins. Heating at normal cooking temperatures does not ensure safety from toxins. Some toxins may be destroyed by heat, but usually very high temperatures are needed, at which the quality of food may be adversely affected.

Under ideal conditions, bacteria follow a growth pattern that can be divided into phases. These phases can be traced on a growth curve which goes through (1) a lag phase, when no multiplication occurs and the bacteria are adapting to the surrounding environment; (2) a log phase, in which rapid multiplication of the bacteria takes place; (3) a stationary phase, when growth and death of the bacteria evens out and there is a competition for available nutrients; and (4) a decline/death phase, when bacteria die faster and practically no multiplication takes place.

Bacteria may multiply rapidly, forming thousands of cells in a very short period of time. Bacterial growth and toxin formation are dependent on several factors, the most important being food, moisture, and temperature.

Food and Moisture

Bacteria require both food and moisture for growth. Food requirements vary with the type of bacteria, although proteinaceous foods are preferred by many bacteria. Moisture is necessary for the bacteria to utilize food, and hence reduction of moisture in foods reduces the chances of bacterial survival. Dry foods such as flour, cereal, and sugar are not favorable media for bacterial growth. Available moisture, referred to as "water activity," within foods is more important than total moisture in the foods. Addition of salt or sugar to water reduces its water activity; thus less moisture is available for the bacteria.

Temperature

Bacteria may be classified by the temperature range at which they multiply:

Mesophiles grow well at temperatures of 59° to 106°F (15° to 40°C), with maximum growth between 86° to 90°F (30° to 32°C). These temperatures fall within the human body temperature range as well as temperature ranges normally prevalent in the foods prepared by any type of foodservice operation. These types of bacteria must be considered when planning sanitation control for a foodservice operation.

Thermophiles grow better at higher temperatures than mesophiles (99° to 140°F or 37° to 60°C). These bacteria may cause problems in foods kept at high temperatures.

Psychrophiles grow best at colder temperatures of about 50° to 65°F (10° to 19°C). Some bacteria are also capable of growing at 32°F (0°C) or less. Psychrophiles may cause problems in foods that are refrigerated or are kept at cold temperatures.

Psychrotrophs will grow at 32°F (0°C), but their optimum temperature is higher, between 65°–85°F (20°–30°C).

As we see, bacteria can grow over a wide range of temperatures, making diligent efforts necessary to maintain high standards of food sanitation. Vegetative cells of most bacteria do not grow below 40°F (4°C) or above 140°F (60°C). This temperature range is described as the **danger zone** for bacterial growth. Refrigeration temperatures slow microbial action to a great extent, and that is why it is preferable to keep food in refrigeration when holding it for a relatively short period of time. For long-term storage, freezing is preferred, since it checks the growth of most microorganisms. However, it should be noted that freezing does not ensure freedom from all microorganisms. Some microorganisms remain dormant during freezing but start multiplying upon the return of favorable temperatures after thawing.

Time

Time and temperature are interrelated as far as the growth of microorganisms is concerned. In general, the longer the time bacteria exist at favorable temperatures, the greater their growth and multiplication. However, some microorganisms grow more rapidly than others at favorable temperatures.

Oxygen

Some microorganisms (aerobic) require oxygen for survival, whereas others (nonaerobic or anaerobic) can thrive in the absence of oxygen. Anaerobic bacteria will not grow in the presence of oxygen and thus do not grow on food surfaces; however, they may survive very well in the inside areas of such foods as pie shells, pudding, or meat loaf. Canned foods are other good media for the growth of anaerobic microorganisms if cans are improperly treated or handled. Vacuum-packaged or tightly sealed containers may also restrict the supply of oxygen. Microorganisms growing on food may do so in the presence or in the absence of oxygen.

pH

Most bacteria survive at neutral pH of 7.0, with minimum values of about 5.0 and maximum of 8.0. However, there are some bacteria that can grow below and above this range. It should be noted that the pH of most foods, particularly perishable ones such as meats, poultry, and dairy products, is close to 7.0, making them good media for the growth of most microorganisms. Acidic and acid-containing foods such as pickled products, cranberry sauce, tomatoes, and sauerkraut are relatively safe, since their pH is lower than 5.0. Cooking processes also affect the growth of microorganisms. Most bacteria and the microorganisms are easily destroyed at a slightly acidic pH of about 5.0. All the above-mentioned factors affect the growth of microorganisms and should be considered in outlining the food-sanitation policies within a foodservice operation.

Viruses

Viruses resemble bacteria in many respects and require similar conditions for growth. There are different kinds of viruses, and they vary in size. Food merely serves as a vehicle of transportation for viruses. Some viruses transmitted through food may cause serious illnesses, such as hepatitis and polio. A common source of reported viral infection in foodservice operations has been seafood, particularly fish and shellfish harvested from polluted waters. Leaky sewage pipes and faulty plumbing are possible sources by which food may become contaminated with viruses. Unlike bacteria, viruses are not complete cells and contain no nucleus or cell wall. Viruses can be carried by food and water, although they can live only in living cells. Once viruses enter living cells within a host, they interfere with cell metabolism and produce more of the virus.

Fungi

Fungi are other microscopic organisms associated with illnesses arising from food contamination. Not only are they prevalent in the atmosphere, but they are common in soil, water, plants, and foods. There are several types of fungi. The ones most commonly causing problems in food are yeast and molds.

Yeasts.   Yeasts are single-celled plants that reproduce by dividing into two by a process called "budding," as in bacteria. Some yeasts are used in food processing. Although yeasts may not be infectious in the sense that they cause illness, they can spoil the quality of food. In some foods they may produce a sticky substance or slime; in others they may cause discoloration or a change in flavor. Yeast thrive extremely well in foods that are rich in carbohydrates, such as starch and sugar. They produce ethyl alcohol and carbon dioxide. The presence of yeasts and the spoilage they cause may be detected by the presence of frothing or an odor of alcohol. Yeasts can be destroyed by heating foods to 136° F (58° C) for 15 min. They can be destroyed quickly at temperatures higher than 136° F. Yeasts will not grow in the absence of oxygen, and they do not pose as much of a problem as other microorganisms.

Molds.   Molds are fungi that are spread by means of spores. They have tubular structures, or "hyphae," that are made up of cells. These hyphae form spores that are carried through air and can grow into molds under favorable conditions. They can spread very rapidly. Spores are not survival devices, as in the case of bacteria, but are a means of reproduction for molds. Molds on foods can often be identified by their velvety, furry-looking, or powder type of growth, particularly on breads and cheeses. Most molds grow at temperatures between 80° to 90°F (27° to 32°C), although many can grow at much lower temperatures. They do not need sunlight to grow and can be destroyed by heat at temperatures above 140° F (60° C) for 10 min. They mainly affect physical properties of foods and can grow on almost any type of food. The problem with molds is that they can grow almost anyplace and at refrigeration temperatures that are considered to be safe for bacteria. Freezing can control the growth of molds but will not kill spores already present in foods.

Parasites

Protozoa

Protozoa are parasitic microorganisms, some of which cause foodborne diseases. They are widely spread in lakes, ponds, and soils. An intestinal disorder prevalent in many developing countries is called "amoebic dysentery" and is caused by the protozoan *Entamoeba histolytica*. The amoebae may be transferred by food contaminated with organisms or by fecal matter.

Trichinae

Trichinae are microscopic wormlike parasites found in farm and domestic animals such as hogs and rabbits. The illness caused by trichinae is called "trichinosis." Most trichinosis in human being is caused by eating raw or improperly cooked pork. Special efforts should be made by foodservice operators to see that pork and pork products are cooked to adequate temperatures, particularly if microwave ovens are used. Cutting, grinding, or slicing of infested raw meat may contaminate cutting boards or other food-contact surfaces. Trichinosis is one of the major problems related to meat in the United States. Federal regulations require that all cured pork be cooked to a temperature of at least 155° F (68° C). The symptoms of trichinosis include nausea, vomiting, diarrhea, profuse sweating, colic, and loss of appetite. The muscle soreness and swelling that develop at the later stages of trichinosis become very troublesome and sometimes life-threatening. Because these symptoms are common to other diseases, they are often overlooked as signs of trichinosis.

BIOLOGICAL CAUSES OF FOODBORNE ILLNESSES

Biological sources of foodborne illnesses include all the pathogenic microorganisms. As described earlier, these illnesses may be classified as food infections that are associated with the physical presence of microorganisms or food intoxications that result from toxins produced by the microorganisms. Certain food products are described as **potentially hazardous foods** from the point of view of food safety. These foods are those that contain substantial amounts of milk or milk products, eggs, poultry, fish, shellfish, and meat.

Although relatively few bacteria are known to cause problems in foods, they are still the most common cause of foodborne illnesses. All possible measures should be taken in foodservice operations to prevent the prevalence and growth of these microorganisms. A description of some of the most common food infections and intoxications and their control measures are described below.

Salmonella Food Infection

The food infection caused by salmonellae is called "salmonellosis." This infection is caused by the presence of a large number of salmonella microorganisms, which may be present in very high numbers in contaminated foods, particularly those rich in protein and carbohydrates. Foods commonly associated with salmonellosis include ham, turkey, chicken, sausage, beef, cream pies, potato salads, and improperly cooked or handled milk and egg products.

Salmonella organisms do not form toxins, so that the infection is associated primarily with the activity of a large number of organisms within the intestinal tract of the affected person. They can grow in a wide pH range (4.0 to 9.0), and the optimum temperature for their growth is 98.7°F (37°C). Human beings, poultry, and wild animals can harbor salmonellae, as can domestic animals, which are particularly known to be carriers. The fecal matter of animals also contains salmonellae. Cracked egg shells may become contaminated with salmonella organisms from soil. Items may already be contaminated with salmonellae when delivered to a foodservice operation.

The symptoms of salmonellosis, which may persist for a long time, are relatively mild and may be confused with those of other illnesses. Common symptoms include headache, nausea, diarrhea, vomiting, abdominal pain, and fever. Other related symptoms include drowsiness, foul-smelling watery stools, restlessness, and muscular weakness. These symptoms become apparent within 6 to 48 hours after ingesting salmonella-contaminated foods. The mortality rate from salmonellosis is very low, although those infected may be carriers for the organisms.

Controls needed for preventing contamination by salmonella organisms in foodservice operations include:

1. Checking foods carefully upon delivery, particularly for any soiled items. Meats may become contaminated with salmonellae at the time of slaughter; cracked eggs at bargain prices may be contaminated with salmonellae; or shellfish harvested from polluted waters may contain salmonellae.
2. Avoiding **cross-contamination,** which is the transfer of microorganisms from one place or item to another by means of such nonfood items as equipment, utensils, and hands. Cross-contamination can occur, for example, when a cutting board that had been used for preparing raw vegetables is not sanitized before using it for slicing cooked foods. It is advisable to have separate cutting boards and separate utensils, such as knives, for cooked and raw food products.
3. Following good personal hygiene. Since the human body may contain salmonellae, all food handlers must follow the sanitary rules pertaining to the washing of hands after using the bathroom, petting animals, etc.
4. Adequate cooking of foods [165°F (74°C) or higher] and storing them below 45°F (7.2°C) to prevent the growth of salmonellae.
5. Control of rodents, flies, cockroaches, and insects that may carry salmonella organisms.
6. Washing hands after handling raw foods.

Clostridium perfringens *Food Poisoning*

Clostridium perfringens is a spore-forming, rod-shaped bacterium that thrives well in the absence of oxygen. The illness caused by *C. perfringens* is considered by some bacteriologists to be an infection and by others to be an intoxication. Although *C. perfringens* is known to produce toxin, a large number of bacterial cells must be ingested to produce the symptoms. *C. perfringens* spores are present in soils and may exist under adverse circumstances for a long period of time. They are also present in human and animal intestinal tracts. Thus, during slaughter, meats are likely to get contaminated with *C. perfringens*. The vegetative cells of this bacterium may be killed at cooking temperatures, but the spores may survive boiling temperatures. They may survive a wide pH range, from 4.0 to 9.0.

Foods commonly associated with *C. perfringens* poisoning include stewed, boiled, or roasted meats; meat-based gravies, pies, salads, casseroles, and dressings. The bacterium is particularly found in foods where heat penetration is slow or inadequate.

Symptoms of *C. perfringens* poisoning are noted within 8 to 24 hours after ingestion of contaminated foods. The symptoms include diarrhea, abdominal pain, nausea, and vomiting. The symptoms normally subside within 24 hours.

Controlling *C. perfringens* depends mainly on its inhibition. Some of the measures of controlling it are:

1. Avoidance of cross-contamination, as it is very hard to eliminate the entry of *C. perfringens* in any foodservice operation.
2. Maintenance of clean food preparation areas so that they are free of dust or soil from fresh vegetables and fruits.
3. Practice of time-temperature control within foodservice operations, to avoid the danger zone.
4. Avoidance of the practice of leaving foods at room temperature.
5. Avoidance of thawing frozen foods at room temperatures.
6. Reheating of foods to an internal temperature of at least 165° F (74° C) or higher. Internal temperatures are more important than the surface temperatures.
7. Division of large batches of foods into shallow containers for rapid cooling.
8. Maintenance of proper time and temperatures of foods held on steam table.

Staphylococcus *Food Intoxication*

Staphylococcus food intoxication is one of the most common foodborne illnesses reported in the United States. The cause of this illness is due to a toxin produced by *Staphylococcus aureus*, which is commonly referred to as "staph." When these bacteria grow in food, they produce a toxin, which, when ingested, results in food poisoning. Human beings are considered to be the primary source of *S. aureus*, which are commonly found on the skin and hands, in nasal passages, and in the throat. These bacteria are carried to foods easily when the skin is affected by boils, cuts, burns, abrasions, or pimples. The toxin produced by *S. aureus* is classified as an "enterotoxin," since it causes inflammation of the intestinal area and stomach (gastroenteritis). The growth of a large number of *Staphylococcus* bacteria will eventually result in the production of a toxin that can survive boiling temperatures. Some of the toxin-producing bacteria can even survive under high salt concentration as well as in the presence of nitrites, both of which are often used in food preservation.

Food products that are cooked or processed can get contaminated easily with *S. aureus*. They provide ideal media for the production of toxin. Processed foods are especially vulnerable, because any competing bacteria in them have been considerably reduced or destroyed. Foods frequently reported to have caused staphylococcal food poisoning include cooked meat and fish products, stews and gravies, custards, pastry fillings, potato salads, and other foods that are much handled as during grinding, slicing, and deboning. It is difficult to detect foods contaminated with this bacteria since the color, odor, and taste are not affected.

The symptoms of staphylococcal food intoxication may be controlled by checking the growth of the bacteria as well as the production of the toxin. Staphylococci can be destroyed and/or prevented from growing by heating foods to at least 140°F (60°C) or above and keeping foods cold at temperatures below 45°F (7.2°C). Since staphylococci can grow rapidly within the danger zone of the temperatures, care should be taken to see that foods are not subjected to long periods of holding at those temperatures and that foods are rapidly cooled before they are refrigerated. Employees with infected pimples, sores, cuts, wounds, and boils, as well as those with respiratory infections, should not be allowed to handle foods until they are well and free of infections. Direct hand contact with foods should be avoided as much as possible. Sanitized utensils should be used to handle foods. Foodservice managers should understand that cooking or heating foods alone does not ensure freedom from staphylococcal intoxication. Sliced or chopped meats, stews, custards, cream fillings, and other foods should be cooled to temperatures below 45°F (7.2°C) as soon as possible. All leftovers should be reheated to at least 165°F (74°C) before use. It should be understood that once *Staphylococcus* toxin is formed, it may not be possible to render the food harmless by heating.

Botulism Food Intoxication

The bacterium responsible for botulism is *Clostridium botulinum*, a rod-shaped, spore-forming organism that can grow in the absence of oxygen. *C. botulinum* and botulism are very commonly known because of the extremely toxic effects, although incidences of botulism in foodservices are relatively rare. Since *C. botulinum* represents a potentially very hazardous microorganism, all precautions should be taken to prevent conditions favorable for its presence and/or growth. Botulism is usually fatal. *C. botulinum* are gas-forming, anaerobic bacteria that can grow at a pH of 5 to 8. They are found in soil, in water, and in the intestinal tracts of animals.

Since *C. botulinum* is an anaerobic microorganism, foods associated with botulism intoxication are those which are subjected to anaerobic conditions, such as home-canned foods and foods that are improperly processed, poisoning such low-acid foods as spinach, green beans, corn, and beets. An indication of the possible presence of *C. botulinum* in canned foods is the formation of gas or a bulging of the can due to the gas formation. Certain types of seafood, particularly tuna, were also found to be associated with the incidence of botulism. The toxin is so potent that even tasting contaminated foods may result in fatal consequences. Even as few as 15 spores of *C. botulinum per gram* at 35° C can produce a lethal test dose in 3 days, and as few as 42 spores can result in a lethal dose in 2 days. The resistance of the *C. botulinum* spores to heat varies with the nature of food, the type and strain of bacteria, the pH, the type of the medium in which spores were formed, the number of spores, and the temperature at which the spores were produced. In an incidence of botulism poisoning in a restaurant in Peoria, Illinois (1983), the contaminated food was found to be sautéed onions. Although onions are not among the foods normally associated with the presence of *C. botulinum*, sautéing them with margarine apparently produced an anaerobic atmosphere in the food. Thus, it points to the potential of certain foods being made anaerobic and the formation of conditions favorable for the growth of anaerobic microorganisms. It is probable that margarine or other fats may coat *Clostridium botulinum* spores during the sautéing heat treatment and provide an anaerobic environment. It is therefore advisable to consume nonacid sautéed foods as soon after their preparation as possible or to properly store them under safe conditions. This outbreak of botulism provided a new dimension to the presence of the *C. botulinum* spores.

Botulism outbreaks may be associated with several factors, the most common being

1. The presence of *C. botulinum* spores in foods, particularly canned foods or those improperly processed.
2. The improper processing of low-acid foods, which provides favorable circumstances for the growth of *C. botulinum* spores.
3. Improper storage or preparation of foods, leading to the growth and development of the spores, and consequently the formation of toxins.
4. Use of improper cooking temperatures that may not be sufficient for the inactivation of the toxin.
5. Ingestion of toxin-forming foods (even in minute quantities).

The symptoms associated with *C. botulinum* intoxication are nausea, vomiting, diarrhea, headache, dizziness, double vision, difficulty in breathing, and progressive respiratory paralysis. Symptoms usually appear within 12 to 36 hours after the ingestion of the contaminated food. Death comes usually within 3 to 5 days. The duration of illness is dependent on the type of toxin and may range from one day to several weeks.

Adequate preventive measures are absolutely necessary to prevent the contamination of food by *C. botulinum*.

1. Never use foods that are canned at home or by other unapproved noncommercial sources.
2. Never accept canned foods if the cans are swollen, dented, or show any signs of internal pressure. There may be other reasons for the swelling of the cans, but to

be on the safe side it is always preferable — and safe — to refuse shipments of such foods.

3. Discard (by incineration or other means) foods showing such signs of spoilage as frothiness, discoloration, and/or foul odor. In no case should the food be tasted.

Less Common Types of Food Poisoning

In addition to those discussed above, there are several other types of microorganisms that may be associated with food poisoning. These are less commonly known because they are relatively rare in occurrence, mild in their adverse impact on human health, and/or symptoms associated with their infection may be easily confused with other types of common illnesses of day-to-day occurrence. One such microorganism is *Vibrio parahaemolyticus*, which causes infection resulting in abdominal pain, diarrhea, nausea, vomiting, headache, and possibly mild fever. This microorganism is mainly associated with seafood and is commonly present in shellfish, crustacea, and underprocessed fish and fish products. Consumption of raw fish is therefore not advisable, particularly when they are imported into the United States. Thorough cooking of seafood and the prevention of cross-contamination are necessary for controlling this infection. Another microorganism associated with food infection is *Escherichia coli*, which may be present in a wide variety of foods. The most common symptom associated with *E. coli* infection is diarrhea, though other symptoms may be present, varying with the type of microorganism. This infection is mainly caused by the lack of personal hygiene and sanitary techniques.

Infectious hepatitis is caused by a virus found in the feces and urine of infected persons. The virus is also found in shellfish harvested from polluted waters. Raw oysters and clams were associated in the past with outbreaks of infectious hepatitis. It can be controlled by purchasing seafood from safe and reliable sources. Also, foodhandlers should be instructed to practice good personal hygiene and good sanitary techniques.

Bacillus cereus causes food intoxication, which can have symptoms that are similar to those of staphylococcal intoxication, including diarrhea, nausea, vomiting, and abdominal cramps. This bacterium is predominantly present in cereal products, particularly rice. Adequate cooking and rapid cooling of foods are recommended to avoid their contamination. There are several species of *Shigella*, which are associated with the bacillary dysentery called "shigellosis." This condition has also been traced to the lack of sanitary conditions and good personal hygiene. A variety of foods may be associated with shigellosis. A rare occurrence of food infection is also attributed to *Yersinia enterocolitica*, which causes the infection called "yersiniosis." Meats, particularly pork, are usually the source of this infection, although other foods may also be associated with it. *Campylobacter jejuni* contaminates food through fecal contamination. Raw meats and poultry become contaminated during processing when intestinal contents contact meat surfaces. Since the microorganism is quite sensitive to stressful environmental conditions it is unlikely to exist in processed edible foods. *Listeria* is ubiquitous in nature, occurring in the soil, vegetation, and water, and therefore is frequently carried by humans and animals.

Listeria monocytogenes is widely distributed in nature and can grow well in raw and pasteurized milk at refrigeration temperatures. It can grow at a wide pH range (5.0 to 9.0). It is relatively heat-resistant and produces a series of toxins. Milk and milk products are not the only sources of recent outbreaks related to *Listeria monocytogenes*. The organism has been isolated from cole slaw, lettuce, meat products, and rice soup with cream. Milk, cheese, and ice creams are potential sources.

Comparative descriptions of foodborne illnesses from biological sources are given in Tables 8.1 and 8.2.

CHEMICAL CAUSES OF FOODBORNE ILLNESSES

Foodborne illnesses traced to chemical sources are most commonly those that are caused by the presence of pesticides, herbicides, antibiotics, fertilizers, metals, additives, or hormones. Several chemicals used in foodservice operations are toxic and may result in chemical contamination of food products. Some chemicals, when in contact with foods or equipment, may react with them to form toxic substances. Pesticides are a common source of chemical contamination of foods. Pesticides are very commonly used to prevent insects or other microorganisms in foodservice operations. Since many pesticides are resistant to breakdown and even minor concentrations may have adverse effects, it is essential to enforce adequate cleaning procedures as well as measures to prevent pesticide contamination. Animals and plants used for foods may have pesticides in their systems, resulting in adverse effects when those food products are consumed. Managers in foodservices have little control over some types of chemical contamination, but efforts should be made to prevent any chance of contamination. Pesticides should be labeled clearly and stored securely and separately from foods. They should be stored, as much as possible, in their original container only.

Numerous chemicals are used in foodservice operations, such as detergents, polishes, caustics, and other chemicals, for which care should be taken to prevent their coming in contact with foods or food contact surfaces. Food poisoning may result from such chemicals. Care should be taken to follow the label directions for their use and for their disposal.

Another important source of chemical contamination may be traced to intentional or accidental additives. These additives, when used in high concentration or in certain forms, may prove hazardous. Some additives recently associated with health problems include nitrites, sodium sulfite, and MSG (monosodium glutamate). Care should therefore be taken to use only those additives that are approved and have been found safe, and these only when necessary. Misuse of additives should be controlled as much as possible.

Metals may also be a source of chemical contamination in foodservices. The presence of lead, mercury, and other heavy metals can cause poisoning. Metals like copper, when in contact with strongly acid foods, may react to form substances that may be toxic, therefore the food contact surfaces and foods selected should be taken into account. Paints and polishes accidentally coming in contact with foods repre-

Table 8.1

Illnesses of Less Frequent or Rare Occurrence

Name of Illness	Causative Agent	Foods Usually Involved	How Introduced into Food	Preventive or Corrective Procedures
Botulism	Bacterial toxin; *Clostridium botulinum*	Improperly processed or un-refrigerated foods of low acidity	Soil and dirt; spores not killed; inadequately heated foods	Do not use "home canned" foods; discard all foods in swollen unopened cans
Typhoid fever; paratyphoid A	Bacterial infection; *Salmonella*; *Salmonella paratyphi A*; *typhi*	Moist foods, dairy products, shell fish, raw vegetables, and water	By food handlers and other carriers	Prohibit carriers from handling food; require strict personal cleanliness in food preparation; eliminate flies
Streptococcus food infection (beta-type scarlet fever and strep throat)	Bacterial infection; beta hemolytic streptococci	Foods contaminated with nasal or oral discharges from carrier	Coughing, sneezing, or poor food handling	Exclude food handlers with known strep infections; thorough cooking of food; rapid chilling of food
Streptococcus infection (alpha type) (intestinal)	Bacterial infection; *Enterococcus* group; pyogenic group	Foods contaminated with excreta on unclean hands	By unsanitary food handling	Exclude food handlers with known strep infections; thorough cooking of food; chilling of food
Bacillary dysentery; shigellosis	Bacterial infection; *Shigella* sp.	Food contaminated with excreta on unclean hands	By unsanitary food handling	Strict personal cleanliness in food preparation; refrigeration of moist foods; exclude carrier
Amoebic dysentery	Parasitic infection; *Entamoeba histolytica*	Foods contaminated with excreta on unclean hands	By unsanitary food handling	Protect water supplies; insure strict personal cleanliness of food handlers; exclude carrier

Illness	Cause	Foods involved	Source	Prevention
Trichinosis	Parasitic infection; larvae of *Trichinella spiralis*	Raw or insufficiently cooked pork or pork products	Raw pork from hogs fed undercooked infected garbage	Thoroughly cook pork and pork products over 150° F; preferably to 160° F
Fish tapeworm	Parasitic infection; larvae of *D. latum*	Raw or insufficiently cooked fish containing live larvae	Fish infested by contaminated water	Cook fish thoroughly; avoid serving raw fish
Arsenic, fluoride, lead poisoning (insecticides, rodenticides)	Chemical toxin	Any foods accidentally contaminated	Either during growing period or accident in kitchen	Thoroughly wash all fresh fruit and vegetables when received; store insecticides and pesticides away from food; properly label containers; follow use instructions; use carefully; guard food from chemical contamination
Copper poisoning	Chemical toxin; copper food contact surfaces	Acid foods and carbonated liquids	Contact between metal and acid food or carbonated beverage	Prevent acid foods or carbonated liquids from coming into contact with exposed copper
Cadmium and zinc poisoning	Chemical toxin; metal plating on food containers	Fruit juices, fruit gelatin, and other acid foods stored in metal-plated containers	Acid foods dissolve cadmium and zinc from containers in which stored	Discontinue use of cadmium-plated utensils as food containers; prohibit use of zinc-coated utensils for preparation, storage, and serving of acid fruits and other foods or beverages
Cyanide poisoning	Chemical toxin; silver polish		Failure to thoroughly wash and rinse polished silverware	Discontinue use of cyanide-base silver polish or wash and rinse silverware thoroughly

Source: Reprinted from the *Foodborne Illnesses*, a publication of the National Restaurant Association.

Table 8.2

Illnesses of Frequent Occurrence

Name of Illness	Causative Agent	Foods Usually Involved	How Introduced into Food	Preventive or Corrective Procedures
Staphylococcus	Bacterial toxin; *Staphylococcus* enterotoxin	Cooked ham or other meat, chopped or diced; cream-filled or custard pastries; other dairy products; hollandaise sauce; bread pudding; potato salad; chicken, fish, and other meat salads; "warmed-over" food	Usually food handlers through nasal discharges, local skin infections (acne, pimples, boils, scratches, and cuts)	Refrigerate moist foods during storage periods; minimize use of hands in preparation; exclude unhealthy food handlers (having pimples, boils, and other obvious infections)
Perfringens	Bacterial toxin; *Clostridium perfringens*	Meat that has been boiled, steamed, braised, or partially roasted, allowed to cool several hours and subsequently served either cooled or reheated	Natural contaminant meat	Cool food rapidly, break down large quantities of food into smaller containers to facilitate cooling; eliminate cross-contamination
Salmonellosis	Bacterial infection. Over 800 types of *Salmonella* bacteria	Meat and poultry, diced foods, egg products, custards, shell fish, soups, gravies, sauces, "warmed-over" foods	Fecal contamination by food handlers; raw contaminated meat and poultry, eggs and unpasteurized milk	Good personal habits of food handlers; sufficient cooking and refrigeration of perishable foods, elimination of rodents and flies

Source: Reprinted from the *Foodborne Illnesses*, a publication of the National Restaurant Association.

sent another form of chemical hazard. Such foods as tomatoes, sauerkraut, pickles, lemonade, and fruit punches should be placed in containers with which they will not have any chemical reaction. Metals like cadmium, tin, zinc, copper, and lead are all soluble, to variable extents, in milk, soy sauce, fruit juices, tomatoes, vinegar, and other types of acid foods. Whenever any acid foods are stored, care should be taken regarding the surfaces they will be in contact with. There are many metals that can get into foods via utensils or cans. Empty cans should not be used for storage of foods. Plastic containers and flexible packages should be used only if they are approved for use and only for the foods that can be safely stored in them, since chemicals may also migrate or interact from these packaging materials. On the other hand, food should never be left uncovered in order to prevent any kind of chemical contamination. Only approved metals and their alloys should be used when buying foodservice equipment. The minimum requirements and specifications of metals as set by the National Sanitation Foundation (NSF) should be followed.

Several antibiotics have been approved for use in foods, such as chlorotetracycline and Terramycin for use with raw poultry. Cooking at adequate temperatures should destroy any residues of these antibiotics. The use of antibiotics in their food products should be checked out with vendors before such products are ordered. Certain hormones are administered to animals which may be present in residual form, and foodservice managers should be aware of their possible presence.

PHYSICAL CAUSES OF FOODBORNE ILLNESSES

Food contaminants of a physical nature are those that are related to physical objects that may accidentally contaminate food products. Foodservice equipment and facilities are subjected to constant wear and tear, and it is essential to see that foods remain safe from physical contaminants that may result in injury, illness, or other related health problems. Good facilities planning and equipment selection are necessary to reduce this problem. Worn-out equipment or its parts should be replaced promptly.

The most common example of contamination by physical sources would be the presence of metal slivers in canned foods introduced by the use of worn-out can openers. These metal slivers may not be detected when cans are opened and thus end up in the prepared food products. Pieces of glass represent another dangerous physical source of food contamination. Since glassware is subject to breakage, care needs to be taken that pieces of glass are not introduced into foods. Normally, accidents occur during the peak hours of production or service, complicating the clean-up process. A good foodservice manager will make it a point to see that prompt removal of all broken glass is undertaken and that all food products liable to be contaminated are discarded. One of the problems with glass is that it can very easily be mistaken for ice. Glass should therefore never be used for scooping ice, and ice machines should be adequately covered. Metal fragments, pieces of wood, string, glass, glass thermometers, paper, styrofoam, and plastics are commonly present near foods and may contaminate them if adequate controls are not enforced.

☐ Food Service Establishment
☐ Retail Food Store
☐ Temporary Retail Food Establishment
☐ Mobile Retail Food Establishment

Establishment Number _____

White – File Copy
Yellow – Establishment Copy
Pink – Inspectors Copy

Name of Establishment _____

Owner or Operator _____

Address _____ City _____ Zip Code _____

Based on an Inspection this day, the items marked below identify violations of the Illinois Food, Drug and Cosmetic Act and/or the Sanitary Inspection Law and Rules Promulgated under these acts. Failure to correct these violations within the time specified may result in prosecution under the Enforcement Provisions of these acts. ● = **Critical Items Requiring Immediate Correction.**

ITEM	X	WT	DESCRIPTION
			FOOD
●1		5	Source, Wholesome, No Spoilage
2		1	Original Container, Properly Labeled
			FOOD PROTECTION
●3		5	Potentially hazardous food meets, temperature requirements during storage preparation, display, service and transportation
4		4	Facilities to maintain product temperature
5		1	Thermometers provided and conspicuous
6		2	Potentially hazardous food properly thawed
●7		4	Unwrapped and potentially hazardous food not re-served, CROSS CONTAMINATION
8		2	Food protection during storage, preparation, display, service and transportation
9		2	Handling of food (ice) minimized, methods
10		1	Food (ice) dispensing utensils properly stored
			PERSONNEL
●11		5	Personnel with infections restricted
●12		5	Hands washed and clean, good hygienic practices

ITEM	X	WT	DESCRIPTION
18		1	Pre-flushed, scraped, soaked
19		2	Wash, rinse water; clean, proper temperature
20		4	Sanitization rinse: clean, temperature, concentration
21		1	Wiping cloths: clean, use restricted
22		2	Food-contact surfaces of equipment and utensils clean, free of abrasives and detergents
23		1	Non-food contact surfaces of equipment and utensils clean
24		1	Storage, handling of clean equipment—utensils
25		1	Single-service articles, storage, dispensing
26		2	No re-use of single-service articles
			WATER
●27		5	Water source, safe: Hot and cold under pressure
			SEWAGE
●28		4	Sewage and waste water disposal
			PLUMBING
29		1	Installed, maintained
●30		5	Cross-connection, back siphonage, back flow

ITEM	X	WT	DESCRIPTION
34		1	Outside storage area, enclosures properly constructed, clean; controlled incineration
			INSECT, RODENT ANIMAL CONTROL
●35		4	Presence of insects/rodents – outer openings protected, no birds, turtles, other animals
			FLOORS, WALLS AND CEILINGS
36		1	Floors: constructed, drained, clean, good repair, covering installation, dustless cleaning methods
37		1	Walls, ceiling, attached equipment: constructed good repair, clean surfaces, dustless cleaning methods
			LIGHTING
38		1	Lighting provided as required – Fixtures shielded
			VENTILATION
39		1	Rooms and equipment – vented as required
			DRESSING ROOMS
40		1	Rooms clean, lockers provided, facilities clean

		FOOD EQUIPMENT AND UTENSILS
13	1	Clean clothes, hair restraints
14	2	Food (ice) contact surfaces: designed, constructed, maintained, installed, located
15	1	Non-Food contact surfaces: designed, constructed, maintained, installed, located
16	2	Dishwashing facilities: designed, constructed, maintained, installed, located, operated
17	1	Accurate Thermometers, chemical test kits provided, gauge cock

		TOILET AND HAND-WASHING FACILITIES
•31	4	Number, convenient, accessible, designed, installed
32	2	Toilet rooms enclosed, self-closing doors, fixtures, good repair, clean: Hand cleanser, sanitary towels/hand drying devices provided, proper waste receptacles, tissue
		GARBAGE AND REFUSE DISPOSAL
33	2	Containers or receptacles covered: adequate number, insect/rodent proof, frequency, clean

		OTHER OPERATIONS
•41	5	Toxic items properly stored, labeled and used
42	1	Premises: maintained, free of litter, unnecessary articles, cleaning/maintenance equipment properly stored, authorized personnel
43	1	Complete separation from living/sleeping quarters, laundry
44	1	Clean, soiled linen properly stored
•45		Management personnel certified Yes _____ No _____

Temperatures: Hot Water Sanitizing _____ Hot Foods _____ Cold Foods _____

Remarks and Recommendations For Corrections

ITEM	CORRECTED BY

Report and Instructions Received By _____

(Signature of Owner or Representative)

Date _____ Time _____ A.M. _____ P.M. Sanitation Score _____ (100 Minus Demerits)

By _____

(Inspector)

IDPH FCC 01

Figure 8-1. Retail food sanitary inspection report. (Courtesy Illinois Department of Health)

SAFE HANDLING OF FOODS

Food safety is an important consideration, and any outbreak of foodborne illness may have devastating effects on the foodservice operation. It is management's responsibility to see that all food handled and practices followed are sanitary. It is advisable to have a set policy on sanitary standards to be followed by everyone within the operation. These standards should be strictly adhered to by employees as well as management. To cover all phases of the operation, sanitary guidelines may be set based on the subunits or functional units within an establishment. It is desirable to have training programs for new employees as well as periodic refresher courses for older employees. Almost every state and city has guidelines for sanitation, and all types of foodservice operations are inspected periodically to determine if they are complying with sanitary regulations. Fines and penalties are imposed upon violation, and certificates/licenses are issued to those who comply with the standards. Some states require that the manager and/or employees working in a foodservice operation be certified in food handling and sanitation. This requirement can be met by taking courses or enrolling in a training program. Several states have their own sanitation training programs. Some organizations, such as the National Restaurant Association's Education Foundation, offer courses in applied foodservice sanitation. Government regulations are designed to ensure food sanitation and safety, but it is the individual operation's responsibility to see that these rules are followed. Inspections are conducted by federal and state agencies to ensure food safety and sanitary practices during the industrial processing of foods. Appendix D contains selected food sanitation regulations from the Illinois Department of Public Health.

Guidelines to be followed and points to be considered for food safety are illustrated in Figures 8.1 to 8.3 according to the common functions carried out within any type of foodservice operation (see Appendix E). Most of the aspects are direct excerpts from federal and state regulations and are self-explanatory. Many states have comprehensive laws dealing with all functions within any type of foodservice operation. A copy of the retail food sanitary inspection report from the Illinois Department of Public Health is seen in Figure 8.1. Many public health departments have publications and other materials available for use in any foodservice operation (Figures 8.2 and 8.3).

Food Purchasing

Federal law requires that all meat (beef, lamb, pork, and veal) and meat products produced in plants be inspected by the U.S. Department of Agriculture. Thus, all such meats should be purchased after assuring that they have been approved by the agency. A certificate, stamp, or approval sign on the package is a common means of assuring USDA approval. Also, foodservice operators should visit those facilities (if possible) in order to inspect the sanitary standards of the plant(s).

Other meats (chicken and turkey, for example) and meat products are inspected

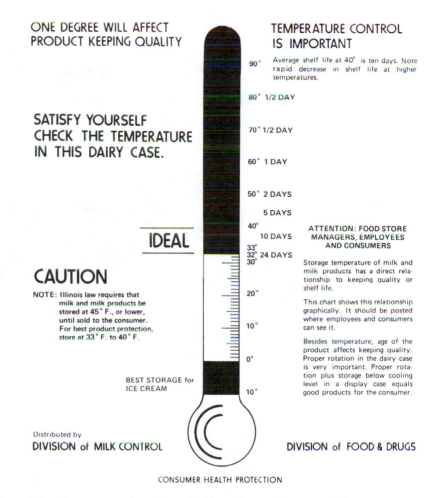

ONE DEGREE WILL AFFECT
PRODUCT KEEPING QUALITY

SATISFY YOURSELF
CHECK THE TEMPERATURE
IN THIS DAIRY CASE.

IDEAL

CAUTION

NOTE: Illinois law requires that
milk and milk products be
stored at 45° F., or lower,
until sold to the consumer.
For best product protection,
store at 33° F. to 40° F.

BEST STORAGE for
ICE CREAM

Distributed by
DIVISION of MILK CONTROL

TEMPERATURE CONTROL
IS IMPORTANT

90° Average shelf life at 40° is ten days. Note
rapid decrease in shelf life at higher
temperatures.

80° 1/2 DAY

70° 1/2 DAY

60° 1 DAY

50° 2 DAYS

5 DAYS

40°
10 DAYS
33°
32° 24 DAYS
30°

20°

10°

0°

10°

ATTENTION: FOOD STORE
MANAGERS, EMPLOYEES
AND CONSUMERS

Storage temperature of milk and
milk products has a direct relationship to keeping quality or
shelf life.

This chart shows this relationship
graphically. It should be posted
where employees and consumers
can see it.

Besides temperature, age of the
product affects keeping quality.
Proper rotation in the dairy case
is very important. Proper rotation plus storage below cooling
level in a display case equals
good products for the consumer.

DIVISION of FOOD & DRUGS

CONSUMER HEALTH PROTECTION

Figure 8-2. Temperatures for milk and milk products. (Courtesy of Illinois Department of Public Health)

by federal and state agencies. Egg and egg products are also inspected. Not all of these foods have mandatory inspection laws, although many manufacturers prefer inspection and certification by regulatory agencies. Similar rules apply to seafood and dairy products. In essence, it should be assured before selecting a vendor that the products ordered are processed under sanitary conditions and that there is an adequate system of inspection. It is never advisable, even if it is economical, to buy such perishable items from local farms or plants that are not subjected to regular inspection.

Sanitary guidelines for food production and service are described in Appendix E.

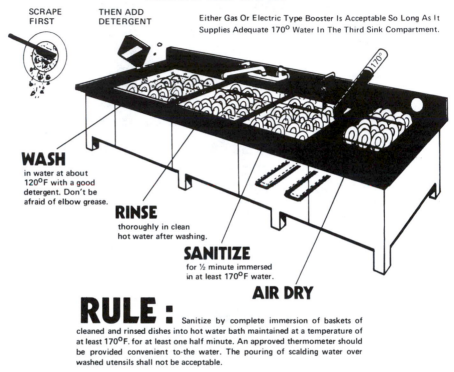

Hand Dishwashing

The password for approved hand dishwashing is WRS.
Learn it and use it!

SCRAPE FIRST

THEN ADD DETERGENT

Either Gas Or Electric Type Booster Is Acceptable So Long As It Supplies Adequate 170° Water In The Third Sink Compartment.

WASH
in water at about 120°F with a good detergent. Don't be afraid of elbow grease.

RINSE
thoroughly in clean hot water after washing.

SANITIZE
for ½ minute immersed in at least 170°F water.

AIR DRY

RULE : Sanitize by complete immersion of baskets of cleaned and rinsed dishes into hot water bath maintained at a temperature of at least 170°F. for at least one half minute. An approved thermometer should be provided convenient to-the water. The pouring of scalding water over washed utensils shall not be acceptable.

REMEMBER CLEAN DISHES ARE GOOD BUSINESS. YOUR CUSTOMER WILL THANK YOU!

Figure 8-3.   Methods and facilities for washing and sanitizing utensils. (Courtesy of Illinois Department of Public Health)

SUMMARY

This chapter describes the role of food sanitation in the management of foodservice operations. It discusses in detail the different types of foodborne illnesses and their causes. Favorable conditions for the growth of microorganisms in foodservice operations are described. A description of the causative agent of the foodborne illness, types of foods susceptible to contamination, and associated symptoms helps in understanding the sanitation needs in foodservice operations.

REVIEW
QUESTIONS

What are the major sources of foodborne illnesses? What is the difference between "clean" and "sanitary"?

Give examples describing the difference between the infection and intoxication.

What are common physical causes and chemical sources of food contamination?

Using the systems approach, show at least one precaution that you will recommend for food handling at various stages of food flow.

Which microorganism is mostly responsible for fatal consequences associated with food contamination?

Among all the pathogenic microorganisms, which one is the most commonly prevalent in foodservice operations?

ASSIGNMENTS

According to the news reports, describe the latest foodborne illness reported to be associated with a foodservice operation. Attach news clippings, if possible.

Visit a foodservice operation and critically evaluate it from the sanitation point of view. Follow the systems approach during your visit. Record and comment on food temperatures of selected food items.

Visit a restaurant of your choice and observe some sources of contamination from the point the food is ordered to the point it is served.

SUGGESTED READINGS

Cichy, R. F. 1984. *Sanitation Management. Strategies for Success.* The Educational Institute of the American Hotel & Motel Association, East Lansing, MI.

Guthrie, R. K. 1980. *Food Sanitation*, 2nd edition. AVI Publishing Co., Westport, CT.

Illinois Department of Public Health. 1983. *Food Service Sanitation: Rules and Regulations.* Springfield, IL.

Institute of Food Technologists. 1988. Bacteria associated with foodborne diseases. A scientific status summary by expert panel. *Food Technology.* Vol. 42 (4).

Institute of Food Technologists. 1988. Virus transmission via foods. A scientific status summary by expert panel. *Food Technology.* Vol. 42 (10).

Longree, K., and Blaker, G. G. 1982. *Sanitary Techniques in Foodservice*, 2nd edition. John Wiley & Sons, New York, NY.

Marriott, N. G. 1985. *Principles of Food Sanitation.* AVI Publishing Co., Westport, CT.

Minor, L. J. 1983. *Sanitation, Safety & Environmental Standards*, Vol. 2, AVI Publishing Co., Westport, CT.

National Institute for the Foodservice Industry. 1985. *Applied Foodservice Sanitation*, 3rd edition. Chicago, IL.

National Restaurant Association. 1979. *Sanitation Operations Manual.* Chicago, IL.

United States Department of Agriculture. Food Safety and Inspection Service. 1989. *A Margin of Safety: The HACCP Approach to Food Safety Education.* FSIS Information Service, Washington, DC.

CHAPTER 9

QUANTITY FOOD PREPARATION

KEY CONCEPTS AND TERMS

standardized recipes
marbling
shrinkage
tenderization
degree of doneness
stocks
gluten
leavening
proofing

The primary function of a foodservice operation is to convert raw ingredients into prepared foods and to serve them in such a way as to satisfy consumers. A blend of science and art is required at various stages of this process. Needless to say, food preparation is the most important part of the system, since all other parts depend on it. The best-planned menu and the efforts of the most efficient purchasing and receiving units may all be negated if food preparation is not up to standard.

The production department is the largest and most critical part of any foodservice operation. A variety of items are prepared by this department in such subdivisions as (1) butcher shop, (2) entrée unit, (3) appetizer/soups unit, (4) vegetables unit, (5) salad unit, and (6) bake shop. Some of these units may be combined. Each division contributes its part, and an overall effort is needed from each unit to produce a quality meal in quantity. Management must assign each item to be produced to the most capable person(s) within that unit. Assignments are communicated by management using a production sheet (Figure 9.1).

STANDARDIZED RECIPES

Recipes that have been tested for quality, quantity, procedures, time, temperature, equipment, and yield are called **standardized recipes.** The recipes are standardized to the extent that when specified conditions and procedures are adhered to, the result is a predictable product. Standardized recipes assure quality control and are effective management tools. Standardization calls for careful assessment, testing, and evaluation of recipes before final adoption. It should be emphasized that recipes standardized for one operation may not be applicable to another operation. Minor variations in equipment and temperature may make a considerable difference. It is essential that testing be conducted on the premises of an operation, using the equipment and procedures that will be used in actual food preparation.

Standardized recipes offer several advantages.

1. Detail ingredients, procedures, and equipment to be used. Thus, a change in personnel does not affect food quality or quantity.
2. Facilitate cost analyses of the recipes.
3. Provide predictable food quality.
4. Facilitate food purchasing, since exact quantities of food and ingredients to be used are known.
5. Permit easier portion control, if serving portions are listed.
6. Help to set selling prices for menu items and facilitate price changes when the cost of ingredients change.
7. Help in work scheduling, since time and procedures used are standardized. Efficient scheduling results in an even distribution of work and job satisfaction.

Date: _____	Function: _____		Manager: _____
Menu Item	Amount to Prepare	Whose Responsibility	Comments
APPETIZERS			
ENTRÉES			
VEGETABLES			
SALADS & DRESSINGS			
BREADS			
DESSERTS			
OTHER ITEMS			

Figure 9-1.   An example of a production sheet.

8. Contribute to consumer satisfaction since quality of food and serving sizes are uniform.
9. Avoid confusion and reduce the chances of poor handling and food-preparation failures, which could prove expensive for the operation.
10. Help train employees in good production and handling procedures.

Standardization Procedures

The standardization of recipes needs careful evaluation and testing. In many foodservice operations, it is undertaken by management with the help of supervisors and/or dietitians. Standardization assures that the operation will have well-documented recipes rather than a vague list of ingredients in the head of a cook or a chef, who may not remain with the operation. Household recipes or small-quantity recipes published in magazines or cookbooks usually are unreliable for quantity production. Every recipe that has been standardized needs reevaluation from time to time.

Standardization involves careful adjustment and readjustment of ingredients and their proportions to produce the most acceptable quality. This calls for subjective as well as objective evaluation. Taste tests should be conducted several times until quality products are assured. Most often recipes are enlarged and tested from smaller quantity recipes. The initial recipe may come from one of various sources such as cookbooks, magazines, journals, commercial food companies, family-recipe files, other foodservice operations, test kitchens, and special community advisory groups. The first step is to prepare the recipe in the minimum quantity for which it was intended. The finished product should then be evaluated. The smaller recipe should be evaluated on the basis of preparation method; ingredient proportion; availability of ingredients; cost, yield, equipment, skill, and abilities of personnel; and its overall suitability for the operation. A careful screening at this point will eliminate expensive large-scale testing at a later stage.

Enlarging Recipes

The original recipe should be multiplied and tested. In enlarging the recipe, ratios play an important role. For example, the ratio between sugar and flour or flour and shortening is very important. The physical form of the ingredients should be carefully assessed. Fresh, chopped onions may be responsible for flavor in a smaller recipe, but it may not be feasible to have chopped onions in larger quantities, as this may change the taste of the finished product. Salt and seasonings need very careful assessment because simple multiplications never work for them.

In general there are two methods that may be followed to enlarge recipes: the trial and error method and the factor method.

Trial and Error Method

Trial and error is applicable to relatively simple recipes in which the ingredients are limited in number. Based on suitability, the original recipe is multiplied— normally twice the size of the original recipe. Yield and other characteristics are evaluated. If the quality and quantity are acceptable, then the recipe is further multiplied. If not, adjustments are made and the recipe retested. This process is continued until desirable quality and quantities are achieved. Special attention should be given to adjustments in processes, such as cooking temperatures, and speed of the mixers. Differences in the desired yield are representative of the need for adjustment and careful evaluation. This method is time-consuming and may be tedious, since several variables are involved and adjustments may be difficult.

Factor Method

In this method, a factor is used for calculation and accuracy of the multiplied ingredients. The conversion factor that is used for multiplication is derived as follows:

$$\text{conversion factor} = \frac{\text{desired yield from enlarged recipe}}{\text{yield from original recipe}}$$

If the desired yield is 60 and the original recipe is 8, the conversion factor would be $60/8 = 7.5$. This factor is used for multiplication as shown in Figure 9.2. All ingredients used should be listed with the amounts given in the original recipe. In order to facilitate calculation, all amounts should be converted to equivalent weights—for example, from cups or teaspoonfuls to ounces. This equivalent weight should be multiplied by the factor as shown in Column 4 of Figure 9.2. This will give the amounts in ounces of the ingredients to be tested in the enlarged recipe. Ounces can then be converted to convenient weights and measures. In this way, the amount of ingredients to be used in the new recipe can be calculated. These calculations give the approximate equivalent weights or measures needed, and adjustments are to be made after careful testing. The factor method facilitates the testing procedure and should not be used in final preparation of the recipe without testing. In order to decrease or increase the recipe yield, similar factors should be used. It should be noted that when recipes are increased, the factor will always be greater than 1.0, and when decreasing the recipe, the factor will always be less than 1.0. The total weight of an enlarged recipe can be checked by comparing it with the total weight of the original recipe. The total weight of the original recipe multiplied by the factor should result in the total weight of the new recipe. If not, the calculations should be carefully rechecked for errors.

Standardization procedures continue as follows.

1. Prepare the enlarged recipe, carefully checking procedures, time, temperatures, and other parameters. Soon after preparation have the product evaluated by a taste panel. Several forms may be used for assessment of the recipe by the panelists. The results may be interpreted based on the type of the data obtained. It may be used (1) for changing special ingredients and procedures to get a better product; (2) for comparative evaluation with other recipes; and (3) for estimating the popularity, acceptability, or marketability of the food product. Thus, this testing may be used in various ways, and the data obtained may prove to be extremely valuable.

1	2	3	4	5	6	7
Ingredients	Original Recipe Amounts	Original Recipe (oz)	Original Recipe (oz × factor)	New Recipe in Weight (oz)	New Recipe, Rounded Weight and Measure	Remarks

Figure 9-2.   An example of a recipe adjustment form.

2. Prepare the recipe at least three additional times to ensure reproducibility of the desired results. Do popularity tests, cost estimates, and yield tests each time. It is advisable to conduct consumer taste tests at this point. If possible, let the recipe be prepared and tested by similar units, such as franchise stores with similar equipment, and assess the results.
3. If positive results are obtained from the above tests and the product quality and quantity are acceptable, the recipe is standardized and is ready for use.
4. Make a recipe card, or enter into the computer, clearly outlining the ingredients, procedures, and other information as shown in Figure 9.3.

Dessert: Pie	**Strawberry Chiffon Pie**			Portion: 8″/10″ pie
Ingredients	7 pies	14 pies	20 pies	Directions
Gelatin	2 oz (½ c)	4 oz (1 c)	6 oz (1½ c)	Soften gelatin in cool water
Water, cool	⅓ qt	⅔ qt	1 qt	
Strawberr-ies, frozen	6 lb 8 oz	13 lb	19 lb 8 oz	Drain berries. Heat one half of juice. Dissolve gelatin in hot juice. Add remainder of juice, and salt. Add berries and cool until partially congealed
Salt	⅓ tb	⅔ tb	1 tb	
Orange juice, frozen, un-diluted	2 oz	4 oz	6 oz	
Egg whites	½ qt	1 qt	1½ qt	Beat until stiff, not dry. Fold into fruit mixture
Sugar	11 oz (1⅓ c)	1 lb 6 oz (2⅔ c)	2 lb (4 c)	
Cream, whipping	⅔ qt	1⅓ qt	2 qt	Fold whipping cream into mixture slightly. Complete folding by hand with wire whip (fold occasionally while dipping into pie shell to prevent streaking)
Pie shells, baked	7	14	20	Measure approx. 1 qt in each pie shell. Let stand until set. Garnish with sweetened whipped cream
Cream, whipping	⅔ qt	1⅓ qt	2 qt	
Sugar	3 tb	6 tb	9 tb	
Vanilla	2 tsp	1⅓ tb	2 tb	

Figure 9-3. An example of a recipe card.

Recipe File

A file of all standardized recipes should be maintained, categorized into entrées, vegetables, soups, desserts, etc. This file should be updated frequently. It is advisable to add costs to each recipe based on the number of servings.

PRINCIPLES OF MEAT COOKERY

In most foodservice operations, meats represent the most important menu item. In fact, the success of many franchise and chain restaurants is based on the meat items on the menu. Meat is also one of the most expensive, if not the most expensive item on the menu. Meats also contribute significantly to the nutrient content of meals. Meat is complete protein and provides most of the essential amino acids needed in human nutrition. It also supplies such micronutrients as iron, phosphorus, potassium, sodium, and magnesium, as well as B vitamins. Adequate care and selection of the best preparation methods are necessary to maintain the flavor, tenderness, color, and palatability of meat dishes.

In order to obtain the best possible products, it is necessary to understand the chemistry of meats. Meats are approximately 75% water. The muscle fibers are in the form of bundles and form the structural units of lean tissue. Connective tissues surround the muscle fibers and help to support the muscle structure. There are primarily two types of connective tissue, collagen and elastin; both are important in cooking. Collagen, which is yellowish-white in color, gelatinizes in the presence of moisture and heat and softens, thus adding to the tenderness and flavor of the meat. In contrast to collagen, elastin is yellow and is very tough; it is not affected by heat and cannot be softened easily. Various types of tenderization methods, primarily mechanical, are often needed to break and soften these tissues. The amount and distribution of these connective tissues vary with the age of the animal.

Fat is present in meats at various points, including the exterior portions, within the abdominal cavity as rolls of fat, between muscles, and within cells. As with connective tissue, the fat content is dependent on the age of the animal and the type of diet that it was fed. To a certain extent, the distribution of fat within the muscle is used in the grading of meats. The intermingling of fat and muscle is referred to as **marbling.** An optimum distribution of fat is desirable, since it melts and adds to the flavor of the meat. In addition to fat, moisture content contributes to the juiciness of meat. Thus, it is important that time and temperature be optimum for retention of desirable quantities of fat and moisture. An appropriate cooking method should be selected to enhance the flavor, color, tenderness, and juiciness of meat. Above all, it is the quality of cooked meat when it reaches the consumer that is most important. Thus, service and delivery methods should ensure that all the desirable attributes of meats are intact when they are served.

Shrinkage is a phenomenon observed in meats when they are cooked. Since meat consists mostly of water, the loss of water during cooking causes shrinkage. All meats will shrink to some degree upon any type of cooking; it is the extent of shrinkage that is of prime importance. A variety of factors are responsible for shrinkage. The most important are cooking time, cooking temperature, and cooking method.

Tenderization of meat is achieved by the use of enzymes, salt, and vinegar or by using mechanical means. The substances act on the collagen and help to tenderize the meat. Such enzymes as papain from the raw papaya fruit, bromelin from pineapple, or ficin from figs have a tenderizing effect. These enzymes are sometimes injected into the animal just before slaughter. Commercially available meat tenderizers contain one or more of these enzymes, spices, and such flavor as monosodium glutamate. In larger portions of meat and where hard connective tissues are present, mechanical means such as pounding, grinding, dicing, chopping, cubing, scoring, or beating help tenderize meats by physically breaking and/or loosening the hard connective tissues. Whatever means are used, they must be effective, since the quality of the finished product depends on texture. Marinating with oils, acids, tomato juice, vinegar, lemon juice, and sour cream also help tenderize meats.

Cooking Methods for Meats

The several methods for cooking meats each results in a different type of flavor. These methods are sometimes classified as dry-heat methods (where no water is added while cooking), and moist-heat methods (where meats are cooked by steam or hot liquids). In dry-heat methods, since no additional water is added, surface caramelization or browning occurs, which results in enhanced flavors. Since surface heating is largely unaccompanied by moisture, and since there is not enough moisture to soften the collagen, meats cooked by these methods should either be tender cuts or should be tenderized. In moist-heat methods meats are exposed to temperatures that are not higher than the boiling point of water, which ensures slow cooking; this contributes to flavor development and tenderization. The moist-heat process can be hastened by the use of steam or pressure. When meat is cooked in water, care should be taken to ensure that the nutrients are not lost in the juices coming from the cooked products. The method selected should be based on the type and grade of meat. The most common methods of cooking various types of meats are described below.

Roasting

Roasting is a dry-heat method in which meats are cooked in various types of ovens such as conventional, convection, and microwave. Large roasts are usually cooked by placing the meat with the fat side up in an uncovered pan. Moderate-to-low temperatures and long cooking times are used for roasting in order to develop the flavor. Lower temperatures keep meat shrinkage to a minimum. In foodservice operations, roasting poses scheduling problems unless the operation has more than one shift. Roasting meats in ovens overnight, while convenient, poses various safety problems, such as those caused by improper handling or power failure. If time and temperature are controlled, the product roasted overnight is of a superior quality with well-developed flavors. The optimum temperature for slow roasting will be a setting of 250° to 350° F. Tender meat cuts are preferred for roasting; these would include the less exercised portions of beef and those meats attached to the backbone portion of the carcass. In the case of veal, lamb, and pork, most cuts are suitable for roasting. It is desirable to start with defrosted meat in foodservice operations to ensure the quality of the finished product, although under certain conditions meats may be roasted without thawing.

It should be noted that internal temperatures are the best indicators of **degree of doneness,** rather than oven settings or external characteristics. The oven-temperature settings will depend on the type of oven used, in addition to the type and cut of meat, the preparation time available, and the seasonings used. A constant low temperature is desirable, since the resulting product is evenly done and is more uniform in color when served. The approximate cooking time and temperatures for

Table 9.1

Cooking Times for Beef

Broiling

		Approximate Total Cooking Time	
Cut	*Approximate Thickness*	*Rare (min)*	*Medium (min)*
Rib, top loin, T-bone,	1 in.	15	20
porterhouse,	1½ in.	25	35
tenderloin	2 in.	35	50
Beef sirloin steak	1 in.	20 to 25	30 to 35
	1½ in.	30 to 35	40 to 45
Ground beef patties	1 in. (4 oz)	15	20

Braising and Cooking in Liquid

Cut	*Average weight or thickness*	*Approximate total cooking time (hr)*
Pot roast	4 to 6 lb	3 to 4
Swiss steak	1 to 2½ in.	2 to 3
Short ribs	pieces 2 × 2 × 2 in.	1½ to 2
Corned beef	6 to 8 lb	4 to 6
Beef shank cross-cuts	¾ to 1 lb	2½ to 3½
Beef for stew	1- to 2-in. cubes	2 to 3

Source: National Livestock & Meat Board.

various cuts of meat are given in Tables 9.1 and 9.2. It should be emphasized that roasts will continue to cook even after they are taken out of the oven. Thus roasts should be removed from the oven at an internal temperature that is slightly lower than desired to allow for the few degrees increase after removing.

Roasts should be sliced 15–20 min after removal from the oven, since this "resting" period permits easier slicing. Roasts have their best flavor right from cooking, so there should not be much time between roasting and serving. Slicing should be done across the grain of the muscle, preferably using a mechanical slicer. For the best quality, the size of the slices should be as thin as possible. Portions of meat should be weighed for standard servings. Refrigeration of cooked roasts prior to slicing results in flavor loss. Likewise, reheating reduces the juiciness of roasts and increases toughness. Considerable amounts of juice are lost in slicing, and with the juice go the flavor components and, more importantly, the nutrients. Care should therefore be taken to utilize as much of the meat juice as possible by adding it back to the meat slices or to the gravy.

Broiling

Broiling is a dry-heat method, and the source of energy may be direct or radiant heat from gas flames, charcoal briquettes, or individual electric units. Relatively

Table 9.2

Cooking Times for Roast Beef

Cut	Approx wt of single roast (lb)	Oven temp (°F)	Interior temp (°F) of roast when removed from oven	Min per lb based on one roast	Approx total cooking time (hr)
Rib, roast ready #109	20 to 25	250	130 (rare)	13 to 15	4½ to 5
			140 (medium)	15 to 17	5 to 6
			150 (well)	17 to 19	6 to 6½
Ribeye roll #112 or #112A	4 to 6	350	140 (rare)	18 to 20	1⅓ to 1⅔
			160 (medium)	20 to 22	1½ to 2
			170 (well)	22 to 24	1⅔ to 2¼
Full tenderloin #189 or #190	4 to 6	425	140 (rare)		¾ to 1
Strip loin, boneless #180	10 to 12	325	140 (rare)	10	1½ to 2
Top (inside) round #168	10	300	140 (rare)	18 to 19	3 to 3¼
			150 (medium)	22 to 23	3½ to 4
Top (inside) round #168	15	300	140 (rare)	15	3½ to 4
			150 (medium)	17	4 to 4½

Source: National Livestock & Meat Board.

tender and thicker cuts are the most suitable for broiling. Prefabricated or "portion-controlled" meat cuts are useful in broiling and result in uniform serving sizes. The most tender and expensive cuts are usually prepared by broiling. The thickness of the meat plays an important part in the quality and doneness of the finished product—thinner cuts show excessive shrinkage and thicker cuts result in nonuniform cooking. The grid markings on broiled meats are considered a sign of quality by many foodservice personnel as well as consumers.

In foodservices, broiling is done in special broilers (rotary in some operations) or a salamander. The meats are placed on racks, with the radiant heat approximately 3 in away from the meat. Turning of the meat ensures cooking on both sides. The temperature, as well as the distance from the heat source, determines the time of cooking and the degree of doneness. The temperature of the heat source may be as high as 1800°F (982°C). The preferred temperature range for broiling is between 300° and 350°F (149° and 177°C). The degree of doneness is achieved at an internal temperature of 140°F (60°C) for rare, 160°F (71°C) for medium, and 170°F (76°C) for well done.

Grilling or Griddling

Grilling is a dry-heat method primarily used for cooking steaks or hamburgers. The fat in the meat itself is enough for cooking. Fat and water are not added, although seasonings may be used. Once the meat is browned on one side, it is turned for cooking on the other side. In some griddles or grills, special provision is made for fat drainage. The cooking temperatures vary, depending on the ambient temperatures, but normally they range from 325° to 350°F (163° to 177°C). The time and temperature of cooking are also dependent on the thickness of the meat.

Braising

In braising, meats are browned in a small quantity of fat. The pan is covered tightly after browning, and the cooking is continued at a low temperature. Braising may be done in the oven, a steam-jacketed kettle, a tilting fry pan, or over the range. The doneness of the meat depends on the internal temperature required for that particular type of meat and may range from 165° to 185°F (74° to 85°C).

Stewing

Stewing or boiling is done by cooking meat in the presence of moisture. Vegetable or cereals may be added to meat for stewing and special recipes may be used. The meat may or may not be browned before stewing. The flavor of the stewed meat is enhanced by the cooking juices. Stewing requires cooking meat at a simmering temperature until it is tender. Steam-jacketed kettles or floor-mounted kettles may be used.

Simmering

Simmering involves the slow cooking of meats in liquid for a long period of time. It is a method that is especially useful for less tender cuts of meats that require longer cooking times for tenderization. The advantage of simmering is that meats can be cooked longer without shrinkage.

SOUP PREPARATION

Soups, when appropriately prepared and served, provide an exciting prelude to a pleasant dining experience. The fragrance, color, serving temperature, consistency, and taste stimulate the appetite. Many foodservice operations are famous for their soups and appetizers. Soups can be served either at piping hot or refreshingly cold temperatures. However, slight variations in temperature may prove to have an adverse effect on the quality of a soup. Thus, although it is not hard to prepare soup, this menu item requires extremely well-balanced spices, good cooking judgment, and careful handling. It is not surprising, therefore, that most foodservice operations have their own way of preparing soups.

Soups are made from basic stocks that can be prepared in numerous ways. A **stock** is a strained and concentrated extract derived by simmering bones, meats, fish, poultry, vegetables, and seasonings in a large quantity of water. In many foodservices, a stock pot is left on the range in which ingredients continuously simmer to produce stock for soups. Slow cooking extracts the flavors as well as gelatinous substances to produce a rich, flavorful base. Several flavor variations can be made by changing the ingredients in the stock. However, proper ingredients, adequate preparation, and care are necessary to produce a good stock for a uniform quality soup. Normally, bones and pieces of meat left over from other items are used in stocks. With portion-controlled meat purchasing, it is difficult to accumulate all ingredients needed for stock and, therefore, there is an increase in the use of commercially prepared soup bases. Several types of bases are available for use in different products. Nevertheless, "homemade" stocks still provide the richest flavor and therefore are highly preferred.

VEGETABLE AND FRUIT COOKERY

In cooking vegetables and fruits, special care and attention are needed to preserve color, texture, flavor, and nutrients. The acidity or alkalinity of the liquid in which they are cooked also has an effect on their organoleptic properties. Most vegetables and fruits contain organic acids which add to the acidity of the media in which they are cooked. Color is affected by the pH of the media. For example, the green color in fruits and vegetables is due to the presence of the green pigment, chlorophyll, which changes color in an acid medium to a dull or olive green. On the other hand, an alkaline cooking medium may intensify the green color. The presence of slight alkalinity may be desirable to enrich the color, a phenomenon that is observed on blanching of vegetables. However, an alkaline cooking medium may have an undesirable effect on the texture of the vegetables as well as a destructive effect on such vitamins as thiamin and ascorbic acid. Cooking times for vegetables and fruits are important. In order to retain their nutrients, vegetables should be cooked for the minimum time.

The red color of vegetables and fruits is commonly due to the presence of the pigment anthocyanin. This pigment is also affected by the pH of the cooking medium. Anthocyanins become bluish-red in acid media and blue-green in alkaline media. Both these colors are undesirable. Thus, care is needed when cooking red cabbage, beets, or similar vegetables. The yellow color of the fruits and vegetables is due to the presence of carotenoid pigments. Corn, carrots, and sweet potatoes contain carotenoids, which are also precursors of vitamin A. These pigments are fairly stable and are not normally affected by the presence of acid or alkali. The flavonoid pigments provide color to white cabbage, onions, and potatoes. They are not affected by the acid medium but generally turn yellow in the presence of alkaline medium.

Care should be taken in cooking all vegetables and fruits to preserve their organoleptic and nutritive properties.

Steaming

Steaming is the most common, as well as the most desirable method for cooking most fruits and vegetables. The texture, color, flavor, and nutrients of fruits and vegetables are better preserved when they are steamed. Steam-jacketed kettles or steamers may be used. Perforated pans that allow the steam to circulate around the food product are useful.

Boiling

Boiling is the cooking of fruits and vegetables in water. The main disadvantage of boiling is a loss of nutrients, particularly if the water left after cooking is not used. Care should be taken to see that these foods are boiled in the minimum amount of water as well as at low temperatures. High boiling temperatures may break up the product. Fruits and vegetables may be dipped in hot water in a steam-jacketed kettle attached with the necessary strainers. Recipes used for boiling fruits may require that the fruits be dipped into syrup or sugar containing water. As seen in canning, the higher the sugar content of the syrup, the less likely it is that the fruits will break up.

Baking

The potato is the most common vegetable to be baked in foodservice operations. Other foods may be baked with equal success. Commonly baked products include apples, tomatoes, green peppers, onions, eggplant, and squash. The foods most suitable for baking are those that are moist. Upon heating, this moisture helps to soften the cellulose in the food. Baking may also produce a desirable crust on the outside due to the carmelization of sugars. Baking temperatures vary and may range from 350° to 450°F (177° to 232°C), depending on the type of product.

Sautéing and Braising

Vegetables are often cooked by sautéing, as for example, breakfast potatoes. Celery, onions, cabbage, and lettuce are often braised. For braising, the vegetables are sautéed in a small amount of fat and then quick-stirred. Vegetables can also be cooked with thickening agents or sauces until tender.

Broiling

Broiling is not the most common method of cooking fruits and vegetables, since a lot of moisture is lost at high temperatures, and the vegetables become charred. Only very tender and moist products broil easily. Bell peppers, tomatoes, and onions are the vegetables most commonly broiled.

Frying

Vegetables can be deep fried or stir fried. Deep frying provides a crisp, desirable texture, as evidenced in french fries. It also results in the carmelization of sugar to provide a desirable crust. Vegetable strips may also be dipped in batters before frying. Many vegetables may be parboiled before deep frying. Vegetables suited for frying include eggplant, onions, potatoes, mushrooms, zucchini, and carrots.

CEREALS AND CEREAL-PRODUCT COOKERY

Most cereal products are cooked by steaming or boiling, which causes starch to gelatinize. Rice can be cooked in a steamer with twice the volume of water. Salt, water, and a little oil may also be added. Macaroni products or pasta are dropped into boiling water and stirred until they are tender.

BAKED GOODS AND DESSERTS

Baked goods and desserts are important in any type of foodservice operation. Only the main principles involved in preparing bakery products and desserts will be discussed here. The principal ingredients used in baking include the following:

Flour.   Although many types of flour are used in baking, wheat flour either alone or in different blends is the usual choice. The protein in the flour responsible for the baked flavor is **gluten,** which absorbs moisture and forms an elastic, strong, and spongy mass—the batter or dough. Gluten has the unique property of stretching to a considerable degree, which is facilitated by the process of kneading. The network of gluten bands formed by stretching becomes firm on baking. Gluten may be developed to form strong or weak bands. Bread, or hard-wheat, flour forms strong structures, whereas pastry, or soft-wheat, flour forms delicate structures. Pastry flour is also called "weak" flour. Thus, the flour used for baking should be selected on the basis of its intended use. All-purpose flour is a blend of 20% soft wheat flour and 80% bread flour.

Shortening.   One of the main requirements of baking is to prevent the sticking of gluten particles, thereby producing the desired tenderness. Hydrogenated fats, oils, butter, and lard are used as shortening in baking. Due to the increased emphasis on cholesterol, many foodservice operations are using vegetable shortenings only.

Sugar.   In addition to sweetening the product, sugars also help to tenderize foods. Different types of sugars are used in baking. Powdered sugars, which are ground sugars to which a small amount of cornstarch is added to prevent clumping, are used for dusting, coating, and icing different types of baked products. Different degrees of grind are indicated by an "X" on the package—for example, 10X is finer than 4X powdered sugar. Regular coarse sugar can be used for coating items such as doughnuts and candies, while finer sugars are used to make cakes, meringues, and desserts that require smooth texture. Brown sugars are less refined than white sugars, and are used in baked products for their special flavor.

Leavening Agents.   Leavening agents provide texture and volume to baked products. **Leavening** must be added carefully and in exact proportions for desired results. Air, incorporated into a product when eggs are whipped to a foam, leavens a batter and when heated swells, causing the products to rise and develop a fine texture. Steam is also used as an automatic leavening agent. For some products a chemical leavening agent, such as baking powder or soda, is added. Cream of tartar is used with soda to form a single-acting baking powder. Several types of baking powder are currently available on the market. Chemical leavening agents release carbon dioxide, which is responsible for the leavening action. Heat also contributes to the leavening action.

Yeast.   Yeast is used for creating carbon dioxide gas and alcohol in some yeast baked products. Yeast growth is at an optimum level at 78° to 90°F (25.5° to 32°C). Yeast is killed at about 140°F (60°C). Yeast is added to warm water before being stirred with other ingredients.

Eggs.   Eggs are used in many bakery products and desserts to enhance the baking qualities as well as to provide flavor, color, volume, tenderness, and nutritional value. They also act as a binding ingredient in batters and doughs.

Depending on the type of baked product—yeast bread, muffins, or breads— ingredients are mixed using large blenders and mixers set at different speeds for specific periods of time. Yeast doughs are allowed to ferment. Kneading and mixing of the dough are done by mechanical mixers. The final conditioning of the bread before baking is called **proofing.** This procedure results in a soft delicate product of increased volume. Most products are baked at temperatures ranging from 375° to 450°F (190° to 232°C). For some bakery products, immediate cooling is required.

Custards are baked desserts prepared from liquids that are thickened with eggs. Souffles are desserts thickened and leavened by eggs and baked at lower temperatures than other baked items. Meringues are made using egg whites and sugar with cream of tartar; they are often used for topping pies and desserts. Pies and pastries are baked from various kinds of flour, shortening, salt, and water. The amount of fat, the blending procedure, and the incorporation of shortening into flour result in the formation of a flaky crust. Preparation methods for different baked products vary, although the principles behind the use of certain ingredients are the same.

SALADS AND SALAD DRESSING PREPARATION

Salads are dishes variously composed of fruits, vegetables, eggs, and meats, usually topped with salad dressings and/or garnishes, often served cold and placed on an underliner. Salads may thus consist of a base, body, garnishes, and dressings. A base, also referred to as underlining garnish, usually consists of salad greens and is used to improve the appearance of the salad and to prevent it from having a bare look. The base also provides for a good contrast in color, as, for example, a green base under a red tomato aspic salad. Bases are seldom consumed. Ingredients that make up the salad, such as lettuce, raw vegetables, fruits, gelatins, and eggs, are referred to as the body of the salad. Garnishes are mainly added for eye appeal and may be composed of a variety of items such as nuts, croutons, meats, fish, cheese, fruits, vegetables, parsley, and condiments. Dressings may be of different colors and textures. They are primarily added for flavor and to help keep the salad fresh, crisp, and juicy. Some of the most popular salad dressings are Thousand Island, French, and Russian.

Recent trends in foodservices are toward more salad use, possibly because salads are becoming popular in nutrition-conscious segments of the population. From the foodservice point of view, salads have both advantages and disadvantages.

Advantages	Disadvantages
They are relatively easy to make.	Maintaining quality is difficult, since most salads need fresh vegetables.
They can prove to be cost efficient if properly planned.	Purchasing salad ingredients needs more than the usual attention, since varietal characteristics and grading changes have to be considered.
They can be made at the last minute or placed on salad bars.	
They provide flexibility in the use of ingredients.	Salads are labor-intensive to prepare, since there are several items, most of which require washing, coring, and cutting. Also, some require careful arrangement on serving plates, which requires skill and labor.
They improve the appearance of other menu items by providing color.	
They add different textures to foods.	
They contribute to the nutrient value of meals.	

Advantages	*Disadvantages*
	Salads are difficult to keep for extended periods of time without sacrificing quality.
	Salads with certain ingredients—eggs, for example—pose a food safety problem.
	Salads composed of fresh fruits and vegetables are relatively expensive. Their ingredients may have fluctuating prices.

Types of Salads

The primary types of salads, based upon their use on the menu, are described below.

Appetizer

Appetizer salads, as their name indicates, are served before meals to stimulate the appetite. They are served in small quantities and are often chilled. Dressings and other ingredients are carefully selected so as to whet the appetite. These salads are often premade tossed, chilled, and/or arranged salads. An example of an appetizer salad would be the shrimp cocktail served in many restaurants and on special occasions. Sometimes small quantities of tossed salad are used as appetizers.

Side-Dish

Side-dish salads are also known as accompaniment salads and may be served as a part of the meal to supplement a main-dish item, normally meat. They should be carefully selected to supplement the flavor, texture, form, color, and overall appearance of the main dish. A contrast in temperature is desirable in accompaniment salads. Side-dish salads are served in larger portions than appetizer salads but smaller than main-dish salads. Normally, vegetables, fruits, and cottage cheese are used. As a general rule, a heavy main course should be accompanied by a light salad and conversely. For example, meat items such as beef and chicken with gravy should be accompanied by light salads. On the other hand, potato, macaroni, and bean salads should accompany light items.

Main Dish

Main-dish salads are intended to be the major part of the meal and are served in relatively large quantities; they are often chosen for lunchtime service. Since this type of salad is the main entrée, it needs careful planning. The nutritive value, as well as the cost, should be considered. Meats and fish make good additions to these salads. Cooked items such as beans, rice, macaroni, and potatoes also can be used. Chef salads, which often are sold as specialty items of a foodservice, contain special ingredients or dressings with sardines, roast beef, or cooked chicken added to make the salad hearty. Type A salads are made with ingredients that meet the minimum nutrition requirements of Type A school lunches. Unique items and their combinations, such as pineapple, avocados, raisins, dates, tuna fish, crabmeat, olives, and mint, appeal to consumers. Arrangement on an attractive serving plate helps make salads appetizing. For example, a glass bowl with julienne strips of carrot, cheese, and meats evenly spread on tossed salad with sardines, olives, boiled eggs, and cherries makes an attractive presentation. Dressings are important in providing flavor, and various types should be made available.

Custom-Made, or Salad-Bar

Custom salads are prepared by consumers using the ingredients offered. Many types of vegetables and fruits can be used. Normally lettuce and other greens are cut and placed as the body of the salad. Various types of salad dressings are available. Garnishes are also provided; selections can include onions, tomatoes, olives, croutons, nuts, seeds, raisins, meats, fish, eggs, pickles, garbanzo beans, cheese, and dried meats. Cold plates and serving utensils are provided for each salad item. Customers enjoy the freedom of choice in designing their own salads. There is a growing demand for salad bars, which are popular in restaurants as well as some franchise chains. At some places, the cost of the salads is determined by weight.

Dessert

Salads can also be used as desserts, and may range in sweetness and caloric content. Light gelatin salads with molded fruits are often preferred for their low-caloric content, particularly when heavy items are included as entrées. Mixed-fruit salads are popular; often fresh fruits are used in these salads. Toppings normally include cream, cherries, nuts, or other fruits. Sweet garnishings or dressings go well with these salads, and syrups or caramelized liquid sugars can be mixed with the fruits used. These salads are normally offered in small-size servings. Dessert salads may also be used as snacks.

Salad Greens

Salad greens are used as the base or as underliners for most salads. Technological advancements in vacuum cooking, dehydrofreezing, rapid transportation, growing methods, and new varieties have made most types of salad greens readily available. Texture, color, and flavor are provided by salad greens. Their freshness is essential to the overall characteristics of salads. It is important to prevent excessive moisture loss from salad greens; wet cloth or paper is often used to keep them moist. Although lettuce is the most commonly used salad green, a number of other available greens are also described below.

Iceberg Lettuce

Also called head lettuce, iceberg is the most often used lettuce in salads. It has a round, firm head with tightly packed bright-green to very pale leaves, which are curly and overlap slightly. It makes a crisp and chunky salad when shredded, cubed, sliced, or quartered. Its juiciness and sweetness add to the flavor of a salad. It is often used as a base ingredient in mixed salads or at salad bars. Variety can be introduced by serving it in different shapes instead of simply tearing leaves into bite-sized pieces. It can be used as lettuce cups, since leaves when gently separated from the head make versatile cups or underliners for salads. Lettuce wedges can be used with special dressings, such as Thousand Island or parslied vinaigrette. It can be cut into thin slices or rafts and used as the base for salads or on sandwiches. Chunks or shreds may be used in tossed salads and many other types.

Romaine

Romaine, also known as cos lettuce, has large, elongated, firm, upright leaves arranged in a cylindrical head. The leaves have a distinctive nutty flavor that is sharper than iceberg lettuce, are crispy, succulent, and slightly pungent. It combines well with other vegetables such as tomatoes and avocados, and the flavor is enhanced by special dressings.

Bibb Lettuce

Bibb lettuce has deep, rich, green and yellow leaves that are soft and velvety. The leaves are arranged like small rosettes which are whitish-green toward the core. It has a distinct delicate, buttery flavor and contributes a sweet texture to a salad.

Leaf Lettuce

Leaf lettuce has intensely green leaves loosely branching off from its stalk. The leaves, which are clustered or pressed together, do not form heads. Large, leafy bunches have flat or curly leaves that are fragile and tender. Leaf lettuce provides a delicate sweet flavor and crisp texture in tossed salads as well as in undergarnishes for molded or cooked salads.

Boston Lettuce

Boston lettuce has a round soft head with medium-sized light-green outer leaves and light-yellow inner leaves. The leaves are tender and velvety. It is very perishable and is not as sweet and tender as other butterhead varieties.

Curly Endive

Endive has a crown of narrow ragged-edge leaves that curl at the ends and have large ribs. Its outer leaves are darkish green in color and are bitter compared to the inner leaves, which are sharp and tangy. The head is yellowish-white with a mild taste compared to the outer leaves. It has a slight prickly texture and bitter flavor, which blends very well with some of the blander salad greens.

Escarole

Escarole is a variety of endive with broader leaves that do not curl at the tips. The leaves are deep green at the edges and pale yellow at the heart. Not as bitter in flavor as endive, it is usually used in tossed salads.

Spinach

Spinach, with its tender, round, and crisp leaves, contributes a unique taste to salads. Its deep-green leaves provide an attractive color contrast. It can be used alone or in tossed salads, where it blends well with a wide variety of dressings.

Watercress

Watercress is a small, dark-green plant with long stems and thick round leaves with a pungent flavor. The flavor is distinctive and and peppery. It can be used in tossed salads or as an undergarnish.

Other Greens

Mustard, kale, dandelion, collard, and turnip greens can also be used in salads.
Some vegetables and fruits that can be added to salads are given in the following lists.

Vegetables

Alfalfa sprouts	Cauliflower	Peppers
Artichokes	Celery	Potatoes
Asparagus	Corn	Radishes
Bean sprouts	Cucumbers	Shallots
Beans, green	Garbanzo beans	Squash
Beans, lima	Garlic	Sunflower seeds
Beets	Mushrooms	Tomatoes
Broccoli	Olives	Turnips
Brussels sprouts	Onions	Water chestnuts
Cabbage	Parsley	
Carrots	Peas	

Fruits

Apples	Cranberries	Kumquats
Apricots	Dates	Lemons
Avocados	Figs	Limes
Bananas	Grapefruit	Melons, cantaloupe
Cherries	Grapes	Melons, honeydew

Fruits

Nectarines	Persimmons	Raspberries
Nuts	Pineapples	Strawberries
Oranges	Pomegranates	Tangerines
Peaches	Prunes	Watermelon
Pears	Raisins	

Basic Principles of Salad Preparation

Although most salads should be assembled as close to serving time as possible, salad greens can be prepared several hours ahead. The quality of the salad greens can be lost very quickly, since they are highly perishable items. Exposure to air, water, heat, and improper handling can cause them to deteriorate. Even heat from human hands has an adverse effect on their quality. The acidity of certain fruits added as garnish may also have undesirable effects. Stainless steel equipment is needed for cutting, storage, and handling of salads. Also, strong vegetables — onions, for example — should be kept and handled separately to prevent the intermingling of odors.

Salad preparation requires a lot of creativity, since contrasts in color, texture, form, and flavor are needed. Salads can be made by using a number of ingredients to provide for the creation of a unique salad specialty or an original food creation. A combination of eye appeal, arrangement, flavor, texture, consistency, dressings, and variety can provide attractive salad dishes. Many types of salads can be included on a menu and can be served in several ways — as appetizers, main dishes, desserts, or meal accompaniments. Leftover vegetable salads can be reused in soups and/or vegetables.

Such fruits as apples, bananas, and peaches when used as garnishes darken on exposure to air due to oxidation. Care should be taken to see that they are prepared as close to serving time as possible and that they are dipped in a slightly acidic solution, such as lemon juice, to avoid discoloration.

Salads should be prepared away from the heated areas of the kitchen, since the heat may cause the wilting of fragile leaves. All serving equipment should be properly cleaned, since traces of dressings and oils impart a rancid odor on deterioration.

Once salads are prepared, they should either be refrigerated or kept moist in order to preserve their crispness. Salad dressings should be added as close to serving time as possible, since dressing may result in wilting of the greens. Also, the dressing may break and look unattractive if added either too heavily or too soon in advance of serving time. Care should be taken in handling salads containing highly perishable items, particularly when cooked and raw ingredients are in contact with each other, as in the case of tuna salad, egg salad, and roast beef salad.

All wilted, discolored, or spoiled leaves should be removed prior to cutting the salad greens. In most varieties, coring can be done by cutting around the core edge with a paring knife. It is preferable to rinse greens in cold running water that has a temperature between 40° and 70° F (4.5° and 21° C). Leaves should be thoroughly washed to remove any dirt or other particles. Where heads are to be used intact, water should be allowed to run gently into the core and all leaves washed thoroughly with running water. After washing, the greens should be placed on a colander for water drainage. Commercially available antioxidants may be used by dissolving the specified quantity in water to preserve the crispness and to enhance the appearance. It is advisable not to leave the greens in water for an extended period of time in order to preserve their nutrients. Excessive moisture also speeds the spoilage process. It is preferable to cover the greens with a damp towel or to place them in a clear plastic bag and store them in a refrigerator for crisping.

Salad Arrangement

Salad arrangement plays an important role in attractiveness. An ample amount of greens with good height is very appealing. Large chunks of lettuce will help to increase the height and the size of a salad. Garnishes and seasonings add to the appeal of the salad, while the color of the dressing adds to its richness. The arrangement should not mask the main ingredients or principal contents of the salad. It should also be remembered that the crispness of a salad is lost if salad greens are cut into very small pieces. Herbs and spices may be added to enrich flavor. Attractive garnishes can be made from raw vegetables; some of these are radish roses, green pepper rings, carrot curls, cucumber slices, mini corns, mint sprigs, and parsley toppings. These garnishes, which are simple to make after a certain amount of practice, can be preprepared and stored. Other garnishes can be created from such leftovers as croutons, toasted slivered almonds, colored coconut, sliced hard-boiled eggs, and sliced pieces of pomegranate. A contrast in color and flavor can be easily provided by creative selection from a variety of foods.

Gelatin Salads

Many attractive dessert salads are made by using a gelatin base. Gelatin, which is a tasteless and odorless protein, is usually extracted from bones, hides, skins, connective tissues, and other cartilagineous substances. It acts as a thickener for cold liquids and is practically unaffected by the acids or alkalis in foods. It should be noted that because of certain enzymes in raw pineapple, figs, and papaya, these fruits cannot be used in the raw state in gelatin salads. These enzymes do not allow the gelatin to gel because they break down the proteinaceous gelatin structure. Although it is very easy to form gels with gelatin, it requires careful control of the time, temperature, and ingredients. The addition of sugars and milk increases the firmness of gels, while the addition of acids or certain solids weakens the gel structure. Large quantities of expensive materials can be lost if gels are not formed because of careless preparation. Various types of flavored and unflavored gelatins are available. In general, plain gelatins must be hydrated or softened in cold water before they are added to hot liquids. Gelatins must be properly softened and dissolved to assure a uniform gel structure. Many new workers or students will need a lot of practice in this crucial step to reduce the chances of failure. Gelatin structures once formed are tough enough to resist breakage in normal blending operations. In hot weather, it may be desirable to increase the proportion of gelatin in salads. When gelatin is completely dissolved in the final liquid, it should be chilled to a consistency similar to that of a heavy syrup and then used for addition of fruits or for other decorative purposes. It should be syrupy enough to hold any suspended fruits or ingredients.

Decorative gelatin molds can be made by pouring syrupy gelatin over prearranged foods on the bottom of the mold. Several layers can be formed in this manner. Interesting salads may be made by creatively using various types of molds to provide interesting shapes and layered ingredients. Endless combinations of gelatins and other foods can be produced by using "swimmers" and "sinkers." Sinkers include such items as oranges, candied fruits, and grapes. Swimmers include fresh fruits, bananas, and nuts. Gelatins can also be made into cubes, flakes, foams, multilayers, aspics, mousses, creams, charlottes, and chiffons.

Gelatin salads once prepared should be allowed to set for approximately 24 hours for best results. Firmness develops after chilled storage. It should be noted that the use of larger quantities of gelatin than required may result in tough gels. Also, the thicker the gel, the more easily it will break. Molded gels should be carefully removed from their containers. Once well set, they can be removed by immersing the mold in hot water for a short time and inverting it. Hot, wet towels may be used instead of immersion in hot water. Gelatin molds should be refrigerated, and special care should be taken with salads containing such perishable items as eggs or fish. Freezing the salads will result in a breakdown of the gelatin structure. Gelatin salads should be served as soon as possible.

Gelatin salads provide versatility, attractiveness, and the opportunity for creative design. In some restaurants, huge gelatin salads are used for decorative purposes and as centerpieces on buffet tables.

Salad Dressings

Salad dressings are sauces that are specially blended to provide flavorful combinations to complement and season foods to which they are added. They enhance the flavor as well as improve the overall appearance of salads. Most salad dressings are emulsions, primarily of oil and vinegar, which are made by combining two immiscible liquids with the aid of an emulsifying agent. For example, in mayonnaise, eggs act as an emulsifying agent by coating the fat droplets and making them immiscible to form an emulsion of the oil and vinegar. The preparation of salad dressings requires careful and slow blending of the immiscible liquids. Emulsions can be temporary or permanent. Temporary emulsions break down after a certain amount of time. Vinegars in emulsions can be replaced by other acid ingredients, such as lemon or fruit juices. Bland oils—corn oil, cottonseed oil, safflower oil, and soybean oil, for example—are used to make dressings. In order to retard rancidity, antioxidants (BHA, butylated hydroxyanisole; BHT, butylated hydroxytoluene; and EDTA, ethylenediaminetetra acetic acid) are added. Although there are several types of dressings, most of them can be classified on the basis of their method of preparation. The four basic types of dressings are described below.

French Dressing

French dressings are temporary or unstable emulsions made of fixed proportion of oil and acid, blended together with different types of seasonings such as paprika, mustard, garlic, sugar, and salt. Salt and seasonings when blended form a temporary emulsion with oil and water. Upon storage the emulsions break down but can be easily reformed by blending. The taste of these dressings varies depending on the proportion of oil and acidic ingredients. Several seasonings can be added to provide special flavors.

Mayonnaise

Mayonnaise is the base for a number of dressings and sauces such as Thousand Island dressing, Russian dressing, and tartar sauce. It is prepared by blending oil, water, egg yolks, and/or whole eggs. Mayonnaise forms a permanent emulsion that does not break down easily. Egg acts as an emulsifier and helps in the formation of stable emulsions. Sometimes gelatin or cooked starch is also used as an emulsifying agent, although these are not as effective as eggs. Mayonnaise is not easy to prepare; proper methods, ingredients, and practice are needed to make a good dressing.

Cooked, or Boiled, Dressings

Cooked dressings are oil-vinegar emulsions that contain much less oil than mayonnaise and are thickened by starch and egg yolk. A starch paste—made from flour, cornstarch, or other thickeners—is added as a thickening agent. Since these thickeners have a tendency to become lumpy, care should be taken to see that they do not coagulate or get scorched while cooking. Thick dressings may be diluted by adding whipping cream or mixing with other dressing ingredients. An evenly blended, smooth, and uniformly seasoned dressing is desirable.

Cream Dressings

Cream dressings contain sour cream, cream cheese, or whipped sweet cream. They are seasoned with vinegar and other ingredients. Several variations are made possible by adding different types of spices and condiments.

PRODUCTION SHEETS

Production sheets should be prepared for items under each food category. Examples of these forms—Summary Requisition Sheet (Figure 9.4), Production Work Schedule (Figure 9.5), Consumption Sheet (Figure 9.6), and Leftover Utilization Plan (Figure 9.7)—are presented on the following pages. These should be used as guidelines in preparing such forms for individual foodservice operations.

Manager: _____

Meal: _____

Date Needed: _____

Meat, Fish, and Poultry			Eggs and Dairy Products			Canned Foods			Fresh Produce		
Type	Amt.	Remarks	Type	Amt.	Remarks	Type	Amt.	Remarks	Type	Amt.	Remarks

Frozen Foods			Seasonings and Spices			Miscellaneous		
Type	Amt.	Remarks	Type	Amt.	Remarks	Type	Amt.	Remarks

Figure 9-4. An example of a summary requisition sheet.

Work sheet for: _____   Date: _____

Article	Amount and size	Time	Job and Special Directions

Figure 9-5. An example of a production worksheet.

257

Menu Items	Amount Prepared	Amount Left Over	Total Cost	Cost Per Serving	Credit Allowed	Adjusted Cost
Date: _____				No. of Guests: _____		
Function: _____				No. of Staff: _____		
Manager: _____						

Menu Items	Amount Prepared	Amount Left Over	Total Cost	Cost Per Serving	Credit Allowed	Adjusted Cost
APPETIZERS						
ENTRÉES						
SALADS & DRESSINGS						
BREADS						
BUTTER						
DESSERTS						
BEVERAGES						
SUGAR						
CREAM						
LEMONS						
MISCELLANEOUS						

Total cost of production: $ _____
Total credit allowances: $ _____
Total adjusted cost: $ _____
Labor cost: $ _____
Food and labor costs: $ _____

Figure 9-6. An example of a consumption sheet.

| Manager: _____ | | | | Date: _____ | |
| Meal: _____ | | | | | |

Product	Number of Servings	If to Be Held and Served at Next Meal, Indicate Whether It Is to Be		If Sold to Another Unit, Indicate to Whom Product Was Given	Major Ingredients
		Refrigerated	Frozen		

Figure 9-7.   An example of a leftover utilization plan.

SUMMARY

This chapter primarily deals with the principles of quantity food production. To start with, the significance of standardized recipes and methods of standardization are described. Principles involved when preparing large quantities of meat items, soups, vegetables and fruits, cereals and cereal products, desserts and bakery products, and salads are outlined in detail. Different methods available for the production of these products are discussed in detail.

REVIEW QUESTIONS

What are the advantages of standardized recipes? Discuss, giving examples.
What is tenderization? How can meats be tenderized?
What are the major differences between roasting and broiling?

From the management point of view, what are some of the disadvantages and advantages of including salads on the menu?

What type of information should be included in the production sheets?

ASSIGNMENTS

List any three quick service restaurants and describe the most common method used in preparing meat items. Contact the manager to obtain further information.

Examine a recipe from a book or a magazine and show how you would multiply it at least ten times. Outline all steps needed for this exercise.

Observe the preparation of one meat item, one vegetable item, one baked product, and a salad in any foodservice kitchen. Describe the methods used and principles of cooking involved.

Make a list of creative food items that can be added to a salad bar. These items should be new and not mentioned in the chapter.

Collect copies of records or blank forms used in the production unit of a foodservice operation and comment on the extent of their usefulness in the management of foodservice operations.

SUGGESTED READINGS

Knight, J. B., and Kotschevar, L. H. 1979. *Quantity Food Production, Planning, and Management.* Van Nostrand Reinhold Co., New York, NY.

Powers, J. M. 1979. *Basics of Quantity Food Production.* John Wiley & Sons, New York, NY.

Shugart, G., and Molt, M. 1989. *Food For Fifty.* 8th edition. Macmillan Publishing Co., New York, NY.

Spears, M. C., and Vaden, A. G. 1985. *Foodservice Organizations: A Managerial and Systems Approach.* John Wiley & Sons, New York, NY.

West, B. B. and Wood, L. 1988. *Foodservice in Institutions.* 6th edition. Macmillan Publishing Co., New York, NY.

Page 262, 263

CHAPTER 10

DELIVERY AND SERVICE OF FOOD

KEY CONCEPTS AND TERMS

portion control
taste panel
centralized service
decentralized service
commissary system
satellite system
cook-chill system
cook-freeze system
cover

Developing technology has made several ways of delivering food to the consumer available. Employing the systems approach that has been followed in this textbook, it is now up to management to see that the food, which has gone from raw through various preparation stages, reaches consumers in the most efficient and appealing manner. The success of a foodservice operation is focused on the service subsystem. Before the food reaches the consumer, several aspects should be checked in the food production area. One aspect is **portion control,** which is extremely important, since even a fraction over serving size can have a cumulative effect. From the economic and psychological point of view, consumers feel they are cheated if unequal portions are served. Effective portion control is also essential because of increasing food costs. Several effective methods for portion control are available for use in any type of foodservice operation.

PORTION CONTROL METHODS

Standardized recipes require effective portion control. The dependable method to use when measuring portions is to serve food using standard utensils such as ladles, scoops, and other equipment. The most commonly used portion control devices are described below:

Standard-sized pans permit portions to be cut or served as needed. Cake pans with specified number of pieces or loaf pans with specified number of portions should be used.

Ladles that are labeled in ounces may be used for serving soups, creamed dishes, gravies, stews, and sauces. The most frequently used sizes of ladles and their equivalent portions are 2 oz (¼ cup), 4 oz (½ cup), 6 oz (¾ cup), and 8 oz (1 cup).

Serving spoons (solid or perforated) may be used, but since they are not specified by number, it is necessary to measure or weigh food to obtain approximate serving size desired.

Scoops may be used for portioning such items as drop cookies, muffins, meat patties, vegetables, salads, and sandwich fillings. The number on the scoop (usually on the rim) indicates the number of scoopfuls it takes to make one quart. Scoop numbers and their equivalent measures are given below:

6	⅔ cup
8	½ cup
10	⅖ cup
12	⅓ cup
16	¼ cup
20	1½ fl oz

24	1⅓ fl oz
30	1 fl oz
40	0.8 fl oz

Portion scales can be used for meat or vegetable portions. Weighed samples can be used for approximation.

Cutting markers are used for pies, casseroles, and other entrées.

Meat slicers, when properly adjusted, provide consistent sliced meat portions.

Egg slicers provide even and attractive egg slices.

Individually weighed, measured, and packed items, such as sandwiches and crackers, provide for efficient portion control.

Individual cups, glasses, gelatin molds, soufflé cups, and custard cups are good portion-control utensils.

It is important to know the equivalent weight and measures for implementing portion control. The most commonly used equivalents are given below, and common can sizes are given in Table 10.1.

3 teaspoons	= 1 tablespoon	2 pints	= 1 quart
16 teaspoons	= 1 cup	4 quarts	= 1 gallon
2 cups	= 1 pint	16 ounces	= 1 pound

Table 10.1

Common Can Sizes

Size Can	Approximate Quantity Net Weight	Cups	Common Uses
6 oz	6 fl oz	¾	Frozen, concentrated juices and individual servings of single-strength juices
8 oz	8 oz (7¾ fl oz)	1	Fruits, vegetables, and specialty items
No. 1 (Picnic)	10½ oz (9½ fl oz)	1¼	Condensed soups, fruits, vegetables, meat, and fish
No. 300	15½ oz (13½ fl oz)	1¾	Specialty items such as beans with pork, spaghetti, macaroni, chili con carne, date-nut bread, fruits, cranberry sauce, and blueberries
No. 303	1 lb (15 fl oz)	2	Used extensively for vegetables, fruits, fruit cocktail, applesauce, and ready-to-serve soups
No. 2	1 lb 4 oz (1 pt 2 fl oz)	2½	Juices, soups, fruits, and vegetables
No. 2½	1 lb 13 oz (1 pt 10 fl oz)	3½	Fruits, such as peaches, pears, plums, and fruit cocktail; vegetables, such as tomatoes, sauerkraut, and pumpkin
No. 3 cylinder or 46 oz	46 oz (1 qt 14 fl oz)	5¾	Juices and condensed soups
No. 10	6 lb 9 oz (3 qt)	12	"Institutional" or "restaurant" size container, for most fruits and vegetables

Recipe: _____   Date: _____

We would appreciate your cooperation in a food-testing research project. Please place a cross on the horizontal line at that point which best describes that attribute in the food.

Appearance

Unattractive   Moderately   Very Attractive
                       Attractive

Color

Unattractive   Moderately   Very Attractive
                       Attractive

Texture

Undesirable   Moderate   Desirable
(tough or too soft)

Flavor

Unpleasant   Moderate   Pleasing
                                          and Fresh

General
Acceptability   Very Poor   Moderate   Very Good

Please turn this questionnaire in as you leave the dining room. Thank you.

Figure 10-1.   An example of a taste panel scoring sheet.

CONSUMER SURVEYS AND TASTE EVALUATIONS

Consumer surveys and taste evaluations should be conducted on a regular basis. They provide a sound basis for management decisions pertaining to the delivery of food. Since there are several factors that have an impact when food is delivered from kitchen to consumers, these assessments provide good feedback. To start with, recipes should be evaluated regularly. Several foodservice operations have test kitchens where recipes are tested and evaluated. Since any foodservice operation is dependent on the popularity or acceptance of menu items, it is necessary for management to have an effective menu-item evaluation system. A **taste panel** of experienced personnel within the foodservice operation may be selected to evaluate prepared products. Since there may be changes in food items delivered (brand names and seasonal variations), it is necessary to conduct periodic evaluations. A form for such evaluations is given in Figure 10.1. It is also advisable to have consumer taste studies whenever new items are introduced, or even for items that are already being served. Samples may be given out at the foodservice entrance or at the table before or during the meal. Testing will generate interest among the consumers as well as provide an incentive for menu development by management.

We would appreciate your cooperation in a class food-testing project.

Name of product: _____

1. How would you rate this product?
   Excellent ☐ Very good ☐ Good ☐ Fair ☐ Poor ☐

2. Have you tasted this or a similar product before?
   Yes _____ No _____ (If yes, where?_____)

3. Was your selection affected by:
   (a) Serving person _____
   (b) Person in line before you _____
   (c) Person who invited you _____
   (d) Recommendation from others _____
   (e) Other reasons (please mention) _____

4. Please rank the reasons for selecting this product using numerals.
   (a) Name of the product _____
   (b) Appearance _____
   (c) Previous experience _____
   (d) Price _____
   (e) Serving size _____
   (f) Curiosity _____
   (g) Taste _____
   (h) Nutritive value _____
   (i) Vegetarian nature _____
   (e) Other (please mention) _____

5. Will you try this product again? Yes _____ No _____

6. Other comments:_____

Please turn this questionnaire in at the cashier's desk. Thank you.

Figure 10-2. An example of a consumer acceptance survey form.

A form for such evaluation is given in Figure 10.2. The forms for consumers' evaluation should be as simple as possible and should contain a limited number of questions. Only those questions that are pertinent and can provide usable answers should be included. Results should be carefully studied. In smaller operations an informal assessment may be sufficient, but in larger foodservice operations, suitable statistical analyses may be required. Action should be taken and decisions made as soon after the surveys as possible.

DELIVERY AND SERVICE

Delivery and service of food may be classified into several types based on the operation. There is some confusion in the literature between foodservice delivery systems and overall foodservice systems. For the sake of discussion, only the delivery systems of typical foodservice operations will be emphasized. Institutional foodservices, due to the nature of the consumers, have set delivery systems which are described in the following sections. Delivery systems are major management decisions and must be chosen early in the planning process. Selecting a system involves major investment, and it becomes difficult to make changes later. Careful assessment is therefore vital before selecting a method.

Conventional System

The most commonly used conventional system has all delivery subsystems located on the same premises. Total production takes place on thes premises from raw to finished state; the food is served within a short time after production. The service may further be divided into two types: (1) **centralized service,** where food is portioned at one place before service and (2) **decentralized service,** where bulk quantities of food are sent by heated or refrigerated carts or modules to various serving facilities on the same premises. More employees and serving equipment are needed in the decentralized system. Centralized or decentralized, in a conventional system all food is prepared and managed by one team. Food distribution costs are limited because the food does not need to be transported over long distances. Since foods are not stored prior to the service, there are peaks and valleys in production

Figure 10-3.   Typical salad bar in conventional cafeteria. (Courtesy of Saga Foodservices)

which make production and labor costs high. An advantage of this system is that foods are freshly prepared and have relatively better sensory quality. A typical salad bar and dessert counter in a conventional cafeteria are shown in Figures 10.3 and 10.4.

Commissary System

Commissaries have centralized production on a large-quantity basis. They have centralized food procurement and production. Prepared foods are then distributed to several service areas. The **commissary system** is also referred to as the **satellite system.** Foods are transported in specialized equipment, usually trucks, used to keep the food hot or cold. Special modules or warmers may also be used. Since centralized large-volume purchasing is employed, this system is cost-efficient. Food is prepared in bulk at one time, hence the quality of food is uniform. It is possible to purchase sophisticated equipment for centralized service, and there is no duplication of equipment. It is also possible to have a test kitchen for the operation, which is normally difficult in a smaller operation.

The disadvantages of the commissary system are related to the fact that food is being transported to different locations and the safety of food may be affected. The impact of temperatures at which food is held may be noted in overall quality. Weather conditions and truck failures may add to the problems. With the rising cost of fuel, it may be necessary to reevaluate this type of system. It is usually suitable

Figure 10-4.   A dessert counter in a conventional cafeteria.

only for large-size operations such as schools, airlines, or military foodservice facilities.

Ready-Prepared System

In a ready-prepared system foods are prepared on the premises and are then chilled or frozen immediately. The foods are readily available for use; hence, they are referred to as **ready prepared.** When foods are chilled, it is referred to as a **cook-chill** system, and when the foods are frozen it is called a **cook-freeze** system. A large storage area and a blast freezer are required to cool the prepared foods. For service, rethermalizing equipment is necessary. The advantages of this system include reduction of peaks and valleys in production and readily available foods. Labor costs are also relatively less because production is on a continuous, but relaxed, basis. The disadvantages of this system include the high cost of a blast freezer and the storage-space requirements. The quality of the food products, particularly sensory quality, may be affected by chilling/freezing and rethermalizing. Also, the number of menu items suitable for this type of system is limited.

Cook-Chill System

Because of some of the advantages of the cook-chill system, it is gaining popularity in institutional foodservices. **Cook-chill** is a system in which food is cooked utilizing conventional cooking methods, rapidly chilled, stored for a limited time, and rethermalized prior to service. Usually the food is rapidly chilled to 37°F (3°C), in 90 minutes or less, stored at low temperatures between 33°F to 38°F (1°C–4°C), for a period of five days, and rethermalized close to the time of service. Day one is counted as the day of production and day five is the day of service.

Cook-chill requires refrigerated equipment specifically designed for blast chilling, ovens specifically designed for rethermalizing, and necessary preparing/preplating equipment and serving utensils. This method requires: (1) complete assessment and adjustment of recipes, since the method requires subjecting food to different hot and cold temperatures; (2) proper scheduling and work production schemes; (3) labeling and dating of all products prepared, for identification and proper rotation; (4) monitoring and recording of all food temperatures and times, for food safety reasons; and (5) special attention to the maintenance of food quality from the sensory and nutritional point of view. The major drawbacks of the system primarily involve (1) the expense involved in equipment purchase, installation, and remodeling; (2) costs incurred in recipe modifications; and (3) food quality and safety, since food is subjected to different times and temperatures. Any failure in the mechanism can result in problems. If all the disadvantages are overcome, there are following benefits: (1) decreased food costs and food waste, since menus are well planned in advance; also, only as much food as needed is removed from the storage; (2) decreased labor costs, since peaks and valleys experienced in conventional systems are eliminated and production is complete well before the time of service; (3)

increased employee satisfaction, primarily because stress is reduced to a great extent; (4) improved flexibility in meal service demands because food is already prepared; (5) efficient use of production space and equipment because all items to be prepared can be scheduled in advance; (6) fewer leftovers due to menu planning; (7) improved customer satisfaction since menu items are available and the chances of substitutions are minimal; and (8) costs savings associated with less labor and inventory costs.

Assembly-Serve System

In the assembly-serve system completely prepared foods are purchased and assembly is done on premises. The system is convenient since no food production is involved. Ready-to-serve packaged foods are brought onto the premises; only heating or minor preparations need to be done. Sometimes ready-to-mix food products are also used. This reduces the labor costs and the time involved in production, service, and sanitation. Certain disadvantages restrict the wide use of this system. It is very expensive, and the food items available are limited.

TABLE SERVICE

Several different types of table service are in current use, depending on the foodservice operation. Theme restaurants usually have their own particular type of service. Service styles become a distinguishing feature of any type of foodservice operation. Common styles of service are discussed below. These styles may also have their own variations based on the policies and geographical locations of foodservice operations.

French Service

French service is distinguished by the fact that food may be cooked, partially cooked, or completed at tableside. The appearance of foods being cooked and the aroma have an appetite-stimulating effect on the customers. Food is carried from the kitchen to the dining room in a special cart *(gueridon)*. A small stove warmer called a *rechaud* is used for keeping food warm as well as to provide an elegant appearance. The food item is completed by cooking, warming, flaming, deboning, slicing, and/or garnishing in front of the food patrons. This service, to be correct, has two food servers waiting on each table. The principal server *(chef de rang)* is responsible for all table-side preparation. The assistant *(commis de rang)* carries the food to the table and dishes back from the table. All food is served and cleared from the right side of the guests except salad, butter, and bread, which are served to the left. Finger bowls, containing warm water with rose petals or lemon slices in it, are also provided. Soiled dishes are carried out after the guests leave. This requires that there be enough room as well as enough dishes when the tables are set. The table setting in this type of service include an hors d'oeuvre plate, napkin, dinner fork, dinner knife, soup spoon, butter plate, butter spreader, dessert fork and spoon, and wine and water glasses.

Russian Service

Russian service is a common type of table service and popular in many restaurants. The table setting is similar to French service. The food is fully prepared in the kitchen and one person serves the table. The food is attractively presented on platters. A plate is placed in front of each guest from the right side going around in clockwise direction. The food server stands on the left side of the guest, shows the food, and then places the desired portion on the guest's plate. Service is continued in counterclockwise direction around the table. Finger bowls/napkins may be used. Dishes are cleared only when guests leave the table.

English Service

In English service, the food is served on platters and heated plates are placed before the host at the head of the table. The host, who serves the menu items to the guests, also carves meat, when served. The host hands dishes to the foodserver, who, in turn, hands plates over to the guests. Desserts may also be served in this manner. Sauces, condiments, and other items are set on the table and are passed by guests when needed.

American Service

American service is less formal than the services described above. The serviceware include two to three forks, a dinner knife, a bread-and-butter spreader, two teaspoons, a napkin, a service plate, a bread-and-butter plate, and a water glass. Foods are brought by an individual server to the table. Soups and appetizers are placed on an underliner and served in the center of the cover. The main item is placed in the center of the cover. Other silverware is added when needed.

Buffet Service

In buffet service, the guests select their meals from attractively arranged and decorated serving tables. Ice sculptures, flowers, centerpieces, and fruit and vegetable carvings are used to decorate the serving tables. Silverware may be located on the buffet table or on the individual dinner table. The guests either serve themselves and/or are served by the chefs and servers standing behind the table.

Salad Bars

At salad bars, salads are placed on long bars with single or multiple arrangements of dressings, condiments, or other ingredients. Guests prepare their own salads and select dressing and other items. Chilled bowls and plates are provided. Sometimes a server is available for help from behind the counter. Smorgasbords are similar to salad bars, except that they have a large variety of items, including entrées. The guests may come back for more food as often as desired.

Counter/Cafeteria Service

Various food items are available on display on the counter and steam tables, and guests select what they want (Figures 10.3 and 10.4). A person behind the counter serves all guests. Trays and silverware are available at the beginning of the line. Beverages may sometimes be dispensed by self-service machines. Guests pay after their selection is completed. At many places, guests are responsible for placing soiled dishes and trays onto conveyors or carts after they finish their meals.

Instructions for table-service procedures are outlined below as an example and as a checklist for the person in charge of service.

Typical Table Service Procedures

The table space allotted to each customer is referred to as a **cover.** This space is based on the type of restaurant and space that is available, and typically ranges from 24 to 36 in. The edge of table, counter, seat, or a booth is called the "edge of the cloth," irrespective of a tablecloth's being used or not. "Set line" is 1 in from the edge of the cloth. All silverware and chinaware is set starting at the set line.

Dinner Plate.   Place 1 inch from the edge of the table.

Knife.   Place to the right of the dinner plate with the sharp edge of the blade turned toward the dinner plate with the tip of the handle placed 1 in from the set line.

Cup and Saucer.   Place to the right of the teaspoon, with the handle of the cup toward the right side of the consumer. Cups may be inverted if the arrangements are for service at a later time, but should preferably be turned before service.

Goblet.   Place above the knife 1 in from above the tip of the blade.

Bread-and-Butter Plate.   Place at the top of the fork (about 2 in above the tines of the fork). Butter knife should be placed neatly across the butter plate with the sharp edge of the knife facing the consumer. The handle of the knife should be toward the right-hand side of the consumer.

Napkin.   Place to the left of the fork. This may vary depending on different factors. Sometimes the napkin may be placed on the plate, or silverware may be wrapped in it and placed either at the left side of the plate or on the plate. One of the recommended procedures for placing a napkin is to place it in such a way that the free edge or hem of the napkin is facing toward the left side of the guest. This provides the consumer or the food server easy access to the napkin for unfolding without inconvenience or embarrassment. Special folding of the napkin to suit the theme or the decor of the restaurant is desirable. Care should be taken that the napkin is folded in such a way that it can be unfolded easily without interfering with the other table settings. If the person serving is required to place the napkin on the guest's lap, the napkin should be picked up with the left hand and evenly spread on the lap.

Dinner Fork.   Place to the left of the dinner plate with the edge of the fork handle 1 in from the set line. The fork should never be placed upside down; the tines should always point upward. More than one fork may be needed for each setting, in which case they should preferably be arranged on the left side of the dinner plate and set according to the sequence of courses on the menu for which these forks are to be used.

Salt and Pepper Shakers.   Place between bread-and-butter plate and goblet.

This description of the setting is given as an example. Once a place setting has been designed, all other settings should be similar and symmetrical in all respects.

The following checklists will help in getting ready for service and properly attending to patrons.

Setting the Table

_____ Tables and chairs placed in their correct positions.

_____ Tables well leveled.

_____ Check size of tablecloth.

_____ Corners of tablecloth covering the legs of the table and not falling between the table legs.

_____ Overlap of the tablecloth even all around the table.

_____ Tablecloths positioned on the tables so that the creases are parallel in the room.

_____ When two tablecloths are used to cover a table, overlap faces away from the entrance to the room.

_____ All covers symmetrical.

_____ Cutlery and flatware cleaned/polished and given final touches before setting on table.

_____ Cutlery and flatware laid from the inside to the outside of cover.

_____ Once cover is laid, other table accompaniments set.

Service

_____ All foodservice made with *left* hand from *left*-hand side of the guest.

_____ A plate with meat or a main entrée always placed directly in front of the guest.

_____ All beverages served with *right* hand from *right*-hand side of the guests.

_____ All food dishes removed from *right*-hand side of the guest.

_____ All beverages removed with *right* hand from *right*-hand side of the guest.

(Note: Change this procedure only if it is inconvenient to follow or is not in line with the theme and style of the foodservice operation.)

A checklist of table-service procedure is given in Appendix F. In a typical foodservice operation, work may be divided based on activities such as production, service, and sanitation, each under a supervisor. Typical responsibilities of these supervisors are given in Appendices G, H, and I. An example of a form used for listing guest reservations is shown in Appendix J.

PERSONAL APPEARANCE

Food servers provide the first and last impressions of any foodservice operation. A good food server acts as a salesperson for the operation, and the success of that operation depends on how many good servers work at the facility.

Uniform

The uniform of attending personnel identifies that person as one who is responsible for service and should be representative of the restaurant. The uniform should have appropriate colors, be suitable to the theme decor of the restaurant, fit well, be suitable for prevalent weather conditions, and should be made of material that is comfortable and easy to clean. In short, the uniform should be such that it facilitates easy and fast movements without causing hazards of any sort. All foodservers should be instructed to keep their uniforms neat and clean at all times. Some of the uniforms made of synthetic fiber blends are durable, easily cleaned, and attractive. Any spots on the uniform should be cleaned as soon as possible. Repairs to torn hems and lost buttons should be attended to immediately to avoid presenting a negative image of the operation to the guests. Pins substituting for buttons are undesirable.

Shoes

Since shoes contribute to the overall appearance of the foodserver, they affect the image presented to the patrons. Desirable shoes are those that are well fitting, comfortable, sturdy, and nonslippery. Since foodservers are on their feet for long periods of time, it is vital that their shoes be comfortable. Clean, polished, and closed shoes with arch supports are safe and desirable.

Jewelry

Jewelry should be restricted to watches and rings. Other types of decorative jewelry should be discouraged because they are not sanitary, do not look professional, and are distracting to consumers. Hanging bracelets, necklaces, and earrings are unsafe since they may drop or dip into foods, which could result in serious consequences.

Perfumes

Perfumes are not desirable since they may interfere with the appetizing aroma of food, or may be undesirable to some patrons. Also, some patrons may be allergic to certain perfumes. Use of light make-up and mild deodorant is advisable.

Grooming

Grooming is part of one's personality and should be given special attention. Good personal hygiene is essential since foodservers are directly or indirectly in contact with the public. Such personal habits as daily baths, brushing of teeth, use of anti-perspirant and mouthwash contribute to a clean appearance, which is a must. Hair should be clean, combed, and covered with an effective hair restraint such as hairnet or a cap. Hands, which are visible and "on display" during service, should be clean and neat. Fingernails should be well trimmed. Nail polish and artificial nails are undesirable. Food servers should always check their total appearance in a mirror before going on duty and at all break periods.

SUMMARY

This chapter focuses on the concepts of delivery and service in foodservice operations. The importance of portion control and methods used for portion control are highlighted. The types of delivery systems used in commercial and institutional foodservices are described in detail. Essentials of good service in a foodservice operation are emphasized.

REVIEW QUESTIONS

List and describe any ten portion control tools that are used in a typical foodservice operation.

What are the major differences between the conventional and commissary systems?

What are the advantages and disadvantages of a cook-chill system?

What are some of the ways by which consumer feedback related to service can be obtained? Explain how this information can be used in the effective management of a foodservice operation.

ASSIGNMENTS

Observe and critically evaluate portion control methods used in a selected foodservice operation.

Design a questionnaire that can be used by a foodservice operation to obtain consumer feedback. Describe what each question is designed to measure and how the answers can be used to improve service.

Visit a restaurant of your choice and critically evaluate the service provided by the staff.

SUGGESTED READINGS

Dahmer, S. J., and Kahl, K. W. 1982. *The Waiter and Waitress Training Manual,* 2nd edition. Van Nostrand Reinhold, New York, NY.

Lillicarp, D. R. 1983. *Food and Beverage Service,* 2nd edition. Edward Arnold Publishers Ltd., London, U.K.

Solomon, E. 1979. *Service Is an Honorable Profession: A Study in Hospitality.* McGarvey's Nautical Restaurant, Vermilion, OH.

West, B. B., and Wood, L. 1988. *Food Service in Institutions.* Macmillan Publishing Co., New York, NY.

CHAPTER 11

FOODSERVICE MANAGEMENT: FUNCTIONAL ASPECTS

KEY CONCEPTS AND TERMS

tactical decision
strategic decision
organizational chart
authority
responsibility
accountability
Theory X and Y
food cost percentage
profit and loss statement
balance sheet
ratio analysis

The most important function in any type of foodservice operation is that of management. The entire system works or does not work on the basis of management and its efficiency. The term "management" may refer either to those individuals who have authority and control over a system or to the function carried by those individuals.

Management may also be considered as a process that is designed to accomplish certain goals, which are achieved by utilizing material and human resources. It involves the decision making, planning, organizing, communicating, directing, motivating, and controlling processes to achieve those goals. Underlying all other management functions is the crucial task of cost control.

When considered from the functional point of view, management involves the utilization of six available resources: manpower, money, material, minutes, machines, and markets, commonly referred to as "The 6M's of Management." A definition of management which is more comprehensive and takes into account all the above factors and which has been developed by the American Management Association, is "Management is that process by which human and physical resources are guided into dynamic and viable organizational units that attain objectives to the satisfaction of those served, and with a high degree of morale and sense of attainment on the part of those providing the service." This definition also fits into the definition of "management" from the foodservice point of view. Some aspects that become clearly evident from this and several other definitions of management are (1) there are goals of management, and management is goal-oriented; (2) management has to utilize all available resources in the most efficient manner; (3) management has to be active at all times; and (4) management should bring about a coordinated effort from all people.

MANAGEMENT RESPONSIBILITIES

The resources available to management in foodservice operations are (1) human, (2) physical (such as equipment and ingredients), and (3) monetary. These resources must be managed effectively in order to achieve the desired goals of an organization. On the other hand, the effectiveness of a management may be evaluated by the way these resources are managed. In utilizing these resources to meet organizational objectives, the important functions discussed below are carried out.

Decision Making

Every manager has to make decisions daily. Decision making may involve one or more of the following aspects: (1) deciding among the choices available; (2)

selecting the future course of direction of an operation on a long-term basis; (3) solving existing problems by utilizing the best possible alternative; (4) interpreting the data from internal and external sources and selecting the best course of action; and (5) adapting, modifying, or changing certain operational parameters. The art of decision making has to be learned by a manager, since the decision made may have long-term consequences and reflect on the management policies of an operation. A step-by-step approach to decision making is highly desirable. The process recommended for decision making includes the following steps:

1. Understand the situation. This is the first step in decision making. A thorough understanding of the problem is essential to arrive at working and lasting solutions. Jumping to conclusions may never solve any problems and may even create additional difficulties.
2. Recognize and analyze the problem. Recognition of the problem will facilitate finding a solution to the problem.
3. Analyze and develop possible solutions to the problem recognized in Step 2. Solutions should in general be specific for the problem. It is preferable to have more than one solution to the problem. The more solutions included in the choices, the easier it will be to make decisions. The solution selected should be workable.
4. Rank the solutions based on merit and feasibility. Estimate the value or the consequences of using each solution. One should be as flexible as possible in developing solutions. Innovative approaches are highly desirable. Every possible solution should be explored and bias should be avoided as much as possible.
5. Based on all factors, choose the best possible solution. Be as flexible as possible. Believe in the solution chosen and plan to take action or serious steps to control the problem.
6. Implement your decision based on the solution selected in Step 5.
7. Follow up on the action. This is probably the most important aspect of the decision-making process. The most common mistake is that after implementing the decision, a follow-up is not done. The workability and the merit of the decision made should be carefully evaluated. This will also help in making further decisions based on the experience gained.

A foodservice manager makes primarily two types of decisions: tactical and strategic. **Tactical decisions** do not require extensive thought and can be made fairly quickly. Many times these decisions can be made by the manager or supervisor without any consultation. Examples of tactical decisions in the foodservice would be the decisions made by a foodservice manager when an employee calls in sick, or when an unexpectedly large group of customers arrives at a restaurant. These decisions have to be made fairly quickly and they have effects which are relatively short-lived. **Strategic decisions** have a long-term impact and therefore have to be carefully thought out and planned. They require consultations and involve people from various levels within the organization. Normally, these decisions are made by higher levels of management. Examples of strategic decisions are the opening of a new section in a restaurant to reduce the lunch time rush and the hiring of additional employees.

Decision making is a process that starts a chain reaction among all affected individuals or groups. If a decision made by a manager is implemented, each employee will make decisions based on the manager's decision. Decisions may be made "individually" or in "groups."

Advantages and disadvantages of group decision making when compared to individual decision making are listed below.

Advantages	*Disadvantages*
More choices for possible solutions can be brought forth in group decision making. Sometimes unique ideas, which are impossible to get by individual decision, may be evolved by group discussions.	Group decisions are time consuming and require advance notice. They cannot be made as quickly as individual decisions. This is their greatest drawback.
It involves those who may be affected by the decision and therefore group decision making provides for their participation.	Decision-making sessions may become lengthy discussions or arguments, and at times it may be impossible to reach any decision because so many individuals are involved.
It provides for a better understanding between employees and management, since by group decision making management shows that it has a genuine interest in solving the problem.	The chances of polarization because of power, status, bias, or personal influence may lead to decisions that are not the best possible solutions.
It provides for better understanding of the problem(s) and permits a greater understanding of the decisions made. It will reduce the rumors that may prevail when individual decisions are made.	Decisions are often made on the basis of satisfying groups, rather than individuals.
Participants, particularly employees, feel good about themselves when they are consulted, and there is a feeling of participation, which is highly desirable in large organizations.	Since the decision-making responsibility is shared, the resulting consequences may not be credited either to management or to the employees.
Employees who have been in the operation for a long period of time may provide valuable solutions based on their experience.	

Planning

Planning is also an important management function. Planning may be defined as that function of management that helps in developing a course of action for meeting the desired objectives, designed to fulfill overall organizational goals. Planning is conducted by various levels of management and may involve different types of plans. Examples of typical plans made within the foodservice operation are menus, production forecast, employee schedules, policy statements, procedures, methods, standards, and budgets. Plans may be informal or formal.

Planning involves the assessment of present environment and actions for adapting the operation to future external and internal environments. Thus planning can be strategic planning on a long-term basis or short-range planning. In the strategic planning process, the life cycle of a product, operation, industry, or a franchise should be considered. This can be charted by observing historical data as well as future extrapolation. Thus planning is as hard as forecasting aspects such as life cycle and the impact of the environment.

Similar step-wise approaches as listed for decision making can be followed for planning. Planning, as with decision making, may be done individually or in groups. The advantages and disadvantages of these types of planning are similar to those outlined earlier for the decision-making function. Good plans are

1. Clear, concise, complete, and specific to the objectives to be achieved
2. Easily understood by all concerned persons
3. Based on the desired and preset goals of the foodservice operation
4. Realistic and based on achievable goals
5. Flexible so that changes may be incorporated from time to time
6. Scheduled with a deadline for completion (preferable but not always possible)

Plans that are well thought out and executed should produce the desired results. An assessment of plans after they are executed will help in future planning.

Organizing

It is important to understand the difference between the terms "organization" and "organizing." Organization may be defined as a system in which individuals work together in a rational, conscious, and orderly manner for the accomplishment of common goals. Organizing, on the other hand, is the function of management which deals with the arrangement, distribution, and conduction of responsibilities in order to accomplish the common goals of an organization. A restaurant or foodservice operation is an organization in which foodservice managers and employees work together to achieve common goals. The manner in which different tasks are assigned to individuals, groups, units, or departments represents organizing within that operation.

The most important task of organizing is to understand the organization or the system itself. All activities and work are to be grouped by kinds, functions, and levels. An **organizational chart** can be drawn to show different functions and levels of activities. This chart is a valuable management tool. The chart may be drawn on the basis of functions or levels of management or both. Organization charts may be drawn in several ways—top to bottom, right to left, left to right, circular, pyramid shape, or a combination of all. Examples of organization charts are given in Figures 11.1–11.4. In planning the organization charts, three aspects should be understood and taken into consideration:

Authority can be defined as right and privilege to expect performance from others. It is primarily restricted to management personnel.

Responsibility is the obligation to complete activities in a required way. This pertains to management as well as employees.

Accountability is to answer for given responsibility.

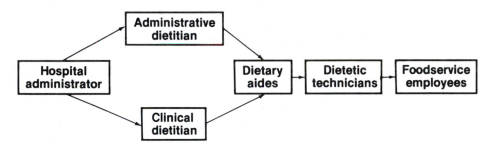

Figure 11-1.   A left-to-right organization chart.

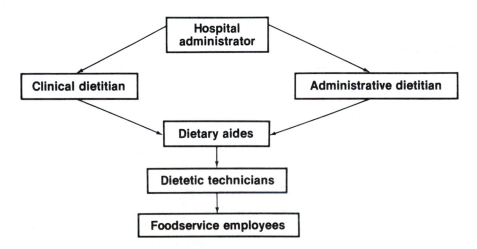

Figure 11-2.   A top-to-bottom organization chart.

Organizational charts should show clearly the flow of authority. There are three types of organizations based on the flow of authority:

Line organization, which has a direct flow of authority from top to bottom. Each position has direct authority over the one below it. In very small organizations, such as a restaurant, all of the employees and supervisors are in line.

Staff organization, which supports the line organization in an advisory capacity; the staff does not have direct authority. An example of this relationship is that between the nursing and dietary departments in hospitals. Each cooperates in carrying out different functions with no authority among them.

Functional organization, which has authority within clearly defined functions. In a foodservice operation, for example, the personnel office may have the authority over recruiting and training all individuals for that particular organization.

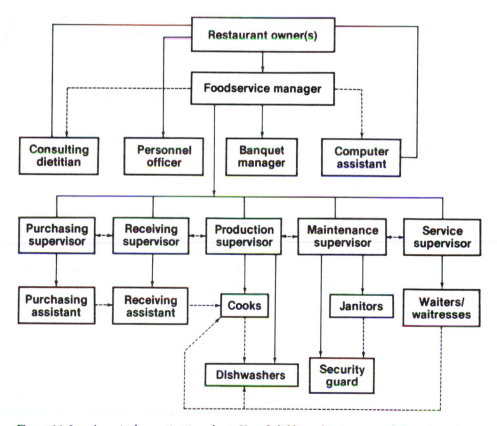

Figure 11-3.   A typical organization chart. Key: Solid line: direct responsibility; dotted line: indirect responsibility.

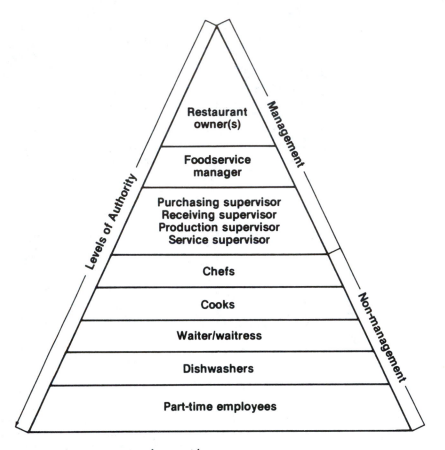

Figure 11-4. An organizational pyramid.

Organizations vary from industry to industry. Some characteristics of hospitality organizations are (1) it is a service industry, with large number of people involved; (2) a high proportion of employees are teenagers, women, minorities, or immigrants; (3) there are relatively smaller units of operation when compared to other industries and each unit requires unit managers; and (4) there is a lot of direct interaction between the consumers and the employees. All these aspects should be considered while planning organizational strategies.

Communicating

Communicating is an important function of management since it keeps the entire organization functioning smoothly and unites the various groups or individuals working within the organization. Thus, communication involves the transfer of information facilitating the conduct of activities within an organization. The basic elements of the process of communication are:

1. *Source.* This is primarily the person(s) who desires to send the communication and who has all the information needed to implement it.
2. *Encoding.* This is the form selected to send the communication, such as a letter or sending a message through an intercom.
3. *Transmission.* This involves carrying out the communication, such as sending a letter or sending a message through an intercom.
4. *Reception.* This takes place when the person(s) actually receives the communication, such as hearing it on a radio, or receiving a letter.
5. *Decoding.* This involves interpretation of the message or communication by the receiver.

Principles of Effective Communications

Words are used for communication, but they do not necessarily carry meaning independently, since they are symbols of expression. Words have to be used in such a way that they carry the proper interpretation of the message as well as the message.

Words also have different meanings to different people. Two people may assign different meanings to the same word depending on their experiences, e.g., "icing a cake" may be literally interpreted in different ways. Cultural backgrounds also provide different meanings to words. Thus, a *careful selection of words* is necessary for effective communication.

The *environment* in which the communication is made has an impact on its effectiveness. Talking to an employee about an important policy change in a noisy kitchen will have less effect than when the same communication is provided in a favorable setting such as the employee dining area. Talking about a procedure just before lunchtime or on Friday afternoon are examples of poor timing. Proper *timing* is essential for the success of any communication.

The educational and social background and feelings of a person should be considered in selecting the format as well as the method of communication. *Emotions* affect understanding. This should be considered by management when selecting the type of communication and its timing.

Facts must be distinguished from opinions in all communications. Often opinions are combined with facts, making it difficult to communicate.

The *communication network* and the number of people involved in the communication process affect the final communication. The role of the "grapevine" should be considered when communicating.

A communication can be made more effective by *actions* than by words alone. Showing how a certain piece of equipment works will have more impact than only having the employees read the manual.

Feedback is a good indicator of the success of a communication. A good communication achieves the desired effect by reaching the person for whom it is intended.

Typical types of communications and the situations for communication with foodservice employees are:

Person-to-person discussions	Paycheck inserts
Group meetings	Letters
Phone calls	Display cases
Bulletin boards	Films, slides, and movies
Handbooks and brochures	Lectures
Conferences and seminars	Electronic displays
Posters and signs	

Effective communication should be well planned and delivered in the most appropriate way. Open lines of communication between employees and manager are desirable. Management should be willing to listen to all concerns of employees. Thus a two-way communication channel will build confidence among employees and will lead to a strong relationship between management and employees in a foodservice operation.

Some points to consider while communicating, either orally or in writing, are:

1. Plan the message. Gather all points to be mentioned and select the main idea of the message.
2. Select the most appropriate time for communicating.
3. Open communication with words that will draw the attention of the receiver.
4. Clarify and outline what you would like to discuss at the beginning.
5. Personalize the message as much as possible.
6. Use words that are commonly understood by the receiver.
7. Cite examples whenever possible to clarify statements and enable the receiver to relate to them.
8. Anticipate questions and objections and be prepared to answer them satisfactorily and politely.
9. Provide ample time for communication and pay attention to receivers' comments.
10. Repeat and close with an emphasis on the key points of the message.

Directing

Directing, as the word indicates, is a management function which guides all activities within a system. Clear directions are those that provide answers to all possible questions. Answers should be provided for:

WHAT is to be done?

WHO should do it?

WHEN should it be done?

WHERE should it be done?

WHY must it be done?

HOW should it be done?

WHO should be contacted with any questions?

If these questions are answered by the planned directions, then they are complete. Many problems arise because of incomplete directions, which may result not only in lost time and/or materials but may generate friction. There are four primary components of directing:

1. Issuing directions
2. Providing information
3. Motivating
4. Following up

In providing directions, the attitudes of management, supervisors, and workers are important factors. Managers, supervisors, and workers all have different attitudes toward work. Two important theories related to the attitudes of workers toward work are commonly referred to in all types of management literature. These theories are known as **Theory X and Theory Y** suggested by Douglas MacGregor. These theories have generated a lot of controversy. The principle of Theory X is that people do not really like to work and so must be coerced, controlled, directed, and/or threatened with punishment in order to get them to work. This theory also assumes an average worker to be lazy. He or she is characterized as one who avoids work, avoids responsibility, is ambitious, and wants security more than anything else. Thus, it is reward and punishment that keep the worker going.

Theory Y assumes that under the proper conditions people will accept and even seek responsibility. Physical and mental effort in work is considered to be as natural as play or rest. According to this theory, employees have much unused capabilities for solving problems. Theory Y recognizes self-direction instead of external control as the principal means of inspiring effort. This theory therefore relies on a worker's desire for self-fulfillment and achievement rather than on the authority of management. In other words, helping employees fulfill their goals will lead to the success of the organization.

Directing involves the ability to lead people, which is dependent on the skills of a manager. Leading is the process of influencing others to act in a way that accomplishes the desired objectives. Thus, an effective leader is one who influences the behavior of the majority of followers to achieve set objectives. Every manager has a different style of leadership, and the attitude of the manager is based on his or her style. The six major types of leadership are discussed below.

1. The supportive leader emphasizes employee participation and job satisfaction. This type of leader involves employees in the decision-making process, planning, and other management functions. Too much interest in employees at the expense of productivity is one of the criticisms of this style of leadership.

2. An autocratic leader plans, controls, and directs all of the work. This type of leader is authoritative and dictatorial in many respects and uses power to achieve productivity. This style of leadership is believed to be effective only in the short run, since the resentment generated by this type of leader leads to employee dissatisfaction and indirectly affects productivity in the long run.
3. The bureaucratic leader governs by the book and is involved in bureaucracy at the expense of morale and productivity.
4. The diplomatic leader is more spontaneous and tries to achieve a balance between getting work done and keeping employees satisfied.
5. The free-rein leader provides freedom to employees and lets the organization run at its own pace.
6. The instrumental leader has talents in working on such procedures as scheduling and routine work and places too much emphasis on routine procedures.

The leadership style selected will be based on several factors; there is no particular style that can be recommended for new managers to adopt. In general, it can be said that an effective manager is one who recognizes that he or she has power, accepts power, and uses it wisely, while keeping in view the goals and objectives of the organization. An effective manager realizes that there is a time for democracy and there is a time for autocracy. A blend of different leadership styles is desirable on many occasions. Tough-mindedness is generally considered a desirable attribute in a successful manager. He or she should visualize and accept things as they are rather than through a sentimental haze.

Controlling

Management must assure that organizational activities conform to the plans designed to achieve set specifications and objectives. Making and overseeing enforcement of regulations are difficult management functions. Too many controls not only affect productivity but also generate resentment against management. However, enforcing conformance is essential for many reasons.

1. Perishable goods have to be handled at a particular time and temperature.
2. There are peaks and valleys in production.
3. Employees tend to lower work standards in the absence of effective controls.
4. Many employees feel uncomfortable when there are no formal rules.
5. Regulations provide a basis for objective employee evaluation and assessment of productivity.

The best controls are those that are the least obvious. A time clock is a good example of an effective but not obvious control. Effective controls should save more time than that spent on maintaining them. Regulations may be functional, such as those related to specific activities or functions, or factorial, based on quality or quantity parameters. Controls that are working effectively should be changed only when necessary.

Effective controls are:

1. Selected for a particular problem
2. Adaptable to changing situations
3. Cost effective
4. Timely
5. Adequate for particular situation
6. Enforceable without any undue complications
7. Contributing to effective management

COST CONTROL IN FOODSERVICES

Because cost control is basic to the successful execution of all other management functions, it is considered here in some depth.

Kinds of Costs

Several types of costs are incurred in any foodservice operation, the most important of which are those for food and labor. The cost of food may be determined by the inventories as follows:

$$\text{value of opening inventory (for a specific period)} +$$
$$\text{food purchases} = \text{total available inventory} - \text{closing inventory}$$
$$= \text{cost of food consumed (for specific period)}$$

The **food cost percentage** is the food cost expressed as the percentage of food sales and can be calculated as:

$$\text{food cost}\,(\%) = \frac{\text{food costs}}{\text{food sales}}$$

Food cost percentage is used as a budgeting tool and for comparative evaluations of financial statements. The food cost percentage varies with the type of foodservice operation. It indicates the amount spent for food out of the total food sales. It may be as high as 40% for a cafeteria or as low as 20% for a luxurious restaurant. Similarly, labor costs may be calculated as:

$$\text{labor cost}\,(\%) = \frac{\text{cost of labor}}{\text{sales}}$$

Food and labor costs are dependent on several factors, including the type of foodservice operation, style of service, menu, and location. The cost of individual menu items may be calculated by using the cost of each item used in the recipe. For

Name: _____	Recipe Yield: _____
Recipe: _____	Actual Yield in Servings: _____
Date Product Made: _____	Size of Servings: _____

Ingredients	Amount	Purchase Unit Price	Small Unit Price	Total Cost

Total Cost _____

Total Food Cost ÷ No. of Servings = Portion Food Cost = $ _____

Desired Food Cost Percentage = _____ %

$$\text{Selling Price} = \frac{\text{Portion Food Cost}}{\text{Desired Food Cost Percentage}} \times 100$$

or

$$\frac{\text{Portion Food Cost}}{\text{Selling Price}} \times 100 = \text{Actual Food Cost Percentage}$$

Figure 11-5. An example of recipe cost sheet.

items that are used in very small quantities, such as spices or seasonings, a fixed cost of about 1% may be calculated. A recipe cost sheet is given as an example in Figure 11.5. The cost of labor may also be calculated along with the cost of recipe.

The most common financial statements used by any type of foodservice operation are: (1) profit and loss statement and (2) balance sheet. These two statements are described in detail in following sections.

Profit and Loss Statement

The profit and loss statement, as its name indicates, is a statement of the status of the account showing profit and losses. A profit and loss statement is shown in Figure 11.6. The first information to be recorded includes food and beverage sales and their totals. Similarly, the cost of food and beverages is to be calculated. Some of the items used in a profit and loss statement are defined below.

Gross profit is the amount after deduction of cost of food and beverages from sales. This will give the total gross profit for the foodservice operation. This is the gross profit and does not take into consideration any expenses.

Other income includes income from sources other than food and beverages, such as vending machines, cigarette, or newspaper sales.

Total income is the gross profit plus other income.

Controllable expenses, as the name implies, are those expenses that can be controlled. These are based on management decisions and are directly related to the efficiency and management of a foodservice operation.

Payroll includes all salaries and wages.

Employee benefits include expenses for medical insurance, compensation, and other benefits paid for the employees.

Direct operating expenses are those items that are directly related to services offered to the customers such as centerpieces, candles, silverware, and napkins.

Music and entertainment expenses are included if these kinds of services are provided.

Advertising and promotion expenses include all kinds of advertising, promotion, and discount expenses.

Utilities expenses are those spent on utilities from all sources.

Administrative and general expenses are overhead expenses that are not related to services offered to the customers, such as office supplies, postage, and telephones.

Repairs and maintenance expenses include all types of repairs and maintenance expenditures.

```
SALES
    Food ........................................    $ ............................    ........................ %
    Beverages ...............................    $ ............................    ........................ %
                                                    ─────────────────────
        Total Food & Beverage Sales ...........    $ ............................    100.00 %
                                                    ─────────────────────
COSTS
    Food ........................................    $ ............................    ........................ %
    Beverages ...............................    $ ............................    ........................ %
                                                    ─────────────────────
        Total Cost of Sales ...........................    $ ............................    ........................ %
                                                    ─────────────────────
GROSS PROFIT
    Food ........................................    $ ............................    ........................ %
    Beverages ...............................    $ ............................    ........................ %
                                                    ─────────────────────
        Total Gross Profit ...........................    $ ............................    ........................ %
                                                    ─────────────────────
OTHER INCOME
    Description ...............................    $ ............................    ........................ %
TOTAL INCOME ......................................    $ ............................    ........................ %
                                                    ─────────────────────
CONTROLLABLE EXPENSES
    Payroll                                          $ ............................    ........................ %
    Employee Benefits                                $ ............................    ........................ %
    Employees' meals                                 $ ............................    ........................ %
    Direct operating expenses                        $ ............................    ........................ %
    Music and entertainment                          $ ............................    ........................ %
    Advertising & promotion                          $ ............................    ........................ %
    Utilities                                        $ ............................    ........................ %
    Administrative & general                         $ ............................    ........................ %
    Repairs & maintenance                            $ ............................    ........................ %
        TOTAL CONTROLLABLE EXPENSES                  $ ............................    ........................ %
PROFIT BEFORE RENT                                   $ ............................    ........................ %
RENT OR OCCUPATION COSTS                             $ ............................    ........................ %
PROFIT BEFORE DEPRECIATION                           $ ............................    ........................ %
DEPRECIATION                                         $ ............................    ........................ %
                                                    ─────────────────────
PROFIT BEFORE INTEREST                               $ ............................    ........................ %
INTEREST EXPENSE                                     $ ............................    ........................ %
                                                    ─────────────────────
PROFIT BEFORE INCOME TAX                             $ ............................    ........................ %
INCOME TAX                                           $ ............................    ........................ %
                                                    ─────────────────────
NET PROFIT                                           $ ............................    ........................ %
                                                    ─────────────────────
```

Figure 11-6. Typical contents of profit and loss statement.

Total controllable expenses include all controllable expenses and are sometimes used as an indicator of management efficiency, since all these items may be controlled by the management.

Profit before rent is calculated by subtracting total controllable expenses from the total income. It is also referred to as operating profit since it indicates the profits made by the operation before calculating other costs.

Rent or occupation costs include rent, occupation costs, real estate taxes, and insurance.

Profit before depreciation is calculated by subtracting rent or occupation costs from the profit before rent.

Depreciation is the calculated cost of expected or actually incurred depreciation or wear and tear.

Profit before income tax may be calculated by subtracting the depreciation cost from the profit before depreciation.

Net profit is the total net profit derived after subtracting income taxes. This is the total profit after taking into account all costs and expenses.

Balance Sheet

An example of a balance sheet is given in Figure 11.7. A **balance sheet** is the balance of assets versus liabilities and capital. It gives an overall picture of the financial position of any foodservice operation. Some of the terms used in a balance sheet are defined below.

Current assets are those assets that can be converted into cash in a relatively short period of time. They commonly include cash on hand, accounts receivable, and inventories.

Fixed assets are those that are of a permanent nature and that cannot be converted to cash while the business is in operation. Examples of fixed income include furniture and land. Their depreciated values have to be calculated for inclusion in the balance sheet.

Current liabilities are obligations that will become due within one year of the balance sheet date and include such items as short-term loans and taxes collected from customers and payable to the government.

Fixed liabilities are equipment contracts payable or notes payable on a long-term basis. They are not payable within one year of the balance sheet date.

Net worth includes invested capital and earnings retained in the business at the balance sheet date. If a foodservice operation is operated as a partnership, it is preferable to show each partner's net worth separately on the balance sheet.

It should be noted that every item has to be converted into dollars in order to be placed in the financial statements. In order to interpret and analyze financial

ASSETS

CURRENT ASSETS
   Cash on Hand .... $
   Cash in Bank .... $

     Total Cash .... $

Accounts Receivable
   Customers .... $
   Credit Cards .... $
   Employees .... $
   Other .... $

     Total Receivable .... $

Inventories
   Food .... $
   Beverages .... $
   Supplies .... $
   Other .... $

     Total Inventories .... $
Prepaid Insurance, Taxes, etc. .... $

     Total Current Assets .... $ _____
Fixed Assets
   Land .... $
   Building .... $
   Depreciation (deduct) .... $_____
   Amount .... $_____
   Furniture, Fixtures & Equipment .... $
   Depreciation (deduct) .... $_____
   Amount .... $_____
   Leasehold Improvements .... $
   Depreciation (deduct) .... $_____
   Amount .... $_____
   Operating Equipment—China,
     Silver, etc. .... $_____
     Total Fixed Assets .... $_____

TOTAL ASSETS $_____

Figure 11-7.   An example of a balance sheet.

```
LIABILITIES AND CAPITAL
CURRENT LIABILITIES
   Accounts payable—trade ........................ $
   Accrued taxes payable ........................... $
   Accrued expenses payable ...................... $_____
      Total Current Liabilities ................................................ $_____
EQUIPMENT AND CONTRACTS PAYABLE ..................................... $_____
LONG-TERM LOANS ........................................................................ $_____
      Total Liabilities ................................................................... $_____
CAPITAL (OWNERS' EQUITY) ..................... $_____
PROPRIETORS' ACCOUNT .......................... $_____
TOTAL NET WORTH ....................................................................... $_____
TOTAL LIABILITIES AND CAPITAL ................................................. $_____
```

Figure 11-7. *(continued)*

statements, various analyses and ratios are calculated by **ratio analysis.** Several types of ratios can be calculated; the most important ones are described below.

Liquidity Ratios help in analysis of an operation's ability to meet short-term obligations as and when they become due. The *Current Ratio* is probably the most commonly used ratio in the foodservice industry. This ratio expresses the relationship between total current assets and total current liabilities. The *Acid Test Ratio or Quick Ratio* is another way of comparing current assets and liabilities. Accounts receivable as a percentage of total revenue represents the portion of revenues that have not been converted into cash and therefore are not available for payment of current obligations. Accounts receivable turnover shows the rapidity of the conversion of accounts receivable to cash. The calculations used for liquidity ratios are:

$$\text{Current Ratio} = \frac{\text{current assets}}{\text{current liabilities}}$$

$$\text{Acid Test Ratio (Quick Ratio)} = \frac{\text{cash} + \text{accounts receivable} + \text{marketable securities}}{\text{current liabilities}}$$

or

$$= \frac{\text{current assets} - \text{inventory}}{\text{current liabilities}}$$

$$\text{Accounts receivable to total revenue ratio} = \frac{\text{average accounts receivable}}{\text{total revenues}}$$

$$\text{Accounts receivable turnover} = \frac{\text{total revenue (total credit sales)}}{\text{average accounts receivable}}$$

Solvency refers to the ability of an operation to meet its debt obligations when they become due, including principal and interest on long-term borrowing. Solvency and leverage ratios are therefore designed to calculate the extent to which an operation is able to meet its debt and how much leverage exists for this possibility. Equations used for calculating solvency and leverage ratios are:

$$\text{Solvency Ratio} = \frac{\text{total assets}}{\text{total liabilities}}$$

$$\text{Debt-to-Total-Assets Ratio} = \frac{\text{total liabilities}}{\text{total assets}}$$

$$\text{Debt-equity Ratio} = \frac{\text{total debt}}{\text{total equity}}$$

$$\text{Number of times interest earned ratio} = \frac{\text{net profit before income taxes and interest expense}}{\text{interest expense}}$$

Activity Ratios show how effectively the assets of a foodservice operation are being utilized. They are also indicative of the efficiency of management and may be calculated using one of the following methods. It should be noted that each method is measuring a different parameter, which should be considered when comparing data.

$$\text{Food inventory turnover} = \frac{\text{total cost of food sold}}{\text{average food inventory}}$$

$$\text{Beverage inventory turnover} = \frac{\text{total cost of beverage sold}}{\text{average beverage inventory}}$$

$$\text{Fixed asset turnover} = \frac{\text{total revenues}}{\text{total fixed assets}}$$

$$\text{Accounts receivable turnover} = \frac{\text{total sales}}{\text{average accounts receivable}}$$

Profitability and Rate of Return Ratios, though not all applicable to all types of foodservice operations, are measures of profitability. They may be calculated as follows:

$$\text{Return on owner's equity} = \frac{\text{net profit after income taxes}}{\text{average stockholder's equity}}$$

$$\text{Return on assets} = \frac{\text{net profit before interest and income taxes}}{\text{total average assets}}$$

$$\text{Net return on assets} = \frac{\text{net profit after taxes}}{\text{total average assets}}$$

$$\text{Profit margin} = \frac{\text{net profit after income taxes}}{\text{total revenue}}$$

$$\text{Operating efficiency ratio} = \frac{\text{gross operating profit}}{\text{total revenue}}$$

Operating Ratios provide important information pertaining to daily operations of foodservice as well as to the efficiency of management. These ratios measure different aspects and are very helpful in assessing various operating parameters of an establishment. There are several ways in which these ratios may be calculated, some of which are given below:

$$\text{Average restaurant check} = \frac{\text{total food sales}}{\text{number of food covers sold}}$$

$$\text{Food cost (\%)} = \frac{\text{cost of food sold}}{\text{food sales}}$$

$$\text{Beverage cost (\%)} = \frac{\text{cost of beverage sold}}{\text{total beverage sales}}$$

$$\text{Sales per seat} = \frac{\text{net sales}}{\text{number of seats}}$$

$$\text{Operating Ratio} = \frac{\text{net profit}}{\text{net sales}}$$

$$\text{Net profit to net worth ratio} = \frac{\text{net profit}}{\text{net worth}}$$

$$\text{Management proficiency ratio} = \frac{\text{net profit after taxes}}{\text{total assets}}$$

Although ratio analysis is a very powerful analytical tool in evaluating financial ability, management effectiveness, operating results, activity reports, and as an aid to management in decision making, it should be used with caution since it has limitations:

1. The ratios are mathematical calculations and do not represent the human side of management. They are good only as far as the comparisons are meaningful.
2. Since ratios are based on mathematical calculations, any error or a difference in reporting system will offset the basis of comparison.
3. The timing of the financial transactions is important in comparing these ratios. Conditions change rapidly in any type of financial business, and this fact should be taken into consideration.

If properly interpreted, however, these ratios can be valuable tools in the hands of management.

SUMMARY

This chapter describes management principles and concepts and their role in the management of foodservice operations. Major management functions are described with key aspects highlighted. Factors to be considered in decision making, planning, organizing, communicating, directing, motivating, and controlling are outlined. Cost controls and ratio analysis are explained. All of these functions are essential to effective management of a foodservice operation.

REVIEW
QUESTIONS

What do you understand by management functions?
Discuss factors to be considered before any decision making.
What are the basic principles for effective communications?
What is the difference in planning long-range and short-range plans?
List advantages and disadvantages of ratio analysis.
What is the difference between (a) Liquidity Ratio and Solvency Ratio and (b) Activity Ratio and Operating Ratio?

ASSIGNMENTS

Interview a foodservice manager and ask selected questions pertaining to each aspect of management. Describe your assessment of the manager's attitude toward the importance of each function.
Draw an organization chart based on your answer to the above question.
Visit a foodservice operation and record all means of communication between the management and the employees.
Analyze a profit and loss statement and calculate at least two of the ratios described in this chapter. Discuss how these ratios can be used in long-term planning and in the overall management of foodservice operations.

SUGGESTED READINGS

Dittmer, P. R., and Griffin, G. G. 1980. *Principles of Food, Beverage, and Labor Cost Controls for Hotels and Restaurants*, 3rd edition. Van Nostrand Reinhold, New York, NY.

Keiser, J. R. 1989. *Principles and Practices of Management in the Hospitality Industry*, 2nd edition. Van Nostrand Reinhold, New York, NY.

Keiser, J. R. 1989. *Controlling and Analyzing Costs in Foodservice Operations*, 2nd edition. Macmillan Publishing Company, New York, NY.

Mill, R. C. 1989. *Managing for Productivity in the Hospitality Industry.* Van Nostrand Reinhold, New York, NY.

National Restaurant Association. 1968. *Uniform System of Accounts for Restaurants.* Washington, DC.

Powers, T., and Powers, J. 1984. *Food Service Operations: Planning and Control.* John Wiley & Sons, New York, NY.

Powers, T. 1988. *Introduction to Management in the Hospitality Industry*, 3rd edition. John Wiley & Sons, New York, NY.

Spears, M. C., and Vaden, A. G. 1985. *Foodservice Organizations. A Managerial Approach.* John Wiley & Sons, New York, NY.

CHAPTER 12

FOODSERVICE MANAGEMENT: PERSONNEL ASPECTS

KEY CONCEPTS AND TERMS

job analysis
job description
job specification
job orientation
training
work improvement studies
chronocyclegraph
stress management
performance appraisal
employee turnover

Personnel management is an increasing challenge for managers in foodservice operations. Human resources will become the number one problem facing the industry in the 21st century. The Department of Labor's Bureau of Labor Statistics projects that the labor force will reach nearly 139 million workers by 2000. Although there will be 21 million more workers than there are today, the growth in the work force will be slower than at any time since the 1930's. The composition of the work force will change. There will be fewer young workers, more women, and more minorities. Managers will have to deal with a different situation. A new way of running things will become necessary, and management will need to follow what is called "managing diversity." Human resources will be a limiting factor in many management decisions. There will be fewer job applicants, fewer trained workers, higher turnover rate, and consequently more jobs staying vacant for longer periods of time.

Personnel management is one of the most important functions of a foodservice operator. Good human relations are necessary for successful personnel management. In any type of foodservice operation, workers come from a variety of backgrounds, and managing them requires extraordinary skills. From the point of selecting employees to their working in the operation, careful management skills are required. In this chapter, only the major aspects of personnel management will be discussed, and only important points will be outlined, since personnel management is a complex subject of study by itself.

RECRUITMENT AND SELECTION OF EMPLOYEES

Because recruiting and retaining employees will become increasingly difficult, all aspects of personnel management need to be given careful attention. The first task to be undertaken by a person in charge of recruitment is to assess the need and outline the functions and requirements of a job. **Job analysis** is a process of obtaining all possible pertinent information about a job and leads to two important aspects that are also described as management tools: **job description** and **job specification.** These terms are used interchangeably by many operations, although a slight distinction may be made between the two.

Job description is a list of duties and responsibilities that are indicative of the type of skills required. It may be in the form of narrative description or an outline. Things to be included in the job description are: job title; location; summary of work; duties; machines, tools, or equipment involved; materials used; supervision required; work conditions; and desired controls.

Job specification is a statement or list of the minimum standards that must be met in order to qualify for a particular job. It normally includes education, experience, training, physical efforts, judgment capabilities, skills, responsibilities, and communication skills.

The job description and job specifications are helpful in screening candidates and in interviewing. Examples of a job description and job specifications are given in Figures 12.1 and 12.2.

After defining the needs of the job, the next task is to look for the places where suitable candidates may be located. An effort should be made to attract as many qualified candidates as possible. The more choices available, the better the selection will be. Advertise the job opening in appropriate publications and in other ways. Advertising for the job must reach prospective applicants. Putting an advertisement in the "Help Wanted" column is good, but a good worker who is currently employed elsewhere may not read advertisements. It is the unemployed worker

---

NAME OF OPERATION
(Location)

JOB TITLE: Cook   JOB CODE;
JOB SUMMARY
   Prepares meat entrées for lunch and dinner
   Responsible for preparation, whenever needed
   Washes all equipment used
   Works under and maintains sanitary conditions
JOB REQUIREMENTS
   A. *Responsibilities:* Responsible for preparation of main entrée and any specials of
      the day
   B. *Skills:* Plan work schedule, assemble all utensils and weigh accurately required
      ingredients, and apply basic principles of quantity food preparation
   C. *Equipment Used:* Ovens, ranges, broiler, steam-jacketed kettles, tilting frying
      pans, fryers, food choppers, and meat slicers
SUPERVISION
   Under supervision of the Food Production Manager
   Supervise Assistant Cooks
JOB RELATIONSHIPS
   Works in collaboration with other cooks
   Promotion to Production Manager after necessary experience
QUALIFICATION
   High School education, preferably with training in foodservice work
   Ability to read, write, and communicate
   Food Sanitation Certification

Figure 12-1.   An example of a typical job description.

```
┌─────────────────────────────────────────────────────────────┐
│                    NAME OF OPERATION                          │
│                      (Location)                               │
│                                                               │
│  JOB TITLE: Cook              JOB CODE;                       │
│  DEPARTMENT: Production                                       │
│  SUPERVISOR: Food Production Manager                          │
│  JOB SUMMARY: Prepares meat dishes                            │
│  EDUCATIONAL REQUIREMENTS: High School or higher              │
│  EXPERIENCE: Preferably in Foodservice and/or Food Production │
│  TESTS: Foodservice Sanitation Certification                  │
│  PHYSICAL REQUIREMENTS: Good health. Capable of heavy         │
│    physical work and lifting                                  │
│  SKILLS: Knowledge of basic principles of quantity food       │
│    preparation. Ability to understand, interpret, follow,     │
│    change, and work with standardized recipes                 │
│  PERSONAL: Neat and clean. Capable of working alone and       │
│    with others under stress. Follow sanitation principles     │
│    at all times                                               │
│  WORK REQUIREMENTS: Willing to work 40 hours per week;        │
│    work on alternate weekends and evenings                    │
│  PROMOTION: Will be considered for promotion to Food          │
│    Production Manager                                         │
│  BENEFITS: Health and Life insurance. Meals and drinks.       │
│    Two-week vacation                                          │
│  SALARY: Negotiable. Based on experience                      │
│  REFERENCES: Required                                         │
└─────────────────────────────────────────────────────────────┘
```

Figure 12-2. An example of a typical job specification.

who will be reading these ads. Other methods that can be used and places where vacancy announcements may be placed include:

1. Recruitment from within
2. Similar operations
3. Radio and television
4. Employment agencies
5. Professional journals
6. Other publications
7. Schools and colleges
8. Religious, social, and cultural organizations

A standard application form is desirable for recruitment because:

1. It provides for acquiring standard information about all applicants, making it easy to compare them.
2. It becomes the personal record of the applicant.
3. It saves time when interviewing.
4. It provides specific information, if the form is carefully designed.
5. It provides a chronological sequence of the work experience.
6. The applicant feels secure in answering questions arranged in logical sequence.

Interviewing

Completed application forms, if carefully reviewed, provide a basis for selecting suitable candidates to interview. The main purposes of the interview include:

1. Personally review, verify, and obtain explanations and additional information pertaining to the applicant.
2. Evaluate such personal characteristics of the applicant as manners, poise, speaking capability, and overall communication skills.
3. Assess the extent of motivation, drive, capability, desire, commitment, and obligation toward the job.
4. Give the applicant opportunity to see the facility and meet with personnel.
5. Provide an opportunity for mutual evaluation of the applicant and the operation.

Before the Interview

1. Determine the goal of the interview.
2. Prepare an outline for the interview.
3. Schedule the interview at a mutually convenient time.
4. Inform the interviewee of the purpose and the kind of interview.
5. Study all the pertinent information about the interviewee.
6. Provide ideal conditions of privacy for the interview.

During the Interview

1. Be yourself.
2. Let the interviewee settle down before beginning.
3. Be direct in your questions when possible.
4. Make your questions open-ended.
5. Try to get pertinent and accurate answers to the questions you ask.
6. Give the interviewee enough time to think about a question.
7. Be a good listener, not a talker.
8. Do not interrupt the interviewee.
9. Make frequent use of "why" and "how."
10. Use simple language.
11. Frame questions in such a way that they do not reveal your opinions or sentiments.
12. When in doubt, summarize interviewee's statements and reconfirm them.
13. Do not put words in interviewee's mouth.
14. Do not hesitate to probe.
15. Be in control of the interview and use your time effectively and fruitfully.
16. At the end of the interview, give the interviewee an opportunity to ask questions.
17. Make all aspects of your contact "evaluative" in nature.
18. Take notes, if necessary, during the interview.

After the Interview

1. Review and organize your notes immediately.
2. Try to evaluate questions you have raised and the answers received.
3. After careful evaluation of facts and attitudes, arrive at a decision concerning employment of the applicant.

Orientation and Training

With the labor shortage, **training** will become increasingly critical. A well-trained employee will be highly motivated. Once an employee is selected and hired, the first day should encompass job orientation. Orientation should involve a tour of the facility and information regarding benefits and policies. This should be followed by training, which can be done either by a manager, supervisor, senior employee, or a training specialist.

Training the new employee is an investment and should be done in a way that yields maximum benefits on a long-term basis. Training is also the first impression that an employee gets of the work itself. It may not be desirable to have the new employee trained by senior personnel or the one who is leaving the position, since the person involved may be a good worker but not a good trainer. Also, the chances of perpetuating mistakes are prevalent in this type of training. The attitudes of the teacher and the trainee are important in the entire training process. On-the-job demonstrations and hands-on experience are preferable to teaching in a classroom atmosphere because of the many practical aspects involved in foodservices. Training may be in the form of on-the-job training, refresher courses, programmed instruction, self-paced studies, or retraining programs.

Retraining of employees at periodic intervals is essential in order to provide a continuing education and to bring the employees up to date with new information and techniques. While training a new or existing employee, the following aspects should be taken into consideration:

1. Lessons should be well organized.
2. Lessons should be easy and interesting to learn. They may be taught individually or in groups.
3. Lessons should be adapted to the capability and speed of the learners.
4. The training schedule should be at a convenient time and location.
5. The training program may include lectures, conferences, seminars, problem-solving sessions, case studies, and/or role playing.
6. The best possible tools should be used for the purpose of training, for example, films, videos, texts, workbooks, computer programs, posters, bulletins, charts, slides, and games.
7. The training program should be assessed and evaluated from time to time. Feedback from employees is very useful in these evaluations.

The advantages of correct training to management are numerous, the most important being

1. Increased production	5. Increased job satisfaction
2. Decreased breakage and spoilage	6. Reduced labor-turnover rate
3. Reduced number of accidents	7. Reduced absenteeism
4. Reduced complaints	8. Increased quality of performance

The advantages of good training to the employees include self-respect; motivation; chances for advancement; increased earning power; and gaining new skills, techniques, and knowledge.

Work Scheduling

Work schedules are plans that distribute the work among different individuals in order to carry out specific activities according to a set time and procedural requirements. The work schedules should be comprehensive yet simple and easy to understand. A well-planned schedule saves a considerable amount of a manager's time, time that may be utilized in performing other management functions. The schedule may be a descriptive outline of work, a tabular form, or a chart. Work schedules should be based on job analysis; the number of workers required for a particular job, menu, or method of preparation; and the type of service. Schedules are necessary for the proper distribution of work loads, for employee reassignments, for determining the areas requiring help, and for filling any vacancies due to unforeseen circumstances. An example of a simple work schedule is given in Figure 12.3.

Work Improvement

Organization manuals, job descriptions, job specifications, and work schedules are all important for improving the work of an employee. Every possible means of work satisfaction and improvement should be provided by management. In order to improve work, the factors responsible for fatigue or stress should be evaluated. Some of these factors are:

1. Psychological, such as dislike for work or dislike for the supervisor or colleagues
2. Low rate of pay and lack of rewards
3. Lack of recess or breaks
4. Monotony of work
5. Poor lighting, heating, and ventilation; high noise level and other environmental factors
6. Improper layout and design of workplace, equipment, and other facilities
7. Hours of work

Function and Position	Monday		Tuesday		Wednesday		Thursday		Friday	
	Time	Employee	Time	Employee	Time	Employee	Time	Employee	Time	Employee
PRODUCTION										
Supervisor										
Range										
Vegetable										
Salad										
Bake Shop										

Week: _____
Date: _____

SERVICE	Time	Employee	Time	Employee	Time	Employee	Time	Employee	Time	Employee
Dishroom										
Service Supervisor										
Supervisor, Counter										
Entrée										
Vegetable										
Soup and Hot Breads										
Salads and Desserts										
Beverage										
Checker										
Cashier (1)										
Cashier (2)										

Figure 12-3. A typical work schedule form.

Name of Worker	Observations										Total	Percent

√ = Productive Work   0 = Nonproductive Work

The total of the percentages of productive work ÷ number of employees = estimated efficiency of the work force.

Figure 12-4.   The sampling method to estimate worker productivity.

Work Improvement Studies

Work improvement studies should be undertaken whenever possible in order to improve the working conditions and to reduce fatigue. Several scientific studies are specifically designed to study work and to assess needed improvements. Some of the studies are described below.

Work sampling is a simple study that involves calculating the amount of work done by randomly selected workers. The percentage of the time spent on productive work is compared to nonproductive work. A chart used for the sampling method is given in Figure 12.4.

A *pathway chart* or *flow diagram* is a scale drawing of an area on which the path of a worker is traced. It involves the measurement of the distance the worker travels to conduct specific tasks. Total length is used in this study. A scale diagram may be drawn while the worker is being observed. Another way of accomplishing this would be to have pins on a drawing board at points a worker is most likely to travel. A string may be used to wind around the pins based on the points travelled by a worker. The total distance may be calculated by measuring the length of the string. This procedure is simple but has many drawbacks. For example, it does not account for the time spent on certain tasks, and it is not possible to use if the foodservice facility is spread out on different floors or areas.

Operation charts show the sequential action of movements without any consideration to the time involved. They are mainly for improving the techniques involved in execution of a task. An example of an operation chart is shown in Figure 12.5. In operating charts, symbols such as small circles are used to indicate transportation, whereas large circles are used for action. Thus, movements are classified in terms of transportation and action. At the conclusion of the study the number of small circles and large circles is counted. Improvements for work are outlined on the basis of reduction of unnecessary transportation and on coordinating the actions of both hands.

Process charts are based on a technique in which steps or events are fully analyzed and divided into categories. At the conclusion of the study all these

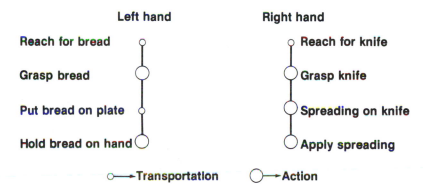

Figure 12-5.   Operating chart showing partial movements of hands in making a sandwich.

different categories are analyzed, based on which improvements are recommended. The symbols most often used in process charts are:

O = Operation
→ = Transportation
D = Delay
∇ = Storage or Hold
□ = Inspection

Present □			**Proposed □**		**Page Number □**		
Summmary	No.	Time	Task or job:				
Operations (0)							
Inspections (□)			Dept:				
Moves (→)			Operator:				
Delays (D)							
Storage or Hold (∇)			Equipment/ Tools, etc.:				
Total:			Date:				
Total Distance:			Analyst:				
Descriptive Notes			Activity		Dist.	Time	Comments
			0 □ → D ∇				
			0 □ → D ∇				
			0 □ → D ∇				
			0 □ → D ∇				
			0 □ → D ∇				
			0 □ → D ∇				
			0 □ → D ∇				
			0 □ → D ∇				
			0 □ → D ∇				
			0 □ → D ∇				
			0 □ → D ∇				
			0 □ → D ∇				
			0 □ → D ∇				
			0 □ → D ∇				
			0 □ → D ∇				
			0 □ → D ∇				
			0 □ → D ∇				
			0 □ → D ∇				
			0 □ → D ∇				

Figure 12-6. An example of a process chart.

An example of the process chart is given in Figure 12.6. A line may be drawn from one symbol to another and the number of O's counted. Improvements are made by recommending elimination of unnecessary actions. The advantage of process chart is that it is easy to use; it analyzes activities, distances travelled, and time spent; it gives complete information; and it may be used for product or work analysis.

Micromotion studies study the movement of a worker's hand by photography. All of the actions of a worker can also be studied. Based on the photographs, actions are divided into various movements. These movements are represented by "Therbligs," which are units named by spelling the name Gilbreth, who is the author of these measurements, backwards. There are primarily seventeen therbligs for which the symbols are:

Sh	Search	PP	Preposition
St	Select	A	Assemble
I	Inspect	DA	Disassemble
TE	Transport Empty	U	Use
G	Grasp	AD	Avoidable delay
H	Hold	UD	Unavoidable delay
TL	Transport loaded	Pn	Plan
RL	Release load	R	Rest
P	Position		

These symbols are used for analyses and, ultimately, recommendations for the work improvements.

A **Chronocyclegraph** is a photographic technique by which hand movements are recorded by attaching lights or reflective objects to the hands. A negative film of the photograph will contain dotted lines which, in turn, are used for analysis of hand movements.

With the popularity of videotaping, work improvement studies may be carried out easily, by using hidden cameras, to avoid possible bias and certain drawbacks of earlier methods.

Standardization of Work Techniques

Standardization of work techniques is essential for successful work simplification. The principles of motion economy can be used to standardize motions, methods and practices, and work space and equipment.

Standard Motions

In order to accomplish motion economy and fatigue reduction, the following aspects should considered:

Both hands should begin as well as complete their motions at the same time.

Both hands should not be idle at the same time except during a rest period.

Motions of the arms should be made in opposite and symmetrical directions and should be made simultaneously.

Smooth, continuous motions of hands are preferable to zigzag or straight-line motions involving sudden and sharp changes in direction.

Ballistic movements are faster, easier, and more accurate than restricted or controlled movements.

Eye fixations should be as few and as close together as possible.

Unnecessary reaching, stretching, and bending should be avoided.

Objects should be lifted by bending knees and avoiding stretching.

Simple, balanced, continuous, and rhythmic motions should be used.

Momentum should be employed to assist the worker whenever possible, and it should be reduced to a minimum if it must be overcome by muscular effort.

Standard Methods and Practices

Plan and organize work well.

Use correct methods and a proper sequence of operations.

Make proper equipment available and preposition around the workspace.

Change job or position when fatigue sets in. Provide short rest periods.

Perform all like operations at one time.

Standard Work Space and Equipment

Organize the floor plan with proper equipment efficiently placed in order to reduce transportation and walking.

Provide a definite and fixed place for all tools and materials. Locate them so as to permit the best sequence of motions.

Adjust the height of the work tables (35 to 36 in) if possible.

Provide adequate and proper lighting and ventilation.

Alternate the workers, whenever possible, between standing and sitting, particularly on prolonged jobs.

Use "drop deliveries" wherever possible.

Relieve the hands of all work that can be done more advantageously by combination tools or foot-operated devices.

Where each finger performs some specific movement, distribute the load in accordance with the inherent capacities of the fingers.

Locate levers, handwheels, and crossbars in such positions that the operator can manipulate them with the least change in the body position.

Make optimum use of momentum, acceleration, and gravity.

STRESS MANAGEMENT

One of the most important aspects to be considered in the workplace is **stress management,** whether it is related to managers or employees. *Stress* may be defined as an impact of several factors associated with work that result in a reaction that adversely affects the physical, psychological, and mental performance of a normal employee. These factors should be assessed and steps should be taken to reduce stress. Some of the symptoms and causes of stress are outlined below:

Management
Attitude of the management
Improper scheduling
Low salaries
Unresolved disputes
High employee- or management-
   turnover rate
Long hours of work
Poor communications

Physical conditions
Poor arrangement of equipment
Poor arrangement of storage areas
Handling materials that cause physi-
   cal discomfort
Poor working conditions
Hazardous equipment and conditions

Co-workers
Uncooperative employees
Absenteeism
Lack of understanding

Customers
Too demanding customers
Inconsiderate customers

Other reasons
Weather conditions
Traffic conditions
Consumer traffic

PERFORMANCE APPRAISAL

Management should plan for the regular appraisal of employees at set intervals. New employees may be evaluated shortly after hiring, whereas other employees may be evaluated on a yearly basis. **Performance appraisals** are useful because they:

Provide a check on employee performance.

Indirectly result in improved employee productivity.

Help in recognizing the achievement of employees.

Provide a basis for salary increase.

Might reduce the employee turnover rate.

Provide an opportunity for any needed corrective measures.

Facilitate the decisions for further training.

Identify good and hard workers.

Several methods may be used for performance evaluation. A point system with weights for each factor or a nonpoint system using charts for different factors may be used. Rank-ordering of all the employees may also be used if the foodservice operation does not have a large number of employees. Forced distribution involves distributing employees into percentiles based on performance. Paired comparisons may also be conducted among two or more individuals. Field reviews and critical incident methods are also suitable for performance evaluation of employees within a foodservice operation. The factors most commonly evaluated include:

Quality of work	Compatibility
Quantity of work	Safe working methods
Knowledge of work	Sincerity
Dependability	Initiative

Based on performance evaluations, corrective measures for undesirable attributes can be implemented.

EMPLOYEE TURNOVER

Employee turnover can prove very expensive for a foodservice operation. The reasons for turnover should be checked carefully. The turnover may be due to (1) workers' decision on their own accord (voluntary), (2) management's decision to terminate the worker for various reasons (involuntary), or (3) the hiring of seasonal employees like students (calculated). Uncontrollable turnovers are those that cannot be controlled by the management as compared to controllable turnovers. Some actions that can be taken to control turnover include:

Assess the exact cause of the turnover.

Evaluate hiring policies.

Provide for effective supervision.

Initiate a good training program.

Conduct regular performance evaluations.

Recognize hard-working employees.

Conduct meetings with the employees.

Evaluate any grievances.

MOTIVATION AND JOB ENRICHMENT

Good management will always try to motivate employees and provide a suitable work atmosphere. The productivity of a foodservice operation is directly based on the motivation of the employees. Some reasons that should be considered by management for providing motivation include:

Create an interest and purpose for work.

Provide for a sense of achievement.

Give as much responsibility as the employee can easily and comfortably handle.

Provide new opportunities for learning.

Provide all possible opportunities for advancement.

Provide good wages and working conditions.

Develop good training programs.

Appreciate employee efforts and achievements.

Understand personal problems and drawbacks.

Become a source of inspiration and an example.

Managers should also evaluate themselves from time to time. Several self-evaluation questionnaires are available. An example of such a questionnaire is given in Appendix K. Several computer programs and software are also available for evaluation of different management functions.

Model Employment Programs

For the purpose of recruitment and retention of foodservice employees of the future, management should be willing to assess some of the model employment programs that will be in place at various operations. These programs will have to be geared toward the composition of the work force expected for the year 2000 and beyond. This force will include increased numbers of women, older persons, minority workers, and handicapped workers. The above-mentioned facts were the outcome of a study done by the National Restaurant Association. Some of the recommendations for the recruitment and retention of these workers include:

Women workers: benefits, wages, flexibility, career opportunities, training and information.

Minorities: image building, recruitment through role models, improved compensation, benefits and support services, and cultural values.

Older workers: sensitivity to prior experience and needs, benefits and compensation, training and advancement opportunities, structure and fit of the job, and information.

Handicapped workers: linkages and information exchanges between employers and agencies serving the disabled, flexibility in approaches to training, compensation, benefits, and special support services, career advancement opportunities, and educating managers and co-workers.

These suggested programs are only some possible recommendations, but it is evident that novel approaches will be needed to fulfil the human resources demands of the growing hospitality industry in the next century.

SUMMARY

This chapter emphasizes the need for efficient personnel management in consideration of the decreasing work force of the future. Discussions focus on the recruitment and selection of employees and factors to be considered in recruitment. After recruitment, points to be considered for orientation, training, and retention are outlined. Standardization of work techniques and work improvement methods are described. Finally, ways to improve productivity, ways to reduce stress, and ways to increase motivation are highlighted. This chapter concludes the stepwise discussion of all concepts essential to foodservice operations and management.

REVIEW
QUESTIONS

What is the difference between job description and job specification? How can each be used in the recruitment of foodservice workers?

What aspects should be included in the orientation of a new employee?

What are the common causes of stress in a foodservice operation? List ways to reduce this stress.

What methods can be used in the performance appraisal of an employee? What are the advantages of performance appraisals?

How can the problem of labor shortage predicted for the future be solved? Discuss some possible novel approaches for the recruitment and retaining of the employees.

ASSIGNMENTS

Write a job description for a position of an employee who will be working in the entrée section of a foodservice kitchen.

Visit a foodservice operation and enquire about the training program for employees. Write a report based on your observation.

Select a work improvement method and comment on its applicability in a foodservice operation of your choice.

Develop a performance appraisal form based on all aspects you consider essential for the productivity of an average worker.

Collect data on labor demographics and suggest novel programs that can be used by the restaurant industry to attract, recruit, and retain well-qualified workers for a decade.

SUGGESTED READINGS

Keiser, J. R. 1989. *Principles and Practices of Management in the Hospitality Industry,* 2nd edition. Van Nostrand Reinhold, New York, NY.

Mill, R. C. 1989. *Managing for Productivity in the Hospitality Industry.* Van Nostrand Reinhold, New York, NY.

National Restaurant Association. 1989. Foodservice Employment 2000: Exemplary Industry Programs. *Current Issues Report* (1/89). National Restaurant Association, Washington, DC.

National Restaurant Association. 1989. Model Employment Programs: Recruitment and Retention of Foodservice Employees. *Current Issues Report* (9/89). National Restaurant Association, Washington, DC.

National Restaurant Association. 1988. Foodservice Industry 2000 *Current Issues Report* (9/88). National Restaurant Association, Washington, DC.

Wheelhouse, D. 1989. *Managing Human Resources in the Hospitality Industry.* The Educational Institute of the American Hotel & Motel Association, East Lansing, MI.

APPENDICES

A. COMMON FOREIGN TERMS USED ON MENUS

TERM	APPROXIMATE PRONUNCIATION	DEFINITION
à la	ah-lah	After the style or fashion
à la carte	ah-lah cart	On the bill of fare; prepared as ordered and priced separately
à la king	ah-lah-king	Served in a cream sauce containing mushrooms, green peppers, and pimientos
au gratin	oh-grah-tan	With a topping of buttered crumbs and cheese
au jus	oh-jù	Served in its natural juice or gravy
béarnaise	bair-nez	In America, a sauce similar to hollandaise, fortified with meat glaze, and with tarragon flavor predominating
béchmel	bay-shaw-mel	Cream sauce
beurre	burr	Butter
bisque	beesk	Thick, rich soup
bordelaise	bawr-d'layz	Brown sauce with butter or fat, meat stock, wine, and seasonings
borsch	bohrsh-ch	Russian soup made of beef stock and beets
brochette	bro-shet	Meat broiled on a skewer
café au lait	cafay-oh-lay	Coffee served with hot milk
café noir	cafay nwahr	Clear, black coffee
canapé	kah-nah-paý	A small piece of toast or fried bread spread with savory foods and served as an appetizer
carte du jour	kahrt-du-joor	Menu of the day
charlotte	shaŕ-lot	A dessert with gelatin, whipped cream, and fruit or other flavoring, in a mold garnished with lady fingers
chiffonade	sheé-fahn-ahd	With finely shredded vegetables
chutney	chuŕ-ni	A spicy relish made from fruits and/or vegetables
compote	kom-poté	Fruit stewed in syrup

TERM	APPROXIMATE PRONUNCIATION	DEFINITION
consommé	kon-so-maý	Clear meat stock served hot or jellied
creole	kree-ol	Prepared with tomatoes, green peppers, and onions
crêpe Suzette	krayp-su-zetté	Thin French pancake rolled and served with a sauce
croutons	kroo-tohn	Small pieces of fried or toasted bread used as accompaniments for soups
demitasse	deh-mee-tahsś	Small cup of coffee served after dinner
éclairs	ay-klaiŕ	French choux pastry filled with a cream filling or custard
en casserole	anh-kahs-roĺ	Baked or served in an individual dish
enchilada	en-chee-láh-dah	Tortilla dipped in hot fat, sauces, and dressings
en cocotte	ahn-ko-coŕ	In an individual casserole
entrée	ahń-traý	A main dish served before the roast or meat course; as commonly used in restaurants may include all main dishes
filet	fee-laý	A boneless loin cut of beef, veal, or pork; or a boneless strip of fish
flambé	flawm-bay	Flamed
fondue	fahn-dú	Baked dish of eggs, milk, cheese, and bread
fricassée	free-kay-say	Meat or chicken stewed and served with thickened sauce
frijoles	fre-hol-ayz	Beans cooked with fat and seasonings
froid	frwah	Cold
glacé	glah-saý	Frozen or glazed
goulash	goó-lash	Thick beef or veal stew with vegetables and paprika
gratin	grah-tan	Brown, baked with cheese
hollandaise	hol-ahn-dayz	Sauce of eggs, butter, lemon juice, and seasonings
hors d'oeuvre	ohr-doé-vr	Savory foods served as appetizers
jardiniere	zhaŕd-n-aiŕ	A mixture of green vegetables
julienne	zhu-lee-eń	Cut in thin and long strips
kebobs	ká-bobs	Marinated lamb and vegetables cooked on skewers
lait	lay	Milk
limpa	limp-a	Swedish rye bread
lyonnaise	leé-oh-nayz	Sautéed with slices of onion
marinade	mah-ree-nahd́	Mixture of oil and seasonings used to flavor and tenderize meats and vegetables
mayonnaise	mah-on-ayś	A salad dressing made with egg, oil, and lemon juice or vinegar
meringue	may-ran-ǵ	A baked dessert made of white of egg and sugar or the topping of pastry
meuniere	moon-yer	Pan-fried and served with brown butter

TERM	APPROXIMATE PRONUNCIATION	DEFINITION
mousse	moose	Frothy dessert made with whipped cream or egg whites
parfait	pahr-faý	Frozen dessert or ice cream in tall stemmed glass with fruit or syrup
pastrami	pahs-tramé-ee	Highly spiced corned-beef brisket
pâté	pah-taý	Highly seasoned meat paste used as appetizer
petit fours	pe-teet-foorś	Fancy small cakes with decorations
pilau/pilaf	pih-lahí	Seasoned rice
purée	pu-ray	A thick-sieved vegetable or fruit; thick-sieved soup
ragoût	ra-goo	A rich stew of highly seasoned meat and gravy
ravioli	rav-vee-oh'lee	Bite-sized noodles filled with meat and other ingredients
rissolé	ree-soh-laý	Browned
roulade	roo-lahd	A thin slice of meat rolled around a filling
sauté	sah-taý	Fried in a small amount of fat
soufflé	soof-flaý	Light, puffed; a light egg mixture served as an entrée or sometimes (when sweetened) as a dessert
spumoni	spoo-mohnee	Rich ice cream in different layers with nuts
stroganoff	strog'an-off	Sautéed beef in sour cream with mushrooms and onions
strudel	stroo'dl	Pastry made of paper-thin flaky dough
table d'hôte	tabll-dohí	A meal served in several courses at a set price
timbale	tám-bahl	Molded vegetable or meats set in custard; sometimes applied to thin batter cases fried in deep fat
tutti-frutti	too-teé-froo-teé	A mixture of fruits
velouté	vuh-lootay	White sauce made from fish, chicken, or veal stock
vol-au-vent	vohl-au-vahń	A puff-paste enclosing a delicate minced meat
Weiner schnitzel	ve-ner-shnit-sel	Breaded veal cutlet served with lemon

B. COMMON UTENSILS USED IN FOODSERVICE OPERATIONS

1	FRENCH KNIFE OR CHEF'S KNIFE
	Most frequently used knife in the kitchen. Can be used for slicing, dicing, chopping, and cutting. Blade is wide at the heel and tapers at the point. Its shape makes it easy to cut by holding the tip against the cutting board and rocking the knife up and down.
2	BUTCHER'S KNIFE
	Used for cutting, sectioning, and trimming raw meats. Has a slightly curved blade which allows for deep cuts. It is heavy and has a broad blade.
3	UTILITY KNIFE
	A narrow, pointed knife about 6–8 inches long. Used for cutting and pre-paring vegetables. Can also be used for carving cooked meat roasts.
4	PARING KNIFE
	The blade is small, about 2–3 inches long. Can be used for removing skins, peeling, trimming, and cutting fruits and vegetables.

5	**BONING KNIFE** Has a thin, pointed blade, about 6 inches long. Can be used to cut around the bones of meat to remove flesh. Its sharp point helps in smooth cutting of meats.
6	**SERRATED KNIFE** Has a long (10–14 inches) serrated blade. Used for slicing breads and cutting baked items.
7	**SLICER** A long slender knife with flexible blade. Used for carving and slicing cooked meats. Its long blade (12–14 inches) helps in carving large pieces of cooked meats.
8	**CLEAVER** Has a very heavy, broad rectangular blade. Used for cutting through bones or chopping meats.
9	**OYSTER KNIFE** A short knife with blunt blade and a dull edge. Has a handle for easy grip. The edge is used for opening oysters.

10	**COOK'S FORK** Has two strong pointed prongs, which are used for lifting, holding, and turning meats and other solid items during preparation.
11	**PIE SERVER** A wedge-shaped offset spatula which can be used for lifting and serving pie wedges from pan.
12	**OFFSET SPATULA** A broad blade offset spatula. Used for turning foods such as hamburger, pancakes, baked food, etc. It can also be used for scraping griddle or grill surfaces.
13	**SANDWICH SPREADER** Has a short blade, useful for placing spreads and fillings on sandwiches.
14	**STRAIGHT SPATULA** Has a long blade with rounded ends. Can be used for a variety of functions, such as spreading, mixing, and scraping.

15	**RUBBER SPATULA OR SCRAPER** Has a broad, flexible rubber or plastic tip on a long handle. The rubber end is used to scrape bowls and pans. Can also be used for folding in egg foams and whipped cream.
16	**WHEEL KNIFE OR PASTRY WHEEL** Has a wheel-type rotating blade. Can be used for cutting pastry, rolled-out doughs, pizza, and other baked items.
17	**GRATER** A hand-operated grater, which consists of a four-sided metallic box with different sized grids. Comes in different sizes. The grid surfaces may be used for shredding and grating items such as vegetables, cheese, coconut, and fruit rinds.
18	**VEGETABLE PEELER** Has a pointed end and slotted blade. Used for peeling smaller quantities of vegetables and fruits. Can also be used for carving fruits and vegetables.
19	**TONGS** Used for picking up foods. They are of different shapes and sizes. Example shown is of spring-type tongs. There are also scissor-type tongs.

20		STRAINER Available in different sizes and shapes. They may have screen-type mesh or perforations on metals. Used for straining.
21		SPOONS: SLOTTED, PERFORATED AND SOLID Large-sized spoons used for stirring, mixing, separation, and serving. Slotted and perforated spoons are used to remove foods from liquids.
22		LADLES Most commonly used utensils in food-service. They have long stems and can be used for measuring, portioning, serving, mixing, etc. Available in variety of sizes. Sizes are indicated on the handle.
23		SKIMMER Used for skimming foods from liquids, for removing solid pieces from soups/stocks, for removing deep-fried items.

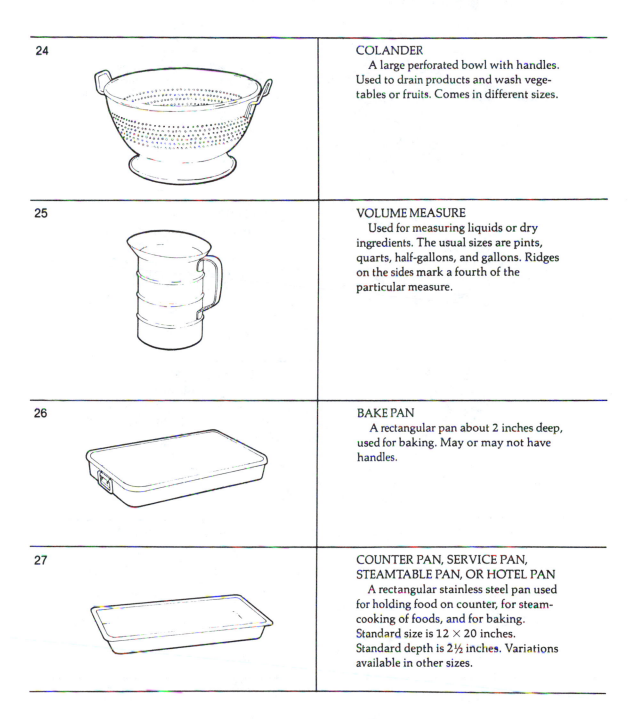

24

COLANDER

A large perforated bowl with handles. Used to drain products and wash vegetables or fruits. Comes in different sizes.

25

VOLUME MEASURE

Used for measuring liquids or dry ingredients. The usual sizes are pints, quarts, half-gallons, and gallons. Ridges on the sides mark a fourth of the particular measure.

26

BAKE PAN

A rectangular pan about 2 inches deep, used for baking. May or may not have handles.

27

COUNTER PAN, SERVICE PAN, STEAMTABLE PAN, OR HOTEL PAN

A rectangular stainless steel pan used for holding food on counter, for steamcooking of foods, and for baking. Standard size is 12 × 20 inches. Standard depth is 2½ inches. Variations available in other sizes.

| 28 | ROASTING PAN |
| | A deep, strong rectangular pan for roasting meats. It is deep in order to collect drained liquids. Also has handles on either side for easy removal from the oven. |

| 29 | SHEET PAN |
| | A shallow rectangular pan. Mainly used for baking cookies, rolls, and similar items. Can also be used for baking or broiling certain items such as fish. |

| 30 | WIRE WHIPS |
| | Heavy wires fastened to a handle to form a loop which can be used for mixing, stirring, beating, whipping, and thinning. |

| 31 | PASTRY BAG AND TUBES |
| | A cone-shaped plastic bag with a narrow end that can be fitted with tubes of different shapes and sizes. These bags may be filled with products used for shaping and decorating. |

32

CUPCAKE PAN OR MUFFIN PAN
A rectangular pan with slots for baking cupcakes or muffins. Available in different sizes based on the number (dozen) of slots.

33

LAYER-CAKE PAN
Used for baking cakes. Comes in different sizes; common diameters are 7 to 9 inches. Some have brackets in the center for easy removal of product.

34

TUBE CAKE PAN
Used for baking air-leavened cakes such as angelfood. Comes in a variety of sizes with removable or nonremovable inside tubes.

C. REQUEST FOR BID PROPOSAL ON FRESH AND FROZEN MEATS

University of Illinois
Purchasing Division
South Oak Street
Champaign, Illinois 61820

Bid Opening: June 3, 199 —, 11 A.M. CST

Bids will be received on the attached form submitted in the Sealed Bid envelope provided herewith or, in cases of emergency or rapidly changing market conditions, by telephone, telegraph (with confirmation to follow exactly as submitted through the media) at the Purchasing Division, 1321 South Oak Street, Champaign, Illinois 61820 [telephone (217) 333–1408] by 11:00 A.M. on the date indicated on these forms. It should be understood that all bids submitted via public media or telegraph or telephone will be handled in a confidential manner until the bid opening hour and date. However, the University assumes no responsibility for inadvertent disclosure prior to the bid opening hour.

It is the intention of the University to place orders no later than the day following the date of the bid opening for expected delivery within four days.

Bidders may make any special offerings for meat items not listed on this proposal. However, such offerings must include, in addition to a firm quoted price, terms and conditions and special or unique conditions for offering such as maximum or minimum quantities available, packaging, age of product, etc. Each such offering will be considered on the basis of its value to the University in relation to current and anticipated related market conditions. The University retains the right to accept or reject any such offering made. Samples of special offers may be required.

Proposals must be signed by an authorized agent of your firm. The sealed bid envelope(s), if provided by the University, is/are to be marked with your company name and return address, all prices quoted must be F.O.B. University of Illinois, Champaign, Illinois. Inquiries concerning the bid proposal can be made to the Food Buyer's office at Central Food Stores, 1321 South Oak Street, Champaign, Illinois; telephone (217) 333–1408.

The University reserves the right to reject any or all bids or any part thereof, to have any formalities in the bidding, and to accept the bid which is deemed most favorable in the interest of the University after all bids have been examined and evaluated.

Meat will be received on the basis of net weight with an allowance for fresh meat shrinkage in transit not in excess of one-half of one percent.

Meat deliveries in boxes must be in 60-pound master cartons. Gross, tare, and net weight must be listed on the *end* of each master carton in order to be visible when palletized.

All beef, veal, and lamb must be USDA graded. Pork must come from USDA No. 1 pork carcasses.

All meats, prepared meats, meat food products, and meat by-products covered on this bid proposal, whether in the fresh, manufactured, or processed state, must originate from animals which were slaughtered or from related product items which are prepared in establishments regularly operated under (1) the supervision of the Federal Meat Inspection Division (MID) of the United States Department of Agriculture (USDA), (2) any other system of meat inspection recognized by the Federal MID, (3) any other system of meat inspection approved by Agriculture Marketing Service of the USDA, or (4) the plant must be in good standing with the Illinois State Department of Agriculture with any known violation corrected.

All products shall be in a wholesome and sanitary condition when delivered. All meat, prepared meats, meat by-products, and meat products shall be individually wrapped, packed, or covered in conventional packages of standard material, in good, clean condition, so that the contents are properly protected. Refrigerated trucks shall be used to transport product, forms, and the truck shall be clean and free from odors foreign to meat. All products will be reexamined at their final destination for cleanliness and wholesomeness as food.

All deliveries shall conform in every respect to the provisions of the Federal Food, Drug, and Cosmetic Act, and regulations promulgated thereunder, and with applicable state, county, and city laws relating to products under contract.

This transaction is subject to Regulations Governing Procurement and Bidding at State Systems Universities in Illinois adopted pursuant to the Illinois Purchasing Act.

The undersigned offers the prices, terms, and delivery herein set forth.

FIRM BIDDING: _____

AUTHORIZED SIGNATURE: _____

DATE: _____

D. SELECTED FOOD SANITATION REGULATIONS

(Illinois Department of Public Health)

FOOD SUPPLIES

Food shall be in sound condition, free from spoilage, filth, and other contamination and shall be safe for human consumption. Food shall be obtained from sources that comply with all laws relating to food and food labeling. Use of home prepared or hermetically sealed food which has been processed in a place other than a food processing establishment is prohibited.

Special Requirements

1. Fluid milk and fluid-milk products used or served shall be pasteurized and shall meet the Grade A quality standards as established by law. Dry milk and dry-milk products shall be pasteurized.
2. Fresh and frozen shucked shellfish (oysters, clams, or mussels) shall be packed in nonreturnable packages identified with the name and address of the original shell stock processor, shucker/packer, or repacker, and the interstate certification number issued according to the law. Shell stock and shucked shellfish shall be kept in the container in which they were received until they are used. Each container of unshucked shell stock (oysters, clams, or mussels) shall be identified by the attached tag that states the name and address of the original shell stock processor, the kind and quantity of shell stock, and an interstate certification number issued by the state or foreign shellfish control agency.
3. Only clean whole eggs, with shell intact and without cracks or checks, or pasteurized liquid, frozen, or dry eggs or pasteurized dry egg products shall be used, except that hard boiled peeled eggs, commercially prepared and packaged may be used.

Reason: To control foodborne illness and prevent food spoilage, which may result from improperly processed, handled, or transported food, food service establishments must be concerned with the sources of the food they use. The sound condition, proper labeling, and

Note: For details of the rules and regulations, contact your local public health authority. The regulations presented here are examples from the Sanitation Requirements.

336

safety of food are basic requirements for the protection of the public health. Accordingly, the provisions of this section are intended to ensure that food in general, especially potentially hazardous food, is obtained from sources considered satisfactory by the regulatory authority.

The use of hermetically sealed, noncommercially packaged food is prohibited because of the history of such food in causing foodborne illness. Additional specific requirements for food supplies, such as the pasteurization of milk and milk products or the use of only clean, whole-shell eggs, are included because these products are exceptionally good media for the growth of pathogens. Labeling requirements, particularly for shellfish, provide assurance that the source of any such food is under the control of a regulatory authority, thus providing for the protection of the public health.

General—Food Protection

1. At all times, including while being stored, prepared, displayed, served, or transported, food shall be protected from potential contamination, including dust, insects, rodents, unclean equipment and utensils, unnecessary handling, coughs and sneezes, flooding, drainage, and overhead leakage or overhead drippage from condensation. The temperature of potentially hazardous foods shall be 45°F or below or 140°F or above at all times, except as otherwise provided in this Part.
2. In the event of a fire, flood, power outage, or similar event that might result in the contamination of food, or that might prevent potentially hazardous food from being held at required temperatures, the person in charge shall immediately contact the regulatory authority. Upon receiving notice of this occurrence, the regulatory authority shall take whatever action that it deems necessary to protect the public health.

Reason: Food, if mishandled, can become contaminated with filth, pathogenic microorganisms and toxic chemicals from a number of sources. Therefore, food protection measures are designed to protect food from being contaminated at all times within the establishment and during transportation. These measures are also intended to prevent the rapid and progressive growth of disease-causing organisms that are naturally present in foods as well as those introduced through incidental contamination in the operation of a food service establishment.

Proper food protection measures should include: (1) Application of good sanitation practices in the handling of food; (2) strict observation of personal hygiene by all food service employees; (3) keeping potentially hazardous food refrigerated or heated to temperatures that minimize the growth of pathogenic microorganisms; (4) inspecting food products as to their sanitary condition prior to acceptance at the establishment; and (5) provision of adequate equipment and facilities for the conduct of sanitary operations.

General—Food Storage

1. Food, whether raw or prepared, if removed from the container or package in which it was obtained shall be in a clean, covered container except during necessary periods of preparation or service. Container covers shall be impervious and nonabsorbent, except that linens or napkins may be used for lining or covering bread or roll containers. Solid cuts of meat shall be protected by being covered in storage, except that quarters or sides of meat may be hung uncovered on clean sanitized hooks if no food product is stored beneath the meat.

2. Containers of food shall be stored a minimum of six inches above the floor in a manner that protects the food from splash and other contamination, and that permits easy cleaning of the storage area, except that:
   a. Metal pressurized beverage containers, and cased food packaged in cans, glass or other waterproof containers need not be elevated when the food container is not exposed to floor moisture.
   b. Containers may be stored on dollies, racks or pallets provided such equipment is easily movable.
3. Food and containers of food shall not be stored under exposed or unprotected sewer lines, or water lines, except for automatic fire protection sprinkler heads that may be required by law. The storage of food in toilet rooms or vestibules is prohibited.
4. Food not subject to further washing or cooking before being served shall be stored in a way that protects it against cross-contamination from food requiring washing or cooking.
5. Packaged food shall not be stored in contact with water or undrained ice. Wrapped sandwiches shall not be stored in direct contact with ice.
6. Unless its identity is unmistakable, bulk food such as cooking oil, syrup, salt, sugar or flour not stored in the product container or package in which it was obtained, shall be stored in a container identifying the food by common name.

Refrigerated Storage

1. Enough conveniently located refrigeration facilities or effectively insulated facilities shall be provided to assure the maintenance of potentially hazardous food at required temperatures during storage. Each mechanically refrigerated storage facility storing potentially hazardous food shall be provided with a numerically scaled indicating thermometer, accurate to plus or minus 3° F, located to measure the air temperature in the warmest part of the facility and located to be easily readable. Recording thermometers, accurate to plus or minus 3° F may be used in lieu of indicating thermometers.
2. Potentially hazardous food requiring refrigeration after preparation shall be rapidly cooled to an internal temperature of 45° F or below. Potentially hazardous foods of large volume or prepared in large quantities shall be rapidly cooled, utilizing such methods as shallow pans, agitation, quick chilling or water circulation external to the food container so that the cooling period shall not exceed 4 hours. Potentially hazardous food to be transported shall be pre-chilled and held at a temperature of 45° F or below (unless maintained in accordance with Section 750.150).
3. Frozen foods shall be kept frozen and should be stored at a temperature of 0° F or below.
4. Ice intended for human consumption shall not be used as a medium for cooling stored food, food containers or food utensils, except that such ice may be used for cooling tubes conveying beverages or beverage ingredients to a dispenser head. Ice used for cooling stored food and food containers shall not be used for human consumption.

Hot Storage

1. Enough conveniently located hot food storage facilities shall be provided to assure the maintenance of food at the required temperature during storage. Each hot food facility storing potentially hazardous food shall be provided with a numerically scaled indicat-

ing thermometer, accurate to plus or minus 3° F, located to measure the air temperature at the coldest part of the facility and located to be easily readable. Recording thermometers, accurate to plus or minus 3° F, may be used in lieu of indicating thermometers. Where it is impractical to install thermometers on equipment such as bain-maries, steam tables, steam kettles, heat lamps, calrod units, or insulated food transport carriers, a product thermometer must be available and used to check internal food temperature.

2. The internal temperature of potentially hazardous food requiring hot storage shall be 140° F or above except during necessary periods of preparation. Potentially hazardous food to be transported shall be held at a temperature of 140° F or above (unless maintained in accordance with paragraph (b) of Section 750.140).

Reason: Proper storage of food assures that there will be minimal contamination of the food from any source, and that the natural growth of microorganisms in the food will not result in foodborne illness. Therefore, measures to prevent the contamination of food must consider the environment in which food is stored and the potential for contamination under these conditions.

These measures are divided into several basic categories which include:

1. *Containers.* Food must be covered in order to provide physical protection of the food. In addition, these covers must be impervious and nonabsorbent to eliminate the possibility of the container being a vector for contamination.

2. *Location.* Food must be stored in a manner that permits cleaning of the storage area and in locations that do not result in a high risk of contamination from other food or from the conduct of normal operations.

3. *Labeling.* To avoid the inadvertent contamination of food in the preparation process, bulk ingredients must be labeled to prevent confusion due to possible similar appearances.

4. *Temperature.* Proper storage temperatures, and the availability of facilities to maintain temperatures are the best available means to control the growth of pathogens. A means for continuously monitoring air (ambient) temperatures is provided by requiring thermometers in or on the equipment.

5. *Cooling.* Since any temperature between 45° F and 140° F presents a hazard to public health in terms of microbial growth, food must remain in the critical temperature zone as little time as possible. The parameters defining the cooling period for foods in storage following preparation set forth procedures and conditions that minimize risk to the public health.

General—Food Preparation

Food shall be prepared with the least possible manual contact, with suitable utensils and on surfaces that prior to use have been cleaned, rinsed and sanitized to prevent cross-contamination.

Raw Fruits and Raw Vegetables

Raw fruits and raw vegetables shall be thoroughly washed with potable water before being cooked or served.

Cooking Potentially Hazardous Foods

Potentially hazardous foods requiring cooking shall be cooked to heat all parts of the food to a temperature of at least 140° F, except that:

1. Poultry, poultry stuffings, stuffed meats and stuffings containing meat shall be cooked to heat all parts of the food to at least 165° F with no interruption of the cooking process.
2. Pork and pork products shall be cooked to heat all parts of the food to at least 150° F or, if cooked in a microwave oven, to at least 170° F.
3. When beef roasts under 10 pounds in weight are cooked in a still dry heat oven, the oven shall be preheated to and held at an air temperature of at least 350° F throughout the process. If cooked in a convection oven, the oven shall be preheated to and held at an air temperature of at least 325° F throughout the process.
4. When beef roasts of 10 pounds or over in weight are cooked in a dry heat oven, the oven shall be preheated to and held at an air temperature of at least 250° F throughout the process.
5. Further, in order to meet the public health requirements for the process as cited above, the following table lists the minimum internal temperature of the beef roasts for the minimum time the roast needs to be held at such temperature:

Minimum Holding Times for Beef Roasts at Various Internal Temperatures

Minimum Internal Temperature (°F)	Minimum Holding Time (min)	Minimum Internal Temperature (°F)	Minimum Holding Time (min)
130	121	138	19
131	97	139	15
132	77	140	12
133	62	141	10
134	47	142	8
135	37	143	6
136	32	144	5
137	24		

6. Beef roasts, if cooked in a microwave oven, shall be cooked to an internal temperature of at least 145° F.

Reheating. Potentially hazardous foods that have been cooked and then refrigerated shall be reheated rapidly to 165° F or higher throughout before being served or before being placed in a hot food storage facility. Steam tables, bain-maries, warmers, and similar hot food holding facilities are prohibited for the rapid reheating of potentially hazardous foods.

Nondairy Products

Nondairy creaming, whitening, or whipping agents may be reconstituted on the premises only when they will be stored in sanitized, covered containers not exceeding one gallon in capacity and cooled to 45° F or below within 4 hours after preparation.

Product Thermometers

Metal stem-type numerically scaled indicating thermometers accurate to $\pm 2°$ F shall be provided and used to assure attainment and maintenance of proper internal cooking, holding or refrigeration temperatures of all potentially hazardous foods.

Thawing Potentially Hazardous Foods

Potentially hazardous foods shall be thawed:

1. In refrigerated units in a way that the temperature of the food does not exceed 45° F; or
2. Under potable running water at a temperature of 70° F or below, with sufficient water velocity to agitate and float off loose food particles into the over-flow; or
3. In a microwave oven only when the food will be immediately transferred to conventional cooking facilities as part of a continuous cooking process or when the entire, uninterrupted cooking process takes place in the microwave oven; or
4. As part of the conventional cooking process.

Reason: Food preparation is the process during which food is least protected due to necessary manipulation and is subjected to potential contamination from many sources within the establishment. Once the food has been contaminated, improper procedures for cooking, reheating or cooling permit the survival as well as the rapid and progressive growth of pathogenic microorganisms. Without adherence to proper sanitary procedures and the maximum use of adequate utensils and facilities, the preparation of a sound, appealing food is impossible.

Food Display and Service of Potentially Hazardous Food

Potentially hazardous foods shall be kept at an internal temperature of 45° F or below or at an internal temperature of 140° F or above during display and service, except that rare roast beef shall be held for service at a temperature of at least 130° F.

Dispensing Utensils

To avoid unnecessary manual contact with food, suitable dispensing utensils shall be used by employees or provided to consumers who serve themselves. Between uses during service, dispensing and incidental utensils shall be:

1. Stored in the food with the dispensing utensil handle extended out of the food; or
2. Stored clean and dry; or
3. Stored in running potable water dipper wells; or
4. In the case of dispensing utensils and malt collars used in serving frozen desserts, stored either in a running potable water dipper well, or clean and dry.

Ice Dispensing

Ice for consumer use shall be dispensed only by employees with scoops, tongs, or other ice-dispensing utensils or through automatic self-service ice-dispensing equipment. Ice-dispensing utensils shall be stored on a clean surface or in the ice with the dispensing utensil's handle extended out of the ice. Between uses, ice transfer receptacles shall be stored in a way that protects them from contamination. Ice storage bins shall be drained through an air gap.

General—Food Transportation

During transportation, food and food utensils shall be kept and packed in covered containers or completely wrapped or packaged so as to be protected from contamination. Foods in original individual packages do not need to be over-wrapped or covered if the original package has not been torn or broken. (During transportation, including transportation to another location for service or catering operations, food shall meet the requirements of Section 750.130, 750.140, and 750.150 relating to food storage.)

Reason: The protection of food from contamination and the maintenance of food at the proper temperatures are critical for the safety and quality of transported food. The special circumstances that arise during the transportation of food make the protection of the food and the maintenance of proper temperatures very difficult and correspondingly increase the possibility of contamination and microbial growth. For these reasons, special attention to sanitary requirements is essential during the food transportation process to provide the necessary protection to the consumer.

PERSONNEL
General—Employee Health

No person, while affected with a disease in a communicable form that can be transmitted by foods or who is a carrier of organisms that cause such a disease or while afflicted with a boil, or infected wound, or an acute respiratory infection, shall work in a foodservice establishment in any capacity in which there is a likelihood of such person contaminating food or food-contact surfaces with pathogenic organisms or transmitting disease to other persons.

Reason: Disease transmitted through food frequently originates from an infected food-service employee even though the employee shows little outward appearance of being ill. A wide range of communicable diseases and infections may be transmitted by infected food service personnel to other employees and to the consumer through the contamination of food and through careless food-handling practices. It is the responsibility of both management and staff to see that no person who is affected with any disease that can be transmitted by food works in any area of a food service establishment where there is a possibility of disease transmission.

General—Personal Cleanliness

Employees shall thoroughly wash their hands and the exposed portions of their arms with soap and warm water before starting work, during work as often as is necessary to keep them clean, and after smoking, eating, drinking, or using the toilet. Employees shall keep their fingernails clean and trimmed.

Reason: In order to prevent the contamination of food and food-contact surfaces, and the resulting potential transmission of foodborne illness, it is essential that employees observe strict standards of cleanliness and proper hygiene during their working periods and before starting work or returning to work after any interruption of their foodservice activities.

General—Clothing

1. The outer clothing of all employees shall be clean.
2. Employees shall use effective hair restraints to prevent the contamination of food or food-contact surfaces.

Reason: Hair restraints and the clothing of foodservice employees play important roles in the prevention of food contamination and food-contact surface contamination. Because of this, hair should be restrained to prevent any possibility of its entering into food. Employees also must not wear clothing that is obviously soiled or difficult to keep clean, because food may be repeatedly contaminated by food debris or other soil from the clothing of food handlers.

Manual Cleaning and Sanitizing

1. For manual washing, rinsing, and sanitizing utensils and equipment, a sink with no fewer than three compartments shall be provided and used. Sink compartments shall be large enough to permit the accommodation of the equipment and utensils, and each compartment of the sink shall be supplied with hot and cold potable running water. Fixed equipment and utensils and equipment too large to be cleaned in the sink compartments shall be washed manually or cleaned through pressure spray methods.
2. Drain boards or easily movable dish tables of adequate size shall be provided for proper handling of soiled utensils prior to washing and for clean utensils following sanitizing and shall be located so as not to interfere with the proper use of the dishwashing facilities.
3. Equipment and utensils shall be pre-flushed or pre-scraped and, when necessary, pre-soaked to remove gross food particles and soil.
4. Except for fixed equipment and utensils too large to be cleaned in sink compartments, manual washing, rinsing and sanitizing shall be conducted in the following sequence:
   a. Sinks shall be cleaned prior to use.
   b. Equipment and utensils shall be thoroughly washed in the first compartment with a hot detergent solution that is kept clean.
   c. Equipment and utensils shall be rinsed free of detergent and abrasives in clean water in the second compartment.
   d. Equipment and utensils shall be sanitized in the third compartment.
5. The food-contact surfaces of all equipment and utensils shall be sanitized by:
   a. Immersion for at least one-half (½) minute in clean, hot water at a temperature of at least 170° F; or
   b. Immersion for at least one minute in a clean solution containing at least 50 parts per million of available chlorine as a hypochlorite and having a temperature of at least 75° F; or
   c. Immersion for at least one minute in a clean solution containing at least 12.5 parts per million of available iodine and having a pH not higher than 5.0 and having a temperature of at least 75° F.

E. SAFETY WORK HABITS

Good grooming habits, neat and sanitary practices, and efficient work practices are essential in foodservices.

Use a hair restraint, preferably a hairnet or cap. Scarves, hairbands, bandannas, and so on are not safe and are ineffective as hair restraints.

Be well groomed, that is, take a daily bath, use deodorant, comb hair neatly, clean fingernails, and so on.

Wear a clean white uniform and comfortable, nonslippery shoes.

Develop the following work habits:

- Wash your hands thoroughly with soap and water every time you enter foodservice areas.
- Keep uniform clean while working.
- Never touch face and hair while working; if you do, wash hands immediately.
- Wash hands after using handkerchief.
- Use a spoon for all tasting and put it in container that will be taken to dishwasher for washing and sanitization.
- Wipe hands on paper towels, never on uniform.
- Try to avoid spilling or splashing; if it happens, wipe it up at once.
- Avoid leaning against tables or ranges.
- Never touch prepared food with hands. Use proper equipment or sterilized gloves.
- Do not touch food contact surfaces.
- Never eat or drink in the food production area and while on service counters.
- Do not *smoke* or chew gum in food production and service areas.
- Organize work efficiently.

Be careful when going through doors. Someone may be on the opposite side coming through in your direction.

Keep floors clean. Wipe spilled water, food, grease, and so on. It may prevent slipping and serious accidents.

Sharp and jagged edges on dishes, silver, equipment are a hazard. Do not allow a sharp knife to become hidden in the pot-washing sink.

Use a *potholder* (not a towel) to prevent burns. Keep protruding pot handles turned in toward work surface.

Sweep up broken glass immediately. Do not pick it up by hand.

Use caution near steam—remove covers or open doors to steamers in such a way that you do not scald hands and face.

Keep range top free of grease. Throw baking soda on a grease fire.

Keep oven doors closed when not in use.

Never leave utensils on the floor.

Always ventilate gas oven for several minutes before lighting it. Check turn-off valve for gas leakage.

Use traffic lanes only. Do not walk through work areas.

Use cutting boards. Cut away from your body and away from fellow workers.

Always use a wooden tamper to push food into a grinder.

If you break glass near food, always report incident to supervisor so that food is removed from use.

Do not store knives helter-skelter.

If a knife falls—get out of its way. Do not grab it!

Handle glasses at the base, silverware by the handles, plates by the edge.

Look where you are going—do not move too fast, especially in congested areas.

Look for open oven doors, thermotainers, and so on.

For safe lifting and carrying, squat down, get a good footing and firm hold, make use of strong leg and thigh muscles, keep back straight. Get assistance when lifting heavy or ungainly objects. Push—do not pull— heavy carts. Carry heavy tray on palm of hand with weight centered over your body.

Use handles on refrigerators and drawers.

Clean blades of cutting machinery immediately after use, replace on machine, and fasten safety guards.

Report all injuries immediately and get first aid.

Report all colds, sore throat, illnesses, cuts, and burns to the supervisor before entering food production or service areas.

F. TABLE SERVICE PROCEDURE CHECKLIST

The following procedures are recommended for maintaining services that are of uniform quality.

1. *The Menu*
    Study the menu thoroughly. The host or hostess will give you a list of menu items, an explanation of what each item is, and the abbreviation you will use on the order card.

2. *Table Assignment*
    The host or hostess will give you your table assignments. Check the tables in your area to be sure that they are completely and properly set

    *   Each plate setting should have silver, bread and butter plate, napkin, and cup and saucer
    *   Each table should have an ashtray, salt and pepper shakers, sugar bowl, and cream pitcher
    *   At the last minute, place iced water glasses at each place setting
    *   At your tray stand, keep a water pitcher and a service napkin for wiping up spills

3. *Seating of the Guests*
    The host/hostess will seat the guests and will give each guest a menu or will tell the guests which table to take and you will give the guests copies of the menu.

4. *Taking the Order*
    After the guests have had enough time to read the menu, ask them what they would like. Write the orders on the card, using the correct abbreviations. Be sure the orders are complete including beverages. There should be a separate card for each guest.

    Collect the menus from the guests and return them to the host or hostess.

5. *How to Serve*
    Serve everything with the left hand from the left side of the customer with the exception of the beverage.

    Beverages are served with the right hand on the right side of the customer.

6. *Service of the First Course and Salad*
    Soups are to be served on an underliner. Place soup spoon or cocktail fork on the right, outside the silver already placed.

    After the first course is served, pick up the salads from the kitchen and serve. If a salad dressing is to be passed, bring it with you.

    When all the guests have finished with the first course, clear the dishes. On your tray stands, stack dishes according to size. After you have cleared your table, take the dishes to the dishwashing unit through the exit door.

7. *Service of the Main Course, Rolls, and Beverage*
    While the orders are being set up, assemble your beverage order (pour milk in glasses). Take beverage and roll baskets from the kitchen to your tray stands.

    Return to the kitchen and pick up your food orders. Set the tray of hot food on the tray stand.

    Carry two dinner plates to the table. Place the first dinner plate in front of the customer with your left hand, then transfer the second dinner plate to your left hand and serve the second guest.

    Serve hot rolls immediately after dinner plates have been served to everyone.

    Rolls: Roll baskets are held with your left hand and offered to each guest from the left. After everybody has been served, return the roll basket to the tray stand.

    Beverage: Serve after the rolls have been served.

    Keep water glasses filled.

    Stay near your tables as much as possible so that you will be available should your guests desire any service.

    Pass rolls the second time while the guests are still eating the main course.

8. *How to Clear*
    Clear everything with the left hand from the left side of the customer with the exception of the beverage.

    When all customers at your table have finished eating, you may clear the tables

    - If the dinner knife has not been placed on the plate by the guest, pick it up and place it across the center of the plate
    - Pick up the dinner plate with your left hand, transfer it to the right hand, holding it behind the customer
    - Pick up the salad plate and place it on top of the dinner plate
    - Pick up the bread and butter plate and place it on top of the salad plate

- Place the dirty dishes on your tray which is located on your tray stand
- Repeat the above process until all dishes on the table have been cleared
- Clear everything except cups and saucers, water glasses, sugar bowl, creamer, ashtray, and silver for dessert. SALT AND PEPPER SHAKERS must be cleared

Take the dishes to the dishwashing unit.

9. *Dessert Service*
Pick up the dessert orders and necessary underliners.

Place any necessary silver (if there is none on the table) for dessert on the right side of the customer

- If the dessert is on a plate, use a salad fork
- If the dessert is in a dish, use a teaspoon

When serving pie, place the plate so that the point of the slice of pie faces the guest.

Refill coffee cups.

Complete the check

- Place the check on small check trays facing down and leave it with the customer
- Guests will pay you; get the correct change from the host or hostess and bring the change back on a small tray to the customer

After guests leave, clear the tables of all dishes and linens. Wipe tables with clean cloth.

10. *Taking Dirty Dishes to the Dishroom*
When taking dirty dishes to the dishroom, stack dirty dishes according to size, e.g., salad plates in one stack.

11. *Miscellaneous Instructions*
When you are not busy, assist other waitresses or waiters.

Keep dining room free of soiled dishes and trays.

Follow One Traffic Pattern: Use one door of dining room for going into the kitchen and the other door for going out of the kitchen into the dining room, whenever possible.

Always leave your station and tables clean and orderly. Return any silver, linen, or food which has been left on the service stand to the proper place. Wipe off the top of each service stand at the end of the meal period.

G. CHECKLIST FOR THE PRODUCTION SUPERVISOR

_____ Several days before the event, go over the recipes and worksheets with the managers. Make suggestions if you feel changes will have to be made

_____ Have a complete list of recipes in your possession all the time

_____ Fill out the production sheets completely. List the food items according to the menu and write the name of the person preparing it, the number of items to be prepared, and at what time the items are to be ready

_____ Initial each item as it is prepared and when it is prepared. Record the time, and mention where they are to be located till served

_____ Check that time/temperature of all items are within the safety range

_____ Check that all ovens, ranges, hot-bread cabinets, hot-holding cabinets, fryers, steam table, etc., are turned on well ahead of the schedule

_____ Check several days in advance to be sure that all equipment, such as pans, skillets, spatula, knives, is available for use

_____ Food items must be ready _15 minutes_ before meal service starts

_____ Turn off equipment when not needed

_____ Stagger preparation schedules

_____ Complete production records of the leftovers. Make sure that food is put on a cart and sorted in proper storage areas. Check with manager on details

_____ Check the cleanliness of the work area. Make sure production workers are cleaning up work areas as they finish

_____ Check the food items on hand during service and be prepared to make quick adjustments

_____ Check to see that accurate portion sizes are being served. Portion controls should be accurate

_____ Check to be sure that all condiments, etc., have been added to the food before service

_____ Make a kitchen counter plan in consultation with the manager

_____ Place all serving utensils on the counter

_____ Have a sample of plate/dish serving in front of the server

_____ Assign production workers on kitchen counter during service. Give all instructions

_____ Have as many items dished up in advance as possible

_____ Provide wet cloths for wiping plates, etc.

_____ Be sure that the plates are nicely decorated prior to being taken into the dining room

_____ Coordinate timing for service of each course of the meal

H. CHECKLIST FOR THE SERVICE SUPERVISOR

———————— Assemble necessary equipment, dishes, and supplies at least 2 hr before service

———————— Discuss with the manager the diagram and plans for service

———————— Train waiters/waitresses on table service. Arrange a separate session. Give all descriptions in detail

———————— Assign tables to waiters/waitresses

———————— Be prepared for any absenteeism

———————— Count the dishes needed for dining room. Put plates and cups in thermotainer. Put cover over them

———————— Get half-pint containers of milk

———————— Turn on the coffee urn and start making coffee half an hour before meal service. Make sure there is enough coffee throughout the meal

———————— Have tea bags available by the coffee stand. Keep hot water ready

———————— Count number of water glasses needed. Leave them right-side-up in racks. Place on cart

———————— Fill glasses with chipped ice and roll cart into the walk-in refrigerator ready for placing on the tables by the waiters/waitresses 15 minutes before guests are seated

———————— Cut wedges of lemon for tea

———————— Prepare iced tea

———————— Fill creamers and store in lower left part of the refrigerator

———————— Fill sugar bowls

———————— Fill salt and pepper shakers

———————— Count and place ashtrays if smoking is permitted

———————— See that dinner plates are hot

_____ Arrange items on trays

_____ Store chilled desserts in the refrigerator and frozen desserts in the freezer

_____ Salad dressings should be placed in appropriate containers

_____ Put butter on plates and keep them in the refrigerator

_____ Rolls or hot breads should be arranged in roll baskets in neatly folded napkins

_____ Have plate covers as well as soup underliners ready for service

_____ Have plate garnishes by the serving counter before service starts

_____ Be ready with counter set up to serve promptly

_____ See that all servers are properly dressed

_____ Always keep a dress in reserve

_____ Change your dress and be ready at least an hour before service

_____ See that all servers are at the station

_____ At each station provide wet cloths, water jugs, etc.

_____ Waiters/waitresses should use stations for keeping trays before and after service

_____ For buffet service, you are responsible for supply and providing help at the buffet table

_____ For buffet service, filled dishes are brought into the dining room *before* partially empty dishes are removed

_____ Arrange tables to suit reservation and put dining room in order a day before the event

_____ Allow room for waiters/waitresses to serve

_____ Set tables with linens and appropriate place settings

_____ Follow table setting plan and check all tables

_____ Double check the names of guests

_____ Have a list of names, menu, and note pads on hand all the time

_____ Set flowers on each table

_____ Follow the procedure for lighting candles, when needed

_____ Fifteen minutes before service set butter plates, rolls, and salad dressings on the tables

_____ Cover all silverware and do not leave it out overnight

_____ Check tidiness of the waiting room and coat room

_____ Arrange decorations in the dining room

_____ Instruct waiters and waitresses to stay at their stations in the dining room when they are not busy

———— Seat guests according to seating chart. You will be assisting the manager

———— Collect and cancel all tickets and give them back to guests. Do not litter the floor with ticket stubs—use small basket

———— Collect checks/cash for those who are paying at the door. Keep the money in a safe place

———— Place a screen—do not lock the door—once all guests are seated

———— Check the coat hangers and coat hanging area for tidiness

———— Be prepared to bring out a booster seat when required

———— Be in charge of all the entertainment, music, etc. Control the tone of music, adjust slides, change cassettes, etc.

———— See that waitresses are entering and exiting through the right doors

———— Thank patrons as they leave and wish them a happy return visit

———— Hand out complimentary gift items, survey questionnaires, etc.

———— After service, see that all service areas are cleaned

———— Rearrange dining room so that it is left in order. Put away or return all decorations. See that tables and other furniture are clean

I. CHECKLIST FOR THE SANITATION MANAGER

_____ Make sure there is a container for garbage and trash. There should also be cans near the sink

_____ See that dish machine is filled with hot water. Prepare silverware container for soaking. (Fill large pan with warm water and add the required amount of detergent.) Make sure machine contains adequate detergent and rinse dry solution

_____ Turn on steam in the dish machine at least 1 hr in advance

_____ Check to make sure proper wash and rinse temperatures are being used. May be necessary to check several times during the service of the meal

_____ Explain dish-sorting procedure to the waiters/waitresses. They must place silverware in pan to presoak, and take all dishes off the tray placing them on the dish machine counter. Salt and pepper shakers, cream and sugars, and dressing containers are all to be placed on counter in front of the dish cabinet. Linen napkins are to be placed in container for counting. Glasses are to be turned upside-down in proper glass racks. Used paper items are to be placed in proper paper container. The waiters/waitresses should use the same tray again, washing if soiled. At the end of use, trays are stacked neatly and then washed and dried

_____ The dishwashers should scrape the dishes with rubber scraper. Stack them in the proper racks, and then using hand nozzle, rinse the dishes thoroughly. The dishes are then run through the wash and rinse cycle in the dish machine. After washing, stack dishes and put away in proper place. Silverware is placed in silver washing container and run through on a flat rack. After final rinse, place silverware on clean towels. Either the dishwashers or the waitresses wipe the silverware and put away in silver containers. Dishwashers are responsible for cleaning the machine and counters after use

_____ After waiters/waitresses have finished clearing the dining room, have them help dry silver and put it away, clean the coffee urn, the coffee pots and water pitchers, count laundry, put away dishes, and wash table tops

Note: Instruct waiters or waitresses to stack dishes according to sizes — all dinner plates in one stack; same with saucers, salad plates, bread and butter plates.

J. LIST OF RESERVATIONS

MEAL: _____

DATE: _____

MANAGER: _____   PHONE NO.: _____

NAME	PHONE NO.	ADDRESS	FOOD PREFERENCE	NO. OF TICKETS	TOTAL NO.

K. MANAGEMENT ASSESSMENT QUESTIONNAIRE

Answer each of the following questions. *Circle* the answer that *most closely* fits your situation. If you do not perform any of the function(s) described in the question, *circle* the answer that you consider as *most appropriate* to that situation.

1. Which one of the following would you use if an employee called in sick?
   a. Have the person *"on-call"* come in
   b. Tell the employee that he/she *must* come in
   c. Work with *short* staff
   d. Have all employees take up *additional* duties
   e. Do that person's job *yourself*
   f. Call scheduled-off employees to *find* someone who could substitute

2. When assigning responsibilities to employees, which one of the following factors is the *most* important?
   a. How long the person has been employed by your foodservice operation
   b. How much interest the person shows in his/her present position
   c. How much experience he/she has, including work outside your foodservice operation
   d. All of the above
   e. None of the above

3. If there is a complaint from a customer about foodservice, how would you normally come to know about it?
   a. Through *wait person* or *food server* or other *employees*
   b. Through *complaint/suggestion box*
   c. Through your *supervisor/boss*
   d. Through letters to editor in the *newspaper*
   e. Through personal contact with the *customer*

4. Which one of the following do you consider the *most* important when issuing orders?
   a. Sounding positive
   b. Being complete and defined

    c. Showing confidence in employee
    d. All of the above
    e. None of the above

5. Portion sizes in your facility are determined by the
    a. *customer*
    b. *person serving*
    c. amount of *leftover food*
    d. serving *equipment or utensils*

6. With which one of the following statements do you most agree?
    a. Individual decisions are time saving
    b. Group decisions encourage enthusiasm and help win support from the employees
    c. Group decisions may facilitate compromises on part of management
    d. Agree with all
    e. Disagree with all

7. Which one of the following *procedures* do you use in scheduling your employees?
    a. Written schedules for a *week* or *longer*
    b. *No* written schedules since you are able to easily memorize them
    c. *Daily* scheduling when the employees come to work
    d. Allow *employees* to make their own schedules and work in areas where they are most needed

8. Which of the following item(s) do you have in your foodservice facility?
    a. Organization *chart*
    b. Written job *descriptions*
    c. Written work *schedules*
    d. All of the above
    e. Items b and c
    f. None of the above

9. If there is a *new* procedure that you want to implement, how would you introduce it to your employees?
    a. By printed memo and procedure
    b. By demonstration
    c. By training the employees
    d. Combination of items a, b, *or* c
    e. By verbally informing senior employee, hoping that the message will be conveyed to the other employees

10. What would you consider as the *most* effective method of increasing job satisfaction among your employees?
    a. Giving pay raises periodically
    b. Promotions based on seniority
    c. Opportunities for more get-together parties
    d. Rewards based on achievements

11. Which of the following actions can be classified as the *most* effective control?
    a. Wearing hairnets or caps
    b. Use of time clocks or other time-keeping devices
    c. Use of standardized recipes
    d. Washing hands with soaps
    e. All of the above
    f. Some of the above

12. Which of the following steps do you think as the *first* and the *most* important in decision making?
    a. Decide on the best solution
    b. Understand the situation
    c. Implement your decision
    d. Pinpoint the problem
    e. Search for various solutions

13. How *often* do you review and update your planning procedures?
    a. Every *week*
    b. Every *month*
    c. *Seldom*, because your plans work well
    d. Every *year*
    e. Whenever *problems* arise

14. Which of the following *terms* are new to you?
    a. Line organization
    b. Staff organization
    c. Functional organization
    d. All of the above
    e. None of the above

15. Are *procedures* for specific tasks (cleaning equipment, etc.)
    a. *posted* near the piece of equipment?
    b. *posted* in manager's office?
    c. kept on *file* for reference?
    d. explained *verbally* to employees?
    e. *none* of the above?

16. An employee is constantly late to work. How would you *handle* this situation?
    a. *Ignore it*, hoping the problem will be corrected by itself
    b. *Talk* to the employee privately and emphasize the importance of punctuality
    c. *Talk* to the employee in front of other employees, since it will be a reminder to all employees
    d. *Fire* him since you might have to face more problems later on

17. Which statement best reflects your attitude toward controls?
    a. Extensive controls are needed to ensure that the employee does a job thoroughly and correctly
    b. Controls are not usually needed. Employees are usually self-motivated and dependable

c. Controls need to be present in moderation so that employees do not feel restricted
d. Controls lead to misunderstandings and so are noneffective
e. Controls are needed for newer employees more than the senior staff members

18. Who is/are mostly involved in your decision-making process?
    a. Employees
    b. No one, you are solely responsible
    c. Your boss
    d. Employees and supervisors
    e. Everyone has input into the process

19. When planning normal functions within your foodservice facility, do you *often*
    a. make plans solely by yourself, taking responsibility for the outcome?
    b. consult your supervisors only?
    c. consult your employees only?
    d. consult your supervisors and employees?
    e. let the employees make a plan first and then you approve or reject it?

20. When do you *revise* job descriptions?
    a. Quarterly
    b. When tasks and responsibilities change
    c. Never
    d. As needed, with regular reviews
    e. Daily

21. When giving directions, which one of the following *patterns* do you normally use?
    a. We're out of coffee! Somebody should take care of it right away!
    b. I want you to make coffee and I'll stand right here while you are making it!
    c. John! We need more coffee. It's chilly outside and more people are coming back for refills.
    d. None of the above

22. When *new and better* methods are introduced in your foodservice, which one of the following procedures do you use?
    a. Implement the method *immediately*?
    b. *Explain* to employees why the old method has been discontinued?
    c. *Discuss* with the employees before deciding to use the new method?
    d. Let some of the older employees *use* the old method?
    e. *None* of the above

23. How often are the reasons for having controls in your facility explained to the employees?
    a. Always
    b. Frequently
    c. Sometimes
    d. Seldom
    e. Never

24. When making a *major* decision, it is best to
    a. do it yourself to assume speed and feasibility
    b. consult all employees who will be involved
    c. do it alone to show your superiors what type of manager you are
    d. pass it on to a lower level of authority
    e. allow the employees to make the decision and then have it reviewed by the manager

25. When forecasting the number of meals or number of customers, which of the following *data* do you use most often?
    a. Profit and loss statement
    b. Previous records of sales
    c. Inventory on hand
    d. Food cost percentage
    e. None of the above

26. How *often* do your permanent employees ask questions about assigned tasks?
    a. Only after initial instruction
    b. Occasionally when they are confused
    c. More often for purpose of clarification
    d. Mostly during the peak mealtimes

27. Which one of the following aspects *fits* into your philosophy of management?
    a. Employee participation and job satisfaction are the main goals
    b. The foodservice organization is more important than the welfare of the employees
    c. A good manager is authoritative and somewhat dictatorial
    d. Motivate employees by selling your ideas
    e. None of the above

28. When is the *best time* to explain the fringe benefit program to an employee?
    a. Friday evening
    b. During peak production time
    c. At a special meeting during the weekend
    d. When the employee is not rushed and has sufficient time during work hours

29. *Effective* controls should be
    a. selective
    b. adaptable
    c. of little concern to the manager
    d. applicable to the situation
    e. obtained by phasing out old controls
    f. items a, b, and d

30. If you receive a customer *complaint*, you should
    a. show sincere concern, find the cause and remove it
    b. ignore it since it is hard to please everyone
    c. form a committee to deal with the problem
    d. insist on evidence to back up the complaint
    e. wait until you receive another complaint

INDEX